Urban Theology

Urban Theology
A Reader

Edited by Michael Northcott, for the
Archbishop of Canterbury's Urban Theology Group

CASSELL

Cassell
Wellington House, 125 Strand, London WC2R 0BB, England
PO Box 605, Herndon, VA 20172, USA

First published 1998

British Library Cataloguing-in-Publication Data
A catalogue record for this book is available from the British Library.

ISBN 0-304-70265-X

Typeset by York House Typographic Ltd
Printed and bound in Great Britain by Redwood Books, Trowbridge, Wiltshire

Contents

Foreword

Five years ago I commissioned a group of urban ministers and academic theologians to reflect on the Church's response to the harsh realities of poverty, unemployment, crime and family breakdown which dominate the lives of people in Urban Priority Areas. The Urban Theology Group was part of the Church of England's response to the call to the renewal of Christian presence and witness in Britain's inner cities by the Archbishop's Commission on Urban Priority Areas in its report *Faith in the City*.

In their first book, *God in the City*, the group drew particular attention to the central role of joyful praise and worship in challenging and transforming the oppressive structures and sinful relationships which create and sustain inner city deprivation, and in empowering the poor in responding to structural and personal sin. In their second book the group conclude their work with a set of readings and reflections which provide a kaleidoscopic portrait both of the harsh realities of life in Urban Priority Areas and of the inspiring struggles of the people of God in challenging sin and injustice in the city with the gospel of Jesus Christ.

The readings in this volume testify to the faithful presence and service of worshipping Christian communities in inner city areas and outer housing estates whose people are haunted by the twin scourges of unemployment and debt. They also testify to the many endeavours of the Church to redeem the city, through the joy of shared faith and worship, and through practical projects to relieve social need and to regenerate the communities and environments of Urban Priority Areas. Above all these readings point to the mission of the Church not only to *be* in the city but to seek the salvation of the city by proclaiming the name of Jesus Christ against the idols which lead people away from the worship and justice of the true God. A rich mine of information and inspiration on the forces which shape the city and on effective responses to urban deprivation by government and voluntary agencies as well as Christian communities, the Reader provides many hopeful pointers to the shape of urban regeneration and Christian witness in UPAs as we approach the third millennium.

† George Cantuar

Preface

This Reader is the outcome of a five-year process of theological collaboration between academic theologians and practitioners of urban ministry which commenced in 1990 and issued initially in the publication of *God in the City* by Mowbray in 1995. That collection of essays with its combination of story, reflection and analysis is designed to chart a new path in urban theology and to exemplify a new way of doing theology in Britain which both draws on the resources of local experience, story and theological reflection in the urban context, and on the skills and disciplines of professional theologians. The group began its work in response to the call in *Faith in the City*, amplified in the follow-up report *Living Faith in the City*, for a concerted effort to identify, understand and represent to the wider church the diversity of local theologies which the Archbishop's Commission had encountered in their visits to Urban Priority-Area (UPA) churches. The group believed that this process of identification and representation would require the publication of at least two books, a collection of stories and essays, and a Reader in urban theology. We hope and intend that the two books will be used side by side and interactively, hence the pointers to *God in the City* which will be found throughout the Reader.

The aim of the Reader is to represent the diversity of local theologies and cultural styles which are to be found in UPA churches and to engage effectively with the social realities of urban deprivation in Britain more than a decade after the publication of *Faith in the City*. The Reader is designed as a study book for at least three groups of people: for people working in UPAs whether as community workers, teachers, members of congregations or clergy; for those living in 'comfortable Britain' who want to understand and be challenged by the reality of social deprivation and the testimony of Christian presence and worship in UPAs; for people in training for ministry and for clergy preparing to work in UPAs.

The themes and shape of the Reader were worked on collectively by the group and demonstrate an intention to link the stories and theologies of urban Christians in contemporary Britain with the stories and reflections of the urban peoples of God in the Old and New Testaments. The Reader is organized around twelve themes. Of the four extracts in each chapter, the first takes the form of a story or narrative. The introductory essay in each chapter is designed both to act as a reflection on a biblical text and to introduce and draw together themes from the selected texts and further reading. (Extracted readings referred to in introductions are given in brackets in bold type, while further reading is given in normal type. Bible passages commencing each chapter are taken from the *Revised English Bible*; the reference numbers at the end of the boxed extracts from *Faith in the City* are to chapter and paragraph numbers in the original report.) This shaping of the material reflects the conviction of many working in UPAs that the contexts and issues of urban life, particularly as these are experienced in the disadvantaged areas of modern British cities, open up the Bible in vital and powerful ways. It also reflects our conviction as a group that social analysis and theological reflection on contemporary reality must always turn us back to re-reading the tradition which we have inherited, and particularly as that tradition has been focused in the witness of the Scriptures.

This Reader is the outcome of a collaborative process, including two meetings and much interchange between members of the group. However, unlike *God in the City*, the final form and composition of this Reader is primarily the work of one member of the group, with strong input and feedback from the members of the group who in its last twelve months included Andrew Davey, the Bishops' Urban Priority Areas Officer, David Ford, Regius Professor of Divinity in the University of Cambridge, Laurie Green, Bishop of Bradwell, Susan Hope, vicar of Brightside and Wincobank in Sheffield, Ruth McCurry, publisher, trustee of the Church Urban Fund and former member of the Archbishop's Commission for Urban Priority Areas, Al McFadyen, Senior Lecturer in Theology and Religious Studies in the University of Leeds and a volunteer youth organizer in a UPA parish in Leeds, Michael Northcott, Senior Lecturer in Christian Ethics and Practical Theology in the University of Edinburgh and non-stipendiary priest in Leith, Peter Sedgwick, Assistant Secretary to the Church of England General Synod Board for Social Responsibility, and Margaret Walsh, Sister of the Infant Jesus and leader of the Hope Community in Wolverhampton.

I am immensely grateful to all members of the group who contributed readings, stories, ideas, and criticisms of drafts of individual chapters, and above all the experience of collaborative theology which the group enabled over a sustained period of five years. The group extends thanks to Archbishop George Carey for supporting us in the last year of our work in preparing the Reader, and to the many urban theologians, college lecturers and urban ministry practitioners who responded to Bishop Laurie Green's mailing, requesting ideas and readings for this volume.

We hope that the fragments of insight and reflection on the pilgrimage of the people of God which we have gathered for this volume will both reflect and extend the Christian mission of building communities of the Kingdom in the inner cities and outer housing estates of post-industrial Britain.

Michael S. Northcott
1997

Acknowledgements

We wish to thank all those who have contributed to this Reader and given permission for their writing to be used.

We have made every effort to trace and identify pieces and parts of work, and to secure the necessary permission for printing. If we have made any errors in text or in acknowledgement, we apologize sincerely.

Biblical passages commencing introductory sections are taken from the *Revised English Bible* (Oxford: Oxford University Press/Cambridge: Cambridge University Press, 1989) and are reproduced by permission.

Boxed extracts in introductory sections from *Faith in the City: A Call for Action by Church and Nation. Report of the Archbishop of Canterbury's Commission on Urban Priority Areas* (London: Church House Publishing, 1985) are copyright © The Central Board of Finance of the Church of England and are reproduced by permission.

1 Theology in the city

Extract from Andrew Davey, 'Liberation theology in Peckham' in Chris Rowland and John Vincent (eds), *Liberation Theology UK* (Sheffield: Urban Theology Unit, 1995), pp. 63–7. Used by permission.

Extract from 'Why do theological reflection?' in Laurie Green, *Let's Do Theology* (London: Mowbray, 1990), pp. 76–7, 91–4. Used by permission.

'A theology for today's city' in *The Cities: A Methodist Report* (London: NCH Action for Children, 1997), pp. 205–14. Used by permission.

'Who is a local theologian?' from Robert J. Schreiter, *Constructing Local Theologies* (Maryknoll, NY: Orbis, 1985), pp. 16–21. Copyright © 1985 by Robert J. Schreiter. Reprinted by permission.

2 Creativity in the city

'A people's astonishing vitality' in Douglas Galbraith, *Music in the Listening Place* (unpublished), pp. 6–9. Used by permission.

Extract from 'Exploring the dynamic of being human' in Robert Warren, *Being Human, Being Church: Spirituality and Mission in the Local Church* (London: Marshall Pickering, 1995), pp. 121–5. Used by permission.

Extracts from Andrew Mawson, 'Community regeneration' in Eric Blakebrough (ed.), *Church for the City* (London: Darton, Longman and Todd, 1995), pp. 122–50. Used by permission.

Extract from David Donnison, *Act Local: Social Justice from the Bottom Up* (London: Institute for Public Policy Research, 1994), pp. 20–7. Used by permission.

3 The shape of the city

'Ronan Point' from Colin Marchant, *Signs in the City* (London: Hodder & Stoughton, 1985), pp. 17–19. Used by permission.

'The great rebuild' from Peter Hall, *Cities of Tomorrow: An Intellectual History of Urban Planning and Design in the Twentieth Century* (Oxford: Blackwell, 1988), pp. 223–7. Used by permission.

Extract from 'The shape of the secular city' in Harvey Cox, *The Secular City: Secularization and Urbanization in Theological Perspective* (London: SCM Press, 1967), pp. 44–9. Used by permission.

Extract from Paul Hackwood and Phil Shiner, 'New role for the Church in urban policy?', *Crucible* 1994, 142–50. Used by permission.

4 Sin in the city

Extract from Anne Power, 'Housing, community and crime' in David Downes (ed.), *Crime and the City: Essays in Memory of John Barron Mays* (London: Macmillan, 1989), pp. 223–7. Copyright © David Downes 1989. Used by permission of Macmillan Ltd.

Extract from Peter Selby, 'Love in the city' in David Ford and Dennis Stamps (eds), *Essentials of Christian Community: Essays for Daniel W. Hardy* (Edinburgh: T & T Clark, 1996), pp. 109–14. Used by permission.

'The struggle with evil' from Austin Smith, *Journeying with God* (London: Sheed & Ward, 1990), pp. 108–14. Used by permission.

Extract from 'Thunder over the city' in Jaques Ellul, *The Meaning of the City*, trans. Dennis Pardee (Grand Rapids, MI: Eerdmans, 1970), pp. 72–8. Copyright © 1970 by William B. Eerdmans Publishing Company. Used by permission.

5 Poverty in the city

Extract from Jeremy Seabrook, 'Living on welfare'. Reprinted by permission of Sage Publications Ltd from Martin Loney *et al.* (eds), *The State or the Market: Politics and Welfare in Contemporary Britain* (London: Sage, 1992), pp. 299–305.

'Love, justice and sharing: a Christian perspective' in Duncan Forrester and Dennis Skene (eds), *Just Sharing: A Christian Approach to the Distribution of Wealth, Income and Benefits* (London: Epworth Press, 1988), pp. 63–70. Used by permission.

Extract from 'Going beyond equality' in John Atherton, *The Scandal of Poverty: Priorities for the Emerging Church* (London: Mowbray, 1986), pp. 93–9. Used by permission.

Extract from 'Relationships of justice' in Hilary Russell, *Poverty Close to Home: A Christian Understanding* (London: Mowbray, 1995), pp. 257–63. Used by permission.

6   Power in the city

Margaret Walsh, 'Organizing for action' (unpublished). Used by permission of the author.

Extract from 'Unmasking the domination system' in Walter Wink, *Engaging the Powers: Discernment and Resistance in a World of Domination* (Minneapolis: Fortress Press, 1992), pp. 96–104. Copyright © 1992 Augsburg Fortress. Reprinted by permission.

Extracts from Gerald Wheale, 'The parish and politics' in George Moyser (ed.), *Church and Politics Today: Essays on the Role of the Church of England in Contemporary Politics* (Edinburgh: T & T Clark), pp. 146–63. Used by permission.

Edited extracts from Austin Smith, 'The Church and powerlessness: an exploration in spirituality', *The Way* **23**, 1981, 199–209. Used by permission.

7   Generations and gender in the city

'Poverty and parenting' in Bob Holman, *Children and Crime* (London: Lion, 1995), pp. 62–4. Copyright © 1995 Bob Holman, used by permission of Lion Publishing plc.

Extracts from 'Families and social policy' in *Something to Celebrate: Valuing Families in Church and Society. The Report of a Working Party of the Board for Social Responsibility* (London: Church House Publishing, 1995), pp. 129–60, are copyright © The Central Board of Finance of the Church of England and are reproduced by permission.

Extracts from Michael Young and A. H. Halsey, *Family and Community Socialism* (London: Institute for Public Policy Research, 1995), pp. 4–11, 13–14. Used by permission.

Extracts from Barbara A. Harrison, 'Women of the Manor – ministry on an Urban Priority-Area council estate' in Elaine Graham and Margaret Halsey (eds), *Life Cycles: Women and Pastoral Care* (London: SPCK, 1993), pp. 145–8, 151–4. Used by permission of SPCK/Sheldon Press.

8   Work in the city

Extract from Malcolm Grundy, *Light in the City: Stories of the Church Urban Fund* (Norwich: Canterbury Press, 1990), pp. 58–61. Used by permission.

Gordon Hopkins, 'The parish church and the industrial worker', *Theology* **69**, 1966, 549–53. Used by permission of SPCK/Sheldon Press.

Extracts from 'Prophetic action: the churches' involvement' in Paul H. Ballard, *In and Out of Work: A Pastoral Perspective* (Edinburgh: Saint Andrew Press, 1987) pp. 152–66. Used by permission.

'London: new life in the inner city' in Mary Lean, *Bread, Bricks and Belief: Communities in Charge of Their Future* (West Hartford, CT: Kumarian Press, 1995), pp. 113–24. Used by permission of Kumarian Press Inc., 14 Oakwood Avenue, West Hartford, CT 06119 USA.

9 Worship in the city

'A service of healing for a hurting world' by Bread for the World, 'A ritual to invite light into areas of darkness' by Mary Robins and 'We are not alone' by Dorothy McRae-McMahon, taken from *Human Rites: Worship Resources for an Age of Change*, compiled by Hannah Ward and Jennifer Wild (London: Mowbray, 1995), pp. 138–42, 273, 292–4. Copyright © the authors.

Extracts from John and Angela Pearce, *Inner-City Spirituality* (Nottingham: Grove Booklets, 1987), pp. 11, 15–19. Used by permission.

Extracts from 'Praxis, prayer and liturgy in a secular world' in Ann Morisy, *Beyond the Good Samaritan: Community Ministry and Mission* (London: Mowbray, 1997), pp. 49–59. Used by permission.

Extracts from 'A worshipping community' in Nicholas Bradbury, *City of God? Pastoral Care in the Inner City* (London: SPCK, 1989), pp. 59–62, 64–71. Used by permission of SPCK/Sheldon Press.

10 Ministry in the city

Extract from William H. Vanstone, *Love's Endeavour, Love's Expense: The Response of Being to the Love of God* (London: Darton, Longman and Todd, 1977), pp. 30–5. Used by permission.

Extract from 'The encounter of the Christian faith and modern technological society' in E. R. Wickham, *Encounter with Modern Society* (London: Lutterworth Press, 1964), pp. 36–42. Used by permission of James Clarke & Co., Ltd.

Extracts from Paul Bagshaw, *The Church Beyond the Church: Sheffield Industrial Mission 1944–1994* (Sheffield: Sheffield Industrial Mission, 1994), pp. 131–8. Used by permission of the author.

Extract from John Tiller, 'The associational Church and its communal mission' in Giles Ecclestone (ed.), *The Parish Church? Explorations in the Relationships of the Church and the World* (London: Mowbray, 1988), pp. 90–6. Used by permission.

11 Mission in the city

Extracts from Helen Bonnick, 'Plaistow Christian Fellowship' in Michael Easton (ed.), *Ten Inner-City Churches* (Eastbourne: MARC Europe, 1988), pp. 179–86, 188–92. Used by permission of Kingsway Publications.

Raymond Bakke, 'Evangelism' in Raymond Bakke with Jim Hart, *The Urban Christian* (Bromley: MARC Europe, 1987), pp. 149–55. Used by permission of Kingsway Publications.

John Vincent, 'Signs for mission' in *Into the City* (London: Epworth Press, 1982), pp. 109–15. Used by permission.

Extract on pp. 300–7 from Jim Wallis, *The Call to Conversion* (London: Lion, 1982), pp. 112–23. Copyright by Harper and Row, San Francisco. Used by permission of HarperCollins Publishers. Copyright © 1981 by Sojourners.

12   Faiths in the city

Elizabeth A. Carnelley, 'Prophecy, race and Eastenders: ministry on the Isle of Dogs and celebrating the difference', *Modern Believing* 36, 1995, 25–9. Used by permission.

'Racism and the proclamation of the Gospel' in Kenneth Leech, *Struggle in Babylon* (London: Sheldon Press, 1988), pp. 206–15. Used by permission of SPCK/Sheldon Press.

Extracts from Greg Smith, 'The unsecular city: the revival of religion in East London' in Tim Butler and Michael Rustin (eds), *Rising in the East* (London: Lawrence and Wishart, 1996), pp. 124–31, 139–43. Used by permission of Lawrence and Wishart.

Extracts from Barney Pityana, 'Towards a black theology for Britain' in Anthony Harvey (ed.), *Theology in the City* (London: SPCK, 1989), pp. 103–12. Used by permission of SPCK/Sheldon Press.

1

Theology in the city

Peter went up on the roof to pray. He grew hungry and wanted something to eat, but while they were getting it he fell into a trance. He saw heaven opened, and something coming down that looked like a great sheet of sackcloth; it was hung by the four corners and was being lowered to the earth, and in it he saw creatures of every kind, four-footed beasts, reptiles, and birds. There came a voice which said to him, 'Get up, Peter, kill and eat.' But Peter answered, 'No, Lord! I have never eaten anything profane and unclean.' The voice came again, a second time: 'It is not for you to call profane what God counts clean.' This happened three times, and then the thing was taken up into heaven.

On the following day (Peter) arrived at Caesarea. Cornelius was expecting them and had called together his relatives and close friends. When Peter arrived, Cornelius came to meet him, and bowed to the ground in deep reverence. But Peter raised him to his feet and said, 'Stand up; I am only a man like you.' Still talking with him he went in and found a large gathering. He said to them, 'I need not tell you that a Jew is forbidden by his religion to visit or associate with anyone of another race. Yet God has shown me clearly that I must not call anyone profane or unclean.

'I now understand how true it is that God has no favourites, but that in every nation those who are god-fearing and do what is right are acceptable to him. He sent his word to the Israelites and gave the good news of peace through Jesus Christ, who is Lord of all.'

Peter was still speaking when the Holy Spirit came upon all who were listening to the message. The believers who had come with Peter, men of Jewish birth, were amazed that the gift of the Holy Spirit should have been poured out even on Gentiles, for they could hear them speaking in tongues of ecstasy and acclaiming the greatness of God. Then Peter spoke: 'Is anyone prepared to withhold the water of baptism from these persons, who have received the Holy Spirit just as we did?' Then he ordered them to be baptized in the name of Jesus Christ.'

(Acts 10:9b–16, 24–29, 34–36, 44–48)

Faith in the City

Are there not signs that, in UPAs as elsewhere in this country, small groups
of people are beginning to follow their own style of theological reflection
and to deepen their Christian understanding in ways that spring naturally
from their own culture and abilities? May such groups not have a contribution to make to the theological thinking of the wider Church as a whole?
May we not expect to see in UPAs the emergence of a theology which
would provide an authentic basis for a Christian critique of contemporary
society? (3.35)

Such a theology would start, not from a conventional academic syllabus of
Christian knowledge or biblical study, but from the personal experience,
the modes of perception and the daily concerns of local people themselves
— priorities which might well be different from those of people of a more
intellectual background. (3.36)

Introduction

The story of Saint Peter's call in a dream to visit the household of a Gentile
Roman centurion in the maritime city of Caesarea is a classic instance of early
Christian 'urban theology'. Caesarea was an important trading centre with a
deep harbour and large public buildings. It had a mixed population amongst
whom there were considerable tensions manifested in ethnic riots between Jews
and Gentiles (recorded by Josephus), and in many atrocities against the Jews. In
the story we read how the leading Apostle of the Jewish Christian Church in
Jerusalem was sent to confirm and welcome the Gentile household into the new
people of God. Peter's vision of the sheet, and then his lived vision of the Holy
Spirit falling on Cornelius and his household, leads to a new theological revelation that 'God has no favourites' and to a new praxis where Peter, the Apostle of
the Jewish Christian Church at Jerusalem, decides to baptize a Gentile household
into the Christian faith, the first recorded instance of such a baptism in the New
Testament. The revolution that this story describes gives it a key place in the
Book of Acts and in the history of the early church.

This dramatic story takes place in a situation of both social and religious
tension which mirrors many of the social and ethnic divisions in cities in Britain
today. For Jews like Peter to enter a Gentile house and to be in physical contact
with Gentiles such as the action of baptism would require was proscribed. A Jew
who even conversed with Gentiles was rendered unclean according to the
religious strictures of the time. The story witnesses to the new things that the
Spirit of God is doing in the church and the world after the coming of Christ, and
the power of the Gospel of Jesus Christ in those empowered and called by the
Spirit to challenge exclusion, to transform division into communion, and to draw
the marginalized into the heart of the community of the people of God.

The story also testifies to the deep theological truth that, despite the exclusions
of the poor from the good life of the city, whether on peripheral housing estates
or in run-down inner city areas, God has no favourites. Human societies and
economic systems may be designed to exclude some and favour others but God's

design for human society recognizes the claim of every individual child and adult, black or white, poor or rich, Muslim, Hindu, Jew or Christian, to a secure and healthy life because every person bears the image of God and is a potential child of God.

The story is an exemplar of urban theology above all because it shows the Apostles discovering that God does new things in new cultural contexts, and that openness to the newness of God involves prayer, spirituality and sensitivity to the action of the Spirit in the self and in the social world. Until the secularization of the universities after the Enlightenment, theology had always been determinatively linked to the life and worship of Christian communities and to the religious disciplines of prayer, spiritual direction and discernment. Modern academic theology has become divorced from the life and worship of the Church, and especially from the spiritual and cultural struggles of urban Christians to discern the way of Christ in the life of the modern city.

The authors of *Faith in the City* suggested that urban theology should be rooted in the personal experiences and concerns of local people, and that such a theology will be an authentic expression of local culture. They contended that intellectual and doctrinal styles of theology are unable to foster indigenous styles of church life and theological reflection in the city. However, despite these observations the report was curiously silent on the actual shape and content of urban theology. Referring to the multiplicity of local theologies in urban areas the commission concluded that they were unable to present a 'theology of the city' and could only point to its emergent, particularistic, diverse and local character. The consequent theological weakness of the report is in marked contrast to the authority which the document acquired in the social policy arena. Though derided by government, the report carried the authority of an institution which was more rooted in, and conscious of, the problems and struggles of poor and unemployed people and urban neighbourhoods characterized by multiple deprivation than any government agency or any group of professionals. It was lauded by sociologists and community activists as a manifesto for urban regeneration and a critique of the individualistic and *laissez-faire* drift of urban policy in the 1980s.

As a critique of *laissez-faire* economics and an argument for more just social policies, the report reflected the strengths of the Christian social tradition in the nineteenth and twentieth centuries as exemplified in the writings of R. H. Tawney. The urban industrial cities of Europe were a new thing in human history and the churches responded to this new way of living with a social critique which emphasized the need to restrain the emergent forces of capital and the divisions between rich and poor which were shaping the new cities. While the churches sought to restrain the worst excesses of capitalism through social critique and charitable works, they were less effective in transplanting the worship and common life of the rural parish church into the working-class communities of the new cities. Indeed, by the early twentieth century it became clear to the clergy of the Church of England, serving alongside working men in the trenches of the First World War, that the gap between the Church and the working classes had become almost unbridgeable. The culture and lifestyle of factory-dominated working-class communities came as a shock to many clergy, who were still drawn from the professional and landed classes and who, unlike Peter in relation to his old religion, were unable to critique the roots of parochial ministry and worship in rural communities and to discern the wisdom of God in the city in ways which both critiqued and connected with the new life of the city. The flight of the Church into social ethical critique of the city, and into attempts to modernize theology, represented an effort to reverse this disconnection but there was a cultural naïveté to these which missed the inherent hopefulness, humanity and spiritual potential within working-class culture, as well as its peculiar forms of sinfulness (Sedgwick).

The rise of the global megalopolis, in many of which upwards of 10 million people live in a confusing proximity, is a further challenge to established modes of theology and ministry. It is crucial for the Church in this new and constantly changing missionary context to be open to the sights, sounds, shapes, symbols and structures of the modern city and the megalopolis, to the voices of its peoples, and especially to the boundaries and divisions which, as in the Cornelius story, exclude some from the good life and the hope of salvation. While sensitive to social divisions, *Faith in the City* evidences a lack of sensitivity to cultural markers and symbols in the neighbourhoods and church communities which the Archbishop's Commission investigated. Similarly, while claiming that 'God, though infinitely transcendent, is also to be found, despite all appearances, in the apparent waste lands of our inner cities and housing estates', the report witnesses more to the disappearance of God than to divine presence in the culture of the inner city. The report was not only theologically weak, but above all it manifested a spiritual lacuna, concerned more with the reorganization of church structures and the reshaping of government policy than with the spiritual and theological discernment of the pathologies and redemptive possibilities of Urban Priority Areas.

Writing ten years after the publication of *Faith in the City*, the authors of *God in the City* identify their theological task as cultural and spiritual discernment, or, in David Ford's words, 'distilling the wisdom' (Ford and Green). While focusing on the reality of daily life in the inner city and the peripheral housing estate, they attempt to move beyond economic and political questions to the distinctively theological task of a 'cultural reading' of urban areas in the light of the Christian tradition, and in particular such dominant motifs as sin, redemption, and sanctification (Sedgwick). This cultural reading can be seen in essays on sexuality, crime, enterprise and children and in an emphasis on church-going, praise, worship and the stories of the people of God as the determinative response of the Church to the inner city.

We may identify a similar process of cultural reading and discernment of wisdom in Peter's role in the Cornelius story. The story indicates that cultural reading, or what is sometimes called contextualization, involves both divine judgement and divine affirmation of human culture: the ethnic exclusions of the Apostle Peter's Jewish culture are judged and overturned while the spiritual experiences of Cornelius and his god-fearing household lead the Jewish Apostle to initiate them all into the sacrament of baptism. The discernment process, which has some similarities with the process of contextual theology described in the extract from Laurie Green's *Let's Do Theology*, may be expressed as follows: 1. spiritual vision and call to mission; 2. cultural judgement and critique of self and society; 3. a new sensitivity to the action of God as Spirit; 4. divinely inspired wisdom; 5. remaking divine worship and retelling the stories of God and God's people. Through this process of discernment Peter's mind was prised open to the new truth that God loves the excluded Gentiles, because he encountered the creator Spirit of God in the alien social world and culture of the Gentiles, and so he was prepared to reinterpret his own long-held beliefs and traditions in the light of the action of the Spirit.

Similarly, urban Christians and urban theologians need to be alive to the action of the Spirit which 'blows where it wills' and to the spiritual yearnings present in the inherent creativity of the cultures, languages, stories and struggles of those who are on the margins of our society. For too long the Western Church has excluded non-Western peoples from full participation in the household of God because of their cultural traditions and styles. Non-Western Christians have only in this century begun to make the Gospel and the Church their own as Christianity becomes rooted and inculturated in their own contexts. There is a similar challenge in relation to the urban poor in the West. We need a church *of* the poor, not a church *for* the poor. Such a church will not look like the churches of the rich or even of the comfortable.

Affirming the poor as the makers of their own history and as theologians in their own right is an essential part of urban theology. As we have seen, this new way of doing theology involves a recognition that theology is the work of the people of God, and not just of academic theologians, priests and preachers. Some British urban theologians have sought to adapt the methods and language of liberation theology as the means to revitalize theological activity 'from below' (Davey). Like their Latin American counterparts, they criticize academic theology not only for its distance from everyday life and the local struggles of ordinary people but also because of its bias towards the rich and powerful, a bias which they also find in the structures of the Church (Schreiter). However, it is now widely recognized that liberation theologians, far from making the poor the agents of their own indigenous spirituality and theology, actually succeeded in imposing a secular Marxist political analysis on the peoples of Latin America. Instead of liberating them from oppressive social oligopolies and ecclesiastical monopolies, liberation theology gave the priests who had traditionally been complicit in social oppression a new mode of priestly authority among the poor. At the same time the liberation theologians were often blind to the spiritual riches of the religions and indigenous cultures of the poor whom they claimed to speak for (Segundo).

In many Latin American countries the poor are turning in growing numbers from the liberation theologies and base communities of the monopoly Catholic Church to the spiritualities and theologies of Pentecostalism and Protestant evangelicalism which have allowed them genuinely to become makers, individually as well as collectively, of their own histories and stories. Through the expressive power of the language of praise and the spiritual and social uplift of the gift of the Spirit Latin American women as well as men are building new churches and small businesses, and becoming healers and preachers as well as local political leaders and community activists (Cox).

The changing religious situation in Latin America is not without parallels in the growing spiritual diversity and religious entrepreneurialism of British cities in the 1990s. Whilst *Faith in the City* was primarily addressed to national government and to the Church of England, the most successful regeneration efforts in inner city areas and peripheral housing estates in the last twenty years have been focused on community enterprises and initiatives which have often been started by local people, and sometimes by local churches, rather than by design or planning from higher authority. This shift from collective to local and individual entrepreneurialism is reflected also in the efforts of local authorities to relocate service delivery on housing estates to local estate management offices, and in buy-outs and local tenancy management agreements.

A similar shift can be discerned in the religious sphere as many new churches, temples and mosques have sprung up or been planted in inner city areas while mainstream churches continue to close redundant churches and struggle to keep open the church buildings which remain. The new churches in such areas are often of an evangelical or Pentecostal tradition, some of them are black-led, and some of them are led by middle-class outsiders who see themselves as missionaries in the new secular environment of the inner city. Like the successful inner city Anglo-Catholic shrines of previous generations, these new churches lay great emphasis on spiritual experience, praise and ritual and on the power of religion to lift people above their social circumstances and to provide moral and theological resources for personal transformation in the midst of otherwise crushing social and personal problems. At the same time other spiritual and social practices have grown up in UPAs, as in other parts of our cities in recent years, including the occult, drug addiction and racist organization which reflect the prevalence of spiritual bondage and social victimization in the modern secular city.

Theological and sociological reflection on contemporary urban life is increasingly open to the diversity, particularism and localism of the sites and places of the postmodern city, and to the spiritual and religious opportunities of this diversity (**Schreiter**). While urban theologians in the past, including some extracted below, celebrated the dominant secular story of social hope and technological progress, they often missed the opportunities for spiritual renewal in the new forms of sociality and community, and the spiritual and moral bondages and demons, which urban living occasioned. Contemporary urban theologians, on the other hand, and indeed some contemporary sociologists, are much more alive to the spiritual and moral problems and possibilities, as well as the social exclusions and opportunities, of the postmodern city. This is reflected in the growing ability of urban theologians to discern the life of God in the particular struggles of Christians to remake their worship, and to regenerate their neighbourhoods, in the midst of these problems and exclusions. Their writings reflect a new confidence in God and in spirituality which earlier generations of urban theologians and urban Christians were in danger of losing. They are not hesitant to argue that worship, spiritual experience and ritual are effective means to address social dis-ease; they are prepared to make direct connections between the Bible as the revealed witness of the Spirit and the stories of the people of God in contemporary cities; they are able to see the local church in the UPA not as marginal to the secular forces which shape the community but as potentially the central player, often the only grassroots organization on an estate, able confidently to host or organize regeneration initiatives (Ford and Green; Sedgwick; *The Cities: A Methodist Report*).

This new-found confidence in God, worship and the local church reflects a theological reorientation even in the midst of the worsening social problems of Britain's cities in the 1990s. Above all, it reflects a spiritual belief in the power and creativity of people, whatever their circumstances, to be empowered by the redeeming work of God in Christ, to experience new life in the gift of the Spirit, and to express that new life both in moral change and in projects of social and community transformation in urban neighbourhoods (*The Cities: A Methodist Report*). The resultant stories of these spiritual and social transformations provide the richest source for an urban theology at the end of this modern century. We hope that in some way they echo the vivid stories and letters gathered in the New Testament of transformation of the first urban Christians and their new communities (Meeks). The centrality of story is reflected in the twelve sets of readings which follow which each commence with a story of social or spiritual transformation, in the conviction that it is in such stories that the wisdom of God for the urban people of God can be truly discerned.

Liberation theology in Peckham

Andrew Davey

In our congregation Liberation Theology has provided an invaluable methodology. Echoing Gutiérrez' description of doing theology as 'critical reflection on Christian praxis in the light of the Word',[1] social analysis has played its part alongside Bible study in understanding some of the pressures and dynamics facing the area and the church. In the context of a series of such studies, we analysed how power was held in the church and society and identified the ways in which interest groups create ideology to secure their position. From there we constructed our alternative futures in the form of manifestos — manifestos which incorporated participants' insights from work with refugees, schools, political parties and credit unions.

The three manifestos that were brought to the session each approached the task from a different angle. The first was concerned with the problems of Peckham and the changes needed locally and nationally to bring about a better society. The second was concerned with how the church must change. The third tried to rewrite Isaiah 61:1–2 and Luke 4:18–19 as the good news for now.

Three important elements emerged in each manifesto:

1. Freedom from fear, freedom from discrimination, equal shares and dignity, 'give children back their childhood', get rid of loan sharks.
2. A radical shift in relationships. The Church of England must listen to the poor, it must work to empower the poor, it must share resources for the good of the poorer parishes.
3. Good news for those who do not know peace, possibility for the hopeless, freedom for those who cling to rules and regulations, and 'to rattle the conscience of those who are comfortable'.

We talked about how our faith helps us discover new possibilities and dream alternative futures. We thought about the sermon we heard on Easter Day, preached by a friend of mine from East Berlin. She contrasted the bad news of the soldiers, bribed by the authorities to say reality was no different, that the disciples had moved the body, and the good news of the women, who claimed nothing would ever be the same again. We thought about how becoming part of St Luke's changed the way people lived and thought — discovering and developing skills, confidence, etc. We decided to put up the manifestos in church and ask people to look at them at Pentecost. The St Luke's congregation was felt to be an important place to create an alternative way of organizing a church as we continued to equip ourselves in ways that might begin to work on making those manifestos a reality. A greater determination to participate and influence things in groups already offering the possibility of change and doing things was felt to be important.

The process enabled some of those involved to articulate experiences of social exclusion as an important stage in self-understanding and valuing people whose stories remain untold and voices unheard. An important element in the process has been attempting to start where the participants are in terms of social location as well as faith and intellectual understanding.

This involves taking seriously instinctive religiosity, particularly among older members, which is often not articulated, and also encouraging the discovery of the liberative strands in their stories and those of their biblical inheritance. The British theologian Andrew Kirk, who spent twelve years teaching in Latin America, encourages English UPA Christians to learn from the Latin American experience 'in the task of reflecting theologically from where they are' in the process of relating Scripture and experience.[2] Like Sobrino he looks forward to

> the church of the poor. No longer does the church come in from outside, as it were, as well defined body to act on behalf of the poor. They now hear for themselves the good news of Jesus and the Kingdom and seek to translate it into action within their fellowship and beyond in the community.[3]

The formation of such a church is the task we set for ourselves at St Luke's.

Social and geographical dislocation is a common experience in Peckham. Those who make up our church congregation have few roots in the area — only two families have any history in the area of more than one generation. Most have family roots in the Caribbean or Africa.[4] There are also local communities which our worshipping community does not draw from, notably Vietnamese and Somali. The rural poor of the Third World have become the concrete-bound dispossessed of the first. That dispossession is not just the experience of poverty and limited social access, but also the stigmatizing of our area and the constant experience of pollution as from traffic, etc.

Walter Brueggemann, when reflecting on OT land theologies, wrote, 'a sense of place is a primary category of faith'.[5] Space becomes place only when there are stories and hopes lodged there. The experience of exile and captivity is the experience of coerced space in contrast with trusted place. 'The central problem is not emancipation but *rootage*, not meaning but *belonging*, not separation from community but *location* within it.'[6]

The strategy for a sustainable, relevant Christian presence among the rootless and dispossessed is the struggle for a community that embraces the fight against captivity and landlessness. These elements have featured in the ongoing process of group work and my own reflection alongside the congregation.

Themes of migration, the search for 'home' and of being an outsider feature regularly in our experience and discussions.

Most of us were brought up with Bible maps which plotted in huge squiggles Abraham's wanderings through the ancient Near East. On one occasion a group plotted alongside such a map their own journeys — from the Caribbean to the Southern States at the height of segregation, from London to Nigeria and back again, from rural Ulster to urban Belfast and then on to London, from the Caribbean to Southport to Balham to Peckham. All roads somehow lead to Peckham, at least in these stories!

Within those stories, we heard of the search for Christian community, of risks taken, of expectations raised and misunderstandings. The community which Abraham and Sarah drew around them seems a paradigm of our experience and aspirations, a place where blessings are shared, strangers are welcomed, faith is passed on, hope takes root, alongside faith being tested to the extreme. A community where people are drawn from traditional cultures has many hazards and pitfalls. It can also have the feeling of a counter-culture apparent particularly when welcoming and hospitality are discussed. Our reflection has also helped with a partnership being created with an evangelical agency working with refugees and speakers of other languages based on our premises.

In our discussions it became increasingly noticeable that those taking part often considered themselves to be on the periphery of institutions, communities and society in general. We spent time looking at how people become outsiders and how those who are insiders maintain control. In this process we used examples from the Gospels, people's own experiences, and the well-known example of the apartheid system in South Africa.

The geographical location, the encounters and the teaching of Jesus in the synoptic Gospels all point to the marginal as key to the coming and presence of the Kingdom of God. On one occasion, we took the three stories of 'children of Abraham' from Luke's Gospel[7] which all point to a concern to include those who, for whatever reason, are denied full participation in the society to which they rightfully belong. Among the marginal, Jesus discovers faith, an honesty to admit to their deficiencies and needs,[8] alongside acute insight into the reality of what makes them marginal. They are the most receptive not only to the message but also to the invitation to create an alternative way of community life, on the periphery, which challenges the hegemony which others wittingly and unwittingly maintain. It is Jesus' practice of 'open commensality' not his parables of the great feast that provokes the severest opposition.[9] This and other symbolic acts (not least at the symbolic level of ritual ideas about impurity) are in essence political action. Such political action is appropriate in a context where the majority of the population are excluded from any type of structural political participation. This approach of the political, which I suspect is a key paradigm for our church life in Peckham, is described in a recent article by Chris Rowland:

> By *political* in this context I mean their relationship to conventional patterns of human interaction and organisation, whether formal (like a Sanhedrin or local body of elders) or informal and traditional (like widely established practices). The political challenge posed by Jesus involved departures from norms of behaviour, status, attitude and access to social intercourse which are typical of a particular society.[10]

The marginalized experience and understand the reality of their situation in a vitally different way from others. From the margins they perceive two realities (or narratives). First, their own immediate reality within which they must struggle for survival and look after their own as best they can. Second, from the margin they also need to understand the systems and language of insiders because it is from there that their own position is determined and the rules of that order are made. Insiders do not need the perspective of those on the periphery because their powerful situation gets them all they need. Jesus attempts to create an inclusive community for those united by suffering and their experience of exclusion. Within that community they experience the possibility of healing and hope. Jesus reinterprets the powerful's world view with outsiders in mind: they shall possess the Kingdom, inherit the earth, receive consolation — this is 'the story of marginality ... retold as entitle-ment'.[11] This is the starting-point of the marginalized's new identity from where lives can be reconstructed. The Jesus community, and the Kingdom that is glimpsed through it, are paradigms of the restructuring of attitudes and systems which are condemned by the very existence of outsiders. There the marginalized come to understand that there can be no security in becoming an insider. Security is to be found in their growing sense of dependence on God and interdependence with each other[12] from which even the most harrowing suffering can be endured. Insiders, that is the rich and powerful, might be called to repent and join this community. It would have been this call to adopt a radical egalitarianism stance which presented the greatest challenge to the readers of the Gospel in Hellenistic culture.

NOTES

1. Gustavo Gutiérrez, *A Theology of Liberation* Revised Version (London: SCM Press, 1988), p. 11.
2. Andrew Kirk, 'Liberation theology and local theologies', in Anthony Harvey (ed.) *Theology in the City: A Theological Response to Faith in the City* (London: SPCK, 1989), p. 24.
3. Ibid., p. 26.
4. The ethnic origins of members on the 1995 electoral roll were 61.5 per cent West African, 24 per cent Caribbean, 9 per cent other African, Asian, Greek, etc.
5. Walter Brueggemann, *The Land: Place as Gift Promise and Challenge in Biblical Faith* (London: SPCK, 1977), p. 4.
6. Ibid., p. 187.
7. I.e. the woman in the synagogue, Zaccheus, Lazarus in Abraham's bosom.
8. Maybe the *New English Bible* rendering of the first beatitude 'Blessed are those who know their need of God ...' isn't that far from the point.
9. John Dominic Crossan, *Jesus: A Revolutionary Biography* (San Francisco: HarperCollins, 1994), p. 69.
10. Christopher Rowland, 'Reflections on the politics of the Gospels', in R.S. Barbour (ed.), *The Kingdom of God and Human Society* (Edinburgh: T & T Clark, 1993), p. 240.
11. This phrase is used by Walter Brueggemann referring to Joshua's speech at Schechem. See *Biblical Perspectives on Evangelism: Living in a Three-Storied Universe* (Nashville: Abingdon Press, 1993), p. 61.
12. J. Kopas, 'Outsiders in the Gospel: marginality as a source of knowledge', *The Way*, 35, 1993, p. 117.

Why do theological reflection?

Laurie Green

I have described elsewhere[1] how, during my ministry in Birmingham, I worked with a group of Christians who began a biblical study of the parables of Jesus, asking what made them such striking stories. They soon perceived that each parabolic story begins with a short account of a situation in life that

seems to present no great challenges. But, then, usually towards the end of
the story, there is a sudden change of gear, and the story whips round and
challenges the hearers. For example, something may go very wrong for the
hero who, after building bigger barns to store all his wealth, finds that his life
is at an end and he cannot enjoy the fruit of his labour (Luke 12:16–21). Or,
as in another example, the villain of the story, having proved himself an
unjust steward, finds himself admired, even though he has used all sorts of
questionable means to secure his own future. He finds that he is applauded
for at least having the sense to realize how critical his predicament has been
(Luke 16:1–8). Sometimes the whole situation in the parable changes, as, for
example, when the farm-workers wake up to find that weeds have sprouted
up in their newly sown crop (Matthew 13:24–30). Or the generosity of a
character in the story passes all known bounds, as when the father welcomes
the squandering rascal of a prodigal son back to his home with open arms
(Luke 15:11–32). On every occasion, there is an unexpected twist in the tale
of the parable — what the Birmingham group began to call 'God's Unexpected'. When that group then looked back at their locality with this
Unexpected in mind, they saw with fresh eyes certain features of the social
landscape which would have been totally unexpected before. They began to
notice the hidden poverty, the generosity of those in need, and the now
obvious injustices of the community. Then they looked back at the Bible and
saw more and more evidence of God's Unexpected — in the birth of Jesus in
a stable, in the death of God's Son as a criminal on a cross, the choice of lowly
fishermen and prostitutes as Jesus' closest friends. As they looked back at the
contradictions in their locality in the light of this, they began to appreciate
that it was exactly these same lowly people whom Jesus, in the Gospels, had
taken as his special friends. Yet they still do not seem welcome in the local
church, and still get the worst deal and least respect in society. But most
dangerous and subversive of all, the group began to feel the urge and the
mandate upon them from the Bible stories to do something about the
situation. So theological reflection on a situation can be a subversive activity
when it begins to point up the contradictions in this manner and then spur a
group to social action.

But it is not only the Bible that can do this. The same sort of challenge to
our situation can also come from elsewhere in our Christian heritage. Some
people have found on entering a beautiful church building that they have had
to start asking questions about the ugliness of their own lives or the situation
that surrounds them. Others have looked at Christian symbols like the
crucifix and have been brought up sharp. Some have received Communion
and been shocked to think how different the equal sharing of that action is
from the unequal distribution of gifts in our own society. If we receive God's
choice wine at the Eucharist and then refuse to give to others of our own
luxury, it takes only a short time of reflection before we sense the contradiction of our actions. There will be many symbols, actions and stories from
the Christian traditions of faith both within the Bible and without it, which
will serve to challenge our contemporary experience, and this reflection
phase gives us opportunity to discern those connections and contemplate
them.

During this reflection phase we will be endeavouring to tease out the
connections of meaning between, on the one hand, our contemporary

situation as experienced and explored and, on the other hand, the great wealth of Christian history, teaching and faith — what I refer to in this article as the Christian faith traditions. So why do we seek to make these connections? First, immersing ourselves in these faith traditions helps us view our experience from the alternative perspective of the Divine. One aspect of this new perspective, which the Christian heritage brings to our contemporary scene, might for example be seen in the fact that in the incarnation God has been experienced by the Christian community in the holiness and otherness of the sufferer and the servant.[2] God seems therefore to see things, to hear things, from the point of view of the sufferer and of those most in need in society. This is a perspective that is rarely appreciated by us, but if we immerse ourselves in the traditions of the Christian faith then we can begin to make this way of viewing things our own, and we can begin to see things to which we were altogether blind before we opened ourselves to these faith traditions. Perhaps this opening of ourselves to God's perspective is something of what St Paul meant when he prayed that we might take on 'the mind of Christ' (1 Corinthians 2:16). But there are also other reasons why, in our theological reflection, we will wish to bring the insights of our Christian tradition to bear upon the findings of our experience and exploration, and so make the connections between that situation and our Christian heritage.

First, there is our wish to check out our contemporary thinking and action against the alternative authority. We are wanting to know whether we are telling the Jesus story or whether we are relating a different story altogether, perhaps one of our own making. We therefore check to see if there are connections between our own experience and the Christian experience through the ages as recorded for us in our great faith traditions. To do this we will need to come to terms with the problem of the tension between faithfulness to the text of the tradition, on the one hand, and contemporary relevance, on the other. If we can overcome this dilemma with integrity and find the connections between our Christian heritage and our contemporary scene, then this will reinforce our faith in our actions and give us the courage to continue.

Another reason for wanting to make these connections with our Christian past is that some of the faith traditions themselves will require checking against the authority of present experience and our understanding of God's present actions. A clear example of this is to be found in the church tradition of the infallibility of the Pope. Our particular denomination within the Church may not accept that tradition as it is commonly understood, and may hold the view that we cannot accept that doctrine as permissible because it does not stand the test of being checked against other traditions (maybe the biblical texts) and, more particularly, against our contemporary understandings of authority and validity.

Yet another reason for wanting to make these connections between faith and life is that it provides occasion for our God-given creative imagination to become inspired in the process of seeking what the traditions have to say to our situation. In this way, the creative spark has its chance to develop in us under the guidance of the Holy Spirit so that we are not simply thrust back into the dullness of an uncritical acceptance of either the tradition or the present situation. Theological reflection provides us with the creative double-edge of reason and imagination.

Finally, we are wanting to contradict those who argue that even for Christians it is not necessary to use 'God-talk' in relation to our contemporary situation because we have appropriate disciplines already to hand in the secular sphere. Our successful practice of the pursuit of meaning and relevant action using theological reflection proves them wrong. In bringing our Christian heritage into connection with our contemporary experience, we guard against a blinkered acceptance of the world. It is this blind affirmation that has hampered many Christians in the past and has led to their uncritical subservience to the injustice of social pragmatism. For while acknowledging that theology of itself does not contain the necessary tools to analyse the internal structures and causal relationships within society, we do maintain with all seriousness that it is only theology that can take the raw material unearthed by our exploration, and work with that material to look for the meaning of it and sense the relationship that the Transcendent has with it. This quest for the Divine is of course the prime motive of the whole exercise, so while the theological reflection may, according to our cyclical diagram, follow on after the experience and exploration phases, it only comes after in terms of methodology, whereas in terms of importance, it precedes them both. So even though we save theological reflection until this later stage of the cycle, we are not allowing the world to lead us by the nose, nor are we content to stop at analysis of the world, but we commit ourselves entirely to the importance of theological reflection, which now becomes possible by virtue of the preceding 'secular' analysis.[3] So we will be allowing ourselves the excitement and adventure of the quest for an undogmatic and unideological faith, by which I mean that we will not come at experience merely to lay upon it the prejudiced dogma of a bygone age, nor open our traditions to a simplistic scientism, but will bring our faith traditions and our felt experience together into a creative mix. This is what theological reflection is all about.

The connections that we will discover between our traditions and our present experience will be of various kinds. First, we may find that our intuition senses certain *similarities* between the faith traditions and the present issue. On the other hand, we may be provoked by the total *opposition* that we see between certain elements of, for example, the Gospels, and the situation. But thirdly, the connections between the traditions and our situation may initially come to us as quite unclear intuitive *hunches* or suspicions. We sense that something is 'on' between elements from each side of the spectrum and we feel that they must connect somehow, although we will need to take time to discover quite how.

In order to do theological reflection, then, we have to develop methods of bringing into juxtaposition our present life experience and the treasures of our Christian heritage, to check one against the other, to let each talk to the other, to learn from the mix and to gain even more insight to add to the store of Christian heritage. However, it has long been recognized that we live in a world that must feel very different from the world in which the great traditional treasures of the faith were born. The Bible, the early Christian creeds, the sacramental and early liturgical life of the Church were all formed and developed in contexts very different from our own. Our modern worldview is so very different that making sense of what was in the minds of those who lived during those early Christian centuries is not always easy. When we first approach the Bible or the creeds we are apt to think all is well, for surely humankind has always been confronted with the same basic issues, and God is the same yesterday as today. Believing this is true, we can immediately be at one with the text. However, the scientific application of scholarly theology has slowly but surely convinced us otherwise, for it is far from easy for us to make the required leap across from our own culture to that of the first Christian centuries and to know the mind of the writers and the first hearers of the scriptural message. In fact, the more we investigate the gap, the more we realize the extent of the difference between our culture and theirs, and the improbability of a late twentieth-century person ever being able to comprehend how people thought and felt in those earlier days and cultures now so far off. And if we cannot fully comprehend the culture, then how can we comprehend an artefact or text that emanates from it? There seems to be a gap between ourselves and these treasures; a gap of time, of culture, of expectation and perception. If I try to straddle the gap I get myself into complex problems of integrity, for when I properly acknowledge myself to be a person from a scientific culture, then biblical talk about being inhabited by demons seems to be a violation of what I know about illness, microbes, genes, and so on. If, on the other hand, I take models from the Bible to look at contemporary political issues, that would seem to do violence to the specificity of the biblical history. If, for example, I want to talk about the city, and use passages about the city from the Bible, I may be forgetting at my peril that in biblical times a city would have had a population only the size of one of our contemporary urban parishes. I stand in danger of overlaying the biblical material with all sorts of modern psychological and sociological paraphernalia that have no place in the original culture, and probably put me miles away from the intended meaning of the text. We are therefore presented with a problem: how can we make the leap, and interpret from one situation to another? This is what theology, in common with other disciplines, calls the problem of 'hermeneutics', the word hermeneutics meaning 'interpretation'.

Our reflective task is to find some way of bridging this cultural gap and seeing connections between the Christian heritage on one side and our present experience on the other — to hear resonances, to ring bells, to sense similarities, to sense opposition, to build up a whole range of sensitivities to the tradition so that we can draw upon it to check our present actions and understandings and see if our own story is part of the Jesus story, or not.

* * *

As we work with the faith traditions in this way we begin to understand how dynamic they themselves are. The traditions of Bible, creeds, sacraments, Church and so on, are not static monoliths handed on in some pure and untouched form from generation to generation, but are changed in all sorts of ways as they pass from culture to culture, from community to community, from age to age. Once we have acknowledged the fact of this dynamism within the traditions, then we really are in a much better place from which to do theology. For once we have fully appreciated the contextual nature of the thoughts and ideologies that come to us within the traditions, then we understand that to start our theological work from anywhere but experience is in one sense quite impossible, since even our conventional 'learned theology' will have emanated from an experience rather than simply a disembodied revelation. With this notion of the fluidity of the tradition firmly in mind, let us recap for a moment so that we can be clearer about how it is proposed that the great variety of exercises and methods that I have just sketched might actually bear upon the situation which we have been experiencing and exploring in our cycle of theology. How do we do it in practice?

Before anything else, we do well in the group to use the set-piece exercises to skirmish around the heritage of the faith tradition in order to remind ourselves of its breadth and vitality. Just remembering that we have all the treasures of Bible, Church, worship, prayer, doctrine and so on, can be an enjoyable experience .... . But then comes the time when the group looks back to the issue at hand and to its exploration. As it considers each element of the analysis in which it has been engaged, it frees its imagination to make those exciting leaps in order to see where the connections can be made. We expect these connections to occur where similarities or antagonisms are perceived between the explored issue and the traditions of faith. These imaginative leaps can be facilitated by any of the [participatory methods[4]], so that the issue is brought under the scrutiny and judgement of the faith traditions. For example, ... towards the end of our analysis in the exploration phase, we teased out the 'dominant values' that seemed to be operating in the situation. We may have decided that in our specific situation the values that were predominant were money, growth and success. In this case, we would now take each value in turn and let it trigger in our imagination any elements from the traditions of our Christian faith that came to mind. We could do the same not only with these dominant values, but for each element and avenue of the exploration until a whole range of connections were made. Each time a Christian faith tradition is thus focused, we can utilize all the participative study methods to get right inside that Gospel story or Church doctrine or hymn or whatever, to tease out even further any other connections that might be made. But of course we will still want to go much further than this in discerning what the connections actually have to teach us.

So the imaginative leap is made — using all the methods described — and we intuitively suspect that there is something in a connection that our imagination has been inspired to see. The Holy Spirit is operative in the process of reflection upon the issue that we have explored, and intuitively suggests that a particular element in the tradition — an element from the Bible, sacraments, church history, and so on — is somehow resonating with the experience in question and has something to teach us for today. So there emerges an *intuition* of what the tradition may hold. We might draw it in the following way.

Reflection

AN INTUITION

The 'intuition' is an imaginative leap which sets up an interplay between the explored issue and the Christian faith tradition so that each is affected by the other. The question starts to arise then of how the tradition we have intuitively thought of may interpret today's experience and what indeed may be the appropriate interpretation from today of that part of the tradition. The intuition sets up a two-way challenge. The next task will be to check that the intuition is not an illusion which might be contradicted by all else that our Christian experience and God-given reason tells us. This checking-out phase can be called exploration, for it will require analysis and a search for meaning, using all appropriate disciplines and tools just as before. So our newly reflected diagram will emerge as follows.

During this new exploration phase, it will be necessary to check out all that we know about the particular tradition, be it a piece of biblical text, a happening in the history of the Church, a doctrine, a hymn, or whatever. We will need to explore its original context and we will endeavour to see how this part of the tradition fits in with all the other segments of the tradition by cross-referencing, analysis and careful appraisal, just as we did earlier when the issue itself was the object of our exploration. There are many academic theological tools at our disposal to help us with this part of the exercise, where the intention will be to explore the piece of the tradition so well that we come to a moment when we can venture to say that the intuition does or does not make some valid sense. So from this careful exploration of the original theological intuition there may well now emerge a 'new witness' from within the tradition that can speak afresh to the situation. Our diagram then begins to complete a fresh cycle, thus:

This new witness will have an authority for the issue we are exploring, and yet will also now be known to have integrity in relation to the whole Christian tradition. It can be put back into the reflective encounter with the issue and must now be taken not merely as a leap of the imagination, but as an authoritative new witness to how God has been experienced in the world.

NOTES

1. Laurie Green, *Power to the Powerless: Theology Brought to Life* (London: Marshall Pickering, 1987).
2. See, for example, John 13 and Philippians 2:1–8.
3. Note also the words of Segundo: 'Any and every theological question begins with the human situation. Theology is "the second step" '. Juan Luis Segundo, *The Liberation of Theology* (Dublin: Gill & Macmillan, 1987), p. 79.
4. These participatory methods are introduced and surveyed on pp. 83–91 of *Let's Do Theology*.

A theology for today's city

From *The Cities: A Methodist Report*

Here, then, are elements for a theology of the city. Its first element is the logic of Election; that sense common to both Jewish and Christian traditions that one's people are not just better than others; they are The Chosen. This perception, at its worst, can be bigoted, paranoid and cruel. Christians can be very bad citizens.

The second element is the experience of Grace. Here is a tradition of spirituality rather than of theology. At its best, the tradition expresses an inward access to the love of God that illuminates the spirit and softens the heart. This generosity of spirit can transcend the logic that dogma imposes. It is possible to risk the notion that God invites us to celebrate a common humanity. Thus, John Wesley, himself impeccably orthodox wrote:

> I wish your zeal was better employed than in persuading men to be either dipped or sprinkled. I will employ mine, by the grace of God, in persuading them to love God with all their hearts, and their neighbours as themselves.[1]

Such a robust and generous spirituality can thrive in the city, where the diversity of our humanity mocks our exclusive instincts on every street corner. The city is a teeming mass of difference, whose reality goes far beyond the pallid clichés that describe urban life as a 'multi-faith' or a 'multi-cultural' experience. There is a rich variety of experience of difference, which Alexandria failed to grasp, and which Manchester nearly failed to grasp. There is an apparent paradox here; the more distinctive is the Christian experience, the less exclusive does Christian behaviour towards others need to be. This experience of the love of God does create problems; but it does not solve them in an excluding way. Christians can be very good citizens.

It is the capacity to engage creatively with others that matters, rather than to rehearse continually the reasons why God has blessed his Elect. Some of the objective, historically based theological realities have already been addressed. . . . [T]he pattern that has emerged over some centuries is one of movement from an exclusive to an inclusive pattern of theology and practice. This movement has become clear over half a millennium. The ferocity of the conflicts of that period are testimony to the difficulty of such a shift.

An attempt has been made here to sketch the ways in which the Church has responded to urban life in the course of its existence. In this way we hope to avoid the temptation to take a given view of the world and simply to interweave some traditional theological terms. The tradition always illuminates contemporary concerns, particularly in the turmoil of urban experience.

We have seen the Jewish–Christian temptation to apocalyptic despair over the city. We have also seen the tendency in the tradition to seek its salvation outside the compromises of ordinary life in the pursuit of an ascetic way. A rather diminished form of this instinct is found in the relative austerity that informs much Christian behaviour, and which often makes it hard for us to accept the raucous vigour of much urban life. As a consequence we tend not to comprehend the degree to which sheer appetite and self-interest drive the city, and we fail to see the elements of trust and hope which inform such self-interested pursuit, and which generate the immense resources required to create and to renew the city. It takes some imagination to feel our mutuality and interdependence as a spirituality of love, when that interdependence is embodied in economic give and take. We find it easy to feel that it is blessed to give, and to receive; but it is generally more difficult to feel the same about buying and selling.

Our brief reflection on the past suggests that God is moving the Church to a more inclusive understanding of the divine purpose. That conviction shapes the following theological observations on the contemporary city. The four theological themes that we wish to raise are:

Creation
Incarnation
Cross and Resurrection
Pilgrimage

CREATION

In the earlier Jewish tradition, creation formed a minor theme in comparison with the choosing of the people of God; in classical Christianity, the theme of creation often serves to introduce that of the Fall. By contrast, contemporary theology speaks of a continuing engagement between the Holy Spirit and the created order, and the city is clearly where that process is seen at its most dynamic and challenging.

Until very recently, the created order was seen as hostile to human purposes. At its hands, humanity generally, and women and children in particular, experienced disease, pain and premature death. Humanity has asserted itself within creation, gained the upper hand for the present, and has wrought great harm upon it. The modern city has also proved hostile to human flourishing, although it is a human creation. Its complexity renders it difficult to plan and to control, without inducing a kind of stagnation and decline that results in the next wave of urban growth moving elsewhere. The process of creative destruction is nowhere more evident than in the city, and it is the great and exhilarating task of Christians to seek to manage that process for the benefit of all its people.

Our historical reflection has drawn attention to the commercial nature of the city. The city requires immense resources to come into being. The simplest city still draws to it that variety of people who build it, service it, profit from it. The city is not just a mass of people living together, nor is it a failed monastery. It is inextricably linked with money and power, and those elements will always be found in great concentration within its walls. Many Christians appreciate that these forces may foster good, but are equally suspicious of the glitter and falsity that sometimes accompany them, and challenge the inhumanity that they frequently mask.

It is hard to be comfortable with the city. It demonstrates in a spatially small area, the depths of poverty and the pinnacles of wealth. Yet the clearest impression given in most cities of the industrial world, certainly in the 1950s and 1960s, has been one of widespread middling prosperity and content-ment. Nonetheless, even in the most favourable circumstances it can seem almost impossible for all a city's inhabitants to work together in pursuit of a common good. Self-interest is so evident in the city that commonality seems continually threatened by selfishness.

The city can be so sophisticated, impersonal and inhuman that it is difficult to see it as a place of blessing and creativity. But God gives us the example of the Body of Christ, of *Koinonia* in the early Church. Our own experience of alienation, homelessness, youth unemployment, and street crime indicate that it is in our shared interest to challenge these injustices. As we have seen, the early Church found it difficult to maintain such a commitment to [*Koinonia*] once it embraced the whole of Roman society, but the challenge remains.

Laurie Green has written well of the particular spirituality of the city:

I sense the majesty, energy and power of God in heavy industry and in that a sense of belonging with God in a solidarity with God's creativity. I feel delighted by a sense of wonder in industry that we have been given gifts to work with such complexity and find comradeship, worth and identity in the endeavour. In the service industries too I find sacraments of God's presence — hospitals, shops, sewers and dustbin collection — all gifts in their fascinating urban complexity. And with every such gift I sense too the challenge and anguish when we get it wrong. When industry becomes unjust; when political groups seek their own aggrandisement; when social services are badly resourced; I still feel God within it all, but now yearning and suffering with his children.[2]

INCARNATION

The second key concept is that of Incarnation. An exclusive theology of the Incarnation makes our sharing in Christ's humanity a possibility only for believers. A bolder doctrine sees Jesus come among us all, as one of us, participating in the common life around him, rejoicing that in him all things hold together, and that the created order serves a recognizably human purpose.

One of the most exciting features of contemporary theology is the exploration of Christian doctrine that now occurs outside the constraints of the classical tradition. Much of this work expands the meaning of those few words in the Epistle to the Colossians: 'Christ exists before all things, and everything is held together in him. He is, moreover, the head of the body, the church' (Colossians 1:17–18). What does it mean for God to have created his relationship with humanity, in the form of Christ, from the beginning of creation? Current reflection on the doctrines of the Trinity and of the Incarnation must inform our thinking about God's relation to the whole of humanity, and especially in its most problematic form, the city. But a spirituality of the city must precede an elaborated theology; it is only when we are moved by the sheer diversity of the city that we feel deeply the experience of God's grace unconditionally among us. That experience creates a new kind of spirituality, which in turn seeks a new kind of theological understanding. If the universe has a human face, then so must the city. It is this conviction that has so powerfully influenced the calling of those who might otherwise have fled the city.

John Vincent has written of a spirituality of incarnation which introduces disciples to a contemporary, secular, identification with Christ:

> First, there is the level of incarnation. We need to confirm ourselves in the areas of need. If we are not there, a few of us need to move there. Second, there is the level of healing. We need people on the ground who will express love and compassion in the face of obvious injustice and victimization. Third, there is the level of parables. We need people, preferably locals, who will take up the gut-level happenings of an area, and hold them up for others to see. Fourth, there is the level of acted parables. We need visible examples, prophetic signs, acted parables, proleptic instances, of what we want, set up for all to see. Fifth, there is the level of disciple-group. We need people really committed to each other, to the place and to the disciplines necessary for significant acting. Sixth, there is the level of crucifixion. We need to be at the places where the oppression of the powers is really encountered and felt, so that we can be borne down by it, as others are borne down by it. Seventh, there is the level of resurrection. We need to be around when old things are raised up, when old things get started again, when the commitments crucified by the enemies are brought to life again. Eighth, there is the level of the new city. We need to be backyard visionaries; plucking from the future the things that all humanity seeks, and digging in bits of them in city backyards.[3]

It is in the city that so many poor, excluded and stigmatized people have discovered their true humanity and their Christian vocation. The Church has a duty to tell their stories and to celebrate them. It is also in the city that many have identified with the poor and excluded and have thereby found their own

calling alongside them. That too is a valid and empowering form of discipleship, and it too calls for rejoicing.

CROSS AND RESURRECTION

In the tradition, the death and resurrection of Christ have been the means by
which we are released from the vagaries of history into an eternal order. We
have seen the tendency within the tradition to retreat from the crudities of
temporal life, not least in the flight from the city. By contrast, it is tempting
to adopt a glib incarnational theology that implies that co-operation between
all people of good will must surely prevail.

On the contrary, God's creation is marked by such profound desolation
that the ordinary processes of renewal, and hope for change, are rendered
thoroughly inadequate. The family growing up in squalid housing, knowing
that its experience of social exclusion is likely to work out relentlessly
through growing children. In the city, the old and frail often eke out the long,
final periods of their lives in a system of Community Care that functions
badly enough in prosperous areas; elsewhere it can be a kind of continual
crucifixion endured in cold, pain and misery. Again, it is a commonplace that
in the robust urban marketplace there are both winners and losers. But the
slow death of a business can blight the lives of a whole family as it fragments
in despair. Added to these are the stories of young people whose lives have
been early blighted by hopelessness, and who experience a long decline into
homelessness and destitution.

It is easy in each of these cases to produce a glib prescription for future
social renewal through better application of existing resources. But such a
response fails to embrace the pain of unbearable personal suffering, felt now.
In such affliction, each day's dawn brings the prospect of the cross. But each
day also brings the promise of that suffering shared with God, and, by his
grace, with others during the course of that day. In this way, each day
becomes both cross and resurrection, but only if Christians are able to share
that suffering with one another, and so be blessed with the experience of
resurrection. Of course, the experience of desolation shared with God and
others is not exclusively urban, but the multiplicity of such suffering in our
impersonal cities is especially intense.

The Cross stands among those who endure inconsolable pain. So too, the
Cross stands in judgement over the whole of human endeavour, revealing the
flaw at the heart of even the most heroically faithful followers of Christ.
Pharisees, disciples, even reflective Christian community workers, have
fallen short of the glory of God. In concrete terms, it is important to
recognize the sinfulness of all humanity, and to resist the temptation to
complacent self-righteousness. The good news of the resurrection is that
faithfulness is taken up into God's greater purposes — the dead are raised!

PILGRIMAGE

A spirituality of Pilgrimage arises in many urban contexts today, not so much
the middle-class notion of personal 'journeys', as the trials of the alien, the

dispossessed, the migrant. Cities themselves are on a journey. They evolve over time, parts decay and others regenerate. But they do persist over long periods of time, an issue that we are particularly aware of with the approaching millennium. It is encouraging to see so many Christian people committed to more than simply the current needs of cities. They also have a pride in the past, and a desire to imagine the future. In every journey of pilgrimage it is important to acknowledge the past, and realize its impact on the present. There is much in the past and the present to celebrate, and there is hope for the future of cities. Like Jeremiah, we have a vision of making our home in Babylon, a world not made according to our wish, but created to serve the divine purpose. It is our calling to work and pray for the good of the city, even if it is the place of our exile.

* * *

As we have seen, the biblical understanding of the city is very diverse ranging from horror to delight. In the Bible the city is depicted as the heavenly New Jerusalem, possible only after the total destruction of the corrupt imperial city. It is similarly seen as Nineveh and Babylon, the cities of pagan gods, harbouring the ritually unclean and morally evil. But Babylon is also seen as the place where the exiled Jewish people can make their homes in hope, and from Jerusalem to Rome the city is the place where the Gospel is hopefully and joyfully proclaimed. The city is both an image of God's presence in creation and also the epitome of human ambition, vanity and greed. It is the product of human creativeness and also the result of an abuse of resources, people and relationships. There are constant tensions between what the city could be and what it is, between the dream and the reality.

While Christians may sometimes feel that they do not fully belong to the city, both Scripture and Tradition challenge us to live with this tension. We should wholeheartedly devote ourselves to promoting the welfare of the city in all its parts, despite our discomfort about some of its activities. Christians are always to some extent exiles.

NOTES

1. G. Davis and G. Rupp (eds), *History of the Methodist Church*, Vol. 4 (London: Epworth, 1964), p. 126.
2. Laurie Green, 'Blowing bubbles: Poplar' in Peter Sedgwick (ed.), *God in the City* (London: Mowbray, 1995), pp. 74–5.
3. John Vincent, *Into the City* (London: Epworth, 1982), p. 136.

Who is a local theologian?

Robert J. Schreiter

The theology that is emerging out of new contexts is engaging the energies of more than professional theologians. Liberation theologies in particular emphasize the role of the entire believing community in the development of a local theology. This same movement, however, has been raising questions about precisely who it is that brings about the development of a local theology. Behind that question lurks a second concern, namely, what are we to call theology itself? This section surveys some of the issues involved with these questions.

The experience of those in the small Christian communities who have seen the insight and the power arising from the reflections of the people upon their experience and the Scriptures has prompted making the community itself the prime author of theology in local contexts. The Holy Spirit, working in and through the believing community, gives shape and expression to Christian experience. Some of these communities have taught us to read the Scriptures in a fresh way and have called the larger church back to a fidelity to the prophetic word of God. What happened over a period of years to the fishing village of Solentiname in Nicaragua is one of the best-known examples of this.[1]

The role of the community in developing theology reminds us also for whom theology is, in the first instance, intended: the community itself, to enhance its own self-understanding. The experience of the development of this kind of theology, especially in liberation models, has prompted others to define theology as the emancipatory praxis freeing an oppressed people. Theology then becomes more than words; it becomes also a pedagogical process liberating consciousness and inciting to action.

If one considers the concrete situation and the expression of faith in situations of oppression, it is hard not to agree with such a contention about the community as author of local theology. Theology is certainly intended for a community and is not meant to remain the property of a theologian class. The expression of faith in theology should make a difference in people's lives; otherwise it is a mere beating of the air. Reflection for its own sake may lead to contemplation, but contemplation should lead to action as well.

Understanding the role of the community in the development of theology shows how the poor become the subjects of their own history. It allows us to understand the special preference the God of Israel, the God of Jesus Christ, has had for the poor in their understanding of the Good News. Through the activity of those communities of the poor on virtually every continent, the whole Christian Church has been profoundly enriched.

Any conception of what is local theology and who brings it about needs to be carefully balanced with a variety of factors. Not everything any community says or does can be called theology: otherwise theology itself becomes an empty concept. The emphasis on the role of the community as theologian has been an important one in correcting the idea that only professional theologians could engage in theological reflection.

In many instances it is helpful to make a distinction between the role of the whole community of faith, whose experience is the indispensable source of theology, and whose acceptance of a theology is an important guarantor of its authenticity, and the role of smaller groups within the community who actually give shape to that theology. In other words, the role of the whole community is often one of raising the questions, of providing the experience of having lived with those questions and struggled with different answers, and of recognizing which solutions are indeed genuine, authentic, and commensurate with their experience. The poet, the prophet, the teacher, those experienced with other communities may be among those who give leadership to the actual shaping into words of the response in faith. Gifted individuals, within the community and working on its behalf, give shape to the response, which then in turn is accepted or not by the community. Looked at in this way, local theologies can thereby more easily avoid the romanticist fallacy, common among folklorists of the early nineteenth century, who saw whole communities actually composing folk songs and epics. More recent research into oral traditions indicates that it is individuals capturing the spirit of those communities who do the actual shaping.[2] This does not play down the important role of those communities; it only puts it in a clearer context.

In sum, then, the community is a key source for theology's development and expressions, but to call it a theologian in the narrow sense of authorship is inaccurate. Significant members within the community, often working as a group, give voice to the theology of the community. Being a theologian is a gift, requiring a sensitivity to the context, an extraordinary capacity to listen, and an immersion in the Scriptures and the experience of other churches. It remains with the community, however, not only to initiate the theological process, but also to rejoin the process of theology in the act traditionally known as reception.[3]

Ordinarily, when one asks the question of who engages in theology, it is the professionally trained theologian who comes to mind. Such a person, schooled in the traditions of a faith community, provides a unique and privileged resource for the shaping of the experience of a believing community.

The problem has been, however, that the requirements of time and energy for immersing oneself in those traditions have often led to a separation of the theologian from the experience of living communities. This problem becomes a hard one for a community to challenge because of the extensive knowledge a theologian needs of Scripture and subsequent Christian tradition, which takes years to develop and is in need of constant upgrading. Yet communities have instinctively felt that such isolation ultimately did not serve the purposes for which theology was intended. How is one to understand the role of the professional theologian in the development of local theologies?

To ignore the resources of the professional theologian is to prefer ignorance over knowledge. But to allow the professional theologian to dominate the development of a local theology seems to introduce a new hegemony into often already oppressed communities. In the development of local theologies, the professional theologian serves as an important resource, helping the community to clarify its own experience and to relate it to the experience of other communities past and present. Thus the professional theologian has an indispensable but limited role. The theologian cannot create a theology in isolation from the community's experience; but the community has need of the theologian's knowledge to ground its own experience within the Christian traditions of faith. In so doing, the theologian helps to create the bonds of mutual accountability between local and world church.

What about the prophetic dimension of the experience of a Christian community? Does not the voice of the prophet suffice for giving expression to the gospel in the community? When one hears the songs, reads the pamphlets, and witnesses the testimony of struggling Christians around the planet, one can honestly wonder whether or not more need be done by way of theology. Is not the voice of the prophet and the praxis of the prophetic community all we need?

The poets in the community, who can capture the rhythm and contour of the community's experience — cannot their work be considered a genuine local theology? Is not some of the more authentic theology, especially that which captures the imagination of the majority of people, to be found in their work rather than in theological monographs or church documents? What role does the poet play in capturing the soul of a community?

Both prophets and poets are essential to the theological process, but that process cannot be reduced to either one of them. Prophecy is often the beginning of theology, and it often exercises judgement on a theology that has developed or been accepted by a community. The poet has the task of capturing those symbols and metaphors which best give expression to the experience of a community. Because a theology is not simply any experience of a community, but that experience of believers coming into encounter with the Scriptures and the authentic experiences of other believing communities, past and present, more is needed. Theology and prophecy are not entirely the same thing. The task of a theology is to expand a prophetic insight in order to engage the full range of issues. Prophetic calls to faithfulness must be tested also on the touchstone of other churches' experience of the Spirit. By the same token, the validity of poetic insight has to be tested on more than aesthetic criteria or resonance with a community's experience. Were a community incapable of sin, this would not have to be the case.

All of this, again, is not to play down the role of the prophet or the poet. Rather, it is meant to help situate their tasks within the larger theological process.

The intense experience of communities often leads them to question the role of outsiders in the shaping of their theologies. In many parts of the world, expatriates have for too long dominated local communities, keeping them (often unwittingly) in a dependent position. Anyone who has worked in another culture knows that parts of that culture will always remain mysterious. One can never know that culture as one does one's own. This has led many cross-cultural ministers to step back from the theological process in local communities, or to be asked to do so by those communities.

Despite the obvious and real problems of paternalism and colonialism, which have frequently marked the expatriate's presence in a culture, the expatriate's role in the development of local theologies has often been quite significant. One wonders if the liberation theologies and the small Christian communities could have developed as rapidly in Latin America without the help of those foreign religious leaders. The expatriate can also be the bearer of the lived experience of other communities, experience that can challenge and enrich a local community. Without the presence of outside experience, a local church runs the risk of turning in on itself, becoming self-satisfied with its own achievements. The expatriate, as an outsider, can sometimes hear things going on in a community not heard by a native member of that community.

In the same way, being a life-long member of a local community does not guarantee insight. One of the disappointments in many local communities has been that having locally born leadership does not guarantee its effectiveness. And local leadership with experience elsewhere often can disdain its own roots and become more oppressive than outsiders. This has sometimes happened with leadership educated outside the local context to the ideals of North Atlantic cultures.

Again, both the insider and the outsider are needed, but they need to be situated within a larger process. What all of this shows is that the task of the development of local theology cannot be committed to one individual or even to one group. The experience of a community can remain amorphous without spokespersons in the prophet and the poet. Yet there is no prophet or poet without a community. The professional theologian can provide essential links to the larger Christian tradition; but local theology has to be more than a mere repetition of that tradition. Outsiders bring important experience, but by themselves can come to exercise hegemony over the community. A rootedness in the community is essential for a local theology, but does not in itself guarantee insight.

All of this underlines how much the theology emerging in local contexts is a communal enterprise. It takes the work of many individuals and groups to be truly effective. This look at some of the individuals and groups is intended to help situate the various roles within that communal undertaking. It helps also to see how complex the development of local theologies is likely to be.

In light of all the things just discussed, is it possible to define more exactly just what is local theology? Obviously it is a complex process, aware of contexts, of histories, of the role of experience, of the need to encounter the traditions of faith in other believing communities. It is also obvious that contexts are complex, that histories can be variously read, that experience can be ambiguous, that the encounter in faith is often dimly understood.

But how do all of these factors interact? I would suggest that their relationship be seen as a dialectical one, using the notion of dialectic in a broad sense. Dialectic is to be understood as a continuing attention to first one factor, and then another, leading to an ever-expanding awareness of the role and interaction of each of these factors.

These factors can be seen as roots feeding the development and growth of a local theology. They must interact to produce the full and living reality. The three principal roots beneath the growth of local theology are gospel, church, and culture.

'Gospel' here means the Good News of Jesus Christ and the salvation that God has wrought through him. This includes, and reaches beyond, the proclamation of the Scriptures. This includes the worshiping context of the local community and the presence of its Lord there. It includes those aspects of the praxis of the community announcing the Good News. It includes that

Word which missionaries find already active in the culture upon their arrival. It refers to the living presence of the saving Lord that is the foundation of the community, the spirit of the risen Lord guiding that community, the prophetic Spirit challenging the culture and the larger church.

But the gospel does not fall from the sky. Our faith is also a *fides ex auditu*, a faith we have heard from others. The gospel is always incarnate, incarnate in the reality of those who bring it to us, and incarnate in those who help us nurture the beginnings of faith. Church is a complex of those cultural patterns in which the gospel has taken on flesh, at once enmeshed in the local situation, extending through communities in our own time and in the past, and reaching out to the eschatological realization of the fullness of God's reign. Thus there is no local theology without the larger church, that concrete community of Christians, united through word and sacrament in the one Lord. The gospel without church does not come to its full realization; the church without gospel is a dead letter. Without church there is no integral incarnation of the gospel.

Culture is the concrete context in which this happens. It represents a way of life for a given time and place, replete with values, symbols, and meanings, reaching out with hopes and dreams, often struggling for a better world. Without a sensitivity to the cultural context, a church and its theology either become a vehicle for outside domination or lapse into docetism, as though its Lord never became flesh.

It takes the dynamic interaction of all three of these roots — gospel, church, culture — with all they entail about identity and change, to have the makings of local theology. Both living spirit and the network of traditions that make up living communities need to be taken into account.

Notes

1. See the four volumes of reflections published by Ernesto Cardenal, the pastor of the community, *The Gospel in Solentiname* (Maryknoll, NY: Orbis Books, 1976–82).
2. Two important works have been A. B. Lord's study of Yugoslav folk poets, *The Singer of Tales* (Cambridge, MA: Harvard University Press, 1960); and Jan Vansina, *Oral Tradition: A Study in Historical Methodology* (Chicago: Aldine Publishing Company, 1961).
3. John Henry Newman, *On Consulting the Faithful in Matters of Doctrine* (New York: Sheed and Ward, 1961), is a classic text in this subject. Reception, a concept borrowed from nineteenth-century German legal research, remains an underdeveloped aspect of theology. Its basic point is that doctrinal formulation requires not only magisterial promulgation, but also positive reception by the faithful.

Further reading

Paul Ballard and John Pritchard, *Practical Theology in Action: Christian Thinking in the Service of Church and Society* (London: SPCK, 1996). Excellent and rounded introduction to practical theology as a disciplined way of reflecting on the practice of the Church in contemporary society.

Georges Casalis, *Correct Ideas Don't Fall from the Skies: Elements for an Inductive Theology* (Eng. trans. Maryknoll, NY: Orbis, 1984: French edition 1977). Perhaps the earliest account of a theological method for a lay theology done by and not for the poor, in contrast to the theology of domination sponsored by clerics and academies.

Harvey Cox, *Fire From Heaven* (London: Cassell, 1996). A fascinating account of the Pentecostal revolution which has swept through the new cities of the twentieth century from Los Angeles to São Paulo and from Singapore to Cape Town.

David F. Ford and Laurie Green, 'Distilling the Wisdom', in Peter Sedgwick (ed.) *God in the City* (London: Mowbray, 1995). The Urban Theology Group practised a collaborative style of theology which brought together urban ministers and professional theologians with the aim of distilling the wisdom of urban Christians, producing stories and reflections which in their fragmentary and distinctive particularity present a kaleidoscopic socio-cultural and theological testimony to the presence of God, and the possibilities of salvation and praise, in the modern and postmodern city.

Trevor Hart, *Faith Thinking: The Dynamics of Christian Theology* (London: SPCK, 1996). An excellent introduction to the nature of Christian theology conceived as the dynamic activity of reflection and dialogue practised by communities of faith. It also includes a consideration of the place of theology in the public world, the quest for public truth, and the task of cultural transformation, as well as inculturation, which theology must engage with in contemporary society.

Anthony Harvey (ed.), *Theology in the City: A Theological Response to Faith in the City* (London: SPCK, 1989). This collection of essays mostly by professional theologians includes a very useful essay on liberation theology and local theologies by Andrew Kirk and a reflection on the nature of urban theology by Anthony Kirk.

Joe Holland and Peter Henriot, *Social Analysis: Linking Faith and Justice* (Maryknoll, NY: Orbis, 1983). A clear and jargon-free introduction to methods of social audit and analysis including power analysis for local churches and Christian communities. *Faith in the City* includes an Appendix A which outlines more briefly a social audit for churches in UPAs.

Wayne Meeks, *The First Urban Christians: The Social World of the Apostle Paul* (New Haven, CT.: Yale University Press, 1983). Using sociological analysis of biblical and extra-biblical sources Meeks manages to reconstruct for the modern reader what it was like to be a member of the early Christian missionary movement.

Peter Sedgwick, 'Introduction: Mapping an Urban Theology', in Peter Sedgwick (ed.) *God in the City* (London: Mowbray, 1995). The decline in manufacturing jobs has led to a loss of hope in the poorest areas of Britain's cities. Lack of hope is related to sin, and the task of urban theology in this context is to identify the redemptive possibilities of urban life when people are empowered by the Spirit of God to recover a sense of belonging and dignity in communities of praise and transformation.

Juan Luis Segundo, *The Liberation of Theology* (Eng. trans. Dublin: Gill and Macmillan, 1977). Includes the clearest exposition of the method of liberation theology, expressed in the form of the hermeneutic circle, and also demonstrates a critical awareness of the limited appeal of liberation theology to the masses, and its tendency to deny rather than to build on popular religiosity.

R. H. Tawney, *The Acquisitive Society* (London: Bell, 1921). Classic text for the developing Christian social tradition and its response to the rise of industrial capitalism and the wealth, and social divisions, it spawned.

2

Creativity in the city

The news that we were rebuilding the wall roused the indignation of Sanballat and angrily he jeered at the Jews, saying in front of his companions and of the garrison in Samaria, 'What do these feeble Jews think they are doing? So they mean to reconstruct the place? Do they hope to offer sacrifice and finish the work in a day? Can they make stones again out of heaps of rubble and burnt rubble at that?'

There came a time when the common people, both men and women, raised a great outcry against their fellow Jews. Some complained that they had to give their sons and daughters as pledges for food to eat to keep themselves alive; others that they were mortgaging their fields, vineyards, and homes to buy grain during the famine; still others that they were borrowing money on their fields and vineyards to pay the king's tax. 'But' they said, 'our bodily needs are the same as other people's, our children are as good as theirs; yet here we are, forcing our sons and daughters into slavery. Some of our daughters are already enslaved, and there is nothing we can do, because our fields and vineyards now belong to others.'

When I heard their outcry and the story they told, I was greatly incensed, but I controlled my feelings and reasoned with the nobles and the magistrates. I said to them, 'You are holding your fellow-Jews as pledges for debt.' I rebuked them severely and said, 'As far as we have been able, we have bought back our fellow Jews who had been sold to foreigners; but you are now selling your own fellow countrymen, and they will have to be bought back by us!' They were silent and had not a word to say.

I went on, 'What you are doing is wrong. You ought to live so much in the fear of God that you are above reproach in the eyes of the nations who are our enemies. Speaking for myself, I and my kinsmen and the men under me are advancing them money and grain. Let us give up this taking of pledges for debt. This very day give them back their fields and vineyards, their olive groves and houses, as well as the income in money, in grain, new wine, and oil.'

(Nehemiah 4:1–2; 5:1–11)

Faith in the City

We have seen evidence of how confidence can be injected. The two Urban Development Corporations, in the London and Merseyside Docklands, have begun to transform areas of outworn derelict land, and silted-up water, into areas which are beginning to thrive once again. There are serious reservations, which we share, about the lack of consultation with, and participation by, local people in the work of the UDCs; about the inadequacy of good public rented housing in the London Docklands; and that much of the investment by the private sector is in non-labour-intensive land uses, such as warehousing. Yet the UDCs are without doubt making a visible impact: for example, through the scheme to convert the Albert Dock building in Liverpool — the largest group of Grade 1 listed buildings in the country — into a new multi-purpose centre, including the proposed 'Tate of the North' art gallery; in the achievement of mounting Britain's first International Garden Festival on the banks of the Mersey, turning spoiled wasteland into a magnificent landscaped garden in two years; in the development of new film and television studies and newspaper printing works, and the plans for a new light railway system to open up transport links and improve communications, in London Docklands. (8.101)

Introduction

Archaeological evidence indicates that the first cities were built in the Bible lands of ancient Mesopotamia in the third and fourth millennia BC. The rise of cities is associated with the growth of all the more complex civilizations in human history, from the ancient cultures of Sumer, Mesoamerica, China and Greece and the early modern trading cities of Venice and London to the megalopolis of modern global capitalism.

Cities were built for a variety of reasons but principal among these seems to have been the collective expression of human creativity through the organization of crafts and manufactures for the embellishment of temples, public buildings and households. Writing, metallurgy, trade and manufacture all had their origins in the development of urban centres of population. Cities were also built for the enhancement of human community, and for physical security and defence, as most ancient cities had walls around them, like the wall which Nehemiah and his friends rebuilt around the derelict city of Jerusalem. But in Nehemiah's account the primary purpose of the work and creativity which are expressed in the rebuilding of the city and its walls is the glorification of the God of Israel, and the restoration of the worship of God in the Jerusalem temple. The purpose of urban regeneration in this story is not simply human security or human creativity but the restoration of an urban society at whose heart is the worshipping community where the trading and creative enterprises of the city are ordered and restrained by the dedication of the Sabbath to worship and rest.

In the Hebrew Bible human creativity is ordered by the worship of Yahweh and the moral demands this worship involves. The first commandment to worship God is accompanied by a prohibition of 'graven images' or the worship of any created or manufactured thing in place of God (Exodus 20:2–5). Worship, the making and remaking of relationships between God and the people, is the central creative work of the Israelite city, giving shape and focus to the working week through the observance of the Sabbath. The worship of the God of Exodus also establishes an ethical shaping to the relationships of Israelite society, as is demonstrated in Nehemiah 5. The God of Exodus is a God who redeems a poor and marginalized people from slavery, and who demonstrates divine opposition to oppression and persecution of one group of people by another. The restoration project in Jerusalem is threatened by a famine. Many of the builders have to mortgage their homes, vineyards and fields, or even their children as labourers, in order to feed themselves while others benefit from their hard times and increase their own landholdings and their wealth in the new city. Mortgages were a common feature of Hebrew society at this time but personal mortgages and poverty were threatening the common project of restoration and undermining the common membership, even kinship, of all the people in Hebrew society. Nehemiah insists that the restoration of the physical city and the temple must also be accompanied by the recovery of social justice, and the liberation of all the people from debt-slavery and hunger. The vision of Jerusalem restored is a vision of a society which has recovered the priority of kinship and the fear of God over monetary gain and rebuilt a divinely shaped community in which every family and household experiences the dignity and freedom which is the just expectation of all God's people who share kinship of the nation of Israel.

Modern cities are a celebration of creativity, and of the powers of human craft and art to create and recreate order, grace, beauty and wonder in the physical shape of concentrated human settlement (Landry and Bianchini). The great public buildings, workshops, warehouses and bridges of Victorian cities were cause for wonder and awe. But the Victorian city gave rise to extremes of wealth and degradation worse even than those described in the book of Nehemiah. The God of the Victorians was a *laissez-faire* God who failed to intervene on behalf of the poor, who blessed the powerful in their amassing of large estates while the new urban poor lived in slums, who blessed the industrialists in their creation of new factories in which the poor and their children were enslaved.

In the twentieth century a more collective and democratic vision of the city emerged, a vision which may also be associated with a more social and non-hierarchical understanding of God, the Spirit of freedom, as celebrated particularly in the Pentecostal churches which have grown so rapidly in the last three decades in cities on six continents. Creativity was exercised by designers, planners, engineers and architects to resolve the problems of public health, housing and transport bequeathed by the Victorians (Landry and Bianchini). Governments also saw their role as being to reduce poverty and inequality, and to advance the health and welfare of the population as a whole through redistributive taxes, health and insurance schemes.

But in the late twentieth century this collective vision of urban–industrial society has been challenged by a more privatized vision symbolized by the choking dominance of the private car on city streets and landscapes, and by the private marketing malls and transnational towers which dominate the retailing and banking centres, and increasingly the out-of-town peripheries, of many contemporary cities. The modern retail or financial park or centre, with its private security guards and camera-festooned car parks, represents a flight from the public realm. Efforts to restore city centres and urban economies through the development of large single-use service, financial and retail centres manifest a lack of creativity and an ethical gap in the vision of the city. They favour styles of development which often exacerbate social division and urban blight for the marginalized, an effect which is clearly evident in the poor communities living cheek by jowl with the glossy new developments in the Docklands area of London. The exclusions of modern regeneration projects are reminiscent of the exclusions which Nehemiah's building project also involved. The wall he and his followers were reconstructing was designed to keep foreigners out, and the Israelites who were invited to inhabit the restored city are first ordered to put away their foreign wives.

Successful efforts at contemporary urban regeneration involve building a partnership between the needs and creativity of local residents *and* the wealth of outside investors. The best examples manifest a rich, creative and complex vision of the centrality of creativity, culture and human relationships to the health of a city, its environment *and* its economy. Experiments in urban renewal from Baltimore to Glasgow have focused on the creation of areas of the city in which cultural, sporting, residential, retailing, banking and workshop activities are mixed together in a creative and relational ferment (**Mawson**; Boyle). This approach sets cultural creativity and human flourishing at the heart of successful cities, and involves the recognition that cities rich in the arts and in liveable spaces which are peopled day and night, and not just by shoppers or bankers from nine to five are attractive to residents, employers and investors. Cities with a vibrant cultural heart and lots of performance space, both inside arts buildings and in open squares or wide pedestrianized streets, are more liveable, and have a higher quality of life.

This approach to urban renewal reflects the recognition that cities are a stage for human creativity, what Jane Jacobs called 'street ballet' and Mumford a 'theatre of social action'. Education, arts, politics, trade, religion are all focused on the city, in modern as in ancient times. The greatest concentration of artists in one place in Europe is in a couple of square miles to the East of the financial centre of the City of London (**Mawson**). The city is a place for show and for seeing — walking out in new clothes, watching the diverse dress of people from a dozen countries walk by a busy cosmopolitan thoroughfare.

Creativity finds best expression in city design when people are empowered to give shape to their own surroundings and where the relationships between people take priority over the other functions of the city. The greatest temptation for the city architect or planner is to fashion it after clean forms or simple functions which bear no relation to the complex patterns of relationships, networks, journeys, designs and meanings through which people individually and collectively construct their environment. The drama, and the safety, of the street are created by the presence and interaction of people who live there. In their daily rituals and interaction they create the order which a city street, with its succession of strangers moving through in cars or on foot, needs in order to be safe and welcoming for its inhabitants (Jacobs). As Jane Jacobs says, a safe street, like a creative space, is one where there are plenty of eyes on the street. Eerily quiet canyons of offices, warehouses or retail malls after closing time, empty subterranean walkways, or windowless streets and walkways beneath blocks of flats on concrete stilts, have insecurity and crime designed into them. People are the best governors of safe space. Where designers exclude people, they create insecurity and opportunities for the criminal.

The worst feature of the peripheral housing estates which were developed to clear the over-crowded housing areas of many British inner cities is that they are just that — *housing* areas. Even today there are many housing schemes where no bank, sports hall or playing field may be found. These were designed as single-use, functional areas and when the complex neighbourhood relationships of work and marketing, culture and leisure, which characterized the former inner cities were stripped away, these new estates were lifeless, culturally barren, and politically and economically marginalized. In *Music in the Listening Place*, from which the extract 'A people's astonishing vitality' is taken, Douglas Galbraith tells the story of how the people of Niddrie/Craigmillar, a large post-war housing scheme on the outskirts of Edinburgh, utilized their aesthetic gifts and creative potential to develop a Festival Society on the estate which mobilized the energy of people in the area not only in cultural activity but also in community organizing for political and economic change to improve the housing and facilities in the area, and challenge the structures of poverty. Mobilizing their own gifts and talents the people of the estate discovered a biblical truth, which is that each person has within them the potential to express the creativity of the creator Spirit. The Craigmillar story illustrates the connection between human creativity and the political economy of urban areas. Today in Craigmillar the housing office is located at the heart of the estate, new sports and leisure facilities have been built on the estate, and the housing has been modernized. However, Craigmillar, like many other large peripheral housing areas, remains economically marginal, its residents experiencing disproportionately the effects of post-industrial unemployment, and the stultifying effects of consequent poverty and lack of opportunity on human creativity.

The biblical vision of human creativity involves transcendence and ethics, celebration and grace. Creativity is seen as a sign of the sharing by humans of the image of the divine creator and as involving the exchange of gifts in recognition of the abundance and wonder of the creation (**Warren**). But the expression of human creativity in the construction of cities and of complex societies must be exercised in such a way as to sustain relationships of justice between all members of the community, relationships which mirror the character of divine justice and compassion. In ancient Israel the more creative and successful farmers or traders were condemned by the Prophets when they used their human advantages to oppress, enslave or impoverish their fellow Hebrews. The destruction of the city of Jerusalem, which Nehemiah tries to restore, is seen by Amos and Isaiah as judgement for the corruption and social divisions of Israel under the late monarchy with its growing military prowess, artistic excellence and bureaucratic and economic complexity.

We may rejoice at the restoration in the 1980s and 1990s of the cultural heart of many Western cities with the creation of pedestrianized spaces or enhanced waterways around which restaurants, art galleries, small business offices or workshops mix with delicatessens and gentrified flats and houses, fostering a new breed of creative entrepreneurs who want to re-people the city. In this restoration city centres are once again becoming liveable places where people want to live as well as work, instead of commuting out to the suburbs in the night and at weekends. This approach is reflected in Andrew Mawson's account of artistic, housing and other projects which developed around the Baptist church in Bromley by Bow (**Mawson**). Creativity in art and in crossing boundaries and building on personal relationships and networks provides a model of the church as catalyst and partner in inner city regeneration.

A truly civilized city will be one in which the exclusions of the urban poor from realizing their creativity and control over their own lives are challenged and reversed, through high-quality education, secure employment and responsive government (**Donnison**). Central to such a reversal will be efforts to mobilize the creativity and inherent giftedness of all the residents of the city in determining and shaping its future, efforts which should be reflected in participative management of the work place, the city centre and the neighbourhood, in effective and challenging education and skills sharing in schools and colleges for poor as well as rich, and in the fostering of relationships of care and reciprocity in households and local neighbourhoods (Atkinson; **Mawson;** *Unleashing the Potential*). The churches as worshipping communities have a vital part to play in sustaining this inclusive and relational vision of creativity in the city centre and the peripheral estate (**Mawson;** Moore). The Christian vision of the potential of every person, made in the image of God, to be indwelt by the creator Spirit of God, and empowered with the gifts of the Spirit to serve the people of God, is a vital corrective to the postmodern exclusion of the new poor from the good life of the restored city (**Warren**).

A people's astonishing vitality

Douglas Galbraith

> Yesterday I saw a stranger;
> I put meat in the eating place,
> Water in the drinking place,
> Music in the listening place.
> And the lark said in her song —
> 'Often, often, often goes the Christ in the stranger's guise.'
>
> (Gaelic rune of hospitality)

They called themselves the Craigmillar Festival Society. It was a strange title for a group whose theatre was as likely to be the debating chamber of the city council or the local planning conference where they pursued the interests of the people of the district. Yet for reasons which will emerge these local activists saw this as the title which most adequately represented what they stood for.

The full story of this remarkable group, whose imaginative programme of community renewal has excited the attention far beyond even the UK, can only properly be told by those local people involved.[1] It is presumptuous for an outsider to try and convey the flavour of this pioneer grass-roots movement in favour of urban renewal, but any story of renewal in Craigmillar must acknowledge its influence. In brief, the Society sought to reverse the reputation and fortunes of a district damned by statistics and the opinion of polite society alike, engaging in political and social action, and combining initiatives for the improvement of the physical surroundings and resources with programmes of community care and development.

The Society's work was backed by the firm belief that the best people to identify local needs and to meet these needs were local people. An early expression of this was the appointment of 'neighbourhood workers'. The sort of people whose personal qualities, contacts and experience already caused others to knock on their doors in time of need, they were given an honorarium, a telephone and some basic training to handle more effectively the wide range of problems which now came their way. Later came the Planning Workshop, when specialists from the universities, local government officials and planners thrashed out issues of concern across the table with local representatives. Similar workshops in education and the arts followed. The idea of 'liaison government' developed, by which the right of local people to have a say in the decisions and in the spending of the money that affected them would be acknowledged by official government bodies. The Society argued that local people felt divorced from those who made the decisions and saw this as contributing to a widespread lack of will, evident both in community and personal life. Skilful use of available funding was made, although the story of the Society is marked by crisis after financial crisis. 'We have got very skilled at discovering what help is available and applying for it successfully,' said the Organizing Secretary.

A milestone was reached when the Society won funds from the European Economic Community — the only non-statutory body in Western Europe to

get an award at that time. Their submission put the question — what are the
factors which have thwarted the good intentions of the original planners of
the district? A solution lay in 'the poor looking at the problems of the poor'.
An action-research project was proposed both to study the causes and to help
solve the problem. It prefigured 'a significant change in politics and economics to yield a more fulfilling society', suggesting that it might be possible, 'by
engaging and activating local people in the planning and carrying out in
partnership with outside agents projects which improve the quality of life',
seeking to do more with the limited public funds and other resources.

But it was one thing to work politically to change the physical environment
and create better opportunities for local people: the people also had to
recognize and grasp these opportunities. While it is important to create
surroundings which make people wake up and live, it is only by releasing and
harnessing the pictures in people's heads that the vision will become a
landscape for living. Thus there grew a unique partnership of politics and
play.

The originating event in the Society's life had been a festival and this had
grown year by year into a colourful, hilarious and indigenous week of
activities in the streets and halls and open spaces of the district. However
important and all-consuming political and social action became, the festival
was always seen at the heart. It 'remains the touchstone of the Society and is
still the generative force that keeps the organization alive, open to new ideas
and forward looking', said Helen Crummy, the founding Organizing Secretary and long-time local resident. It made for a more effective engagement
with local issues as audiences and participants alike glimpsed in live productions the type of vision elusive at public meetings. Further, as people took to
the stage or the street, they often discovered a talent they did not know they
had, an identity they had not recognized, a worth in the eyes of others. They
could come to see that they had something the community needed — and
that the community needed them. The festival thus, in Helen Crummy's
words, provided a 'field force for social action': it was the key which
unlocked the creative talent within the community. The festival also high-
lighted the shortcomings of the district. Some had nothing to celebrate.
Others had potential which needed training and fostering, while there were
few opportunities for doing this. Social change was needed to bring this
richness to its full expression. Thus was the festival locked in again to
political action.

This is not to suggest that festival productions consisted of polemic and
propaganda. In the annual Community Musical, prepared and created by
local groups and schools, script writers sought to include the experience of
the past as well as analyses of the present and visions for the future. The
musical about the ring road was entitled 'Hormits and Termits', the strange
name given to a seventeenth-century derelict house which also lay in the path
of the road — not in the immediate district, it is true, but not too far away!
As the bulldozer went about its demolition work, the crumbling walls
exposed characters from the past who led the audience into situations from
the city's history which bore helpful similarities to the struggle of the
contemporary community. One of these was 'Half-Hangit Maggie Dickson'
who, having been 'hanged' in 1724 in Edinburgh's Grassmarket for the
alleged murder of her child, was found by her pall-bearers taking their

refreshment at a Craigmillar hostelry on the way to her burial place to be still alive. Her song reflected the local community's own hopes:

'You can't keep a good woman down
The news is all over the town
You tried but you failed
To keep Maggie jailed
Underground'.

This musical had its starting point in an environmental issue. In subsequent years topics included education, unemployment, and community arts, and — one year — the housing shortage. That year happened to be the six hundredth anniversary of the building of the local castle and it coincided with a local overcrowding crisis. It was believed that lack of will on the part of the authorities had prevented a large number of local flats from being repaired and made ready for occupancy (six hundred was the estimate, as it happens!), forcing young couples to live with parents and in-laws as well as 'stranding' old people in blocks of flats where most units lay unoccupied. In desperation, the 'council' gives the keys of the castle to a needy family before whose eyes its history begins to unfold — Sir Simon Preston in the time of Edward 'the hammer of the Scots' forced to walk barefoot to London when the castle was taken in an English raid, Mary Queen of Scots signing Darnley's death warrant, Red Jess the witch — a woman of vision misunderstood, the earl murdered in his bath, and a host of others, their various trials and triumphs in counterpoint to the struggle of the present-day community to transform the neighbourhood. Adults and children sang:

'Don't let's hang around, move it along!
Man the battlements, take it by storm.
We can make it
Just the kind of
Place where
Every–
One will want to be–
Long'

Another year the plot had its starting point in the report of a national study which showed that, given present social conditions, one in ten children in Scotland was 'born to fail'. The hero was a teenage member of a local gang who was blessed with a creative imagination and whose ability to participate in past events offered him a foothold in the present. The message to the community was that its most precious asset was its high proportion of children, and that to realize this asset there was a need for bolder educational provision with the important addition of local community encouragement and nurture:

'Imagination more and to spare;
Hang on to us and we will take you there.
LOOK AT YOUR CHILDREN, WE'LL TELL YOU TRUE —
YOU'D BETTER LISTEN, FOR THERE'S
VERY MANY
MORE OF
US THAN
YOU!'

An underlying theme in all these musical productions was the conviction that the best people to identify the problems and suggest solutions were the people of the district, not in place of those in authority but in partnership with them. But before this 'liaison government' could work, the people had to accept the responsibility, and the authorities helped to see the limits of their power.

An interesting feature of the festival was that the plots and scripts were devised and written by those who at other parts of the year were writing documents, preparing cases, debating issues, confronting institutions. The interchange of information and argument, passion and humour thus served both to bring the arts down to earth and to make politics creative. Small wonder that the city's environmental Cockburn Association dubbed the Society, and the people it represented, 'a new voice in the Scottish consciousness'.

Helping to form the festival was also to have a far-reaching effect on the church. In giving hospitality to this distinctively local initiative (the church building doubled as community theatre, a member of the team ministry acted as musical director) a 'listening place' was formed in the midst of the community, gradually divesting of its cultural clothing a church used to speaking and operating in certain time-honoured ways, and encouraging it to respond not only in new words but in the structure and quality of its life.

NOTE

1. Helen Crummy, *Let the People Sing* (Available from Dr Helen Crummy OBE, 4 Whitehill Street, Newcraighall, Musselburgh EH21 8RA).

Exploring the dynamic of being human

Robert Warren

A response to both grace and celebration is the desire to give expressed in creativity. It could also have been called work, service or ministry. However, 'creativity' is a more holistic and inclusive term. It points to our nature as creatures made in the image of God who both celebrates (Day Seven) and creates (Days One to Six). Such creativity is central to the first creation, and the new creation, understanding of our being made in the image of God. To be human is to share in both aspects of the divine nature, to *celebrate* and to *create*. Creativity is distorted today alike by the consumer culture and by the notion that 'creativity' is what we do in our 'leisure time'. However, to be human is to be creative and we need to practise — and help others to experience — the essential creativity at the heart of all we do and are. Parents create families and family life, clergy create Christian community. Plumbers, teachers, those who work in factories and in offices, politicians and athletes are all engaged in creativity. ...

Using the term 'creativity' can help to shift the attention of the inherited model of church from an inward looking church-life focus to the outgoing whole-life focus of the emerging church. This shift to a whole-life focus was well expressed recently by the Archbishop of Canterbury:

> A copernican vision is required of us to see at the centre of God's mission not the splendid work of church life but the equally splendid wilderness of the world — where there are few places for Christians to hide, where moral or ethical signposts are blurred or non-existent and where we are outnumbered by the indifference, the unholy and the uncultured despisers of our day ... It will require a radical change of attitude from us all. It will mean being prepared not to jettison all that we have for the sake of something new and different but of humbly accepting that the local church must come second to the needs of those serving Christ in the world and the real needs of the communities in which we live.[1]

There is a need in the church today for a shift from a focus on 'the work of ministry' to the more important matter of 'the ministry of work'. ... Engaging in creativity, both as individuals in the whole of life, and as a church in its corporate activities, is at heart participating in God's mission. The ultimate creativity is the sustaining and renewal of each individual life, all human society, the whole creation and cosmos. Creativity, so understood, is the expression of the dominion (as distinct from domination) that is part of our nature as those made in the image of God. It is the work of the Kingdom which Jesus did and called his disciples into. It involves working for justice and peace and for a just sharing of the earth's resources. It will involve confronting the principalities and powers that frustrate the will and goodness of God reaching the life of groups and individuals. It will, of necessity, because it is a spiritual work, require prayer through which we can find God's direction and our part in the midst of a multitude of 'good ideas' and passing enthusiasms.

> Prayer is not a pious instrument by which we move God to baptize our enterprises; it is entering the strength of him who moves history and binds the powers that be.[2]

However, in drawing attention to the spiritual roots of creativity we need to guard against any 'spiritualizing' tendency which would narrow creativity to one sphere of life. All life, all relations, all expressions of artistic ability and human culture are included in the creativity which reflects the image of God in and through us.

A church functioning in the affirmation of its members' creativity will need sufficient pastoral networks for people to be known well enough to discern the areas of creativity to which, in the wider society as well as in the life of the church, they are being called. It may well find itself linking with other churches to support groups engaging in particular issues from educational provisions to wealth creation and from the health service to genetic engineering. It is likely to be a church forging partnerships with agencies working in specific areas, such as homelessness, drug abuse or the rehabilitation of offenders. The first sign of its prophetic nature is much more likely to be found in what it is quietly doing than in what it is loudly denouncing; though confrontation is part of the call to bring about creative change. Such a church is, as already noted, likely to travel light as far as its own structures are concerned.

Such creative engagement with the whole of life will inevitably involve working with others. In doing so the church, and the individual Christian, experiences a further dimension of the image of God, namely the social, trinitarian, nature of God. Furthermore, involvement in such creativity as has been previously identified is likely to draw others into an experience of grace and into a desire to celebrate.[3] It is this which is fundamental to the building of community. In this work of community building the church participates in the Trinity, for the dynamic of a missionary congregation living in the image of God expresses the nature of the God revealed in the person of Christ — *giving, celebrating, creative* and *love-in-community*. Tragically this is what in international, national, industrial and domestic affairs, our world so often lacks; namely the gift of life-giving community.

> Unable to engage our interior lives, we are incapable of engaging the interior lives of other people. Not knowing ourselves, we are unable to reveal who we are before the face of another person. And we are unable to receive them in their personhood since we are out of touch with our own.[4]

> Trapped in our tradition of rugged individualism, we are an extraordinarily lonely people. So lonely, in fact, that many cannot even acknowledge their loneliness to themselves, much less to others.[5]

To this end, the development of communities of faith is crucial. Too easily, as was said in identifying the chief marks of the church in inherited mode, we see the church as an organization rather than a community.

> At the same time, the political, social, and economic institutions of government are changing radically as well. Larger and more impersonal, they are increasingly competitive, specialized, bureaucratic, and out of touch with the people. Created to serve humanizing forces within society, they tend to evolve into alienating structures with dehumanizing programs.[6]

As networks rather than institutions are the means through which people increasingly relate to one another, it is vital that the church itself discovers how to become a network of loving relationships. In this process it will need to discover how to be an empowering, forgiving and conflict-handling community. For many who have lacked stable relationships, the church may well find itself fulfilling the role of family and natural community in a setting when both of them have collapsed. It will not be easy and will require a significant amount of its skilled leadership to be active in this area whilst simplifying all the time its organizational structure.

Notes

1. Quoted from Yvonne Craig, *Learning for Life: A Handbook of Adult Religious Education* (London: Mowbray, 1994), p. 1.

2. Melba Maggay, *Transforming Society* (Oxford: Regnum Books, 1994), p. 71.
3. This is a very similar pattern to the 'service, worship, discipleship' of the *Isaiah Vision*, though the order here is different. See Raymond Fung, *The Isaiah Vision: An Ecumenical Strategy for Congregational Evangelism* (Geneva: WCC Publications, 1992).
4. John Kavanaugh, *Still Following Christ in a Consumer Society* (Maryknoll, NY: Orbis Books, 1991), p. 8.
5. M. Scott Peck, *The Different Drum: Community Making and Peace* (London: Arrow, 1988), p. 58.
6. John Westerhoff III, *Living the Faith Community: The Church that Makes a Difference* (Minneapolis, MN: Winston Press, 1985), p. 8.

Community regeneration

Andrew Mawson

I was introduced to Santiago Bell by a friendly journalist whom I knew through my work on Central America and Liberation Theology during the early 1980s. Santiago is a Chilean exile who once worked with the famous educationalist Paulo Freire and had paid the price of putting this theology to work. He had been responsible for establishing various community initiatives in Chile during the Allende administration. A former governor of a province, Santiago was arrested in 1973, following the *coup d'état*, tortured and imprisoned along with thousands of others.

In prison he was ordained a deacon and called to share a humble liturgy of bread and water with his nine companions. Through this meal he kept his sanity whilst being brutally humiliated. In an article in *The Independent on Sunday*, written for our exhibition at the Concourse Gallery in the Barbican in 1993, Santiago recalled how he had been beaten and tortured and forced into near madness in solitary confinement: 'They made me eat shit with a spoon. People say that this has made me wise. Well, I would rather be stupid and not have had the lesson. I learnt things but they were all dark things.' Strangely that darkness has shed much light in Bow.

Because his paternal grandfather was Scottish, Santiago and his wife and six children were eventually released into exile in Britain. His life destroyed, he was now reduced to doing odd jobs in people's houses. When we first met I instantly recognized his artistic potential. His portfolio presented a master craftsman who was capable of earning a large salary in the West End. He asked simply for a workshop space to continue his craft and one that could be open to members of the local community. It was clear that this creative process he was initiating would also be the route through which he would find his own healing. The church members unanimously agreed to give Santiago a derelict space to the side of the church hall. Within weeks he had turned it into an orderly workshop with beautifully designed hand-made benches, which echoed the attention to detail of his art. It was not long before the congregation also recognized his priestly gifts and this renegade Catholic was invited by the members to share in my ministry and administer here, as he had done in prison, the sacred mysteries.

We had no money and for the first eight months Santiago earned nothing. He simply opened his door and began work. We undertook no publicity, Santiago's view being that the community would discover this oasis for itself. He was right. One of the first people to come was a young man called Daniel who lived in a squat next door. He was building eccentric furniture for Janet Street-Porter's house and needed Santiago's skill and tools to complete the commission. Santiago obliged and the first relationship was established, amid suspicions as to what I was exactly about.

Daniel was followed by his near neighbour, Su, a young woman requiring space to build a small sailing boat. She asked for permission to use the derelict hall. Ethel, an elderly member, with her usual youthful spirit suggested to the church meeting that Noah built a boat so why shouldn't Su do so in our hall. This seemed a perfectly reasonable line of argument to me. Through the process of building the boat our relationship became established. Su, I soon discovered, had encountered a zealous Pentecostalist teacher at school who had tried to convert her; this had led her, a bright girl, to be totally suspicious of anything Christian. It was some considerable time before she could fully trust that Santiago and I had no hidden agenda. Certainly our early conversations over afternoon tea in her house, viewing the magnificent greenhouse under plastic, which Ebon, who shared the home, had constructed, were memorable times.

The real breakthrough came when one morning I arrived to find a small jar of flowers on the floor outside the workshop door. On a note was written 'With many thanks for the use of the workshop, wild flowers of Bow, Su.' Here was a kindred spirit. Su may have had little time for the church, but she certainly rang bells with both Santiago and me. The first important community relationship outside the church membership had taken root. Her insight and connections were to prove crucial in the months ahead, for Su was to point us to the real possibilities that lay on the doorstep.

It was during these months that I became increasingly convinced that the role of the church in such urban areas, where high-rise living produced a dehumanizing privatization of life, must be as a catalyst to bring together in concrete ways the variety of people who lived cheek by jowl and yet often seemed unaware of each other. Surely to create community was an historic calling of the Church. To establish a human context, a space, which people could enter and explore together the connections that existed between them — was not this theology in action? I was also now encountering considerable pastoral demands. I could not cope alone; we needed a corporate response to be effective.

I became concerned to create a concrete environment in which ordinary people's lives, from diverse racial backgrounds, would cross and interact. Care was taken not to control the interplay but to create the arena in which real human integration, that was visibly evolving, could take place. The cafe, the dance school, the workshops and the nursery have many tales to tell of this growing integration, amid the inevitable conflicts that occasionally resulted between both individuals and groups. On the whole the experience has been friendly and open and people have been generous with each other. The church's position was clear: we supported an equal opportunities policy and were open to all people of whatever race or creed. When local parents refused to join in the local Muslim Eid festival at the school and withdrew their children, we purposely attended. The church has since hosted numerous Bengali festivals and Muslim prayers in the church space where the Eucharist is shared. We conclude each Sunday liturgy with the words: 'Living God, we thank you for this heavenly banquet prepared for us and all the peoples of the earth.' The message, in a context where there is serious racial tension, is clear among locals who know us. Others of a more traditional Christian mindset worry considerably about this policy. We have also sought to take an independent political stand. Our view has been, in a changing climate, that a bird with one wing never flies. We have remained vigilant and open.

* * *

It would be dishonest not to admit that the middle classes locally have had an important part to play in all the developments of Bow. Without them we would never have started. One of my concerns about much of the Liberation Theology I had witnessed in action in Central America was the often unstated role that this social group played in any social change. They were the ones who were economically flexible enough to engage in social change. 'The poor', I observed, usually had too many pressing demands placed upon them to be able to change their lot in any real way. Indeed, experience often led them to be fatalistic.

I realized that we needed to bring together a creative mix from the new diversity of life that was now evolving in east London. The compartmentalization of local communities was a reality, be they working class, middle class, the elderly, the young, the New Age Travellers or the Bengali youths. People on the whole had few opportunities where their lives could truly cross and engage, creating understanding and tolerance. The irony of the neighbourhood system of local government, introduced during this time by the Liberal Democrats, is that it often exacerbates the mindset of the ghetto.

* * *

Both Santiago and I have always known, since the early days, that the project was about the present; we said that it was not 'for ever'. What matters is not the building of an edifice which outlasts us all, but to live life to the full now. When I eventually leave Bow I would like to say that we played the game with some success; now let someone else appear and possibly build something different. This would not be a sign of failure, but a realistic response to the fast-moving and unpredictable environment in which we are living. The worship area itself is designed as a tent, the pegs can be easily pulled out. The project as a whole is simply a movement in time and space; let us enjoy it for what it is.

The Bromley by Bow Centre, as we are now known, has today become a unique venture at the crossroads of community, the arts, education, health, environment and liturgy. The formerly derelict buildings have been extended and are now used by over 600 people each week. We employ a staff of forty and run a budget in excess of £700,000. Until recently the project has been very local, but we are now faced with the pros and cons of increasing national significance. Today the Centre comprises the following elements: a range of art workshops; a Bengali language project; a nursery; a toy library;

creche facilities; a community cafe; an art gallery; a church; until recently the Janet Viola School of modern dance; a health project; offices; a community garden.

We have in recent years hosted a visit by HRH the Princess of Wales, along with three government ministers and the permanent secretary from the Home Office. We are now embarking upon a 3-acre park development which will include a new health centre to provide the main primary health care for the area. Until now local GPs have operated in run-down premises and it has proved impossible to attract high-quality doctors into the area. This integrated development, we hope, will address this problem. Over the years I have buried some who have died before their time who, had they received adequate primary health care, might still have been alive today. It is hoped that this initiative will be a practical response to this human need.

The policy of the Centre today remains one of enabling. We aim to make concrete those ideas which would otherwise remain only potentials within the community. We have embraced creativity and artistic endeavour as central to the task. Tower Hamlets has probably the largest artistic community outside New York and we have sought consciously to engage this community in our model of urban regeneration. We now run art workshops in stained glass, woodwork, stone sculpture, pottery, life drawing, wood sculpture and mosaics. We have had gallery space in the City of London and in 1993 we held an exhibition in the Concourse Gallery, at the Barbican; two hundred works of art were on display, provided by local people and professional artists. Lord Ennals and Lord Peyton, to whom I will always be grateful, hosted two private views sponsored by British Gas and the Post Office. Pentecost '95 and The Great Banquet were launched at this event.

We have been concerned to design helpful spaces in which people can live and work, recognizing the truth that we are all profoundly influenced by the physical spaces that we occupy. I have increasingly come to the conclusion that our built environment deeply affects the way people live and behave in the inner cities. Alice Coleman in *Utopia on Trial*[1] all too clearly demonstrates this fact. The spaces in Bow have therefore been designed as artistic expressions in themselves.

We have an unusual approach to organizing our artistic work, by which we encourage local artists, who are committed to working with local people, to work from the Centre. Establishing their studio space on site creates a sense of openness and also enables the project to have a 'critical mass' of artistic activity. We also now work extensively with people with disabilities, enabling them to explore their artistic talents alongside significant local artists and volunteers. The integrated nature of these workshops reflects the diversity of the local community and prevents making ghettos of people labelled by their particular problem. One group has, for example, made a set of ceramic plant pots for the garden they helped to design and build. The garden has won local prizes as well as the Shell Better Britain Award for the London Region. In September 1991 the garden was formally opened by Mrs Carey, the wife of the Archbishop of Canterbury. Dr Carey was born locally and some of the plants come from Lambeth Palace, the second largest private garden in London.

The liturgical space stands at the centre of the buildings and is surrounded by an art gallery, a day nursery, a toy library and creche facilities. This unusual and flexible area converts quickly into a theatre or large open space. Courses have been run in this context on a wide range of topics, including parenting and child-birth (sponsored by the Body Shop), and singing classes are held twice each week. Stephen Goode, a local parent, and his wife, Yvonne Begley, were responsible for developing our child-care facilities initially from a small co-operative nursery that they ran from their home. The nursery, now under the able management of Jo Monteith-Hodge, is still run by the parents. Ten years on, at a recent AGM, parents were asking if their children could remain until they were five because they recognized how important this facility had become in their children's development. One parent indicated that she did not know of any other nursery facility which mixed children's play with the arts, culture and community at such an early age. Clearly the integrated philosophy of the nursery, developed initially by Stephen and Yvonne and at the time resisted by Social Services, has now become recognized in its own right. Finbar, the last of their four children, is now to move on to infant school, but they have left us with a legacy, a model of child care, which offers lessons for the future.

* * *

In 1993 I was asked by Sir George Young, Minister of State for Housing, to join the Board of the Tower Hamlets Housing Action Trust. This quango has, in my view, the real opportunity to improve the quality of housing in one of the poorest areas of the borough. The sum of £80 million has been allocated and the project is now up and running under the very able leadership of David Gilles (Chief Executive) and Dr Michael Barraclough (Chairman). I was asked to join the Board to share more widely our experience of community development in Bromley by Bow and our involvement in high quality, cost-effective community buildings. Notwithstanding the legitimacy or otherwise of quangos, I have to admit that this very capable group of people, working with the residents, is likely to produce some first-rate housing. Whilst not perfect, this process is teaching me a great deal about larger structures and how they can be made to work effectively. Frequently Tower Hamlets has experienced mismatch between the rhetoric and action of both the main political parties and the people have paid the price. A far more rigorous assessment of the consequences of particular beliefs and decision-making needs to be undertaken if public money is to be spent more effectively in the future. The Housing Action Trust will provide an interesting experiment to see if we can be any more effective.

The McCabe Educational Trust was launched by its Patron, the Right Reverend Dr George Carey, Archbishop of Canterbury, in June 1991 at Lambeth Palace. Its first initiative was Project Sinai, which takes young people from the inner cities of Britain to the Sinai desert to experience at first hand the beauty, history and complexity of the Middle East, while at the same time helping them to discover the roots of the three monotheistic faiths that are increasingly in contention in urban Europe. This project has given our activity-based approach to education an international perspective and our first trip from Bow, which included people of eight different nationalities, proved to be a major success. In 1994 the project took ninety-two young people from contexts as diverse as Belfast, Glasgow, Toxteth in Liverpool and Sheffield. In 1995 the Trust is supporting 100 young people from London to take part in the project, as part of the Pentecost '95 celebrations.

One of our major concerns in recent years has been to develop methods of working which actively influence social policy and the integration of wider community policies. In April 1991 Jean, a young mother with two children, died after a protracted illness. In the months leading up to her death the statutory services involved had failed to organize or provide care for either her or her family, though, in my opinion, she was a member of one of the most vulnerable groups in Britain. Workers at the Centre kept a detailed record of the missing care and provided much of it themselves. Jackie, five months pregnant, would each morning go in to bathe Jean. As a result of a report, written by Allison Trimble, following Jean's death, an enquiry was called in the Board Room of the Royal London Hospital. After a series of difficult, and not always co-operative, meetings, a new pilot study was implemented based on the 'key worker' model of care which we had proposed.

From the earliest days we resisted creating a context in which people became dependent upon us or anyone else. The scale of pastoral problems that we confronted demanded that we stimulate a supportive community who would care for each other. The Church, if it is seriously engaged, can in my experience have a key role to play when so many caring agencies are dominated by professional vested interests rather than by human need. The minister or priest has few career prospects or legal responsibilities and as such can cast a critical and objective eye over the realities of care in which she or he needs to be a partner.

Perhaps our major impact has been to start a wider process, stimulating a sense of value and belonging in a local context, celebrating its richness rather than concentrating endlessly upon its many problems. ... What we have developed in Bow is a particular model of social engagement which seeks to be holistic in its integrated approach. ... If we are serious about exploring this ecumenical model that may be able to take us beyond the 1990s then the Church must maximize its potential to be a catalyst both for community involvement and for change. Certainly for many it will demand a radical mental adjustment but, at its simplest, it will need also to take seriously the gospel imperatives to be generous, tolerant, open and truthful with our neighbours, for we are told that love of neighbour and love of God are the two greatest commandments of all.

The design of the church in Bromley by Bow is a statement of our theology in a project which seeks to be holistic in its approach to both structures and individuals. The symbols of the Eucharist sit at the centre of our life. We hold hands and share the peace each Sunday. We break the bread and share the wine, serving each other as a symbol of our Christian community. We take bread from the cafe and light the seven-day candle, as a sign of the presence of God among us. In a fragmented and often racially tense context we seek to bring people together, to open channels of communication and to be a 'presence' in the midst of God's world. We struggle to be a parable of what the Kingdom of God may be about.

The multi-coloured triptych at the front of the church speaks of the ecumenical nature of our church life. Catholics, Anglicans, members from Free Church traditions share their lives with new members who have few church roots. We all recognize that we live in a new historical situation, in which the Church must seriously review its mission, and our concern is to reflect theologically upon this urgent matter in a concrete context. To be concerned for 'the poor' in our community is a complex matter. It is not possible to implant models developed in the Third World, we must discover our own and this is central to our mission in Bow.

How do the bread and wine shared on a Sunday relate to the children's play in the nursery, the toy library and creches, and the human drama which unfolds just a stone's throw away from the table on which they are offered? I have suggested that our physical context is not unlike the medieval cathedral, where often the liturgical centre was surrounded by the market-place of life, the cosmic drama in the midst of mundane human activity. If it is true, as I have implied, that 'we are the environments we live in', powerfully and subtly influenced by them, then the impact of all this is, I suspect, considerable upon many levels of the human spirit and particularly upon the many people who pass through this space each week.

The worshipping life of the church is no longer hidden behind oak doors and frosted glass, but can be seen from the street. The stone angels, made in the workshops, fly over the children playing in the nursery. The very liturgical space is the theatre of their play. The theologian Rubem Alves reminds us how loaded with liturgical significance children's play is, as indeed Our Lord reminded us. There are few liturgical spaces in London, I would guess, that are so central to human living.

The liturgy that we have written embodies this broad ecumenical under-standing. We have taken what we consider to be the most helpful aspects of the historic Christian liturgical tradition and created our own liturgy and service book, in which children, adults and strangers can take part. We share mid-week prayer each Wednesday evening by candlelight. We have recognized that the traditional rhythm of regular Sunday worship is over in our community. This is why the church had virtually collapsed by 1984.

I see my role as minister essentially as a person who shares bread and wine and the gospel stories with those who choose to listen. There is no obligation. The church space is free and open for people to share their lives and anxieties, with no hidden agenda. If people choose to become members, as some have, that is fine. The church is very much like the workshops in this respect, open to all. As a result of this tolerant attitude the church has grown from the ten elderly members in 1984 (eight of whom have now died) to twenty-five, plus six children. There are strengths in being small, and, in a diverse local community where a third of the population come from Bangladesh, we are realistic about the size of the worshipping community. Our worship provides a focus, a hub around which both activity and our reflection can revolve.

Because of our close relationship with the community many have shared in our liturgy and have, as I explained, written their own liturgies over the years. Some of these have been of astounding beauty and understanding. The church's liturgical life is no longer a compartment separated from the wider community's life, but sits naturally in the market-place of secular East End living. For this reason we resist simplistic divisions and categories that institutions often wish to place upon us.

The Church's ecumenical vision can have no walls or partitions, for on the death of our Lord the curtain of the Temple was torn from top to bottom. We are one world, one capital city, one community, who must look together, through the glasses of our different traditions, out to the ocean which borders the islands that together we have made. The church in Bromley by Bow is drawn to the conclusion that it is only here will we discover the God whom we have seen in Christ, who always comes to us, as his parables about the Kingdom of God suggest, from the future.

NOTE

1.   Alice Coleman, *Utopia on Trial: Vision and Reality in Planned Housing* (London: Hilary Shipman, 1990).

Act local: social justice from the bottom up

David Donnison

The processes which create great concentrations of poverty in particular neighbourhoods arise partly from the failings of past urban policies: the building of poorly serviced public housing estates with few jobs within easy reach, the concentration in these places of many people who are having a hard time — the homeless, lone parents, people coming out of prisons and long-stay hospital care — and from failures to maintain buildings and their surrounding environment. Together, these can lead to high turnover, squatting, vandalism and the erosion of constraints on behaviour maintained by more stable communities.

Now that by deliberate policies this country has created a public sector of the housing market which, in many cities, consists largely of people living on state benefits, any big housing estate is likely to be a poverty-stricken neighbourhood. Thus special steps must be taken to improve local opportunities, to diversify housing and tenures and to integrate these communities more closely into the rest of the city.

Meanwhile there remain inner city areas of run-down housing, public and private, owner-occupied and rented, which have been badly neglected. They may offer a first foothold in the housing market for recently arrived migrants, together with cheap business premises for people starting their own enterprises. If they are to be renewed and diversified without damaging vulnerable people, local residents have to be actively involved in planning for these areas.

This kind of social polarization and segregation would not be allowed to happen if it did not, at least in some respects, suit powerful people quite well. Housing managers may find it useful to have a 'Siberia' in which space can always be found for people with urgent needs, and which also serves as a kind of punishment camp for poor rent payers and troublesome tenants. Police chiefs, who know they cannot eliminate drug traffickers, may find it convenient to concentrate the trade in a low-status area where they can keep an eye on it and middle-class citizens will not be disturbed. As the populations of economically failing cities decline, those responsible for health and education services have to find hospitals and schools which can be closed without politically damaging protests. Planners need reserve supplies of land and buildings which can be brought forward for redevelopment or neglected till they are required. Meanwhile powerless people and their children have to live out their lives in these landscapes of despair.

It follows that purely technical or commercial solutions will not work. Initiatives which are to put these things right must be launched by political leaders who have the authority to change public priorities and focus resources in new and sustained ways on such areas. They will need support from central government and the national taxpayer — a point we return to below. If the area to be renewed is a large one, it will need a local committee or agency capable of pulling together the efforts of the private sector and the many different public services operating there, and gaining support from local community groups and the central government. Women, people with disabilities and the varied ethnic groups often found in such areas must gain a voice in the project. There are encouraging examples of such initiatives led by local authorities and the central government. No single formula can be guaranteed to work: success depends on the people involved.

Local residents must be given an independent voice in the formulation of priorities through some association or an umbrella group speaking for existing associations, with resources which enable them to hire their own staff and to own some of the initiatives and enterprises that will be set up. Again, we have seen encouraging examples of this kind.

The private sector has an interest in the social and economic regeneration of deprived areas — an interest best carried forward by focusing on particular places in collaboration with local authorities and community groups, as Scottish Business in the Community has tried to do, not riding roughshod over local people in pursuit of killings in a fickle property market.

Local needs, resources and traditions differ, even in areas which appear uniformly deprived. In some, people will give first priority to housing (as in Manchester's Hulme estate); in others it will be jobs and training (as in Moss Side, next door), or culture and celebration (as in the early days on Edinburgh's Craigmillar estate, and, on a larger scale, in Derry), or economic opportunities coupled with the reduction of violence and crime (as in Glasgow's Barrowfield estate). Given time and some support, people will usually take up all these issues — together with welfare rights, child care, mental health and other issues.

The flexible way in which the Government has sought bids for public funds from the new Single Regeneration Budget shows that this lesson is being learned. The broad objectives are clear, but the initiators of such projects and their first priorities are expected to vary from place to place.

Political action will be needed to ensure that the public services which have to respond to these demands work effectively together for neighbourhoods with special needs. Left to themselves, each agency will usually retain a different pattern of area management, making it impossible for their staff even to talk about — let alone act for — the same area. If regeneration projects focused on areas with special needs are not just to sweep social problems around the urban map, their priorities have to be built into the operations of mainstream services in ways which will prevent the emergence of new problem areas as soon as old ones are improved. Areas entitled to priority treatment need to be agreed by all services, and their requirements built into the priorities of Education, Health, Training, Housing, Planning, Transport and other services. That is bound to be difficult at a time when more and more of these services are being contracted out to independent agencies or placed in the hands of semi-independent quangos. Local politicians, securely based in the communities which elected them, have greater authority than anyone else to call upon these agencies to adopt priorities of this kind, and to call upon a future Parliament to give civic leaders greater powers to make such priorities effective.

We have stressed the importance of focusing attention on areas with special needs; but, within a framework of that kind, public services must be capable of operating at many different scales. A housing co-operative usually works best when it is small, serving perhaps 200 or 300 households; an urban secondary school needs a much larger catchment area with at least 5,000 people living in it; a modern health centre may serve an area three times as large; and a training and placement programme that is designed to give people the best opportunities for work will serve a region extending beyond even the larger cities. The complex requirements of a strategy which has to operate at these different scales make this a task for civic leaders responsible for a whole city or county.

* * *

New patterns of governance and voluntary action are developing to give hitherto neglected people a voice in local and public affairs, to make public service staff more directly accountable to them, and to extend genuine rights of citizenship. These initiatives include:

- The creation of voluntary bodies with local branches designed to act as advisers, advocates and pressure groups. Some speak for people with particular needs — like women's refuges, Age Concern and many more. Some, like the tenants' and residents' associations, speak for their neighbourhood or housing estate. Some speak for larger groupings of poor people in general — like the Child Poverty Action Group. Local authorities have found various ways of supporting and responding to these groups.
- The deconcentration or outstationing of public services in smaller, more accessible offices from which a team of staff from different services operate with greater commitment to a local community in which they are better known and more exposed.
- The creation of new, community-owned or at least community-based, agencies providing particular services such as the credit unions, and the management and ownership co-operatives which have developed in the housing field. More ambitious development trusts of various kinds have an open brief to develop a wider range of services and enterprises.

- The development of community enterprises, producing and trading like other businesses, but on terms which make them accountable to their local communities while feeding back any profit made into the development of the enterprise or to benefit the community. These can in principle serve any kind of place, but they have made a particularly important contribution in deprived neighbourhoods where they have helped people who have been out of work for a long time to find a way back into the labour market.
- Attempts to link up some of these initiatives in ways which begin to create new forms of governance linking providers and users of services in new ways. Some of the more venturesome examples are to be found in Islington's neighbourhood offices, to which active neighbourhood forums of local people are attached, and in Tower Hamlets' neighbourhood councils which work through neighbourhood offices and smaller 'one-stop shops' in consultation with local tenants' associations. Other authorities are experimenting with similar strategies, sometimes in selected areas of deprivation (as in Glasgow, for example) and sometimes wall-to-wall across their territory (as in Manchester, for example).

As power begins to be handed over at the local scale to community groups it becomes very important to foresee problems of incompetence, dishonesty, discrimination and other abuses of power which may arise, to discuss these frankly with community representatives, to work out agreed methods for monitoring and auditing their operations, and to train them to deal with such matters. There is no magic about 'community': civic leaders have to ensure that the basic tasks of government are still performed.

Critics of community-based projects often complain that they are 'not really representative'. In fact, they are often more representative than municipal councillors are — in the sense of resembling the communities they serve in age, gender, race, and so on. But that is not their main purpose. The main questions should be: 'Are they efficient and effective?' and 'Are they accountable?' — to their staff and customers, to their funders and backers, to the law and the community at large. Those questions must be answered at three different levels:

- At the local, day-to-day level: where, for example, do the aggrieved customers and staff of a housing co-operative go if they feel badly treated?
- Over a somewhat longer term and larger scale: to whom, for example, can the neighbours appeal if they believe the co-operative is polluting their street or competing unfairly with local enterprises?
- At the larger, city-wide scale: who ensures that the co-operative does not act in racist or financially dishonest ways?

Exactly the same questions must be asked of the growing numbers of quangos appointed by central government to wield great powers at the local level: development agencies, hospital trusts, the Housing Corporation, and so on. Only if accountability can be assured at all these levels will people gain rights, not only as customers concerned with the quality of the services they get, but also as citizens, concerned with the way in which their society is developing. Local councillors empowered to speak for the whole community will have to play a central part in those processes if the poorest people are not to be further excluded.

This leads us to the central phase of the processes we have traced: the stresses imposed on people who are being excluded from the mainstream of their society — and particularly the hardships of families and young people.

A society can still respond at this stage in ways which ease or exacerbate such hardships. If (as has happened in Britain) lone parents living on income support are placed in flats which no-one else will live in because they are impossible to keep warm at a price which people living on low incomes could afford, if the discretionary grants which used to help such people pay for fuel are eliminated and VAT is added to their fuel bills, if the local school is closed and school meals deteriorate, then the hardships of these families grow worse. But none of the policy changes which have exacerbated these hardships were inevitable. Things could instead have been made easier for them.

A similar story can be told about the ways in which social security and housing benefits have been withdrawn from young people between the ages of 16 and 25, while at the same time economic changes were making it harder — in many places impossible — for them to find jobs which confer any sense of the dignity of labour. The rise in homelessness, addiction and crime which has occurred since the mid-1980s was widely predicted. But again, none of these policy changes were inevitable.

Many of the policies suggested by these examples would have to be initiated by central governments, but there is scope too for action to be taken at a local scale. Many municipal and health authorities in Britain are now trying to formulate more systematic anti-poverty policies and the local authorities have set up a National Local Government Forum Against Poverty to help in carrying forward this work.

Much of the action required under this heading has already been outlined. The ways in which deprived communities respond to hardship depend partly on their social composition, and that can be shaped, wittingly or unwittingly, by urban policy. If housing is provided in a place where public and commercial services are poor, the environment is neglected and good jobs are hard to find, then the more successful families will move out to rent or buy a home elsewhere and more hard pressed people will take their places. If turnover then rises and the sense of community decays, crime and fear are bound to become more widespread. Only a comprehensive, long-term programme of regeneration will arrest this kind of social decay. To provide training and jobs alone will hasten the outflow, enabling some people to pay off their debts and buy their way into better neighbourhoods while others are left in a community even more deprived than before.

People may respond more or less creatively to exclusion and injustice. How they respond will depend heavily on the way in which they are treated by the politicians and officials whom they encounter. For every creative, community-based project there is usually at least one support worker, chosen by the community but paid from public funds, and, somewhere in the background, at least one supportive official, empowered to devote a lot of time to helping the activists, with the backing of local politicians.

Too often, official initiatives to renew and regenerate stricken parts of a city's economy are launched, and then local people are asked to participate in them — quickly. The procedures decreed for Estate Action and City Challenge projects permit no other approach. It rarely works well. Individuals and communities lying fairly close to the bottom of the scale we outlined which runs from apathy to creativity will be suspicious of invitations to 'consult' and 'participate'. They've heard it all before; and, in their experience, nothing much gets done. Moreover, people lacking long experience in the rituals of government are seldom at their best in large meetings with formal agendas. Initiatives which are designed to respond to their needs and feelings, and to help them to play effective parts in the action will usually provide the best starting points and training grounds for what may later become more ambitious community-based action. Initiatives which tap the vigour and imagination of women often do best of all — possibly because their commitment to their children makes them more determined than men to fight for a better future; possibly because they have depended less on wage labour to give their lives meaning and so they are less demoralized by unemployment. There are many encouraging examples of this kind ranging from community colleges to food co-ops.

Many renewal and regeneration projects cannot — or are not allowed — to proceed in this informal way. For them it may be better frankly to explain that there will be one stream of decisions leading to action which has to proceed according to a tight timetable. Every effort will be made to consult people about those things, and to respond to their views or explain why that is impossible; but they will not 'own' that stream of events or be able to delay them for long. Meanwhile there will be other developments which can proceed according to a more relaxed timetable, and the community will be helped to take over full ownership of those parts of the work.

Further reading

Dick Atkinson, *The Common Sense of Community* (London: Demos, 1994). Argues that self-reliant self-governing communities are the best regenerators of cities and that devolving power to tenants, residents and neighbourhoods over housing, schools, and the local environment is the surest strategy to the recovery of democratic and crime-free cities.

David Boyle, *Building Futures: A Layman's Guide to the Inner City Debate* (London: W. H. Allen, 1989). Incisive account of regeneration projects in inner city areas from arts projects to housing refurbishment, and from Baltimore to Glasgow.

N. Deakin and J. Edwards, *The Enterprise Culture and the Inner City* (London: Routledge, 1993). Argues for the retargeting of public subsidies for the regeneration of derelict inner city land onto job creation and skills training for poor and unskilled people.

David Harvey, *The Condition of Postmodernity* (Oxford: Blackwell, 1990). Examines the substitution of ethics with aesthetics in the 'spectacle' of postmodern city planning.

Jane Jacobs, *The Death and Life of Great American Cities* (New York: Vintage Books, 1966). This classic work argues that cities are best constructed by their residents, not by planners. Thus neighbourhoods in which people — as pedestrians and as residents — take priority over other demands for space such as roads are safer and less prone to crime and disorder.

M. Keith and A. Rogers (eds), *Hollow Promises: Rhetoric and Reality in the Inner City* (London: Mansell, 1991). A critical examination of the social and economic effects of the shift of urban funding from ethics to aesthetics, or from people-oriented to property-oriented programmes in the 1980s.

Charles Landry and Franco Bianchini, *The Creative City* (London: Demos, 1995). Presents a number of case studies of cities in Europe which have put people and creativity first, raised the quality of life, and thereby have attracted and generated more jobs.

Gill Moody, 'Life in the City', in Peter Sedgwick (ed.) *God in the City* (London: Mowbray, 1995) pp. 9–15. The release of creativity in the city is identified with partnership between denominations and agencies, governmental and non-governmental, in the regeneration of the city and in the recovery of confidence amongst urban Christians.

Paul Moore, *The Church Reclaims the City* (London: SCM Press, 1968). Prescient text on the retreat of the churches in America from the city to the suburbs and a powerful exposition of the vital role of downtown churches, neighbourhood churches and church sponsored social work in the Church's reclaiming of the city.

Lewis Mumford, *The Culture of Cities* (London: Secker and Warburg, 1938). From one of the century's foremost thinkers on the nature of cities, in this book he emphasizes that the physical organization and planning of the city — transport, buildings, etc. — should be subservient to human social needs and local communities.

Michael Schluter and David Lee, *The R Factor* (London: Hodder and Stoughton, 1993). Presents a relational vision of human society and government and contends that at the heart of the good society, and the good city, is a network of relational communities of neighbourhood, work and governance.

Peter Sedgwick, 'Enterprise and Estrangement', in *God in the City* (London: Mowbray, 1995) pp. 163–77. Argues for a social understanding of wealth creation where the encouragement of individual enterprise and creativity are not realized at the expense of the common good. Worship is seen as the key to reconnecting individual creativity with the creativity and the justice of God: 'the hope which there is in worship must seek a dialogue with the secular hope found in entrepreneurial activity, so that the two worlds of economics and Christian faith are neither seen as separate realities nor one identity'.

Unleashing the Potential: Bringing Residents to the Centre of Regeneration, (London: Joseph Rowntree Foundation, 1996). Reviews successes and failures in regenerating deprived public housing estates. Argues that tenants must be at the centre of the planning of improvements to housing, public service delivery and local economic revival. Contrasts the best practice in local estate regeneration with the continuing tendency on many estates for outside agencies and workers to ignore the voices and initiatives of residents, and for money putatively targeted at UPA estates to be spent elsewhere.

Ken Warpole and Liz Greenhalgh, *The Freedom of the City* (London: Demos, 1996). Argues that efforts to restore the aesthetics of the built environment of the city must be matched by efforts to encourage good citizenship and wider participation in political and decision-making processes.

3

The shape of the city

See, I am creating new heavens and a new earth! The past will no more be remembered nor will it ever come to mind. Rejoice and be for ever filled with delight at what I create; for I am creating Jerusalem as a delight and her people as a joy; I shall take delight in Jerusalem and rejoice in my people; the sound of weeping, the cry of distress will be heard no more. No child there will ever again die in infancy, no old man fail to live out his span of life. He who dies at a hundred is just a youth, and if he does not attain a hundred he is thought accursed!

My people will build houses and live in them, plant vineyards and eat their fruit; they will not build for others to live in or plant for others to eat. They will be as long-lived as a tree, and my chosen ones will enjoy the fruit of their labour. They will not toil to no purpose or raise children for misfortune, because they and their issue after them are a race blessed by the Lord. Even before they call to me, I shall answer, and while they are still speaking I shall respond.

(Isaiah 65:17–24)

Faith in the City

To describe the pattern of urban growth and dispersal is relatively simple. To explain it is far more complicated. Obviously urbanization was closely linked to industrialization. Migration from a rural to an urban economy has been the central force of population movements in the modern age. The Anglo-Saxon countries led it in the nineteenth century, just as they have been leading the counter-trend towards suburbanization in the period since the Second World War. The pull of jobs and opportunities was strong for at least a century-and-a-half. Urban industry attracted more industry. The city became the magnet for human populations all over the industrializing world. (1.13)

Today the metaphor of the magnet is misleading. To be sure, the city centres remain as a focus for commerce and trade, with many new shopping centres and precincts having been developed in recent years. There are also protected pockets of prosperous material life in parts of the inner cities. And there are city jobs for qualified commuters. But for the most part opportunities for jobs, for housing and for the desired amenities of social services, shopping, schools, and leisure have shifted out of the industrial city. Migration has been selectively reversed, and the inner city is increasingly the territory of the left behind in the scramble for comfortable survival. (1.14)

Introduction

The Bible is full of images of the city, both positive and negative — the city of Jerusalem, surrounding the shining Temple on the hill, restored and renewed as in this passage from Third Isaiah, the dream of every Jewish exile; the cities of Egypt, Babylon and Assyria where the Jews knew slavery and forced migration; the city of Rome where St Paul was martyred, and after him Peter, and which is described in the Book of Revelation as the new Babylon, seat of the Emperor and ruler of the anti-Christian Roman Empire.

The narrative shape of the Bible constantly moves from garden to city, from rural to urban. The descendants of the nomadic farmers of Eastern Mesopotamia — Abraham, Isaac and Jacob — emigrated from Mesopotamia and Egypt into the plains and trading cities of Canaan where they found the Promised Land. The life of Jesus in the Gospels takes the form of a gradual movement from rural to urban, from the village of Galilee to the towns of Judea such as Capernaum, and ultimately to the city of Jerusalem. The early Church, though dominated in its leadership by rural fishermen, became most firmly established not in the rural communities of Palestine, which seem to have resisted the radical ethic of Jesus of Nazareth and his Jewish interpreters, but in the cities and large towns of the Eastern Mediterranean where Paul presented a Gospel ethic of community and liberation from religious or social exclusion which was shaped by and directed towards the experience of the ethnic migrants, slaves and small traders who were his frequent and most receptive audiences.

Migration and movement are key elements in the shaping of the modern city. Much rural–urban migration originates in changes in land use, and particularly the enclosure of lands for commercial farming, plantations and the establishment of large estates, changes mostly sustained by powerful city-based vested interests and property owners. Rural–urban migration is linked to the growth of cities as centres of economic power and commerce and the tendency of powerful cities to extract surplus from the surrounding countryside, often to the detriment of rural inhabitants and even the health of the land. The consequent overcrowding of cities and the impoverishment of the economy, and even the soil, in rural areas are two sides of the same coin. The visionaries of the early modern city saw this dysfunctional connection and sought to find ways of recovering harmony between urban and rural life, thereby overcoming the problems of both (Howard; Geddes).

Ebenezer Howard's vision of the planned Garden City was influential in the emergence of the town planning profession in Britain and North America, and also in Europe. The key elements to his vision were the balancing of town and country, industry and agriculture, housing and green open spaces, and the sharing of the wealth of the city through effective local democracy and the municipal ownership of land. Like Patrick Geddes, the modern prophet of the human scale self-build city, Howard believed that ordinary people were the best designers of their own environments, and that this could be achieved through individuals working together as small groups of artisans and self-builders, through co-operative municipalism, lending from local building societies, recycling of taxes from local businesses and regional agriculture, and through the extension of local democracy.

Town planning in the late nineteenth and early twentieth centuries saw the building of garden cities and suburbs, some of which remain monuments to a modern but human scale vision of urban living, low density, integrating people with nature. But after the Second World War planning became more grandiose, centralized and bureaucratic, and reflected the priorities of mobility, speed and industrial manufacture rather than the needs of families or the health of the environment (Le Corbusier; **Hall**). Many cities have been devastated by Le Corbusier's vision of traffic speeding by tower-blocks on elevated motorways, streets in the sky which provided modular cells — 'machines for living' — where the worker would form no long-term attachment to place and be all the more available as a mobile unit of labour for work in factory or city office. Many of Britain's town centres were more damaged by this vision than they had been by the German *Luftwaffe* and millions of people in cities throughout the world were decanted from houses or traditional tenements with their gardens or shared but enclosed greens to the anonymous blocks, windswept tunnels and bulldozed flat grounds of Le Corbusier's disastrous vision (**Hall**).

People dream of a softer more organic city, not zoned but interactive, multi-layered, with eateries, offices, homes, workshops, gardens and even farms in related not separate areas, a city which looks as if it has always been there, which integrates naturally with the landscape, which provides safe play areas for children, broad pavements for walking to work and for leisure, eating *al fresco* and sitting out on warm summer days, a city which encourages human inter-action, which is built around human-scale communities, fosters neighbourliness and discourages crime.

The failures of so much post-war planning resulted in government attempts to restrict the influence of local authority planning departments, which had grown immensely in power and significance since the Second World War, and to free up land for private developers, particularly through the new Urban Development Corporations. But with planners out of the way untrammelled commercial pressures produced offices and expensive homes in places like London's Dock-lands, but no affordable housing for local people, ineffective transport infrastructure, no community facilities, and the cityscape was once again of towers — this time in glass and aluminium — which rival the earlier planners' concrete towers in their inhumanity and ugliness (**Hackwood and Shiner**).

Another response of the planners to their failure to conceive people-friendly cities was the involvement of citizens in extensive participation exercises in the design of new developments and the rehabilitation of older areas. A more radical approach to popular planning emerged in the 1980s where local communities themselves organized to purchase and develop sites such as the Coin Street Site in London. Tenants groups or community organizations, including some churches, are increasingly involved in attempts to plan, build and renew their own environs, and to provide affordable housing for local people in a recognition that buildings and cities work best when they are built by local people in relation to their own needs as they see them (**Hackwood and Shiner**; Wates and Knevitt).

At their best, cities provide redemptive space in which people experience the freedom of true citizens, and the richness of social, cultural and spiritual being. At their worst, they offer a nightmare of environmental and economic depriva-tion. Theological and biblical reflection on the meaning of cities reflects this ambiguity in the nature of the city, as both place of human fellowship, centre of religion, trade, creativity and the arts, and as centre for the quest for wealth and military power, and of those economic and social forces which oppress minor-ities and the weak, ravage nature and ultimately undermine human flourishing.

Salvation and oppression are both possibilities for the modern city as for the ancient. But the history of the modern city is of economic and social and bureaucratic systems which frequently put speed or money, property, design or production before people (**Hackwood and Shiner**).

The Isaiah vision is of a city in which people come first, where they live in their own houses, their children do not die in infancy, and they have economic security and experience good health and long life (Fung; Mumford). Isaiah's prophecy of the rebuilding of Jerusalem is a vision of urban regeneration which has inspired generations of rural migrants, city designers and social reformers. As we have seen, the prophets frequently linked the fall of Israel and Judea to foreign powers, and the exile of their peoples, to unethical dealings between wealthy city dwellers and poor farmers, and to the tendency of urban-based societies to trust in economic and military might rather than in the Lord who gifted the land and its riches to a people who were called to love justice and share the fruits of the earth fairly. Isaiah's restored city is one where the sins of greed and avarice, lust for power and oppression of the weak are redeemed and the Lord's blessing has returned.

The Christian city of the Middle Ages bore some relationship to this vision. It was spatially ordered around the iconic focus of the Cathedral, and its economy and society frequently ordered around the hallowed time and relationality of the monastery. The Christian city sought to reflect in stone and trade and relationships the household ethic of the early Christians, but the conflict between this ethic and the machine-ordered world of the masses in the industrial city was to break the older urban vision of the secular interpenetrated by the sacred (Sennett). The modern city, just as it so often reduced the human to the function of a machine, excluded the spiritual vision of human relationality from the public square. The consequence was the retreat in British and North American cities from the city centre to the distant suburb where its conflicts and ills were banished by wealth, and the continuing contemporary retreat from the public square to the comfort of the designer interior of the private home whether in the suburb or the gentrified city centre (Neuhaus; Winter).

The constant temptation for Christianity in the modern city is to follow this retreat from the public to the private and to submit to the 'suburban captivity of the churches' (Winter). The Isaiah vision establishes an unambiguous link between the biological and economic conditions necessary for the good life, and worship of God in truth and sincerity (Fung). It conceives of the people of God as a community who seek the security and welfare of the city as a whole and are not content with private satisfaction — whether material or spiritual — alongside public squalor, unemployment, homelessness and the other growing problems of our increasingly divided cities. The Isaiah vision confirms the calling of the Church to minister and prophecy in the public square as well as the private household, to minister to communities of workers facing the ethical challenges of the city centre as well as to the residents of the distant suburb. The Isaiah vision establishes the importance of mission and ministry in every area of the city and especially in those parts of the city where people continue to live in exile, to inhabit houses designed for machines and not people, who have no land or olive trees, no secure employment or income to feed their children, who have a poor diet and poor air quality, unsafe streets and diminished chances of health and long life.

Ronan point

Colin Marchant

Ronan Point, one of 123 tower blocks in Newham, is both a local landmark and an international symbol. It replaced the tight-knit rows of terraced housing built for the incoming dockers and industrial workers during the 1880–1900 population explosion. They were swept away by the combination of war-time blitz and peace-time planning. The new 'street in the sky' immediately cut neighbourhood ties and created acute social problems.

In 1968, I was awakened by the sound of emergency vehicles travelling past our home. When I arrived at the foot of Ronan Point the cause of the jagged hole high up in the building was not known. Two of our older Church members lived there and I went with them to pack a suitcase as the tower block was evacuated. Later I returned to stand with the silent crowds. A week afterwards I buried one of the victims.

Since Ronan Point is just down the road I watched the reconstruction, knew the fears of returning tenants, and heard of the final verdict of structural insecurity. In 1984 the block was evacuated and abandoned.

Here, for me, is an inescapable, ever-present symbol of the significance of housing. In that one building is carried the story of human needs, social change, broken hopes and personal frustration. Focused here are the dilemmas of local authority planning, national policy and family needs.

In 1977, nearly 1.8 million people lived in 450,000 high-rise flats in Britain, all of them built since 1953; 92 per cent of these dwellings were built in large towns and cities. Within each tower block is a cluster of pressures — shortage of land, the power of the planners, the new-technology dreams of the architects, and the building industry investment in pre-fabricated methods.

The truth is that whole sections of our community will never be able to buy their own homes and have little choice about where they will live. Options narrow as private landlords disappear, council waiting lists lengthen and financial cut-backs slow down new housing.

Young people wanting to stay in the inner city face acute difficulty in acquiring council housing, see a decreasing (and expensive) supply of private lets, and often face a creeping gentrification in which the higher purchasing power of incoming buyers overwhelms the resources of the poorer-paid local people.

Even plans designed to ease pressure — Housing Benefit, Fair Rents, Tenants' Protection — end up by confusing tenants and restricting choice. Add to this the social effects of tower blocks, the wholesale break-up of communities by redevelopment, the competing claims of host communties and immigrants, and the central position of housing as a key to the inner city problem becomes clear.

It is an ever-present segment of the urban kaleidoscope. Home is a place to live, a base camp for life, a family centre and an accepted essential. Yet in 1982/3 our local council statistics showed that the monthly average of fifty-nine families rehoused from the waiting list was swamped by the 239 families who joined the list. Furthermore, only one in ten of the houses let had a garden. In this one London Borough 26,000 dwellings are substandard and 14,000 lack basic amenities such as an inside toilet or bathroom.

Within the statistics are the people. I know a road sweeper who retired to discover that his landlady insisted on him leaving his rented room at his old work hours. One day I discovered him huddled on a seat outside the post office: that experience pushed me into the world of housing associations and sheltered housing. I know a young couple who spent the first year of their marriage apart — then made their first home together in a double flat at Lawrence Hall.

The people suffer frustration and impotence, as expressed in this local paper report:

> Sky flat families went on the march last week armed with banners — and a song sheet. The Christmas Carol 'Silent Night' suddenly became 'Silent Strife, Tenant's Life'. And even the Beatles would have been proud of this one:

> > Oh, you'll never get to heaven (echo)
> > In a council flat
> > 'Cos a council flat
> > Ain't where it's at.

> > Oh, you'll never get to heaven
> > On a council scheme
> > 'Cos a council scheme
> > Is just a dream.

The great rebuild

Peter Hall

In 1955 the Conservative Government, in the form of Housing Minister Duncan Sandys, launched a major slum-clearance programme that was to run for nearly two decades, and simultaneously encouraged local authorities around the major cities to designate green belts in order to contain urban growth; coupled with a birth rate which started unexpectedly to rise that very year, this soon produced an impossible land-budget arithmetic.[1] Land acquisition costs rose, especially after changes in the law in 1959. The big cities, many of which were not averse to keeping their own people rather than exporting them to new and expanded towns, read all this as a signal to build dense and build high.[2] The big builders were ready to move in, and sold their ability to solve the cities' housing problems fast through package deals.[3] And the government, despite a barrage of protest from Osborn at the TCPA, obligingly gave them the special subsidies they needed for the job: from 1956, three times as much for a flat in a fifteen-storey block as for a house.[4] Dutifully, the proportion of high-rise in the total public-housing programme rose year by year: units in five-storey and more blocks were about 7 per cent of the total in the late 1950s, as much as 26 per cent in the mid-1960s.[5].

In all this, there were extraordinary contradictions, even in individuals. Richard Crossman, who as Sandys's successor nearly a decade later spearheaded the Labour Government's accelerated slum-clearance and housing drive, could record in his diary that he did not like the idea of people living in huge blocks of high-rise housing, yet almost simultaneously encourage even bigger programmes of destruction and industrialized building: 'In conversation I asked why it was only 750 houses they were building at Oldham; why not rebuild the whole thing? Wouldn't that help Laing, the builders? 'Of course, it would', said Oliver [Cox], 'and it would help Oldham too'. ... I drove back to the Ministry ... warmed and excited.'[6]

The London County Council's immensely prestigious Architect's Department, under first Robert Matthew, then Leslie Martin, provided a model in the early years; it had an unusually free hand, because the Ministry's ordinary cost sanctions did not apply to it.[7] It first produced 'the great Corbusian slabs' which culminated at the end of the 1950s in Alton West, Roehampton, the most complete homage to — and only true realization of — La Ville radieuse in the world; then began 'the era of the high towers, slimmer, less oppressive, and of course more highly subsidized':[8] 384 of them, in all, completed between 1964 and 1974. After the reorganization of 1965, the new boroughs made their own distinctive contributions like Southwark's huge megastructures in north Peckham, later to become some of London's most problematic blocks.

Some few among the great British provincial cities tried to compete in prestige. Two AA graduates headed the team that developed Park Hill, the great wall of deck-access flats that juts like a fortress above the centre of Sheffield and that, it must in fairness be said, is still highly successful with its tenants. Glasgow hired Basil Spence for the Gorbals and then built huge towers up to the city's edge; here, where the tenants all had a totally unEnglish tradition of high-density tenement living, there were few consistent problems with the design except for those with children, unsurprising since four in five children lived above the fourth floor.[9] But there were many other places where the architect was uninspired or non-existent, and where tenants found themselves uprooted into hurriedly constructed system-built flats lacking amenities, environment, community; lacking, in fact, almost anything except a roof and four walls.

The remarkable fact was how long it took for anyone to see that it was wrong. In order to appreciate why, it is necessary to do something that for anyone born after 1960 requires an effort of imagination: to appreciate just how bad were the dense rows of smoke-blackened slums that the towers replaced. The fact that later on the bulldozers started to remove sound and savable houses may obscure the fact that most were neither. As Lionel Esher says, 'even the preservationists saw the great mass of our Victorian "twilight areas" as expendable. Six years of war had reduced those parts of London and the great provincial cities to a sinister squalor that recalled the darkest passages of Bleak House.'[10] In Ravetz's words, 'For two full decades ... any social disbenefits of clean-sweep planning and its transformation of the town passed unremarked [other] than by cranks, a few people with residual ideals from the 1940s, or those who lamented the passing of the old on artistic grounds.'[11] It was not the fact of clean-sweep planning that began to be criticized, but the form it took.

Accentuated by the media after the disastrous collapse of Ronan Point, an east-London system-built tower block, in a gas explosion of 1968, the criticism soon became deafening. In fact the subsidy system had been recast the previous year, and local authorities were already phasing out their high-rise blocks. Now, everything was suddenly wrong with them: they leaked, they condensed, they blew up, the lifts did not work, the children vandalized them, old ladies lived in fear. All of this had some basis: Kenneth Campbell, in charge of housing design at the LCC and GLC from 1959 to 1974, listed three failures, the lifts (too few, too small, too slow), the children (too many), the management (too little).[12]

But, in fairness to the Corbusians, some things should be said. First, though some London estates were directly inspired by the master, and some of these proved design disasters, many others up and down Britain were bought off the peg by local authorities too lazy or unimaginative to hire architects and planners of their own. It was Crossman, visiting Wigan as early as 1965, who commented on its 'enormous building programme' of 'an appalling dimness and dullness', adding that 'they have built a Wigan that in 2000 will look just as bad as the old 1880 Wigan looks in the eyes of the 1960s'.[13] Second, Corbusier never advocated putting people (as distinct from jobs) in high towers; his proletarian housing would have looked more like Manchester's huge Hulme Estate, the biggest urban renewal project ever carried out in Europe, which consisted of medium-rise blocks but also proved a design disaster. In fact, the architectural fashion that followed the high-rise era — high-density low-rise — had proved a failure in Glasgow immediately after World War Two[14] and would later be criticized just as severely:

> High-density low-rise in practice meant mobs of children in echoing bricky courtyards, and mobs meant vandalism. ... They became 'hard-to-let', i.e. lettable only to the poorest and most disorderly families, who seldom had cars to occupy the now mandatory basement garages, and whose children wrecked the few they had.[15]

Ironically, this too was a Corbusian solution. All of it missed the real criticism, which was of design solutions laid down on people without regard to their preferences, ways of life, or plain idiosyncrasies; laid down, further, by architects who — as the media delighted to discover — themselves invariably lived in charming Victorian villas. (When later some actually lived in the places they were designing, as did Ralph Erskine's site architect Vernon Gracie in the famous Byker Wall at Newcastle, it was a matter for comment.) The main result of this failure, of which Corbusier is as fully culpable as any of his followers, was that the middle-class designers had no real feeling for the way a working-class family lived. In their world,

> Mum isn't isolated at home with the babies, she is out shopping at Harrods. The children, when small, are taken to Kensington Gardens by Nannie. At the age of eight they go to a preparatory school and at thirteen to a public school, both residential. And during the holidays they are either away in the country, or winter-sporting, sailing and so on: golden and brown in the playful wind

and summer sun. At any rate they are not hanging around on the landing or playing with the dustbin lids.[16]

The rich, then, could always live well at high densities, because they had services; that is why those quotations of Corbusier were so telling. But for ordinary people, as Ward says, the suburbs have great advantages: privacy, freedom from noise, greater freedom to make a noise yourself. To get this at a high density requires expensive treatment, generally not possible in public housing. Above all, the problem is one of children: for 'unless they get a chance to play out their childhood, they are certainly going to make a nuisance of themselves when they are older'.[17] And this is especially true, as Jephcott concluded in 1971, for families with children that are less well equipped educationally, living in high-density high-rise: 'local authorities should discontinue this form of housing except for a limited range of carefully selected tenants or in cases of extreme pressure'.[18] Corbusier, of course, was blissfully unconscious of all this, because he was both middle-class and childless.[19]

NOTES

1. Peter Hall (ed.), *The Containment of Urban England, vol. 1. Urban and Metropolitan Growth Processes, or Megalopolis Denied* (London: Allen and Unwin, 1973). E.W. Cooney, 'High flats in Local Authority Housing in England and Wales since 1945', in A. Sutcliffe, *Multi Storey Living: The British Working Class Experience* (London: Croom Helm, 1974), p. 160.
2. Cooney, *op. cit.*, pp. 161–20.
3. Ibid., p. 168; P. Dunleavy, *The Politics of Mass Housing in Britain, 1945–1975: A Study of Corporate Power and Professional Influence in the Welfare State* (Oxford: Clarendon Press, 1981), pp. 72, 114.
4. Dunleavy, *Politics*, p. 37; Cooney, 'High flats in Local Authority Housing', p. 163.
5. Cooney, 'High flats in Local Authority Housing', p. 152.
6. R.H.S. Crossman, *The Diaries of a Cabinet Minister. Vol. 1: Minister of Housing 1964–66* (London: Hamish Hamilton, 1975), p. 81.
7. Dunleavy, *The Politics of Mass Housing in Britain*, p. 170.
8. L. Esher, *A Broken Wave: The Rebuilding of England 1940–1980* (London: Allen Lane, 1981), p. 129.
9. P. Jephcott, *Homes in High Flats: Some of the Human Problems involved in Multistorey Housing* (University of Glasgow Social and Economic Studies, Occasional Papers No. 13) (Edinburgh: Oliver and Boyd, 1971), p. 140.
10. Esher, *A Broken Wave*, p. 45.
11. A. Ravetz, *Remaking Cities: Contradictions of the Recent Urban Environment* (London: Croom Helm, 1980), p. 89.
12. Esher, *A Broken Wave*, pp. 129–30.
13. Crossman, *Diaries, Vol. 1*, p. 341.
14. G. Armstrong and M. Wilson, 'Delinquency and some aspects of housing', in C. Ward (ed.), *Vandalism* (London: Architectural Press, 1973), pp. 74–9.
15. Esher, *A Broken Wave*, p. 134.
16. C. Ward, *Housing: An Anarchist Approach* (London: Freedom Press, 1976), p. 51.
17. Ward, *Housing*, p. 54.
18. Jephcott, *Homes in High Flats*, p. 131.
19. H.A. Anthony, 'Le Corbusier: his ideas for cities', *Journal of the American Institute of Planners* (1966), 32, 286.

The shape of the secular city

Harvey Cox

Theologians have spent themselves in well-intentioned forays against the 'depersonalization of urban life', often fed by a misunderstanding of Martin Buber's philosophy of 'I and Thou' relationships. In contrast to those who utilize his categories in a different manner, Buber himself never claimed that *all* our relationships should be of the deep, interpersonal I–Thou variety. He knew this experience was a rich and rare one. But Buber did open the door for misunderstanding by neglecting to study with sufficient thoroughness the place of types of relationships which actually constitute most of our lives, a point to which we shall return shortly.

A recent survey by some Protestant ministers in a new urban high-rise apartment area where they intended to establish house church groups illustrates the misplaced emphasis on I–Thou relationships that has marked modern Christian theology. In conducting their study, the pastors were shocked to discover that the recently arrived apartment dwellers, whom they expected to be lonely and desperate for relationships, did not want to meet their neighbours socially and had no interest whatever in church or community groups. At first the ministers deplored what they called a 'social pathology' and a 'hedgehog' psychology. Later, however, they found that what they had encountered was a sheer survival technique. Resistance against efforts to subject them to neighbourliness and socialization is a skill apartment dwellers must develop if they are to maintain any human relationships at all. It is an essential element in the shape of the secular city.

In condemning urban anonymity, the ministers had made the mistake of confusing a preurban ethos with the Christian concept of *koinonia*. The two are not the same. The ministers had wanted to develop a kind of village togetherness among people, one of whose main reasons for moving to high-rise apartments is to escape the relationships enforced on them by the lack of anonymity of the village. Apartment dwellers, like most urbanites, live a life in which relationships are founded on free selection and common interest, usually devoid of spatial proximity. Studies have shown that even friendship patterns within a large apartment complex follow age, family-size, and personal-interest lines. They do not ordinarily spring from the mere adjacence of apartments. Thus, to complain that apartment people often live for years just down the hall from another family but do not 'really get to know them' overlooks the fact that many specifically choose *not* to 'know' their spatial neighbours in any intimate sense. This allows them more time and energy to cultivate the friends they themselves select. This does not mean the apartment dweller cannot love his next-door neighbour. He can and often does so, certainly no less frequently than the small-town resident. But he does so by being a dependable fellow tenant, by bearing his share of the common responsibility they both have in that segment of their lives shaped by residence. This does not require their becoming cronies.

All this means that the urban secular man is summoned to a different *kind* of neighbourliness than his town-dwelling predecessor practised. Much like the Samaritan described by Jesus in the story he told in response to the question 'Who is my neighbour?' his main responsibility is to do competently what needs to be done to assure his neighbour's health and well-being. The man who fell among thieves was not the next-door neighbour of the Samaritan, but he helped him in an efficient, unsentimental way. He did not form an I–Thou relationship with him but bandaged his wounds and made sure the innkeeper had enough cash to cover his expenses.

Urban anonymity need not be heartless. Village sociability can mask a murderous hostility. Loneliness is undoubtedly a serious problem in the city, but it cannot be met by dragooning urban people into relationships which decimate their privacy and reduce their capacity to live responsibly with increasing numbers of neighbours. The church investigators who shook their heads over the evasiveness of the apartment dwellers had forgotten this. They had come to the city with a village theology and had stumbled upon an essential protective device, the polite refusal to be chummy, without which urban existence could not be human. They had overlooked the fact that technopolitan man *must* cultivate and guard his privacy. He must restrict the number of people who have his number or know his name.

The small-town dweller, on the other hand, lives within a restricted web of relationships and senses a larger world he may be missing. Since the people he knows also know one another, he gossips more and yearns to hear gossip. His private life is public and vice versa. While urban man is unplugging his telephone, town man (or his wife) may be listening in on the party line or its modern equivalent, gossiping at the kaffee-klatsch.

Urban man, in contrast, wants to maintain a clear distinction between private and public. Otherwise public life would overwhelm and dehumanize him. His life represents a point touched by dozens of systems and hundreds of people. His capacity to know some of them better necessitates his minimizing the depth of his relationships to many others. Listening to the postman gossip becomes for urban man an act of sheer graciousness, since he probably has no interest in the people the postman wants to talk about. Unlike my parents, who suspected all strangers, he tends to be wary not of the functionaries he doesn't know but of those he does.

How can urban anonymity be understood theologically? Here the traditional distinction between Law and Gospel comes to mind. In using these terms we refer not to religious rules or to fiery preaching, but to the tension between bondage to the past and freedom for the future. In this sense Law means anything that binds us uncritically to inherited conventions, and Gospel is that which frees us to decide for ourselves.

As the contemporary German theologian Rudolf Bultmann once wrote, Law means the 'standards of this world'.[1] It is what Riesman calls the power of 'other-direction' driving us toward conformity to the expectations and customs of the culture, enforced in a thousand small, nearly unnoticeable ways by the people who make our choices for us. When Law rather than Gospel becomes the basis for our lives, it militates against choice and freedom. It decides for us, thus sapping our powers of responsibility. Similarly, Gospel in a broader sense means a summons to choice and answerability. It designates not merely the verbal message of the church, but also the call which comes to any man when he is confronted with the privilege and necessity of making a free and responsible decision, not determined by cultural background or social convention. Our use of the

Law–Gospel dialectic here suggests that it has a broader relevance than is ordinarily accorded it in theology. It suggests that in the historical process itself man meets the One who calls him into being as a free deciding self, and knows that neither his past history nor his environment determines what he does. In the anonymity of urban culture, far from the fishbowl of town life, modern man experiences both the terror and the delight of human freedom more acutely. The biblical God is perceived in the whole of social reality, and Law and Gospel provide us an angle of vision by which to understand secular events, including urbanization. The God of the Gospel is the One who wills freedom and responsibility, who points toward the future in hope. The Law, on the other hand, includes any cultural phenomenon which holds men in immaturity, in captivity to convention and tradition. The Law is enforced by the weight of human opinion; the Gospel is the activity of God creating new possibilities in history. Law signifies the fact that man does live in society; Gospel points to the equally important fact that he is more than the intersection of social forces. He feels himself summoned to choose, to actualize a potential selfhood which is more than the sum of genes plus glands plus class. Man cannot live without Law, but when Law becomes wholly determinative, he is no longer really man.

From this perspective, urbanization can be seen as a liberation from some of the cloying bondages of preurban society. It is the chance to be free. Urban man's deliverance from enforced conventions makes it necessary to choose for himself. His being anonymous to most people permits him to have a face and a name for others.

This is not an easy thing to accomplish. The challenge of living responsibly within segmental relationships is formidable, especially for those who have been reared in small-town or traditional cultures. Often a nagging sense of guilt plagues the urban man with rural roots because he cannot possibly cultivate an I–Thou relationship with everyone. Unfortunately the church, largely bound to a preurban ethos, often exacerbates his difficulty by seeking to promote small-town intimacy among urban people and by preaching the necessity of I–Thou relationships as the only ones that are really human. But this represents a misreading of the Gospel and a disservice to urban man. Relationships among urbanites do not have to be lifeless or heartless just because they are impersonal. Jane Jacobs in her *Death and Life of Great American Cities* has caught the flavour of urban neighbourliness exceptionally well. It necessitates learning how to enjoy public relationships without allowing them to become private:

> Nobody can keep open house in a great city. Nobody wants to. And yet if interesting useful and significant contacts among the people of cities are confined to acquaintanceships suitable for private life, the city becomes stultified. Cities are full of people with whom, from your viewpoint, or mine, or any other individual's, a certain degree of contact is useful or enjoyable; but you do not want them in your hair. And they do not want you in theirs either.[2]

Theologians would do well to appreciate this characteristically urban 'togetherness' so aptly described by Jane Jacobs and to see in its impersonal, even anonymous, interrelatedness an authentic form of corporate human existence in the urban epoch.

We need to develop a viable theology of anonymity. In doing so, it might be useful to add another type of human relationship to Buber's famous pair. Besides 'I–It' relationships, in which the other person is reduced to the status of an object, and in addition to the profound, personally formative 'I–Thou' encounter, why could we not evolve a theology of the '*I–You*' relationship? Buber's philosophy suffers from an unnecessary dichotomy. Perhaps between the poles of the two types of human relationship he has elaborated we could designate a third. It would include all those public relationships we so enjoy in the city but which we do not allow to develop into private ones. These contacts can be decidedly human even though they remain somewhat distant. We like and enjoy these people, but as Jane Jacobs says, we 'don't want them in our hair, and they don't want us in theirs either'.

The danger with an I–Thou typology is that all relationships which are not deeply personal and significant tend to be swept or shoved into the I–It category. But they need not be. The development of an I–You theology would greatly clarify the human possibilities of urban life, and would help stall attempts to lure urban people back into preurban conviviality under the colour of saving their souls.

The development of such a theology would help expose the *real* dangers inherent in urban anonymity, as opposed to the pseudodangers. Technopolitan possibilities *can* harden into rigid new conventions. Freedom can always be used for antihuman purposes. The Gospel can ossify into a new legalism. But none of these hazards can be exposed if we continue to insist on judging urban life by preurban norms. Despite its pitfalls, the anonymous shape of urban life helps free man from the Law. For many people it is a glorious liberation, a deliverance from the saddling traditions and burdensome expectations of town life and an entry into the exciting new possibilities of choice which pervade the secular metropolis.

NOTES

1. Bultmann's discussion of the Law can be found in his *Theology of the New Testament* (New York: Scribner, 1951; London: SCM Press), Section 27, pp. 259–69. The best discussion of the broader significance of the Law is found in Friedrich Gogarten's *Mensch zwischen Gott und Welt* (Stuttgart: Friedrich Vorwerk Verlag, 1956), especially Section I and the first part of Section II.
2. Jane Jacobs, *The Death and Life of Great American Cities* (New York: Vintage, 1963; London: Cape), pp. 55–6.

New role for the Church in urban policy?

Paul Hackwood and Phil Shiner

If we examine the achievement of property-led regeneration, it is apparent that it has failed to deliver the goods for indigenous communities. This is the market economy idea of 'trickle down': that large-scale physical redevelopment would stimulate local economic development. Some of these large prestige projects such as London Docklands and Canary Wharf, the International Convention Centre and Broad Street Regeneration Area in Birmingham, and elsewhere, the projects produced by urban development corporations, have simply left local people even more deprived and divided. We have the unwelcome image of prestigious multi-million developments set alongside communities dependent upon charitable trusts for the provision of basic community resources. But it gets worse. Birmingham City Council's regeneration of the City Centre was achieved only by raiding the education and housing capital programme to finance the interest on the capital borrowing for its prestige project development. Over £380m expenditure produced pathetically small outputs in terms of the creation of employment and training opportunities for local people.[1] By this analysis one can see that the poor are not just irrelevant to this approach: they end up paying for it. We must learn from these experiences.

The Church should take the lead in promoting a new agenda for 'community empowerment' as it would appear that no political party has sufficient belief in ordinary people. Everyone is talking about 'community' and 'empowerment' but what do these terms actually mean? More crucially, what would 'community empowerment' mean for those with a fundamental belief in people, and an overriding concern to tackle the causes of social exclusion and alienation? What we advocate below is one small part of a complex jigsaw of social policy issues which impact upon one another. The response to each part must be right. How many of these lend themselves to principles of 'community empowerment'?

We start with our belief in the innate potential of ordinary people. From there we see how crucial it is to achieve linkage between physical, social and economic regeneration. Present programmes do not facilitate this process and it is a fundamental weakness. We must retain a clear vision of the type of social regeneration that could be achieved by a people-led approach. There must be a major shift in power to the local community and major cultural changes, both at central and local government level. Until there is this fundamental change in culture and approach, given the present private sector domination, regeneration will never be effective.

It is at this stage that we begin to outline an existing framework and process set out at greater length recently by Nevin and Shiner.[2] This argument for cultural changes and the change necessary to the process of regeneration, government mechanisms and funding regimes, starts with the following aim: 'to engage local communities in the development of policies for the regeneration of their own areas within the context of wider national and regional strategies for urban and economic development'.[3] In this we are concerned to see local residents enabled to plan and implement their own regeneration strategies based on their own assessment of the needs and priorities of their community. At the level of local government the cultural changes necessary involve local government officers learning to enable people to do things for themselves, rather than doing things for them. There needs to be a recognition of the fact that there is a long development process to enable latent skills and talents to develop, and to facilitate a process that produces local community activists. Local government needs to adopt different notions of success and realistic timescales in which the regeneration process can take place. More fundamentally, at central government level we cannot conceive how a people-led approach can emerge within the present culture. If we are serious about empowerment in the context of urban regeneration, we must ensure that it happens. To that end we advocate a framework and a process that combines the best of central direction and planning whilst being a bottom-up process that remains responsive to the local situation.

Therefore, we advocate that a new Directorate of Community Affairs (DCA) be established to replace the existing Inner Cities Directorate of the Department of Environment. The DCA should be staffed by civil servants with a proven track record of work with communities, and would take over the administration of all the urban expenditure programmes currently in the control of the Inner Cities Directorate. The DCA would have a strategic role and would provide a link between urban, community and economic development programmes, and the policies of other government departments and divisions within the DoE.

Additionally, it would assist local authorities in creating community development strategies which are consistent with strategic and development plans. Its prime objectives in terms of urban regeneration would be to facilitate and enable people-led regeneration schemes. The DCA would be able to 'call in' a plan for a scheme if the process of developing the community was being compromised or subverted.

We see the need for this central agency to hammer out the principles and good practice of empowerment and then to work closely with local communities to facilitate the process in the local context. The primary aim of the National Community Regeneration Agency (NCRA) would be to achieve the social, economic and physical regeneration of inner-urban and deprived areas by people-led schemes. It would have a wide remit that would include responsibility for a new grant, approval of plans for funding, project appraisal and the continual process of establishing principles of good practice. At the local level the NCRA would ensure that local people's views and needs were translated into people-led plans.

What we want to see is a process that translates local people's views about what is needed in their area together with their vision as to how these needs might best be met, into a people's plan which is then implemented. We recognize, of course, that in areas that have strategic implications for the district or region, it would not necessarily be appropriate for the community to lead the process. On the other hand, they should, at least, be in a position of real equality in these larger schemes of regeneration. In smaller schemes, for instance, those for peripheral council estates, we see no reason why the community should not lead. To that end we see the need for Community Regeneration Units (CRUs) which would produce a people-led plan for regeneration. The CRU would consist of local people, professionals, local government officers and members, voluntary sector representatives and others. Once prepared — and that process may take considerably longer than allowed under present funding regimes — the plan would be submitted to the NCRA for funding.

Present funding regimes do not allow for the crucial community development work that must [precede] schemes of regeneration. We see the need for the pre-release of fees for that work. In addition, in larger schemes where the people are to be in an equal role there must be funds available for the preparation of people's plans. One fundamental principle of community development is that access to information and knowledge equals power. To begin to correct the present gross imbalance of power, we see that the community should have access to funds for fees so that they can assume a purchaser–provider relationship with the private sector and professionals. Once a people-led plan was approved it would receive a community regeneration grant. The primary principles in approving funding would be whether the process had been followed and whether what was proposed was reasonable. The emphasis on need and empowerment makes this approach the antithesis of the present one. We recognize the importance of flexibility as communities start from different stages of development and 'the community' can mean different things in different areas to different people.

This people-led process to regeneration connects also with several theological themes which have come to the fore in recent years in urban theology.[4] A move away from a substantive theology in which a dogmatic deposit of faith is applied to the diverse situations encountered in urban ministry, to a procedural theology where insight arises not from the application of timeless truths but from listening to the context in which God speaks. We will explore this under three headings, Location, Form and Truth.

THE LOCATION OF OUR THEOLOGY

Urban theology is a contextual theology. As urban theologians we are not so much engaged in a theology which focuses on specific issues like poverty or crime but rather a theology that is a way of doing things in relation to our context. To ignore the reality of those socially excluded from society is at best irresponsible, at worst it makes us purveyors of the ideologies and interests which seek to keep God, theology and faith separate from the day to day reality of people's lives. If we are to engage in responsible theology in the city then we must identify ourselves with those who are victimized and oppressed by the 'culture of contentment' which characterizes our society. It is this 'location' which enables the church to be an instrument for change in our cities but only in so far as the agenda of particular churches arises from local people.

THE FORM OF OUR THEOLOGY

Professional models of working in many different disciplines tend to 'apply' previously developed ideas to new situations. This is true in terms of urban planning and theology. The vitality of local communities has thus been lost as their experience and ideas have been forced into alien patterns of expression. Faith and discipleship in most inner city congregations are as a consequence ways of avoiding the work rather than ways of living out an authentic Christian life. To regenerate communities can be a theological process, a process which seeks to identify those degrading and dehumanizing features of life in society which are contrary to the will of God, so that they can be acted upon and a practical response can be made. Theology's main purpose here is to serve critical Christian practice, in worship, service and prophecy, and on to political action.

THE TRUTH OF OUR THEOLOGY

Inner city areas and peripheral estates are a significant testing place for authentic faith in God. They are the location *par excellence* for the testing of truth, for the claims of our faith and our policies for change, our interpretations of the Gospel, and our action as an institution. In our inner cities and peripheral estates we find those who have been socially excluded, victimized and silenced by our talk and action. We need therefore to be attentive to these areas in order to ask questions about our own truthfulness. From this follows the test for not only our theology but also our urban policy, how far we are prepared to attend to the self-definition and agendas set by people who live in these situations rather than responding to the questions and issues set by our own agendas.

CONCLUSIONS

We start with a fundamental belief in people which we understand is a crucial part of a Christian faith. Therefore, we seek to translate this belief into practical policies to empower people in schemes of regeneration. We see that more practical policies are needed to flesh out a new vision and approach for community empowerment. The Church must have faith and trust in local people and seek to facilitate the creation of a new radical agenda of empowerment. We understand that this may be truly liberating and, therefore, 'good news' for people. We are realistic about the difficulties of establishing this new approach both in respect of people-led regeneration and also in other aspects of a full policy on community empowerment. However, we do at least commend these ideas for wider discussion.

NOTES

1. P. Loftman and B. Nevin, *Urban Regeneration and Social Equity: A Case Study of Birmingham 1986–1992*, Research Paper No. 8, Faculty of the Built Environment, (Birmingham: University of Central England, 1992).
2. B. Nevin and P. Shiner, 'Britain's urban problems: communities hold the key', *Local Work* 50, October 1993 (Manchester: Centre for Local Economic Strategies).
3. We are grateful to Bob Colenutt and Austen Cutten for a sight of their draft paper 'Community Empowerment and Urban Policy'.
4. What follows owes substantial acknowledgement to Dr Al McFadyen at the University of Leeds, Department of Theology and Religious Studies.

Further reading

Asa Briggs, *Victorian Cities* (Harmondsworth, Penguin, 1968). A portrait of five English Victorian cities, and Melbourne, which begins with a very useful survey of the ambivalence of Victorian attitudes to the city, whether as a place of hellish squalor, ugliness and human misery, or as opportunity for the expression of social progress and the celebration of a new form of public and civilized life.

David Clark, *Urban World/ Global City* (London: Routledge, 1996). Over half the world now live in urban areas. Clark examines the global effects of urbanization and urbanism.

Raymond Fung, *The Isaiah Vision: An Ecumenical Strategy for Congregational Evangelism* (Geneva: WCC, 1992). An influential study of the implications of Isaiah 65 in the delineation of a holistic approach to the mission of the local church.

Patrick Geddes, *Cities in Evolution: An Introduction to the Town Planning Movement and to the Study of Civics* (London: Ernest Benn, 1915). Geddes' vision of the city was as a social and potentially civilizing space, not a collection of factories and houses. He urged the democratic empowerment of industrial workers and urbanites and their involvement through education and public consultation in the planning of cities with a high quality of environment and housing, clean air and access to improved rural areas.

James Gilbert, *Perfect Cities: Chicago's Utopias of 1893* (Chicago: University of Chicago Press, 1991). An imaginative reconstruction and critique of the different visions of the city which emerged in this great industrial metropolis, including an account of Dwight Moody's vision of the evangelical metropolis and of urban evangelism.

Ebenezer Howard, *Garden Cities of Tomorrow* (London: Faber and Faber, 1965). Classic work which argued for a new balancing of town and country, industry and agriculture, housing and green space which inspired the Garden Suburbs and New Towns of the early and mid-twentieth century, and the formation of the Town and Country Planning Association.

Le Corbusier, *The City of Tomorrow and Its Planning* (London: Architectural Press, 1938). Tremendously influential account of the city as essentially the site of mass production, of houses as machines for living and as repetitive cells for workers, and of motorways on stilts as the ideal movement corridors.

Hugh McLeod, *Religion in the Victorian City* (Oxford: Oxford University Press, 1974). Seminal study of the adaptation of the churches to the new urban context of industrial Britain which draws on a wealth of social history.

Lewis Mumford, *The Culture of Cities* (London: Secker and Warburg, 1938). From one of the century's foremost thinkers on the nature of cities, in this book he emphasizes that the physical organization and planning of the city — transport, buildings, etc. — should be subservient to human social needs and local communities.

Richard John Neuhaus, *The Naked Public Square: Religion and Democracy in America* (Grand Rapids: Eerdmans, 1984). Argues that government without spiritual moorings will always tend to be oppressive, and to substitute economistic or other purposes for the ethical orientation towards the common good which is the test of good government in the Hebrew Bible.

Wollf Schneider, *Babylon is Everywhere: Reality is Man's Fate* (London: Hodder and Stoughton, 1963). Substantial theologically informed study of the nature and development of cities. Remarkable for its range of sources and ideas, from ancient Egypt and Israel to contemporary North America and Northern Europe.

Richard Sennett, *The Conscience of the Eye: The Design and Social Life of Cities* (London: Faber and Faber, 1990). A luminous exploration of the nature of the city which is theologically and aesthetically rich.

Peter Stubley, *A House Divided: Evangelicals and the Establishment of Hull* (Hull: University of Hull Press, 1995). Insightful account of the different ways in which the Church of England, Catholics and dissenters responded to the social problems of an emerging industrial city, from Sabbatarianism and Temperance to education and Sunday Schools.

Nick Wates and Charles Knevitt, *Community Architecture: How People Are Creating Their Own Environment* (London: Penguin, 1987). Argues that the built environment works better when the people who live in it are actively involved in designing, building and managing it and includes many case studies of successful self-build and community planning projects.

Gibson Winter, *The Suburban Captivity of the Churches: An Analysis of Protestant Responsibility in the Expanding Metropolis* (Garden City, NY: Doubleday, 1964). A pioneering work of urban theology which combined sociological analysis of the emerging shape of modern cities with a critique of the flight of the churches from ministry and responsibility for the whole of life in the city from the financial, government and manufacturing sectors to the outer suburbs.

4

Sin in the city

Go up and down the streets of Jerusalem, take note; search through her wide squares: can you find anyone who acts justly, anyone who seeks the truth, that I may forgive that city? People may swear by the life of the Lord, but in fact they perjure themselves.

How can I forgive you all this? Your children have forsaken me, swearing by gods that are no gods. I gave them all they needed, yet they committed adultery and frequented brothels; each neighs after another man's wife, like a well-fed lusty stallion.

Have you no fear of me, says the Lord, will you not tremble before me, who set the sand as bounds for the sea, a limit it can never pass? Its waves may heave and toss, but they are powerless; roar as they may they cannot pass. But this people has a rebellious and defiant heart; they have rebelled and gone their own way.

They did not say to themselves, 'Let us fear the Lord our God, who gives the rains of autumn and spring shows in their turn, who brings us unfailingly fixed harvest seasons.' But your wrongdoing has upset nature's order, and your sins have kept away her bounty.

For among my people there are scoundrels, who, like fowlers, lay snares and set deadly traps; they prey on their fellows. Their houses are full of fraud, as a cage is full of birds. They grow great and rich, sleek and bloated; they turn a blind eye to wickedness and refuse to do justice; the claims of the fatherless they do not uphold, nor do they defend the poor at law.

(Jeremiah 5:1–2, 7–8, 22–28)

Faith in the City

The city has always both challenged and threatened. Jeremiah called the people of God in exile 'to seek the welfare of the city' even though the reference was to Babylon with all its connotations of evil. The city in human history is synonymous with civilisation: yet now we investigate it as a point of breakdown of Christian society. Civicism is the name of the principle that all citizens have equal rights and duties: yet urban priority areas are a symbol of contemporary inequality. (1.3)

Vandalism may often be a protest against the inhumanity of the environment and an attempt to soften some of its harshness. In some places this aspect of vandalism has been channelled into positive directions through community arts programmes. ... Our experience suggests that where a community is constructed on a scale small enough for human relations to be conducted, and for the environment to be cared for by people who live within it, the destructiveness diminishes. (14.16)

The growth in material goods available in modern society has increased the opportunities for theft and damage, particularly when goods are very accessible, like cars on the streets and goods in self-service shops. ... Since our society encourages consumerism and exposes all its members to attractive life-styles through the mass media, yet severely restricts real opportunities for many, particularly if they are black, female, poor or handicapped, it is not surprising that respect for law should be weakened. (14.22)

Introduction

In Liverpool in 1996 a bright and courageous young priest was knifed to death outside his Vicarage at midnight by an ex-convict whom he had been trying to help. In Birmingham in 1996 a young woman was dragged kicking and screaming from a crowded shopping street into a car, driven a short distance to a quiet back alley, and repeatedly raped and assaulted by three young men. Nobody on the crowded street protested verbally or tried to intervene to prevent the kidnapping. In every large city in the United States and Britain, and in many Third World cities, the homeless live in the doorways of the city centre, crouched in blankets on the edge of crowded city streets, surrounded by people throughout the day who hardly acknowledge their existence. On many urban priority estates in Britain residents live in constant fear of crime and violence. The incidence of burglary, knife-point muggings, drug pushing and drug taking, prostitution, dangerous driving, vehicle theft, vandalism, violent assaults and rape is greatest in the poorest estates of Britain. The generalized fear of crime in modern urbanized Britain is at its most extreme, and most justified, in UPAs (**Power**).

The freedoms, anonymity and individualism of the city have a terrible downside and from Babel and Babylon to Rome and Rio de Janeiro cities are associated with much which is most violent, sinful and evil human experience. The face-to-face rural communities of the past with their extended kinship networks and subsistence livelihood may have been confining, uncreative, gossip-ridden and parochial but homelessness, drug pushing and unresolved crime were rare phenomena in communities where everyone knew everyone else. People had a claim on their kin, and, failing that, on their parish or trade guild, a claim of common humanity which is increasingly denied in the faceless bureaucratic and economic structures of modern cities (Bookchin).

Structural and long-term unemployment, and the poverty associated with it, are also implicated in the growing incidence of urban crime and violence. The great majority of burglars, thieves and muggers who are convicted by the courts are unemployed, and frequently return to unemployment after their prison sentences. Unemployment is a form of bondage and a denial of human dignity to which crime and deviance are an inevitable response, especially when the income gap between those out of work and those in secure employment grows as fast as it has in Britain and North America in the last two decades (Farmington; Currie). There is a collective and structural character to poverty and unemployment, and hence to the crime, addiction and violence which deprivation and the absence of work occasion.

But anonymity and unemployment are not enough to explain the current levels of crime in modern cities. The unemployment and poverty in London or Liverpool in the 1930s did not occasion the levels of crime and violence which we see today. Furthermore, crime and deviance in modern urbanized societies are by no means limited to the poor and the unemployed. One-third of young men in Britain today acquire a criminal record by the time they reach the age of 30, and these are just those who have been *caught* committing crime (Farmington). The majority of crimes such as burglary and mugging go unsolved. Violent crime and theft may be prevalent in urban priority areas but fraud, corruption, insider dealing, tax evasion, drug taking and drug dealing, consorting with prostitutes, and illegal arms trading are just part of the growing catalogue of corporate and individual crime in the private offices and public squares of the city centre and the privatized malls and housing areas of the suburbs.

Jeremiah identifies a series of sins in the streets and public squares of the city of Jerusalem including not only oppression of the poor, but also economic fraud, corruption in the legal system, lust for power and wealth, the adulation of war and violence, sexual immorality, and idolatry. The lust for power and wealth shown by the monarchy, armies, traders and landowners of the cities of Israel and Judah before they were overrun by Babylon is seen as a principal reason for their downfall. For where these tendencies dominate, oppression, immorality and debt slavery abound, and the ethic of justice for the whole community, which is central to the covenant between Yahweh and the Israelites, is abandoned.

But for Jeremiah sin has a deeply spiritual, as well as an ethical and economic, character. The prophet sees direct relationships between human self-assertion and the worship of idols, and between rebellion against the true God and the prevalence of sin in the city. The Israelite monarchy and its wealthy acolytes idolized their riches and the instruments of their social and military power, adopting the cult of Baal which reflected the values of self-assertion, domination and materialism (**Wink**). These values arose, and were sustained in relations of exploitation, greed, immorality and disrespect between persons in Israelite society.

Sin is seen by Jeremiah as a disturbance to the whole network of relationships in which human life is constructed: relations with God, with other persons, and with nature and the environment. The failure to worship God as Lord of creation, and to keep his commandments, results not only in human injustice and depravity but also in the subversion of the created order and its regular provision of food and water in due season (Jeremiah 5:24–25). Spiritual and social, individual and political, economic and sexual, embodied and cerebral, human and non-human — Jeremiah's account of sin in this chapter engages all of these aspects of the corruption of life.

This holistic understanding of sin is an important corrective to individualistic or moralistic accounts of the experience of sin and deviance in the modern or late modern city (McFadyen). Some identify the personal failings of the poor as the origin of most crime and deviance. Some identify the rise of sexual licence and the decline in authority as explanations for the prevalence of crime in the city. Some point to the secular character of modern urban life and argue that it is the failure to worship God which is the cause of the ills of the city (**Ellul**), while some point to the rising levels of inequality and social injustice in modern urban society. Some argue that it is the inherent facelessness and dehumanizing and non-participative character of mass urban societies which explains the disaffection of urban people with law and authority (**Bookchin**). But the prophet finds the structures of sin in the whole gamut of individual, social and environmental experience.

The Jewish and Christian traditions are profoundly marked by the prevalence of reflection on the multifarious character of sin and evil in the human condition. In contrast to Islam, which commends a straightforward model of submission to law as the form of moral order, or to Buddhism which commends detachment from ego as the essence of goodness, Christianity affirms the complex relational character of sin, and of redemption from the order of sin. Biblical and theological reflection on original sin and bondage sustains a structural and social understanding of sin, while at the same time pointing to the bondage to sin, manifest in particular in idolatry and in distorted perceptions of the self and the other, which individuals acquire in a world of fallen relationships. This relational understanding of sin and redemption is vital for an understanding of the multiple layers of sin and suffering, and also of hope and goodness, which we encounter in modern urbanism. The misery of the ghetto or urban priority area is but the counter-side to the flight from social responsibility, the denial of relationality and community, or the insatiable greed, which may be encountered in the suburbs, private apartments, and boardrooms of the capitalist city (**Bookchin; McFadyen**). The poor are sinned against as well as sinning.

As in the days of Jeremiah, a besetting sin of the modern city is the sin of idolatry. Modern urban culture is organized around the production and consumption of *things*. The idols of consumerism dominate the landscape of the modern city, the private car being the most classic example. The car, seen by Henry Ford as the vehicle of liberation for the masses, has become a symbol of oppression, pollution, danger and gridlock for the residents and increasingly the commuters of the modern city, particularly in urban priority areas where deaths from road accidents, especially among children, are higher than in any other part of the city, and where the cult of the car takes criminal form in 'twocking' — taking without consent (**Selby**). The multiplication of small mobile private spaces in vast numbers, and roads and flyovers on which they travel through cities, has subverted the shared good of effective public transport systems in many cities, especially in the USA and Britain. The car has also destroyed the peace and safety of the city environment, an environment which originated to defend its inhabitants from the vicissitudes of life beyond the city walls. Modern city streets may be wide but they are not 'free' nor 'public' in the classical sense. The pedestrian leaves the narrow pavement for the wide road at his or her peril. The car is a classic instance of idolatry, what Marx called commodity fetishism, because it exalts the commodity over the person, the object over the human (**Selby; Kavanaugh**).

Car showrooms, shopping malls, advertising hoardings and neon signs all symbolize the ambiguous lure of consumerism in modern cities. In their design, and in the images and symbols they purvey, they express the vibrancy and colour which are one of the great attractions of modern cities to urbanites and non-urbanites alike. But the vibrancy and colour of this commodified form of exchange sustain a structure of exclusion and inclusion where access to the good life is in cash or credit. The temples and icons of consumerism represent commodities as the means of human fulfilment and flourishing. The greatest danger of consumerism, as with all forms of idolatry, is that by substituting relations to God and persons with relations to commodities and created things it corrodes the true source of human flourishing (Kavanaugh; Wuthnow), which according to the Hebrew and Christian traditions (and according to modern studies of happiness) is the sustaining of relationships of loving reciprocity between loving, conscious beings, human, divine, and, some would add, non-human.

Many who live and work in UPA areas testify to the relational riches of these communities. Vulnerability and the genuine sharing of life stories, struggles and triumphs are often greater amongst UPA residents than amongst those who live in the suburbs, defended by the space, services and facilities of their private houses from extensive engagement in community relationships except by personal choice (Walsh). But the relational giftedness of the poor is subverted by another set of oppressive relationships manifest in the structures of sin, and especially the commodity and money forms which sin takes in modern urban cultures.

Debt and drug addiction are two of the most prominent structural and personal forms of bondage in the UPA: debts incurred to feed, house, heat and clothe the household, and debts incurred to meet some of the aspirations which consumerism defines as the icons, or idols, of the good life; drugs which often lead to addiction — alcohol, amphetamines, cannabis, crack — to provide a measure of escape, of self-transcendence, from the impossible gap between aspiration and indebted reality which is the form of deprivation in an affluent consumer society. Individual failings, individual bondage and weakness of will are clearly evident in decisions over debt and drugs as not all UPA residents are either in debt or use the escape of drugs. But the structures of sin are also manifest in the pervasion of these patterns of life in the UPA (Selby).

The poor person may pay a 'legal' rate of interest of 50 per cent or even 200 per cent on a loan to feed her household until the next giro cheque, there being no regulation against excessive interest rates beyond the prohibition of the use of force by creditors. The rich borrow money at little over the cost of inflation. The poor borrow money to buy food and clothes, toys and shoes. The rich borrow money to buy houses and cars, foreign holidays or stereo systems. Debt is the structure of sin which connects both groups, but, as with all sinful structures, it disadvantages one group over another, and subverts the common humanity which both groups share.

The complex individual, spiritual, social and structural account of human sin in the Jewish and Christian traditions resists the utopian promises of the city of towers of the kind which tempted the builders of the mythical tower of Babel (Ellul), just like its modern counterparts in the financial centres and housing schemes of London or New York. The strength of human self-assertion in the structures and idols of the modern city is ironically connected to the spiritual vacuum which characterizes the human experience in the modern city (Bookchin). In asserting our humanness through the exaltation of progress in material achievement, the modern city subverts our humanness and those goods of human flourishing for which money and consumerism are poor substitutes — sociability, mutual care, loving community, worship of the true God.

Redemption from sin in the city involves divine judgement and spiritual discernment in relation to the idols of materialism and power, and divine grace in the struggle for liberation from addiction, from debt slavery, and from the flight of responsibility, of rich for poor, of the poor for themselves, of poor men for their children. Redemption from sin in UPA areas will also involve mobilizing their relational strengths in the creation of counter-structures to the structures of sin: structures of community praise and festival which enable true worship, self-belief and self-transcendence instead of idolatry or drug dependency; structures of local economics, such as credit unions or housing co-operatives, which encourage saving and sharing and recycle money within the UPA economy thus breaking the vicious cycle of debt dependency; structures of community organizing which actively engage the structures of sin and crime through engaging the politics and economics of the larger city; structures of education, skills sharing, care and neighbourly vigilance which attempt to reconnect people disconnected by their struggles for individual survival or the fear of crime (**Walsh**).

In addition to these counter-structures and stories, the struggle against sin in the city can also be seen in a range of government and commercial initiatives which have become established practice in urban regeneration in the last twenty years — crime reduction programmes involving community police and local people in enhanced awareness and reduced tolerance of crime; traffic calming and improvements for pedestrians and public transport users; the refurbishment and rebuilding of public housing in ways which discourage crime and enhance ownership; the involvement of industry and commerce, as well as local government, in the environmental improvement of derelict inner city areas; community arts projects and community care programmes which enhance creative and people skills in UPAs (**Power**). However, alongside these initiatives has gone a continuing drain of economic resources from the poorest areas in Britain, which seems to indicate that structural sin needs more radical treatment than current regeneration strategies. As well as giving local people more say in the running of their own communities there needs to be a rebalancing of economic power between local communities and powerful global economic forces and corporate actors.

Christ in his ministry of teaching, healing and deliverance struggles with sin in demonic, bodily, natural, social and political forms (Castro). The conclusion of his struggle with the sources of power at his trial and crucifixion in Jerusalem gives us grounds for believing that God is present in the pain of the city as well as in the struggle for justice, and that in the deep law of creation, reasserted in the Resurrection, good will triumph over evil, and the principalities and powers will be dethroned. But redemption in the midst of the city is a redirection, not a final destiny. The promise of salvation is revealed in the story of the Church through the ages as a new form of life within the structures and fallen powers of a sinful society. The struggle to resist and engage the structures of sin in the modern secular city is enabled and sustained by the Spirit of God who is active in restoring creation wherever human beings and communities resist evil and affirm the good, just as the Spirit was active in the Resurrection of Christ from the dead.

Housing, community and crime

Anne Power

Penrhys Estate [in South Wales] has 930 houses in an area of severe industrial decline. In 1986 there were 350 under-five-year-olds, about 700 five to fifteen-year-olds and 300 older teenagers living on the estate. About 300 tenancies a year were vacated. Of the last fifty-five lettings, only five households had any member in employment. Two-thirds of all new tenants with children had only one parent.

A full-time local housing office and repairs team were set up on the estate in 1984. General conditions improved gradually but significantly. However, the overriding problems of unemployment, poverty and crime were not resolved by a good housing service. The jobs that arose on or around the estate either required qualifications or were part-time. In general, people lose £1 of welfare benefit for every £1 they earn.[1] If the job itself is only part-time and arduous, such as litter picking, there is little inducement to take it as wages are very low — about £80 a week for full-time, unskilled work. It proved difficult to recruit enough part-time caretakers as a result, although over the three years of the Project, fourteen permanent jobs in the housing team have been given to residents.

Early in 1985 a group of youths locked themselves into the community centre, let off all the fire extinguishers and terrorized resident leaders, the caretaker and other staff. It was several hours before the police regained control. In October 1985 the local police base was ransacked by a group of youths, most but not all from the estate. In January 1986 there were twenty-seven reported break-ins to houses. If this rate were replicated over a year, one-third of all households would be burgled within twelve months.

Reported crime on the estate was more than double the rate for the Rhondda valleys as a whole. Four per cent of the Borough's population experienced 10 per cent of its reported crime.[2] Crime levels climbed steadily until 1986, faster in Penrhys than in the rest of the valleys. By June 1986, Penrhys experienced *over* 10 per cent of the Borough's reported crime.

Many sections of the community were determined to beat crime. A residents' crime watch was formed but folded and then started up again under new leadership. The Tenants' Association was unusually active and strongly led but involved only a minority of residents directly. Leading spokeswomen of the Tenants' Association had an inexhaustible commitment to the improvement of the estate in all its aspects and for all its residents. But the exceptional strength and qualities of their leadership led them to be regarded by some officials as unrepresentative and over-assertive. Again and again the crevices appeared: glue-sniffing, vandalism and organized crime re-emerged. There were a few households on the estate with a history of crime and violence which were very difficult to deal with. A small group of youths — about five in all — were beyond the control of their parents, the schools or other residents.

Without debarring from the estate those few individuals and households whose behaviour cannot be contained or restrained, it is hard to see a way forward. It is also hard to pinpoint why or how they should be excluded. But they should not be housed precisely in the area where defences are lowest, where their behaviour had the most damaging impact and where they themselves stood least chance of adapting. That they needed to adapt to survive was beyond question because most people found them unbearable to have as neighbours. In that circumstance, they either had to adapt or move out of reach.[3] Such extreme situations can often end in violence; on this estate an elderly resident was assaulted and seriously hurt when he tried to stop youths breaking in. The two ring-leaders received heavy prison sentences, after which a period of relative calm ensued. Because of concerted action by the residents who gave evidence, the housing office, which backed the residents, and the police, it was possible to stop the spiral. This experience echoes the suggestion that 'police action should in general be initiated by the public rather than the police themselves'.[4]

The morale of residents and estate staff rose as the level of fear diminished. There was a general sense that the extremes of bullying had been blocked at least for a while. One clear result has been a sharp reduction in criminal damage over two years, an offence which is still on the increase elsewhere in the Rhondda; there has also been a 60 per cent reduction in burglaries on the estate between 1986 and 1987.

Not only has the incidence of burglary and criminal damage decreased according to police records, but the local estate office receives only a fraction of the requests for glass, and door and lock replacements. The management performance of the local office improved steadily until arrears began to fall. Only 2 per cent of the property was empty in spite of the high turnover and low demand, and there was virtually no backlog of repairs any more, thanks to the job performance of the local team almost doubling. The Borough Treasurer recently calculated that repair workers in the local team were covering 50 per cent more jobs to the houses than the rest of the Borough repairs service.

The Council found itself in the strange position of arbiter of peaceful living conditions, enforcer of minimal standards and support for the residents who were prepared to hold out for enforcement of the law. This in the end involved saying no to bullies and making it stick. Francis Reynolds, in reference to the Omega estate, underlines the Council's ultimate responsibility on unpopular estates both as landlord and as the only local body with sufficiently wide and democratic powers.[5] Alderson, in his famous exposition 'Policing Freedom', suggests that social policy and informal controls within communities are likely to have far more impact than formal policing on the incidence of crime.[6]

The change occurred over a period of two years through a series of stages. After the incident of the attack on the local police station, twenty-four-hour beat patrols were introduced with support from the Residents' Association and the co-operation of the local housing office. A youth employment scheme recruited twenty young estate residents to work on environmental improvements. A resident-run youth club was established. Nine part-time caretaking posts were filled by residents.

The performance of the local housing office played a central role in creating a sense of the possible. A change in policing style in favour of a permanent local police presence reinforced the residents' need for peace and security. The residents' ability to influence events and be heard changed the way the estate was perceived by residents, by housing staff and by police. A way had to be found to enforce some of the basic social norms in order for any sense of community to survive. Otherwise the potential leadership within such a vulnerable and exposed community would have been crushed. It is not easy now for 'anything to go'. To quote Alderson, 'policing is not only seen as a matter of controlling the bad but also includes activating the good'.[7] It is hard to pinpoint the change. More policing, local projects involving and employing local youth, a cleaner, a more cared-for environment, a reduction in empty dwellings and much greater satisfaction with prompter repairs all contributed to a change in residents' attitudes.

NOTES

1. There are complex and finely printed rules about 'income disregard' which normally means that you can only earn about £4 a week before you lose £1 for every £1 earned.
2. South Wales Constabulary, June 1984. All reported crime figures in this section are derived from South Wales Constabulary Collaters' Office, Ton Pentre.
3. G. White's *The Worst Street in North London: Campbell Bunk, Islington, Between the Wars* (London: Routledge & Kegan Paul, 1986) contains a valuable discussion of this issue based on an Islington street in the 1930s.
4. D. Downes and T. Ward, *Democratic Policing* (London: Labour Campaign for Criminal Justice, 1986), p. 62.
5. F. Reynolds, *The Problem Housing Estate: An Account of Omega and its People* (Aldershot: Gower, 1986), p. 76.
6. J. Alderson, *Policing Freedom* (Plymouth: McDonald and Evans, 1979); see also Downes and Ward, *Democratic Policing*, p. 40.
7. Alderson, *Policing Freedom*, p. 38.

Love in the city

Peter Selby

DEBT: THE BINDING OF THE FUTURE

Among the economic statistics that are eagerly awaited each month is the level of consumer debt. A significant increase in consumer debt is regarded as a sign that the economy is reviving, and is greeted with appropriate exultation by those responsible for the direction of economic policy. This is in some ways odd at a time when in other areas 'Victorian values' are in vogue: evidently thrift and prudence are not necessarily high on the list. Yet the reason for this very positive attitude to consumer debt is that it is regarded as a reasonable index of public confidence: people will only borrow more, so the argument runs, if they are more confident in the future, if they expect their jobs to be secure and the property market buoyant. This very positive view of debt does not extend to public debt, government borrowing, which is regarded as a very negative phenomenon. It applies only to private debt, the debts of individual consumers. (It is worth noting in passing that the use of 'public' and 'private' in relation to debt is a particularly flagrant example of the individualism that accompanies a failure to identify the 'direction of society' and remedy its 'pathological deviations'; after all, how many individuals' debts does it take, and how large do they need to be, before they cease to be 'private'?)

It needs first to be pointed out that a large proportion of personal debt is not voluntary 'consumer debt' at all, and therefore in many cases the view that debt is a sign of renewed confidence in the future is (in the derogatory sense of the word) a myth. Persons in receipt of benefit do not borrow from the social fund out of a sense of renewed confidence in the future but because of desperate need in the present. (In this respect the debts of the poorest members of society resemble the indebtedness of the countries of the two-thirds world.) Furthermore, the escalating indebtedness of students does not betoken the sense they have of their steadily improving career prospects on graduation but of the necessary price of higher education. Any talk of indebtedness as a sign of confidence masks the large areas of society where it is simply a sign of desperation.

Yet a critical examination of indebtedness which confined itself to its effect on the poorest sections of the community would be too limited. For surely as important as the causes of indebtedness are its effects. A rising level of personal indebtedness in effect mortgages the future of the whole of society: it is itself the creator of social needs and the producer of great shifts in social attitudes. On the one hand, all of us who contract debts for whatever purpose limit our future freedom of action: the pattern of our future life is largely determined if we have considerable debts to pay off. On the other hand, since we borrow against the hope of a rising standard of living and against the expectation of a steady increase in the price of property, those expectations *must* be met and those results *have* to be produced. As a result it is likely that whatever a government does in pursuit of those goals will be willingly accepted, whatever may be the accompanying costs in civil liberty or social justice. The current policies of lending money to the poorest and increasing student loans will have many effects, but a principal one will be social control: what chance of students being in the vanguard of social criticism if they all have huge debts to pay off?

To make this point is not to mount a doctrinaire attack on all forms of borrowing and lending, but to draw attention to the fundamental dynamic involved when the ideology of debt and the amount of it pass without examination. That dynamic is revealed in that original transaction by which those without food entered slavery:

> When that year was over, they came to Joseph the next year, and said to him, 'We cannot hide it from my lord: the truth is, our money has run out and the livestock is in my lord's possession. There is nothing left for my lord except our bodies and our land. Have we to perish before your eyes, we and our land? Buy us and our land in exchange for bread; we with our land will be Pharaoh's serfs. But give us something to sow, that we may keep our lives and not die and the land may not become desolate.' (Genesis 47:18–19)

The slavery which is the background to the Exodus and thus to the history of redemption results not from invasion or colonization, but from debt. Whether as a result of that folk memory or because of other experiences, the Bible enjoins stringent controls on debt, on rates of interest, on the lengths to which creditors might go in seeking repayment, and on the length of time during which a debt could remain in force. Behind this is certainly the recognition of the dynamic of power that is involved in involuntary indebtedness, and more seriously still the effect that it has on the future freedom of action of the debtor. All the efforts of the ancient equivalent of social policy were directed at ensuring that debt was not a means to exploitation or to depriving others of their freedom for the future.

Thus the presentation of Christ as *redeemer* was not simply created out of the imagination, but was drawn from the deepest memories and contemporary experience of a people who knew what debt could accomplish and saw it as the reverse of the freedom which new life in Christ was intended to be. Lending and borrowing can, when the transaction is undertaken by two voluntary and equal participants, facilitate the best use of available resources; but it can only do that if its highly dangerous capacity to bind the future and impose the will of the creditor on the debtor are recognized and controlled. The point has a particular importance in a situation where most who enter credit transactions do so in the fond belief that they are doing so voluntarily: the pressures of an economy based on acquisition are such that the avoidance of debt is almost impossible, and the constraints of indebtedness on the future freedom of the debtor are so grave as to be something we hardly dare notice.

Ahead of us in the pursuit of the sociality symbolized by escalating debt is a society composed of two more or less clearly defined sections. On the one hand, there are those with so much to lose and to protect that their capacity to see their own future as an open sphere of freedom is severely diminished; and, on the other hand, there are those whose indebtedness has been forced to a level far beyond anything they might be expected to repay — they will be those with nothing to lose, whose future is simply a continuation of the bondage they already experience, and whose investment in society's good and society's laws will become minimal. Such is the effect of unrestrained debt on the very possibility of maintaining the fabric of anything called society.

* * *

The nature of debt comes to the surface very quickly in any game of 'Monopoly': the possibility of buying and selling in fantasy the names of famous city streets is one that some find exhilarating; but it is not so easy for losers to have that same sense of power — rows of upturned property cards marked 'mortgaged' are hardly ever the sign of a player with confidence in the future or much chance of surviving. (Such 'games' can also be 'played' in a way which demonstrates the way in which world trade works.) The game surely survives because it is easier to relish the fantasy of large winnings than to savour the bitter fruits of bankruptcy.

Such a game is of course a caricature, a bringing into high relief of the reverse of that 'social transcendental' of which Hardy speaks.[1] Any attempt to propose that a city might be built upon some other foundation, some form

of social relation other than that between debtor and creditor, will immediately be branded either as sheer idealism or as the attempt to re-establish
some form of repressive socialism long presumed dead. Such objections
reveal the degree to which the economy now prevailing over our urban life
rules in our minds and commands what amounts to worship. That economy
and its rules constitute a social transcendental other than God, an object of
worship made by human beings, an idol chosen instead of the possibility
represented by the Christian picture of love.

> We have already noticed how close is the relationship between ancient cities
> and idols — gods made by men — because they bear the same names. It is
> precisely by this creation of idols that the city closes herself up to God. Now
> she has her own God — the gods she has manufactured, which she can hold in
> her hands, which she worships because she is master over them, because they
> are the surest weapon against any other spiritual intervention.[2]

What Paul teaches, and what God has offered in Christ, is indeed a social
transcendental which is in direct contrast to what such idols offer. It is a love
which opens history up towards the future instead of locking the future up in
an unequal distribution of power and resources by the fantasy of unlimited
possibilities of affluence. For if that is the future in which the city chooses to
lock itself, it has indeed defended itself well against any possibility of
'spiritual intervention'. Such a 'society' is defended against all change except
the unlikely one of revolution or the already evident signs of internal
disintegration wrought by crime and social disorder. The links between
acquisitiveness and crime, especially in the ambitions of young men, are well
displayed by the example of Beatrix Campbell's account of 'joyriding':

> Joyriders' communication systems were built around the community on the
> one hand and technology on the other ... Radio scanners gave the joyriders
> greater knowledge of police manoeuvres than the police could reciprocate.[3]

And she makes the point that only a fundamental consideration of the
meaning of car crime and the way in which it connects crime and personal
wealth will have any effect:

> In the absence of any challenge to the connections between the car cult, the
> potency of its pleasures, and their very identity as men, the criminal justice
> system was unlikely to impinge on these young offenders.[4]

The attempt to speak of love in the face of such realities runs the severe risk
of sounding like a retreat into romanticism. The fear engendered in many
parts of our urban environment, the places where nobody dares go, is such
that it is hardly surprising that love is separated in our minds from anything
that might be expected to be known in society, and the effects of those
ideologies which have attempted to achieve sociality by planning and then
imposing their plans is hardly encouraging. As Hardy writes: 'Given the
ideologies and events of modern times, one might readily doubt whether
there could be a transcendental sociality in the real world which was either
Godly or fully human.'[5] Yet it is in the face of that fact of our modern worldview that Paul writes to the Corinthians of a way of being together that opens
up the possibility of a new history. He speaks of a sociality that has to be real,
to be practical; it starts, in the mind of Paul, with the church as the

community brought into being on the basis of the love revealed in Jesus, one that redeems those who were enslaved and whose future was constrained as a result of their indebtedness to false socialities. Paul's vision is of a society in which we shall 'owe no one anything but to love one another' (Romans 13:8).

If the social transcendental called love is to begin with the church, it cannot end there; and the social project called 'church' has to be based on ideas and processes which might have the capacity to undermine that alternative sociality operative in society at large. In constructing our life as church we have to take account of the pressure upon the church's members to conform to the life of the world and participate in its social reality. One of the realities which we may assume, therefore, is that our congregations will be composed of people who know something about love — and who also know a lot about debt.

So a start would be to talk about that reality openly and begin to see how any possibility of being responsive to the call of God's future has been constrained for us all by the ways in which we have placed the future Christ offers in bond; we might even discover that more significant than the agenda created by the loss of the Church Commissioners' millions would be the agenda created by all the years when they gained — at whose expense?

And while we do that, we shall also need to carry out another part of making the social transcendental a practical reality. We require the rehabilitation and control of the economy of debt: to bring it within the bounds of mutuality, equality and concern for its effects. We must support those institutions like credit unions which enable the needy to borrow without thereby losing their freedom of action and/or their ability to speak out and question the roots of their impoverishment.

It is doubtless fruitless to speculate whether Jesus taught his followers to pray to have their debts forgiven as they forgave their debtors (Matthew 6:12), or to pray to have their sins forgiven as they forgave those who sinned against them (Luke 11:4) or both. What is beyond doubt is that those who experienced the social reality he created found that they could only describe it as a place where people who had previously been burdened by a debt they could never meet found themselves the recipients of treasure beyond price. There were others too who observed that new society; they decided such a world would be too hard to control.

NOTES

1. Daniel W. Hardy, 'A magnificent complexity: letting God be God in church, society and creation', in Daniel Ford (ed.), *Essentials of Christian Community* (Edinburgh: T&T Clark, 1996), pp. 307–56.
2. Jacques Ellul, *The Meaning of the City* (Grand Rapids: Eerdmans, 1970), p. 54.
3. Beatrix Campbell, *Goliath: Britain's Dangerous Places* (London: Methuen, 1993), p. 257.
4. Ibid., p. 269.
5. Daniel Hardy, 'Created and redeemed sociality', C. E. Gunton and D. W. Hardy (eds), in *On Being the Church: Essays on the Christian Community* (Edinburgh: T & T Clark, 1989), p. 28.

The struggle with evil

Austin Smith

When I see the liberation of the powerless suggested by Christian writers as an example — amongst others — of the ethical application of Christian faith, I find it quite extraordinary. It is quite scandalous that such a term as 'fundamental option for the poor' should be a theologically debated topic: in terms of the hopefulness of the kingdom of God, there is no option of any kind, let alone a fundamental one. For the Christian faith there is simply no choice in the matter, a confrontation with evil and the identification and purging of it are at the heart of the human and Christian journey. But the purgation does not apply only to my own personal journey: it is an obligation to be honoured with regard to the ideologies and structures of this world and especially so, when such ideologies and structures oppress, alienate and stigmatize the powerless.

To be sure, on a personal level, we always live with a measure of self-seeking which is destructive. Thus our lives are, or should be, always caught in a process of purification. On a very simple and daily level I cannot find union with another, develop a personal friendship, unless I face the ever-present danger of self-seeking. And only too often, for all of us, there is the temptation to rationalize our selfishness. This is not to suggest that such an ongoing purification process should become an obsession; and it is certainly not a programme for a pessimistic view of myself which ends up in a form of spiritual paralysis. But I suggest that it is precisely in the constant effort to reach out beyond myself to the other that I shall find grounds of my purgation. In other words, the denial of my own tendency to a form of self-protection, which can spiritually devour me, is to be found in my willingness to exist with, act with and, above all things, suffer with the other. The preposition is so important. That is to say, I can act *for* the other and yet easily preserve my own comfort. When I exist with, act with and suffer with the other I am drawn into the other's life agenda. Such a drawing in, when it is authentic, means a self-purgation which, whilst truly leading me to a personal self-understanding, stops short of unhealthy introspection. Rather, I come to grips with an evil which forever haunts me and sometimes possesses my life. To cast evil out of myself demands that I enter into a givenness to another. Thus there are not two separate processes, one which purges evil from myself and another which leads me to reaching for and loving another; there is rather one process which is the product of two distinct, though inseparable parts.

On a personal level, then, if the tension I have spoken about is to be resolved, there must be both the recognition of evil and the casting out of evil. I must struggle to exorcise from myself all that belongs to the reign of selfishness, and this can only be achieved by a givenness to the world which is around me. Such a taking hold of myself, in the face of my own self-seeking, in order to lose my life for the other, is the ground of my willingness to grapple with the forces of evil in history.

At the very heart of the mission of Jesus, without sin though we understand him to be, his own casting out of evil in his world, both in cosmic and personal terms, was his own total givenness. I can never forget the sense of silent awe which takes hold of a Christian congregation as it sings the words, '*Et homo factus est*.' Certainly the awe may be seen rooted in the sense of the mystery of God become man, but it is surely something much deeper than this, for the self-emptying of the Godhead made manifest in Jesus is a declaration of the very process I have referred to. God became man, existed with, acted with and suffered with his world, to underline, on the one hand, the spiritual emptiness if such a givenness is not at the heart of the building up of the kingdom and to exemplify, on the other, the wonder of a vision which has this givenness as its basic demand. Indeed, it is the root of all hopefulness. It is a statement which, in so many words, articulates the belief that 'things can be better, that things can be different'. In a despairing world this may appear totally unreal, but in a hopeful world it is the cry of authentic progress.

At this stage of my own priesthood and religious life I find the introspection of so many Church programmes wearisome. Of course, there are also wonderful examples of reaching out to that larger world, but I do wonder if we have lost some of the energy, not to say the excitement of, the 'Signs of the Times' theology. Whenever the signs are somewhat ambiguous, do we retreat into a world of self-protection? I feel that this is where the trouble is. I have already mentioned this question of ambiguity and also the dangers of too many qualifications and parentheses. To struggle with the oppression of the poor, the powerlessness of the powerless and the marginalization of the stigmatized, is to struggle with the forces of evil. To be sure, there will be times and events which cause ambiguities in such a struggle, but confronting such ambiguities may lead us on to a path not only towards the liberation of the oppressed, but towards a simplification of the very life of the Church itself. In other words, the Church's act of transcendence in existing with, acting with and suffering with the oppressed, is its moment of purification. This is to be found not only in its prayer, its penance, its pilgrimages, but in its identification with the prayer of the powerless, the suffering of the powerless and the journeying of the powerless towards a better life. One cannot leave the latters' demands of life to reports, sermons and specialized apostolates. The starving Ethiopian child brushing insects from her eyes may well call us to immediate acts of charity; she is also a sign of a divided world of affluence and deprivation. And that divide is a sign of the kingdom of Satan.

The movements of liberation amongst the powerless of our world, with all their ambiguities, signify an energy born of utter frustration to utter the name, 'I am'. They also offer the world, and especially the Christian world, not simply a new context for the formulation of a Christian social doctrine, but rather a bleak picture of the landscape of contemporary evil. Having received that picture, perhaps having had it thrust into our hands, we must hang it in the galleries of our speculative and pastoral theologies, gaze at it day by day, in order to deepen, motivate and determine our mode of existence with, action with and suffering with, the powerless in their struggle for liberation.

TRANSITION FROM EVIL TO LOVE

The junction of the inner city, in my journey as priest and religious, has brought me a certain sense of bewilderment. The *word* bewilderment comes from the verb to bewilder, 'to lose in pathless places'. In using this term I do not speak of myself, but my sense of the 'lostness in pathless places' experienced by those who are marginalized in our world. But I am bewildered, in a world with so many resources, by the phenomenon of their bewilderment. The inner city population is that sector of society which is

> placed at a disadvantage by law, by social stigma, by discrimination or by the changing requirements of the labour market ... The Inner City is ... of far more than local interest. It is the bombardment chamber where the particles generated and accelerated by the cyclotron of a whole society are smashed into each other. It is a very good place to learn about the destructive forces inherent in ... society.[1]

The problem here is that too many people view such a phenomenon as an inevitable consequence of the pursuit of the good of the majority. But much more dangerous is the rider to this argument: God is made to bless or, at least, approve of this situation in a superficially Christian context. Avoidable suffering is made to appear unavoidable.

For better or worse, we remain heirs of that period of history known as the 'Enlightenment'. Basically, its philosophies held that if we could realize a world in which the human subject would attain control over and harmony with the forces of nature, we would all arrive at 'the best possible world'. And further, insofar as a God was to be invoked as part of this human effort, then that human struggle was God's will. The outcome of such a philosophy of life left the struggle, and indeed the definition of the harmony to be achieved, in the hands of the political, social, economic and cultural so-called élite of our world. As far as Christians are concerned, however, in such a view God is manipulated. Whatever the evil, they will say, good will come. This means that the racism, economic poverty, social and political powerlessness which are suffered by the marginalized of our society are blasphemously caricatured as the outcome of God's will. Avoidable evil is projected as unavoidable, that millions should be isolated and left desolate the consequence of the pursuit of a better world.

The consequence of this unholy alliance between reason and God is that those who call for liberation are portrayed as disturbers of the peace, destroyers of the common good and irrational agitators with no object in view but the simple act of agitation. They are seen as opposed to a reasonable political, social, economic and cultural target for society and, when God is invoked in rather vague Christian terms, opponents also of the so-called Christian or godly values of society. To soften the hard face of a seductive rationalism, those who are willing, find themselves called to confront such problems in terms of charity, sometimes clothed in the doubtful garments of self-help philosophies and schemes. In such a programme social justice slips off the agenda altogether.

The ultimate outcome of such a social and political vision is the victimization, not to say the criminalization, of the powerless. At the root of this process those who are the sufferers and victims become the constant topic of an unhealthy form of conversation: they are 'talked about'. This unhealthy conversational content claims for itself reason and, if the occasion should arise, the sympathetic approbation of God. The fatal response of the Church, in such situations, would be to make Innercityism a specific apostolic or evangelical target and leave the proponents of such a philosophy without rebuke or challenge. This would be a failure to respond to the inner demands of a 'Signs of the Times' theology and to realize that the liberation of the powerless is also the liberation of us all.

I do not think many of us, in these days, consecrate suffering in the name of God, but I do think we are still a long way off applying our more enlightened approach to suffering in a social context. We may perhaps seek some kind of solidarity with the struggle against physical and mental disability, but not with the struggle against social suffering. Whatever the case, the value of the struggle is measured by the criterion of 'who pays the bill'. Even in the case of physical and mental disability, the frail of our world are subjected to economic criteria. The radical response to social suffering can be authentically expressed only in an act of solidarity with the loneliness and desolateness of those who are socially marginalized, stigmatized, alienated and discriminated against within our inherited paradigms of power.

Too often, in the Christian pilgrimage, the struggle with evil has been perceived and defined within the boundaries of personal failure, accountability, contrition and penance. One must not, of course, attempt to escape the essential personal nature of evil. Systems did not light the crematoria of Auschwitz — human wills and hands were needed. But the logic of those systems was so structured that the system justified, and indeed motivated, the human beings who perpetrated the crimes. In other words, though at the root of all human action one finds human beings, the energizing force in creating a system is a philosophy and a mode of action. One may, indeed, go through a personal conversion of heart in life, but if the evil from which I am converted is rooted in a specific system or structure, the system and structure must also be dismantled. If we live in a system which agrees, at least implicitly, that, in order to prosper, certain levels of powerlessness are unavoidable, then I must struggle against the system itself. To reduce the whole problem to the conversion of individual human hearts results in a failure to resolve the tension between my own personal struggle for liberation and the demand upon me to join hands with the powerless in their struggle for liberation from social powerlessness. The struggle is against and concerns an evil which engulfs us all and is rooted in inherited ideologies and institutions which secure and perpetuate a system of social power with exclusive access to political, economic and cultural resources. I must seek union with God in a union with those who socially suffer; that act of union must purge me of my self-seeking and self-securing; and, at a much deeper level, their struggle for liberation must become a moment in God's grace which illuminates for me the choice of more profound human and Christian values. I must seek to 'exist with, suffer with and act with' the oppressed in the cause of their liberation. In Gospel language I must make a transition from personal and social evil to personal and social love.

NOTE

1. Paul Harrison, *Inside the Inner City* (Harmondsworth: Penguin, 1983), pp. 24–5.

Thunder over the city

Jacques Ellul

But it is in these cities that we must live. We human beings. We who are Israel and then the church. Such is our environment, as is the world itself. We must not forget that the city is the symbol of the world, especially today, when it has become the synthesis of our entire civilization.

To the captives from Israel, dragged off to the very heart of the city, to Babylon, the symbol of symbols, Jeremiah wrote:

> Thus says the Lord of hosts, the God of Israel, to all the exiles whom I have sent into exile from Jerusalem to Babylon: Build houses and live in them; plant gardens and eat their produce. Take wives and have sons and daughters; take wives for your sons, and give your daughters in marriage, that they may bear sons and daughters; multiply there and do not decrease. *But seek the welfare of the city where I have sent you into exile, and pray to the Lord on its behalf, for in its welfare will you find your welfare.* ... I will fulfil to you my promise and bring you back to this place. (Jeremiah 29:4–7, 10)

In this city we are captives. That is the first thing we must understand. As Israel in her Babels, the church is in captivity. And we know that this is even the essential goal of the cities — to make every man captive. And as with every prisoner, escape seems to be the ideal goal. Get out. Destroy the prison, or at least get outside its walls. This is the first reaction: if the city truly came from man's hands for the reasons revealed in God's Word, if a curse is truly resting on her, then she is the great enemy of all dwelling on the earth. Moreover, the end has been announced and we must first of all flee this place of perdition. We must settle elsewhere, for outside the city the same curse does not reign. Then we must fight the city, destroy it, revert to an agricultural, a rustic civilization. If it is true that there is more virtue in country living, we must bring about God's judgements with our own hands.

This is a logical reaction, but God is not logical in what he tells us. And far from asking us to destroy Babylon, he asks us to preserve her alive. God will bring about his own justice alone. Babylon will fall by the condemnation decided by God when God will decide it. He will choose the day and the hour, and it is not by the hands of men that the act of God will be accomplished; or if it is by human hands, it will be done unconsciously, without man realizing that he is fulfilling such a task. Man's duty is not to execute God's judgements. Man's duty is not to establish God's justice in God's stead. On the contrary, all of the Bible's teaching is there to show us that God establishes his own justice. We know that God has condemned the city, but we have no reason to presume on this judgement, putting ourselves on a level with God. For are we not inhabitants of the city? And just like all the other inhabitants of the city, do we not have our own part of the condemnation to accept since we are all dependent on each other here behind our walls? Let us avoid such a terribly simplistic notion as a clear separation between good men and evil men, right and wrong. The judgement of God is not separation of good and evil, but annihilation and re-creation. And this makes us completely powerless to realize any of God's judgements, powerless to annihilate the power of nothingness which the city represents, and incapable of re-creating.

Moreover, we have seen the meaning of God's judgement, and not only do we have nothing to do with its execution, but neither do we have any power to add to it. God's condemnation is sufficient in itself; we have no personal condemnation to add against the city. We have no supplementary human reasons to discover — neither favourable to the city, which is directly contrary to the teaching of the Bible, nor unfavourable to the city, which is just as faithless. In either case, we accomplish not God's will but the teaching of the city: we have substituted, by this act, ourselves for God. And when our pretended obedience to God pushes us out beyond his will, our action falls into the long line coming down from Adam, and takes the form, for example, of the sin of Ahaz (Isaiah 7). We have no right to replace God, to make ourselves judges of the world's sin. This temptation would lead us to obey exactly that same will which incited the builders to construct their cities. Thus, far from taking God's side by our works which are already cursed, we are in reality, although we think we are destroying the cities, only working on their side.

This is not the road God asks us to follow. Astonished, we see that, on the contrary, our job is to lead the life of the other inhabitants of the city. We are to build houses, marry, have children. What a happy ground for conciliation, for that is exactly what the city is asking of us! What a mediocre vocation, so disappointing in its lack of heroism and so reassuring in its apparent ease! And thus we are to continue from one generation to the next, assuring, it would seem, that very stability and depth which men were seeking when they built the cities. Are we to do nothing differently? There is one thing which is not asked of us, and that is to *build* the city. We are to live in the city already existing. But we are asked neither to materially found a new city, nor to participate in spiritual building projects, that is, to share in that which forms the very being of the city. This must be made much more precise. For we are clearly told to participate materially in the life of the city and to foster its welfare. The *welfare*, not the destruction. And the welfare of the *city*, not our own. Yes, we are to share in the prosperity of the city, do business in it, and increase its population. We are to defend it because our solidarity is there. But it is the solidarity of the captive with his jailkeeper. We must make it beautiful, because it is a work of man. And because it is such, God looks down even on it with love. Who knows if in this cursed environment, man's work cannot also sing to the glory of the living God? This question is now possible since Nineveh repented before Jonah's preaching and a new door was opened.

But we will never understand the incomprehensible contradiction between

God's curse and the order given us unless we remember that this city-dweller with this work is already the object of God's good will, that this sinner has already been called to become, against his will, a witness for righteousness. Although he is naturally incapable of understanding anything good and true, he has nevertheless received from God's word (even if he understands nothing of it) his role as a witness, dependent, bound to that word. For he is already the object of God's great work in the resurrection, he already belongs *objectively* to Jesus Christ. This is only an eschatological reality, the meaning of which we have yet to study, but it already exists here and now, and it is in terms of it that we must take the way of obedience while participating in man's work, which in turn becomes an involuntary witness of God's work.

However, this participation cannot be total, with no limiting conditions. It does not consist of integration into the urban system. It is not absolute and eternal goodness. He who would live in such a way would nevertheless remain a captive; the place he works would still be his prison. It would also be a place of non-communication, as we have already seen, making preaching an empty and wasted effort. That is why we are not first asked to preach and convert Babylon, but rather to pray. Involved in a battle on a spiritual plane, a battle comparable to Abraham's battle for Sodom, our duty is to pray for the good of the city. Thus our task is to defend this counter-creation before God. We must ask God to take away this condemnation which we know so well, and herein lies our liberty in relation to the city. It is our accomplishment of this act which shows that we are not captives like the others. This is the exact line of separation between ourselves and the city.

Some are captives of the spiritual power which has embodied itself in the city, and they help to strengthen the city's specifically anti-redemptive tendencies, although by so doing they are physically free and in full accord with the powers of the world, full of success in their projects even though the curse reigns. The others are physical captives, bound prisoners, working against the dominations, refusing to go along with the game as the angel of the city would like, obstinately attached to an incomprehensible faithfulness, and praying for the welfare of the city. But it is a welfare different from that which the city looks forward to and desires. The welfare they pray for means another kind of success. By their prayer, the very meaning and quality of the city run the risk of change. I have said 'run the risk of change' rather than 'will be changed', for the reason behind the city's construction runs the risk of being eliminated, while the city itself stays on.

But how is such a thing possible? It is beyond human strength, and only at Nineveh is such a thing shown as happening, with God's intervention. But our task is not to spend time pondering this success, but to obey our orders, and by doing so we enter into combat with the power of the city itself. This decision to follow God's orders puts us in a position much more dangerous than any other we could occupy. For our prayer and the action it implies bring on Satan's vengeance. In fact we are exposed to many vengeances whose motives will not be evident. We will be looked upon as adversaries of public welfare or as enemies of the human race and our efforts for the good of the city will be interpreted as a will to destroy it. And the accusation is in fact true if the city is considered only from the angle of its spiritual power. Thus a secret thread is woven into the visible side of the city's fabric, and its design is not clearly seen. But on the reverse side of the city's history, on the inside of the cloth, this is the thread which appears as the surest link, and the true design.

We are asked to act thus not for the city itself, but (and this of course will appear supremely selfish to outsiders) for ourselves. For the church. The city can go on because it contains men who are bearers of God's word. And this, let us not forget, is the exact meaning of Abraham's prayer for Sodom. The only worth of these men resides in the fact that they are bearers of God's word. And the city can go on only because it contains such men. And by them it in turn temporarily becomes a bearer of the Gospel. Our welfare is bound up with hers, and so we must work for it, both materially and spiritually — not for our own peace, our own satisfaction, our own established security in the city, but for the good of the Word we have to announce to the world and which needs to be upheld.

As servants of the Word, we must for its sake accept working with what revolts us, hurts us, and breaks our human hearts, for blind refusal is a disservice to the Word of God, and this Word declares forgiveness with judgement, not a judgement without pardon. And the life of the city is dependent on such an attitude. Jonah was angry when the city was not ruined and destroyed, both because the city was evil and because God's prophecy seemed to be false. Since the facts contradict it, who is to say whether this Word against Nineveh was true or not? Have there not been critical students of history who, to explain the lack of evidence for this conversion of Nineveh, have suggested a pretended conversion? And it is in fact easy to visualize the attitude that the men of our time would take toward a prophecy which is not fulfilled! What an argument against God! And we can understand how sad Jonah could be because of what appeared to be a betrayal of God. Jonah's attitude is ridiculous, but it is nevertheless possible that the first steps toward conversion could have turned into play-acting when the Ninevites saw that nothing happened! At least if fire and brimstone had showered down on Nineveh there could have been [no] argument. But no salvation, either. And Jonah's task is ours, permanently. We must unceasingly proclaim God's curse and judgement on the city; but we must also pray to God that it will not happen, that he have pity (Should not I pity 120,000 men?), that he grant life to the city, that he make of it something to his glory. We must do this even at the cost of looking ridiculous and being embarrassed.

The life of the city is entirely dependent on this faithfulness, on this righteousness, which is not ours. 'By the blessing of the upright a city is exalted ...' (Proverbs 11:11). Here is a power which the builders had not foreseen! But the city is built neither for it nor by it. Nevertheless, God reveals to us that it has a decisive role to play in the city's history, decisive but not definitive; for our situation has not been completely changed. Jeremiah's letter shows us that we are still in a period of waiting. Although we live in the city, our efforts on its behalf are still subordinate to the awaited moment when the city itself will be overthrown by God, when the proclaimed judgement will take effect, when we will leave the city with all those called and chosen of God, when God will take us to our true homeland, out of our land of exile, out of our prison. And then it will be proper no longer to oppose the city's destruction. Then it will be proper to separate ourselves from it. But not before. We must wait.

And this situation of ours is also radically different from that of the other inhabitants of the city, its builders. Theirs is a closed world, a world for which nothing else is expected. A world which is reaching man's perfection. A finished counter-creation, to which nothing else can be added. And inside its walls are men who think they have found a secure home, the only one, their Eden. Man protected against attacks from the outside, in a security built up in walls and machines. Men who live artificially contrived lives (just as artificial as their world of concrete and steel), which go on without a hitch, imperturbably, in three-eight time, and where there is no room for adventure, where nothing more is expected. And it is into this world that we are asked to reintroduce an attitude of waiting — not an empty hope for better days, not a desire for more power and security, but a hope for certain very precise events, known by us for a long time, but out of our jurisdiction because they do not depend on us. Anxiety and hope mixed together. And we must bear them to the heart of the city, where the battle rages. For such an attitude is the very ruin of what the city was built for. Our waiting attitude, if it is constant and true, if it reaches our very hearts, is the very ruin of the spiritual power of the city.

Further reading

Murray Bookchin, *The Limits of the City* (Buffalo, NY: Black Rose Books, 1984). A powerful examination of the subversive effects on human relationships and communities of the economic processes which drive rapid urban expansion.

Emilio Castro, *Sent Free* (Geneva: WCC, 1981). A holistic account of the mission of Jesus and of Christians, a mission which is shaped by the personal *and* social character of sin and evil, and by the holistic struggle against evil and its consequences in the ministry of Jesus.

Elliott Currie, 'International developments in National Association for the Care and Resettlement of Offenders', *Crime and Social Policy: Market and Society and Social Disorder* (London: NACRO, 1992), pp. 105–22. Argues for a direct connection between the dramatic growth in property crime in the United States and Britain since 1979 and sharp rises in income inequality, unemployment and job insecurity.

David Donnison *et al.*, *Crime and Social Policy: Report of the Crime and Social Policy Committee of NACRO* (London: NACRO, 1995). Argues that focused strategies dealing with the causes of crime — poor parenting, poor education, bad housing, poorly designed estates, low income, unemployment — are more effective in crime prevention than the creation of more punitive regimes for offenders.

David P. Farmington, *Understanding and Preventing Youth Crime* (York: Joseph Rowntree Foundation, 1996). Authoritative investigation of the causes, and possible cures, of youth crime and delinquency which links the growth in youth crime to economic deprivation, poor housing and unemployment as well as to family breakdown, poor parenting and failures in moral and educational formation.

John Francis Kavanaugh, *Following Christ in a Consumer Society* (Maryknoll, NY: Orbis Books, 1984). Theological exploration of idolatry and commodity fetishism in consumer societies and their contribution to a culture of economic victimization as the down-side of materialism.

Alistair I. McFadyen, 'Crime and violence. The UPA as the place of the demons?', in Peter Sedgwick (ed.) *God in the City* (London: Mowbray, 1995), pp. 178–90. Argues that the structures of sin which are made visible in the prevalence of crime, violence and addiction in UPAs are spiritual as well as social in their origin and effects. The answer to structural sin and disorder is a vision of society modelled on the creative and relational being and action of the triune God. In this perspective society is an organic network of reciprocity and mutuality and critiques the denial of reciprocity in the spirituality of materialism.

Robert Wuthnow (ed.), *Rethinking Materialism: Perspectives on the Spiritual Dimension of Economic Behavior* (Grand Rapids, Michigan: Eerdmans, 1995). Economically informed theological reflections on the consumer society and the quest for material affluence, the essayists pose particularly sharp questions to our apparently insatiable desire for money and material security, and what this desire is doing to our own souls, as well as to the world's poor.

5

Poverty in the city

There was once a rich man, who used to dress in purple and the finest linen, and feasted sumptuously every day. At his gate lay a poor man named Lazarus, who was covered with sores. He would have been glad to satisfy his hunger with the scraps from the rich man's table. Dogs used to come and lick his sores. One day the poor man died and was carried away by the angels to be with Abraham. The rich man also died and was buried. In Hades, where he was in torment, he looked up and there, far away, was Abraham with Lazarus close beside him. 'Abraham, my father,' he called out, 'take pity on me! Send Lazarus to dip the tip of his finger in water, to cool my tongue, for I am in agony in this fire.'

But Abraham said, 'My child, remember that the good things fell to you in your lifetime, and the bad to Lazarus. Now he has consolation here and it is you who are in agony. But that is not all: there is a great gulf fixed between us; no one can cross it from our side to reach you, and none may pass from your side to us.' 'Then, father,' he replied, 'will you not send him to my father's house, where I have five brothers, to warn them, so that they may not come to this place of torment?'

But Abraham said, 'They have Moses and the prophets; let them listen to them.' 'No, father Abraham,' he replied, 'but if someone from the dead visits them, they will repent.' Abraham answered, 'If they do not listen to Moses and the prophets they will pay no heed even if someone should rise from the dead.'

(Luke 16:19–31)

Faith in the City

Poor people in Britain are not of course as poor as those in the Third World. But their poverty is real enough none the less. For poverty is a relative, as well as an absolute, concept. It exists, even in a relatively rich western society, if people are denied access to what is generally regarded as a reasonable standard of living and quality of life in that society. (9.3)

Poverty is not only about shortage of money. It is about rights and relationships; about how people are treated and how they regard themselves; about powerlessness, exclusion, and loss of dignity. Yet the lack of an adequate income is at its heart. (9.4)

Income support policies are a first step to doing justice to those members of our society who are poorest, and who are most likely to be concentrated in UPAs. (9.7)

Yet in recent years social welfare and taxation policies have tended to benefit the rich at the expense of the poor. (9.8)

Introduction

The parable of Dives and Lazarus has long been a stumbling block to interpreters of the Gospels who seek to harmonize Christian teaching with the dedicated pursuit of wealth, especially in modern capitalist and market-dominated societies. The parable is set in a society where a small minority of rich merchants flourished through collaboration with the Roman occupiers of Palestine while the majority languished, like Lazarus, in debt, economic insecurity and ill health (Mealand).

The parable also reflects the Hebrew tradition concerning the dangers of inequality and wealth, a tradition which Jesus draws on many times in his teachings and parables (Wallis). According to this tradition, wealth represents a grave danger to the soul of the person who possesses it because the wealthy are distracted by worldly cares from the worship and love of God, and from their spiritual destiny, hence the famous saying of Jesus that it is 'harder for a camel to go through the eye of a needle than for a rich person to inherit the kingdom of God' (Luke 18:25). This is why the parable represents the rich as moral reprobates while the poor are regarded as the rightful subjects of God's love and favour. God is biased towards the poor because they are more likely to understand their dependence on their creator and to worship God, and also because their poverty is evidence of oppression and sinfulness amongst those who have cornered for themselves too much of the good gifts of God's creation. The rich refuse to acknowledge their dependence on the generous creator relying instead on their power to amass resources for their own luxury and aggrandizement.

Jesus himself prefers poverty to wealth as a state of life, frequently praising those who give up possessions for the sake of the Kingdom, while warning the rich that their wealth may lead to their eternal ruin (Pobee). But throughout his ministry Jesus also resists the effects of inequality and poverty. He admonishes the corrupt and the wealthy, warning them of the judgement to come, as in this parable, while healing the sicknesses of the poor and the outcast. He condemns or caricatures the taxes and debts imposed by the Roman authorities and their Jewish collaborators, proclaiming the good news of the kingdom where debts are forgiven, the poor are blessed, and the lowliest are invited to the heavenly banquet.

This moral attitude to wealth and poverty is retained and developed in the Christian tradition, in the practice of sharing of possessions and almsgiving in the early Church, and in the warnings against wealth and luxury in the teachings of monks and theologians (Gonzalez). Modern attitudes to wealth and poverty, where wealth is seen as a state of blessing and poverty as evidence of moral failure, represent a complete reversal of traditional Christian ethics, and of New Testament attitudes to wealth and poverty (Pobee). This reversal finds ultimate expression in the cultural explanations of poverty favoured by underclass theorists who argue that poverty, crime and unemployment are all forms of behaviour which predominate amongst illegitimate children and their parents, while the wealthy are those who live in traditional families and who teach their children to work hard and obey the laws. The poor are said to be poor because of their want of morality while the rich enjoy the fruits of their virtues of family life, enterprise and avarice (Murray). In the morality of the New Right poverty is a consequence of personal or familial sin while wealth is a social symbol of warranted individual beatitude (Katz; Field).

Such modern theories and attitudes not only deny the gospel of the kingdom as represented in this parable, but they also neglect the social and collective origins of poverty. In the modern world, as in the ancient world, though on a much larger scale, the untrammelled pursuit of wealth is clearly linked with the growth of scarcity and of poverty. The promise of capitalism was that as capital owners marshalled their control over land, labour and natural resources, initially causing great social upheaval and destitution, the system would eventually spread its benefits to all citizens of capitalist societies through the growth of employment and the cash economy. But the new spectre of post-industrial unemployment, and the persistence of poverty, both relative and absolute in industrial and post-industrial societies give the lie to this promise (**Atherton**). In the last two decades Britain and North America have experienced massive increases in inequality with income differentials of 500 to 1 now common in many post-industrial cities. These inequalities are not only relative but absolute, manifest most clearly, as in the story of Dives and Lazarus, in health inequalities. The modern urban poor have a shorter life expectancy than the comfortable, experience higher rates of infant mortality, and higher incidences of cancer, heart disease and viral infections.

The parable reminds us that God's economy is an eternal economy. The mirage of economic security in this life fools Dives into neglecting the balance between earth and heaven, as well as ignoring the needs of his neighbour Lazarus. In a similar way, the modern consumer society generates exclusion as well as luxury, and the mechanisms of exclusion — secret bank accounts, unaccountable corporations, ghettos and defended suburbs (Harrison). As in the parable they are two sides of the same coin: wealth and poverty, exclusion and inclusion, heaven and hell. But the Kingdom of God upturns these dualities, unravels the iron laws of economics, and challenges the gods of the here and now. The punishment of poverty in this life is reversed in the parable of Dives and Lazarus with the promise of paradise in the next.

But this heavenly reversal is not the end of the parable's meaning for the complicity of the rich in the ill health and indignity of poverty has two possibilities for redemption in this life. The first is that the rich recognize that their wealth creates obligations and is not won without cost to others like Lazarus whose poverty is linked to others' excess. The denial of his neighbourly connection with Lazarus is the cause of the judgement which Dives experiences. Where the rich establish corporations, advertising agencies and media conglomerates to persuade governments, viewers and voters that natural resource use and wealth accumulation should have no limits, and should carry no social obligations, the guilt of the rich is great indeed, and the danger of judgement is also great. It is the vocation of the Church to forewarn the rich of this.

Poverty is an offence against the dignity of persons because by denying the poor an adequate income the poor are excluded from relationships of respect and recognition (**Atherton**). This is why Jesus' offer of recognition to those whom his own religion excluded was so important. But in the Hebrew tradition, which Jesus inherited, the denial of dignity and livelihood is also an offence against God the creator who made all persons equal, with equal rights to the feast of life. The denial of those natural rights to creation's gifts is a sinful denial of God's justice in creation (**Forrester and Skene**). This social and collective sin can only be overcome when the rich learn to share their power and their wealth, and to reconnect their lives with those who are poor. The recognition of the relationship between rich and poor who live in the same society, and of the relational connection between wealth and poverty, is the prerequisite, according to this parable, for the redemption of the sin of avarice.

According to the parable, this redemption arises from worship, and from restored relationships in the worshipping community. When we worship and praise the God of justice and love, and in particular when we hear the stories of Abraham, Moses and the people of God in the reading of the Bible in worship, we cannot avoid the plain sense of Scripture that God chose an enslaved and poor people to be his followers, that God favours the poor over the rich, the down-trodden over the powerful, the meek over the mighty (Wallis). When the first urban Christians worshipped, often in the houses of the rich who were the only ones with enough space to enable them to meet together in private, they recognized the obligations of wealth and the giftedness of the poor. The early Church where this gospel story was read and retold was a church which laid great emphasis on the needs of the poor, and on the church as a society in which these needs were not ignored. The internal economy of the Christian society was formed around the sharing of wealth and property with those in need, a reflection of the divine economy which established an abundant earth from whose fruits and riches no-one should be excluded (**Forrester and Skene**). The early Church witnessed to the power of the risen Christ and his Spirit to reconnect those whom sin and society had alienated one from another.

The true worship of the God who is in Jesus involves the breaking down of the walls of division between rich and poor, slave and free and the reconnection of each to the other in communities of solidarity, and in a common quest for the good life for all God's children. And here is the second possibility for redemption of the comfortable; when they establish mechanisms by which their comfort and accumulated wealth are materially shared so that no-one is denied dignity, health and access to the good life. After the Second World War, when Britain, like much of Europe, was massively indebted because of the cost of the war, the Christian socialist vision inspired a system of welfare and social security which, while never generous, at least ensured that all those who had together fought for freedom from totalitarian tyranny should experience freedom from the tyranny of poverty in their own society. But fifty years later, when corporate profits, gross national product and personal incomes have never been higher, many have adopted the view that we can collectively no longer afford taxes which effectively redistribute wealth, and a welfare system which guarantees a decent standard of living to all whether in or out of work (Field). According to New Right economists the redistribution of wealth through the welfare and tax systems is an undue restraint on the processes of wealth creation, and is increasingly unpopular with voters (Katz). This collective shift to selfishness and greed is the clearest evidence of the advance of secularism and the demise of the influence of the Christian

Gospel, and the parables and teachings of Jesus, over our modern public life and culture (**Russell**).

The readings which follow indicate the extent and character of poverty in modern Britain, its links to the demise of welfarism and to the failures of industrial capitalism to fairly distribute the fruits of production and employment, and they demonstrate the cultural and moral approbation which the comfortable tend to heap on the poor, including comfortable social scientists (**Seabrook**). They also demonstrate that the prophetic voice of Christians is not silent (**Atherton; Forrester and Skene**), that Christian communities and theologians are still capable of speaking in modern parlance the traditional Christian ethic which regards the reduction of poverty and the quest for social equality as the divine vocation for a Christian society (**Russell**).

Living on welfare

Jeremy Seabrook

Marie has gone into hiding. In her long experience of dealing with the caring agencies of the state, she has learned that the only way to get attention is by means of creating high drama that the authorities cannot ignore. Violence, danger, self-damage, children at risk — there is an increasingly competitive clamour for attention. Anything less will not be considered sufficiently urgent for action.

It's actually a good place to hide: shielded from the busy road on the edge of the city, you go down about twenty steps and find a fortress-like low-rise building from the late 1970s, a hexagon, with cobbled courtyards and beds of silver-green conifers and pyrocanthus. Marie's flat is secure, with an extra Chubb lock which she keeps closed whether she is out or at home.

Marie is here temporarily, having abandoned her flat and gone to a women's refuge some twenty miles from where she was living. Her husband, Greg, had left her only a few months after their marriage. She had always known it wouldn't work. 'I tried to talk him out of it, but he didn't want to know. He thought getting married makes people love each other; getting married is the surest way of finding out you don't.'

It wasn't Greg who had beaten her up; he is not a violent man. Within a few weeks of being married, he spent a month in gaol for breach of parole, and within four weeks of release he had left home. He had returned, saying he wanted to start again, and Marie, who is a placid, good-natured woman ('They can see me a mile away,' she says deprecatingly about herself), agreed to try once more.

Six weeks later, there had been a row, and he left home for good. To make matters worse, he went to live with Marie's best mate, Tina, and her boyfriend, who lived on the same estate, no more than 300 yards away. One weekend, Marie's parents had come to stay, to cheer her up and help with the three children. Her father had parked his Reliant Robin three-wheeler outside the flat. On the Saturday morning the car had gone. Scouring the estate for it, Marie had called at Tina's, and found the garage door open with Ted working on her father's car. She challenged Tina, and asked her if she knew her father's car had been nicked by Greg. Tina said it was news to her, and promised to make sure that Greg would return it straight away.

Later in the afternoon, Marie went to get some ice-cream for the children. She saw her father's car parked outside the shop, driven by a stranger. This woman said she had just bought it. She had paid £100 cash. She was told that it was stolen: Marie's father produced the papers. The woman went to the police.

Tina believed that Marie had told the police that the car had been in her garage and that Greg had taken it. For Tina, the idea that her mate had grassed on her was too much: she had a few drinks and worked herself up into a state of fury and indignation. In fact, the police had called on Marie, and asked to see Greg; she had told them she didn't know where he was. All she said was, 'If you find him, keep him away from me or it's me you'll be arresting for murder.' The policeman replied, 'That's all right, it isn't a crime to kill a Taylor' (Greg's surname). As soon as the police left, Tina arrived. As Marie opened the door, she had rushed at her, beating and bruising her, breaking her nose, tearing out some hair and blacking both eyes. Marie's father tried to intervene, but was no match for Tina's rage.

Marie rang the women's refuge where she had retreated earlier when a boyfriend had given her a good hiding. There was no room, but she was told to try the refuge in the next city. Her father drove her there in the car which he had repossessed. 'I was the only woman there who'd been beaten up by another woman,' says Marie. 'They thought I must be a lesbian.'

After a few days, she was temporarily rehoused in her present flat. The two younger children are with their father, who has just remarried, and Marie is here with her 10-year-old, Stephanie. After the shock and the extremes of emotion, Marie says she now feels empty. She finds herself confiding in Stephanie, telling her things that she knows no 10-year-old ought hear. 'But I can't help it. Stephanie says she's never going to get married. I just don't know how to get through the days.' In the same block Marie has started a friendship with a man in his fifties, who has brought up two boys on his own. His wife left him ten years ago, and he determined not to let the children go into care, because he himself had been brought up in a Dr Barnardo's home, where his memories are of being always cold and hungry, over-punished and under-loved. He urges Marie not to let the two younger children stay with their father, but to keep the family together. He is now semi-retired, and does a part-time job driving a lorry. 'The curse of my life now is loneliness. My youngest is now 15, he's got his own life. The older boy has left home. It hurts when they grow away from you, but I'd rather lose them this way, through their choice, rather than through mine. People thought I was mad, a bloke on his own bringing up kids. But I wouldn't want any kids to go through what I did.'

Marie's secret dread, and what tempts her to leave the younger two with their father, is that she finds it increasingly hard to cope with the three of them together. Her first husband is now working on a Community Programme scheme; he can give them the firm hand she feels she lacks. 'With me, they just run wild.' Stephanie is difficult enough; she goes into long sulks, sits under the table and will not speak for hours at a time. She is teased at school because she wears jumble-sale clothes; today she has gone to school in a pair of plastic sling-back shoes with the heels sawn off. The other children have called her gipsy and flea-bag.

It has required great strength for Marie not to return to the flat, and not to signal to her friends where she is. 'I always get in with the wrong people.' She wonders what has happened to the flat. 'There's nothing in it I care about. I don't want to see it again. They tried to put pressure on me to go back, because the flat is in a joint tenancy with Greg, but now I've been told that they will rehouse me here, so I won't have to go back. I want to start a new life. I'm thinking of changing my name. I don't want to be reminded of anything in my past. There's only one trouble. Where the kids are with my first husband, they've got a lodger; and he's an old flame of Tina's. Tina's old flames, there's enough of them to start a forest fire, they're everywhere.'

The Social Services have been good to her here; and she is getting more from the DHSS than she received in her former home, £37 a week plus Child Allowance. She has a big box of Meredith and Drew's broken biscuits which she got on the market for £2. In the kitchen there are two meat pies in silver foil ready for the evening meal. She can buy frozen chops and ox-tail and bacon from the butcher's for £5 to last the week. It costs 62p for her and 31p for Stephanie to go into town.

'I'm finished with men,' she says. She reflects on her relationship with her father, which had never been particularly happy. 'He always preferred my brother. He never took any notice of my girls; it wasn't until Kevin was born that he noticed I had any kids at all.'

We go over the bridge to meet Stephanie out of school; eighty-six steps, past the cement works that has coated all the trees and pavements with a film of grey dust; over the busy main road, and then a pathway bordered with trees, where Marie says dirty men are always lying in wait for the children. The graffiti on the bridge say 'Karen is a Slag, Jason and Kelly shagged here', 'Women Don't Want Equality — They Just Want Your Jobs'.

Many people have observed the relative apathy or quiescence of the poor in recent years, in spite of the inner-city riots. At the same time, there has been an increase in crime and violence, combined with a decreasing level of political activity and protest. What seems to have happened is that the images and symbols of wealth are so pervasive and insistent that the rich are not so much objects of resentment as models of aspiration and hope. If there are more crimes, greater violence, a more ready breakdown of relationships, much of this is contained within the poor communities themselves, with relatively little effect on the mainstream of social life. Some of the poor have learned to play the system, as though it were a kind of refined roulette wheel; others have set out, often parodying the values of enterprise and initiative of the dominant culture, to get, by fair means or foul, the money without which a decent life is not possible; but the vast majority accept the curtailed and diminished possibilities that being 'on benefit' implies. It is not, on the whole, public disorder and protest that characterize the lives of the poorest, but their acceptance of the often imperfect structures of caring, it is their patience and endurance, their extraordinary longanimity; which all suggest how little has changed beneath the constantly shifting surface of things.

There is now a significant core of people in Britain who have grown into adult life as dependants of the welfare state. They have come through childhood on what was National Assistance, later Supplementary Benefit, into adult unemployment, and have now brought up their children in similar circumstances. The conditions in which many such people live are familiar, not only to social workers, but to any viewer of those TV documentaries of which they are so often the subject: the hard-to-let estates with the barricaded shops, the rank grass and half-wild dogs, the broken windows and burgled meters, the jumble-sale clothes and Social Services Department furniture, second-hand cookers and foam mattresses; 'existing, not living', as they will tell you.

There is something both upsetting and disturbing about dependency upon the caring agencies of the state (the dwindling benign effects of which are so frequently counteracted now by its multiplying agencies of control). This is not to suggest that there is anything morally bracing about leaving the poor to fend for themselves, to make their own accommodation with unemployment, disablement and death: this will merely fill the towns and cities with beggars, as any visitor to the cities of the South is immediately aware. It isn't even that the labyrinthine and sometimes impenetrable workings of the welfare system itself are the source of the wrong (although they are no help either), or even their not particularly well rewarded and often resentful custodians and administrators.

What makes life on welfare so cruel — and it is a different kind of cruelty from that in societies where there is no welfare provision at all — is the context in which that system of relief has to operate. For dependency on welfare is only another aspect, a more intensive version of a wider and more institutionalized dependency that pervades all the rich industrial societies; and that is the ever-extending and more total dependency upon money and what it will buy. It is not welfare, but the growing, indeed, it sometimes seems, boundless power of money and our increasing reliance upon it that is the true cause of the loss of autonomy and independence in people. This is what more and more constrains human — as opposed to entrepreneurial — initiative, stifles creativity, directs great areas of activity through the severe filter of the markets. The spoiling, the degrading and exclusion of the freely given, the spontaneously offered, the mutually exchanged service, the monetizing of all the things that human beings have always provided for each other without cost, leads to a slow shrinking of that realm of social intercourse not subject to market and commoditized relationships.

It is a commonplace in the critique of conventional economics that this measures only the cash transactions of the official market economy: all private sector production, employment, consumption, investment and savings; all state and local government expenditure and income. That this is supported by a cash-based 'underground' economy is also recognized. But all this, in turn, rests upon the non-monetized 'counter-economy' as Hazel Henderson calls it,[1] which subsidizes the GNP sector with unpaid labour, do-it-yourself, bartering, social, family and community structures, unpaid household work, parenting, voluntary work, sharing, mutual aid, caring for the majority of the old and sick, home-based production for use, subsistence agriculture. All of this, of course, is sustained by the natural resource base, which absorbs so many of the external costs of the official economy as well as many of those of the counter-economy.

What we have lived through in the West has been the accelerating passage of non-monetized activity into the formal economy. Being on welfare illuminates the extent to which the poor have also been penetrated by this dominant process (and market penetration is precisely what the ugly jargon suggests, a form of violation). For them, the last penny is accounted for before it even reaches their hands. The sense of impotence in the presence of money all used up in advance is what makes of welfare so shaming and unfree an experience. The poor, more than anyone else, feel the limitations of lives in which all human abilities are in the process of being superseded by the supreme ability — the ability to pay. Such processes can occur only in societies in which a majority of the people have access to a rising disposable income; enhanced purchasing power masks the decay of other, human powers and possibilities. While the rich seek out more and more ingenious things to spend their money on, the poor are increasingly stranded, excluded, set apart; and this process is experienced by them as both arbitrary and violent.

One of the reasons why so many young people leave school able neither to deal with the institutions of the society that shelters them, nor to respond to its most elementary demands is because their understanding has been not aroused, but smothered by that superior knowledge that money can buy, and without which, as they will readily tell anyone who asks, you can do nothing; as though money itself were the key to all human activity. Buying and selling have long since ceased to be simple negotiations over daily necessities: they have become the locus where action, invention and creativity are extinguished. The decay of human possibilities is written into the very structure of the market economy. This perhaps helps to explain the increase in crime and violence as society gets richer, a development which has puzzled so many commentators and observers. Far from being 'mindless', it has a precise cause, and is a response, not merely to an absence of material things, but to more violent underlying processes of expropriation and loss.

As we become more dependent upon money, we feel more disempowered, and thus more prey to terror at the thought of any change or diminution of what we have. Our much-cherished 'standard of living' is a kind of life-support system, which in fact indicates very little about the *level* at which we live, but everything about the *way* in which we live. Faith in the rising income attaches us securely to a marketplace which suggests to us, prompts, inspires us even, in the spending of our money. In other words, the marketplace becomes the focus of all hope of increase and enlargement in our lives.

No policy for improving the condition of the poor can be effective if it ignores the wider context. Such a policy would need to look at ways, not of deepening our subordination to the cash economy, but of seeking to release us, where possible, from it. It would propose a process of reclamation of all that we can freely offer each other without the mediation of money; would seek to regain as many freely exchanged services and commodities as may be; it would consider reducing the marketplace to a minimal role in our lives, not allowing it free passage into deeper and deeper places in both heart and imagination.

The projection onto welfare of a major disabling influence on people's lives has gone unchallenged, and for an obvious reason. Because the alternative to the market economy appears so bleak — that state planning of those clumsy mechanisms that fail the people in Socialist countries which are so crude and cumbrous — this does not mean that the market economy is therefore perfection and beyond critical scrutiny. Yet this is what has happened. The inadequacies of existing alternatives make the market system the object of a taboo. Indeed, it is proclaimed as the surest guarantor of our liberties; it is celebrated as the finest ornament of Western civilization.

Beyond a certain level, the extension of market transactions into human lives becomes damaging, corrosive, destructive. Because there is no limit to the needs, satisfactions and consolations which can be turned over to the markets, no individual can ever possess enough money to achieve them all. When everything is for sale, we want everything; and yet we still want for so many things. Security, sufficiency, mutuality remain elusive, for they are not to be found in the realm of monetary satisfactions. Commodity substitution for our deepest yearnings is a profanation of our humanity; and this is what the poor, of both North and South, are trying to say to us.

NOTE

1. H. Henderson, in P. Ekins (ed.), *The Living Economy* (London: Routledge & Kegan Paul, 1986).

Love, justice and sharing: a Christian perspective

Duncan B. Forrester and Dennis Skene

At the level of personal relations some patterns of distribution are compatible with, or even encourage, loving relationships, while other patterns impede or obstruct the growth of love. For example, the relationship between a beggar and the person from whom he solicits alms is so structured as to make virtually impossible an authentic, caring relationship. The passerby is invited to give a paltry sum as a kind of bribe to persuade the beggar to go away and terminate the embarrassing relationship. There is no way within this encounter of meeting the beggar's deeper needs, which are, as with everyone, for care, respect, affection and a recognition of worth as well as for material resources. Neither buying off the beggar with a couple of coins, nor refusing to give alms, should ease the conscience of the passer-by. It is the system which creates and tolerates such poverty, and the parody of authentic caring relationships involved in beggary, which are wrong. They offend against the conviction that the beggar is the neighbour we have been given to love as ourselves.

Christianity is centrally concerned with relationships and with community. Our relationship to God and our relationship to our fellows are regarded as inseparable from one another. Salvation understood as the healing of our relationship with God must show itself in renewed relationships with our fellows. Healed — healthy — relationships must express themselves in the way we share things, in patterns of distribution. Distribution and community are inseparable in the Christian tradition. Hence we can only discuss distribution in the context of community, fellowship, *koinonia*.

From the beginning, Christians have found it necessary to think of God as more like a community than an isolated person, a fellowship held together by the closest and most intimate love and sharing. God's own inner being is love. The God who loves us is love from all eternity. God could not be God without being love; love is the essence of the divine community which Christians call the Holy Trinity — utterly reliable, constant, unchanging. There is no fickleness here, no arbitrary, unpredictable blowing hot and cold. In God, the Father, the Son and the Spirit are in perfect harmony, unity and diversity bound together by love and sharing, a model and source of what community might be and ought to be, fellowship without domination, love expressed in lavish sharing.

God's love 'spills over' upon his creation and particularly upon the women and men made to live in love with God and with one another. But human self-centredness has broken and denied love; human beings have become separated from God and from each other. Alienation, destruction and death are the inevitable consequences (Romans 3:10–18). In Jesus Christ we see the definitive manifestation of the love of God, shown in his sharing of the human condition, entering into the fullest and most costly fellowship with human beings in all their lovelessness and need: God loved the world so much that he gave his only Son (John 3:16). In Jesus Christians believe God is at work restoring community and bringing the lost back into fellowship.

Jesus fulfilled his task by entering the human situation and plumbing its depths. He emptied himself, and took the nature of a slave (Philippians 2:7), that is, he shared in a special way with the poor, the alienated, the marginalized, and the rejected. His identification with people restored for them what they had lost — wholeness, health and dignity, hope and faith: life in its fullness, in fellowship with one another and with God. When he saw crowds of hungry people, harassed and helpless, let down by all those who should have been responsible for their welfare, he was 'moved with compassion' for them, because they were as sheep without a shepherd. The word commonly translated into English as 'moved with compassion' or 'filled with pity' is far stronger in the Greek. There it literally means 'to feel in the guts' — Jesus so shared the lot of the poor, hungry and powerless, of those who were manipulated by the leaders of society, of the despised and fearful, that he felt it as his own, he made their condition and destiny his.

In the gospel stories we see instance after instance illuminating the nature of God's love and showing how closely it is connected with sharing, with restoration of community, and with changes in people's attitudes and behaviour. Again and again we read how Jesus' behaviour surprised and shocked the religious, wealthy and influential people because he drew outcasts, prostitutes, sinners, cheats and all sorts of riff-raff into fellowship with himself, because he shared his table and his food, his time and his heart with people reckoned to be impure, with the marginalized, and with the excluded. He drew the lost and the bewildered with fellowship and shared himself with them. And in this sharing people were encountering the love and life of God. The feeding miracles were exemplary acts of distribution: 'You give them to eat', he said to his disciples (Matthew 14:16). And Jesus shared more than material resources with needy people — although the material food and drink were important both in themselves, as ways of meeting human need, and as signs of the bread of heaven and the water that slakes the thirst for ever. He shared himself, in countless convivial or costly ways, culminating in the cross. And the mode of Jesus' sharing deserves attention; he accepted people in all their diversity, he swept aside stigma to encounter the person within the label, he broke down social divisions and overcame ancient hostilities and suspicions.

Again and again in his teaching Jesus shows how bad distribution obstructs and destroys fellowship with God and with our fellows. In this life a great gulf has been created between the rich man and Lazarus, because the rich man in his luxury did not notice or respond to the needs of poor Lazarus lying at his gate. The gulf could have been bridged by the rich man reaching out to share his material resources with Lazarus as a sign of his love to the neighbour God had given him, and his obedience to the God of justice. But his failure in earthly, human fellowship results after death in an unbridgeable gulf between the rich man and Lazarus, their lots now reversed, and between the rich man and his God (Luke 16:19–31). The story of the Rich Young Ruler also shows in stark terms how wealth unshared obstructs fellowship: it is almost impossible (but with God all things are possible!) for a rich man to enter into the quality of loving, sharing relationships with God and with others which are characteristic of the Kingdom (Mark 10:17–31). The gospel of the Kingdom calls people to participate in the life of God, to enter into the fullness of community. And this participation involves sharing.

The costly reconciliation of the cross was the supreme act of community creation. The second chapter of the Letter to the Ephesians argues that through the blood of Christ those who were far off have been brought near, strangers have been brought into fellowship, and ancient dividing walls of hostility have been broken down. Suspicion and hostility have been brought to an end so that both Jews and Gentiles, and by implication all other antagonistic social groupings, are 'no longer strangers and sojourners, but fellow-citizens with the saints and members of the household of God' (Ephesians 2:13–22). The Letter to the Hebrews speaks of Jesus on the cross bearing abuse outside the camp in solidarity with the rejected, the despised, and the marginalized. And believers are called to join him and them in fellowship there, and share his abuse (Hebrews 13:12–13). Finally, the resurrection of Jesus is God's affirmation that the new community cannot be destroyed and is valid for all.

According to the Genesis creation narratives, and indeed the whole witness of Scripture, God did not create human beings as isolated, self-sufficient entities, but as persons-in-relationship, in fellowship with God, with one another, and with the whole creation.

First, God created people in the context of the whole creation, which Calvin speaks of as 'the theatre of God's glory'. People are set as stewards, responsible to God for the flourishing of other creatures. Human stewardship excludes any idea of absolute ownership: God's gifts in the creation are to be used, enjoyed, cared for, and shared for the sake of community. Only God owns things in an absolute sense; he entrusts things to human beings to be used and distributed in accordance with his will, in fulfilment of his purposes of love. Throughout the Old Testament it is made clear that the creation is to be delighted in, and that material goods of all sorts, including land, are to be used responsibly to help the user and others, particularly the poor and weak, to flourish. Hoarding and accumulation by individuals in such a way that others are deprived of what they need are uniformly disapproved.

Second, God created human beings for fellowship: 'It is not good for the man to be alone' (Genesis 2:18). The image of God, it has been suggested, is reflected in the fellowship between woman and man (Genesis 1:27). In isolation a person is incomplete; only in fellowship, delighting in one another, loving one another, is God's creative purpose capable of fulfilment. And the central relationship is between God and the people God has made. The God-centredness of the creation is emphasized in the institution of the sabbath. According to the story, this is the day when God rested after the work of creation, and ever since it is a time set apart from the labour of life to enjoy the good creation, to delight in fellowship, and to remember that 'goods' are in fact gifts to us rather than the fruit of our efforts on which we have an absolute claim.

Third, the creation story, and in particular the affirmation that people are made in the image of God, is a strong statement that the original and proper situation is one of equality. Everyone is of the same infinite value in the eyes of God. There is in the created order no hierarchy or ranking, no inferiority or superiority, no dominance or subordination. The kind of fellowship which is God's original and final purpose for human beings, the condition for true human flourishing, is that human beings should be treated as equally significant, equally important, equally entitled to love, equally capable of making a distinctive personal contribution to the enrichment of the community.

When Christians affirm the equality of all human beings they are asserting an equality of worth. Each and every individual is entitled to respect. This belief is rooted in the conviction that God has endowed each person with infinite worth as people created in his image. God in Christ gave himself for all equally, and the heart of Christian ethics is to love God and your neighbour as yourself. The neighbour is to be treated as an equal, with his needs and interests put on a par with one's own. This has clear distributional consequences. Absolute equality of resources is not demanded, but there must be such a redistribution as will allow human relationships to flourish. An insistence upon a more equal sharing of goods within the community is one important way in which we can recognize the status and claim of the other people God has given us to care for and love.

The story of the 'Fall' is a way of indicating that a fatal flaw has entered into the created order. People in fact amass belongings at the expense of others, use possessions to destroy fellowship and the justice on which community depends, and arrogantly claim absolute ownership, putting their trust in belongings and attempting to find their security in possessions. This attitude to possessions is denounced in the Bible as idolatry. The communal harmony of creation is disrupted by the lust for power, dominance and control. People become alienated from God and one another, estranged from the creation, which becomes a threat or a tool rather than a delight.

An immensely influential model of what it means to be the People of God is rooted in the story of the journey out of bondage through the desert to the Promised Land. This motif is repeated again and again throughout the Bible, and is still today a powerful image of the kind of community that the Church represents and offers to the world. 'The land flowing with milk and honey' is reached after the testing wilderness experience, but then a further goal lies ahead, and another, and another, until at last the final goal, 'the city, that has foundations, whose builder and maker is God' is attained (Hebrews 11:10).

The pilgrim community does not settle down. The people are on the move towards a goal, and their whole life and activity can only be understood in the light of that goal. On the way, pilgrims discover what it is to be a community, a fellowship of aliens and exiles seeking their true homeland, and kept alive by hope. On the journey they learn to trust, support and understand one another; pilgrims depend on one another, and must have confidence in one another. Estranged and crippled fellowship becomes true community in the pedagogy of pilgrimage.

People on a journey travel light and must sit easy to possessions. It is absolutely necessary for people on the move to share. And the desert is not only a place of threat and danger, but above all a place of scarce resources, in which, the Exodus account is at pains to emphasize, God gives enough for all *provided* it is shared fairly. The stories of the manna — the bread from heaven — and the quails suggest that God provides for the needs of all, but not for greed. God's gifts are to be used, shared and enjoyed, not amassed or stored. The needs of each individual and family were met, so that there was neither scarcity nor waste. Hoarders are frustrated — 'He that gathered much had nothing over and he that gathered little had no lack' (Exodus 16:18). Accumulation is unnecessary and impossible — a kind of reminder that security lies in relationships with God and one's fellows rather than in amassing of possessions.

At the heart of the life of the pilgrim community is worship, the celebration of their relationship with God and with one another. God is with them, but is not a possession of the community. And yet the people again and again turn from God and from their goal, longing for the 'fleshpots of Egypt', the security of bondage, and abandoning the risky quest for the Promised Land. The height of their turning away from God was when, in Moses' absence, they took their jewellery and made a Golden Calf, a god, who was their possession, their plaything — the very epitome of the idolatry of material things, or riches. Here was mammon worship at its starkest and its most degrading, but also at its most obvious: then as now there were more subtle and unsuspected ways to worship material things and deny the living God who leads his people to their goal.

Going beyond equality

John Atherton

Without reasonable access to material resources most people cannot grow into the fuller maturity which is so intimately a part of human fulfilment. In society today, income is the most important of these resources although in no way does this detract from the increasing significance for living of health, education and housing.

Most moralists and Christians underestimate this contribution of income to human life. At best they give it a purely instrumental value as the means for purchasing the essentials of life. At worst, and indeed normally, they regard it with moral suspicion. Their view of what is necessary for human fulfilment has centred instead on the human spirit, on the virtues of freedom, courage and creativity but often detached from the realities of ordinary life. They have rarely made moral sense of the value of income for human living.

The understanding of the poor beginning to emerge from this analysis, corrects this moral imbalance in three ways. First, it reveals the supreme importance of adequate incomes for sustaining any kind of normal and moral life *in contemporary society*. Survey after survey has shown that what the poor lack most is money. To neglect that reality is to base attitudes, theories and policies on defective premises. Second, it points to the importance of economic resisting power for movement towards fuller lives. Without such a power-base it becomes virtually impossible to have any effective say over matters which either personally affect one's life or the running of society as a whole. Third, it suggests that a concern for incomes is an essential and proper vehicle through which values and preferences are promoted. Money as adequate benefits and wages becomes 'a symbol for a society which enables a man to live his life without fear of poverty and family disaster. Other things are as important as freedom from want. But a society that guards its members from want is likely to do its other tasks well. Social security has thus become a touchstone for the future'. It recognizes income as the supremely relevant moral currency for a wage society.

If income is so important for understanding what it means to be fully human, then what would an adequate basic income for all amount to? Such an understanding of income has to take account of at least two things. On the one hand, it needs to recognize that any estimate of income levels must relate to generally accepted standards in a particular society at a particular time. On the other hand, it needs to accept that a basic income is preferable to past and present concerns for minimum incomes. A concern for minimum standards inevitably generates a minimalist view of humanity which is detrimental to us all. A basic income guaranteed for everyone provides an essential base from which human fulfilment can be pursued. It does not guarantee fulfilment but at least it makes it possible.

What does such a basic income mean? It suggests an income sufficient to guarantee physical survival, to give people the basic means for making and carrying out decisions, and to allow the formation of free and equal relationships within the family and society. In other words it would provide the generally accepted standards of food, clothing, housing and heating, and the ability to participate in the normal activities of that society. It would enable a person to live a self-respecting life as 'a matter of right not grace'.

A basic income suggests, too, the importance of developing detailed and realistic costings of all the matters which are essential for any kind of pursuit of human fulfilment in contemporary society. Such a costing will inevitably relate to more than the traditional poor. It will also need to take account of lower one-income families with young children who are often vulnerable to poverty even when on incomes of £5–6000 per annum. It will mean, too, replacing the costings of Rowntree, Beveridge and Supplementary Benefit with the more accurate estimates of income needs currently being developed by people like Piachaud and Townsend. But it will also mean in all probability developing a form of payment which combines income payment with a taxation system. Various ways of achieving this have been discussed over the years. For example, it could be achieved by guaranteeing to every citizen through a negative income tax system certain cash benefits. If the allowed benefits even with the addition of earnings are less than a certain level then instead of paying tax you would receive benefits sufficient to take you up to the accepted base-line. Everyone would therefore receive a basic non-means-tested income to which for example, part-time earnings could be added. (It is a major nonsense that the retired are allowed to earn significant sums and dignity in addition to their basic pensions, while the long-term unemployed remain inactive and in penury because they are essentially limited to their supplementary benefit.)

If the pressure of growing poverty and rapid industrial change is questioning old ways of putting and doing things, then how can we move beyond traditional ideals and values like equality? Move beyond them we must, since so often, and especially in the case of equality, they produce either-or stances which fuel those divisions associated with the existence of poverty in an affluent society. Yet any movement forward would be unwise to neglect equality's emphasis on the quality of relationships between people and communities. How therefore can ways be found to foster relationships between social groups, areas and individuals which both avoid and reduce divisions and promote common concerns? How can people learn to handle together those redistributions necessary to initiate and sustain such changed relationships?

Some of the answers to these questions have begun to emerge from this study of poverty. An examination of the predicament of the poor in an affluent society suggests an understanding of what it means to be human which is relevant to poor and affluent alike. It includes three important points about relationships and how they can be encouraged to develop which could contain truths about relationships which move beyond values like equality.

First, the emerging understanding of what makes people people asserts the supreme importance of men and women as human beings above any recognition of them in relation to their occupation or income. It points to a view of people which moves through and yet always beyond material resources. It therefore emphasizes that essential humanity which all men and women share. In no way contradicting the reality of the individual, it rather affirms 'not only that exceptional men should be free to exercise their exceptional power, but that common men should be free to make the most of their common humanity'.

Second, this understanding of people underwrites the importance of certain values traditionally associated with promoting their humanity, but fashions them through the realities of ordinary life. For example, it defines freedom as having the resources to choose; it defines it in terms of increasing 'the range of alternatives open to ordinary people, and the capacity of the latter to follow their own preferences in choosing between them'. Such access to resources and relationships inevitably requires a more equitable sharing of opportunities if people are to grow into individual and social fulfilment. It requires, with regard to income distribution, the recognition of minimum and maximum income levels. By reformulating in these ways traditional values like freedom and equality, this understanding of an essential humanity also allows people to avoid not simply some of the conflicting views centred on these two values but also that wasteful demand to be committed to either one or the other. It is neither particularly helpful nor accurate to argue that liberty is more important than equality, or vice versa. A view of the essential humanity of people is needed which moves through and beyond both.

Third, this understanding of people shows the vital importance of finding ways to redistribute access to resources. Although individuals 'differ profoundly ... in capacity and character', they are equally entitled 'as human beings to consideration and respect'. The well-being of a society is therefore only likely to be increased 'if it so plans its organization that, whether their powers are great or small, all its members may be *equally* enabled to make the best of such powers as they possess'. The redistribution of access to employment, housing, education, income and wealth can mean nothing less than this.

In each of these three points about relationships ways are offered of translating problems associated with poverty into ideals and values associated with promoting the fulfilment of men and women. They offer everyone the opportunity to form purposes in life, to engage in relationships, and accordingly to nourish self-development. They move beyond values like equality to a view of relationships increasingly influenced by a growing commitment to a wider and more common good based on our understanding of humanity. They translate what are fundamentally religious and moral matters into today's society through categories which emerge from taking the poor seriously. They offer to all a view of what people really are and can be.

Facing up to poverty and industrial change has driven us to examine their implications for an understanding of essential humanity. To address such an underlying issue in this way clearly affects a whole range of matters. For example, it confirms the importance of the reasons why we are involved with poverty, based as they are on the nature and significance of people. It suggests too, the need to re-formulate the motivation and shape of practical caring and what it means for society. ... However, perhaps the most important implication is for the Christian understanding of what is involved in people being people in contemporary society. Clearly, a Christian anthropology will include far more than what this study reveals. Yet what it has indicated is the supreme importance for people of the availability of resources and the opportunity to develop relationships. That understanding has been based upon the reality of actual human experience and not upon abstract theories or false perceptions and attitudes.

To reach this conclusion is of profound theological significance. For the importance of these assertions about basic humanity and its fulfilment is derived for Christians from the understanding that Christian belief and discipleship are concerned precisely with the realities conveyed by these assertions about resources and relationships. It is this belief and these realities which invest the assertions with a supreme significance. *It is therefore through them, and indeed principally through them, that God is to be found and served.* Addressing them in this belief is what Christianity and Church life must now be about.

The effect of this conclusion on Christian anthropology is far-reaching. It means that the assertions about the importance of resources and relationships for human living should now be considered in relation to all the central images which make up the Christian view of man. The traditional two-fold belief that people are made in God's image and people are also sinners needs unpacking into the current scene with the help of these contemporary assertions. Such an approach to the understanding of what it means to be human becomes a more comprehensive and realistic assessment of the nature and potential of people in relation to today's pressing social and human problems. Without an analysis of the poor and the development of the test of 'poverty impact statements' that conclusion would neither have been reached nor maintained. That is why the poor must be taken seriously. Without them none will attain to a full understanding and defence of what it means to be human.

Relationships of justice

Hilary Russell

Poverty fetters people socially and psychologically as well as materially. It goes beyond the lack of physical resources. It can also mean being trapped; lacking opportunity, fulfilment and security; having no recognized contribution to make. It can mean living in appalling housing in a blighted neighbourhood, suffering from constant chest infections as a result of damp conditions or asthma aggravated by a polluted environment. It can mean being in bed and breakfast accommodation, isolated but also lacking privacy; living, cooking and sleeping in one room, without anywhere safe for the children to play or quiet for them to do homework. It can mean always running short at the end of the week, having a restricted diet, never being able to afford to have a holiday or treat the children. It can mean feeling on the scrap-heap and humiliated by having to depend upon state benefits or handouts from charities, family or friends.

Poverty arises not because poor people are inherently lazy or incompetent. No doubt individuals are, but so are those who are not poor. It stems from the economic and social character of society. There is now a division between those who are manual or non-manual workers in primary labour market jobs and those who are not. On the whole, the former will have access to decent housing, schooling and health care. However, the long-term unemployed and those in insecure, low-paid employment are increasingly excluded not only from a sufficient income but from these other essential components of an adequate lifestyle in the Britain of the 1990s. There are young people who do not know what it is like to have a job; women struggling to bring children up alone; ethnic minorities for whom exclusion is reinforced by discrimination; and those whose poverty and insecurity are carried into old age. These are the groups most dependent upon welfare and consequently most vulnerable to welfare cuts and sanctions.

Given this analysis of poverty, it has to be treated as a systemic problem, not as something marginal. It requires preventive change not just amelioration. The reason for the failure of so many attempted remedies is that they have tried to contain the problem (and the poor) and patch matters up rather than attack the root causes. To realize that poverty and growing inequality are symptoms of a malfunctioning society opens the way to recognizing that arguments for eliminating poverty do not rest on compassion or social justice alone. There are also sound pragmatic reasons based on the self-interest of the non-poor majority.[1] These are concerned with the social and economic waste and the social fragmentation that result from a divided society.

Poverty and exclusion are extremely expensive, both directly in terms of transfer payments — social security benefits — and indirectly in the opportunity costs of failing to develop human potential to the full. There is a common interest in cutting these costs and, therefore, in providing social frameworks which will maximize the opportunities for individuals to develop their talents. In economic terms, this is expressed as human capital which is recognized as a vital component of national competitiveness. When Howard Davies, Director-General of the Confederation of British Industries (CBI), called for a concerted attack on poverty and investment in better education and training to bring the long-term unemployed closer to the labour market, he did so because it makes economic sense. He wanted to close Britain's skills gap with the rest of the world.[2]

This argument goes against the thesis of the political right for whom efficiency necessarily leads to inequalities, so that society faces a trade off between equality and efficiency. They argue that redistribution policies have disincentive effects and lead to loss of efficiency. However, even in solely economic terms, this is disputable. In several policy areas, redistributing the resources of society can result in positive gains for all because

> the impact of the redistribution on the productive contributions of the poor leads to greater economic efficiency. This benefits not only those who can now find work, or work more productively: there are external effects in this case too as tax revenues rise and benefit expenditures fall, allowing lower tax rates (or better public services) for all.[3]

Redistribution here applies beyond income. Although transfer payments lessen inequality, they only alleviate the problem, not solve it. Insofar as they also stigmatize and subordinate people, welfare measures can exacerbate inequality and reinforce feelings of a lack of self-worth even while they relieve some of the material pressure. On the other hand, redistributing the means for people to participate fully in the economy and society would remove the need for perpetual income redistribution. It would also release society from the burden of costs accruing from the results of material deprivation — the costs of exclusion — such as mental and physical ill health and anti-social behaviour.

This leads on to the other line of pragmatic argument in favour of minimizing poverty, which focuses on the social disorder that follows in the wake of growing levels of poverty and inequality. Perhaps in a rigidly hierarchical society, inequalities could be accepted as legitimate, with the poor man quite content to be at the rich man's castle gate, so that social cohesion was not threatened. However, in a society which apparently offers mobility and opportunity, those at the wrong end of a widening divide are more likely to express some form of resentment. Such discontent is scarcely politicized in this country but is expressed in crime and conflict. Thus it is in the majority interest to curb socially divisive inequalities.

So far the response has been largely one of trying metaphorically and literally to pull up the drawbridge and shelter behind it, which can only be effective in the short term, if at all. At one extreme, there are 'no-go' areas; at the other, private enclaves of high-tech security. Stores and shopping precincts are monitored by cameras. Homes are fitted with alarms, window locks and security lights. Chain-link fences encircle factories and industrial estates. Security guards patrol them. It is all too easy for these physical security measures to be seen as the 'keep out' signs of a wider exclusion for those on the wrong side of the fence, shut out from the economic activity inside and the material security or social recognition that goes with it.

Not only are the financial costs of exclusion escalating, but other sorts of damage are taking place. Shops close down because of repeated break-ins. Potential investors are deterred from bringing their businesses to areas which have, or are reputed to have, a high crime rate. People are afraid to go out at night, or leave their homes unattended, or live alone. Mistrust grows and fear of the stranger. Although very often it is those living in the poorest neighbourhoods who are also the chief victims of this phenomenon, the consequences of the boredom and resentment of those people cut off from economic success diminish life for everyone.

> If we listened to the poorest, not only those living on minimum income but those who never take part in anything, those who feel inadequate and excluded from mainstream society, they would reveal everything in our society that crushes or tramples people down. They would ensure that all change, all progress and all political trends are used for everyone's benefit. Their experience could teach us the demands of a true democracy, where all citizens have rights, where all citizens are heard, because they are human beings.[4]

If poverty is rooted in economic and social structures and processes, action against poverty must address it on a number of levels — access to education, training and job opportunities; housing and nutrition; enhancing self-esteem and the confidence to participate in community life. In sum, this means reasserting the full citizenship of those in poverty. The material base for citizenship assumes an interrelationship between three major institutions: the labour market for employment, the family for practical and emotional care, and the welfare state as a source of cash and services.[5] A large section of this book [Poverty Close to Home] has been concerned with the major changes that have taken place within these institutions as we have moved from an industrial to a post-industrial society, and their profound implications for the intensification of poverty:

- The labour market has polarized; patterns of male and female involvement in the labour market altered: insecure employment and unemployment have grown. At present all the signs are that with a continuation of current policies, unemployment will remain around at least 2 to 3 million.
- Accompanying these labour market developments and the increasing preoccupation with material consumption in advanced industrial societies has been disruption in former patterns of family life. Families are more likely to be physically distanced, with grandparents, aunts and uncles less

likely to be on hand to share in child care and adult children less available to give support to ageing parents. More marriages break down. More people remarry and start second families. More children are apparently at risk of neglect and abuse.

- The welfare state is overstretched as a result of higher demands on it and reduced public funding. Some of its functions have been hived off to other agencies or put within the realms of private provision. As a result, although it has been a significant buffer against further erosion in social cohesion, people are increasingly being asked to find alternative routes to meeting basic material, health, education and social care needs. The poor lose out again.

All these changes have altered the patterns of dependence and independence. Citizenship for all, therefore, needs to be rethought and poverty addressed via these institutions.

Materially, there are two key challenges: to give people labour market security and to tackle their right to a decent income. Both depend to some extent upon reconnecting the wealth creation in the hands of private companies and large, often multi-national corporations, with the rest of society. It is not a matter of disparaging this sort of wealth creation — a criticism sometimes (justly or unjustly) levelled at church leaders. Rather it is a question of recognizing that it has a social as well as a private role. It arises out of, and is made possible by, society as a whole and must feed back into society's overall well-being. In the past, a large part of the connection was in the mass employment industry provided. However, while advanced technology has increased productivity, it has also cut the traditional link between investment and jobs. Higher investment is now more likely to be labour saving than labour generating. We saw this first in manufacturing, but it applies increasingly in any information processing situation. In other words, wealth creation (in the narrow sense) requires a smaller employment base. It therefore provides a living for fewer people, with a consequent loss of taxation and spending power. This results in a smaller revenue stream to the public purse to fund other activities, necessary for the public good and which would themselves generate more employment and promote greater money circulation. We cannot just write off the public sector as 'unproductive'. It *is* productive of many essential and desirable social goods. Rather it is a question of rebalancing the way that the whole economy works for social as well as private ends.

Within the labour market, most attempts to get people into work rely upon supply-side policies, such as improving infrastructure, developing human resources through training programmes, promoting regional policies. Nevertheless, the question of whether full employment is achievable still has to be asked. And, what would full employment mean in today's type of labour market? Would it still rely considerably on part-time and insecure jobs which on their own could not provide a sufficient level or security of income? The report of the Commission on Social Justice summarizes proposals for the reduction and eventual elimination of long-term (over 12 months) unemployment. It gives seven conditions:[6]

- a high and sustainable growth rate in demand;

- low inflation entailing pegging average money earnings in line with productivity;
- a large and competitive tradable sector to ensure a full employment level of demand;
- greater intensity of employment through expanding non-tradable, labour-intensive sectors, such as personal services, and greater flexibility in hours of employment;
- re-integrating the long-term unemployed into one labour market using measures such as high quality help with education and training, wage subsidies, childcare, sponsoring small-scale entrepreneurs, regenerating the most disadvantaged areas;
- developing tax and benefit systems providing incentives instead of disincentives through greater flexibility, less reliance on means-tested benefits and a gradual reduction in taxes on employment, especially less skilled and lower paid jobs;
- a new balance between employment and family across life cycles through arrangements such as employment breaks for men and women for family needs or additional training and flexible retirement packages.

Clearly such an agenda needs translating into firm policy proposals, but at least its principles are sufficiently broad to address this basic need to re-align employment, the family and the welfare state.

The second challenge is to ensure that everyone has a decent income. There are a number of proposals for basic income schemes to give each individual a tax-free state payment, irrespective of employment or family status, age or gender.[7] Such basic income would be 'a citizenship-based share of national income'.[8] The idea is attractive not just as an anti-poverty strategy but also because of its underlying principle of ethical collectivism, 'the idea that we are all equal inheritors of society's productive capacity and contributors to society's current production whether through full-time or part-time employment, through personal, familial or other unpaid carework, or in other ways'.[9] But proposed schemes tend to suffer from problems of complexity and practicality as well as affordability. In any case, a single policy instrument cannot solve all the interwoven problems associated with poverty. Such arguments for distributional justice in income cannot be detached from issues to do with the labour market, the family and other aspects of the welfare state.

Alongside these economic and social trends, there has been a change in the nature of politics.[10] Geoff Mulgan argues that politics have suffered a demise for a number of reasons. One is the passing of the Cold War. The rubble of the Berlin Wall also buried the old competing ideologies. While it had communism to oppose, the anachronism of the New Right was obscured. Although at first apparently vindicated by the Soviet collapse, New Right economics have since been found to have few answers to post-industrial forms of economic organization and political expectation. Also, the nation state is now a less obvious vehicle for dealing with many political issues. For example, basic income schemes tend to take national sovereignty for granted whereas nowadays such proposals should consider the future of income policies and rights within the European Union. Some issues, too, have extended into hitherto non-political arenas. Global economic and ecological questions transcend national boundaries; at the other extreme, personal lifestyle, gender and identity, domestic and neighbourhood issues slip through the national net. Politics has become either everything or nothing. All issues are political yet formal politics and political institutions have weakened. In other words, the context of politics has changed and with that change comes the need to redefine — re-imagine — democracy and democratic structures.

This is closely related to the issue of citizenship because those with less economic stake in society are also those with least say and those for whom democratic participation risks being an empty ideal. In any case the national picture has changed over the past fifteen years. Much Government policy in the 1980s, though it purported to minimize the role of the state, in fact centralized power by curbing the autonomy and spending power of local authorities and constraining other intermediary institutions such as trade unions. On the other hand, many local authorities are moving towards greater decentralization in their management of local services, taking planning and implementation nearer to residents. There have also been some urban policy moves by Government towards bringing in 'the community' as a full and active partner, though such talk of 'the community' should not distract from the more fundamental issues of citizenship. There is a long way to go to make such participative democracy a reality for most people and to bridge the credibility gap which often exists at both parliamentary and local council level between elected members and their constituents.

NOTES

1. See for example, Geoff Mulgan, *Politics in an Antipolitical Age* (Cambridge: Polity Press, 1994), pp. 48ff; Andrew Glyn and David Miliband (eds), *Paying for Inequality: The Economic Cost of Social Justice* (London: IPPR/Rivers Oram Press, 1994); *Social Justice: Strategies for National Renewal*, The Report of the Commission on Social Justice (New York: Vintage, 1994).
2. Howard Davies in an interview before the 1994 CBI Annual Conference, reported in Larry Elliott, 'CBI chief urges action on poverty', *Guardian*, 3 November 1994.
3. Glyn and Miliband, *Paying for Inequality*, p. 14.
4. John Penet, *ATD Fourth World Journal*, Spring 1994, p. 3.
5. Maurice Roche, *Rethinking Citizenship: Welfare Ideology and Change in Modern Society* (Cambridge: Polity Press, 1992).
6. *Social Justice: Strategies for National Renewal*, pp. 155–7.
7. See for example, Hermione Parker, *Instead of the Dole* (London: Macmillan, 1989); T. Walker, *Basic Income* (London: Marian Boyars, 1989).
8. Bill Jordan, *The Common Good: Citizenship, Morality and Self-Interest* (Oxford: Basil Blackwell, 1989), p. 119.
9. Roche, *Rethinking Citizenship*, p. 185.
10. See Mulgan, *Politics in an Antipolitical Age*, pp. 7ff.

Further reading

Frank Field, *Losing Out: The Emergence of Britain's Underclass* (Oxford: Blackwell, 1989). Analyses the roots — cuts in social benefits, poor education, wealth redistribution from poor to rich through tax changes and middle-class welfare, long-term unemployment, reductions in manual jobs, growth in part-time working — and the dangers of the creation of a class of people who are increasingly unable to participate as citizens and consumers in mainstream society.

Justin Gonzalez, *Faith and Wealth: A History of Early Christian Ideas on the Origin, Significance, and Use of Money* (San Francisco: Harper and Row, 1990). Explores the themes of poverty and wealth, property and ownership in the New Testament and the early Church Fathers demonstrating the consistency of early Christian warnings against wealth accumulation as both a spiritual and a social problem, and the call of Christians to relieve the effects of such accumulation amongst the poor.

Paul Harrison, *Inside the Inner City: Life Under the Cutting Edge* (London: Penguin, 1983). A powerful account of the reality of poverty in Britain in the 1980s using personal testimony and academic analysis to chart the down-side of affluence and the meanness of the political response to the persistence of poverty in Britain.

Michael B. Katz, *The Undeserving Poor: From the War on Poverty to the War on Welfare* (New York: Pantheon Books, 1989). Charts the rise and fall of the stigmatization of poverty, the racial dimension of the underclass debate: Katz identifies contradictions in the statistical evidence on which underclass theories are based, and argues for a more sociologically complex understanding of poverty and cultural enclaves.

Joanna Mack and Stewart Lansley, *Poverty in Britain in the 1980s* (London: George Allen and Unwin, 1985). Important collection of evidence of the deepening problems of the poor in Britain in the 1980s indicating in particular declining health amongst the poor and their children which give the lie to claims that absolute poverty has been eradicated.

David Mealand, *Poverty and Expectation in the Gospels* (London: SPCK, 1980). An excellent introduction to the teachings of Jesus in the Gospels on poverty, property and the New Testament vision of the Kingdom of God as a just and equitable society.

Charles Murray, *The Emerging British Underclass* (London: Institute for Economic Affairs, 1987). Trenchant and polemical statement of the cultural theory of poverty, identifying illegitimacy, crime and unemployment as the key determinants of poverty, but also identifying these with the immorality of the poor, and in particular the demise of two-parent families, the decline of respect for persons and property, and the absence of a work ethic. The book also includes critical responses to this thesis.

Not Just for the Poor: Christian Perspectives on the Welfare State. Report of the Social Policy Committee of the Board for Social Responsibility (London: Church House Publishing, 1986). Theologically and sociologically informed defence of the Welfare State which argues that decent income provision through state benefits, in a context of high and continuing unemployment, is essential to prevent society from becoming dangerously divided.

John S. Pobee, *Who Are the Poor? The Beatitudes as a Call to Community* (Geneva: WCC, 1987). In a luminous theological exposition of the New Testament parables and gospels relating to poverty Pobee contrasts the African understanding of community, which he finds in the New Testament, with the denial of relationality and community of modern affluent societies with their extreme economic divisions.

Jim Wallis, *The Soul of Politics: A Practical and Prophetic Vision for Change* (London: HarperCollins, 1995). Argues that the biblical option for the poor requires a new reformation in which churches put the poor at the centre of their policy decisions and mission programmes and remake the economic and spiritual connections between rich and poor both locally and globally which affluence and secularism have hidden or denied.

Margaret Walsh, 'Here's coping', in Peter Sedgwick (ed.), *God in the City* (London: Mowbray, 1995) pp. 27–51. Personal stories from a UPA in Wolverhampton which illustrate powerfully the worsening reality of poverty resulting from reductions in spending on housing and reductions in the value of benefits in the 1980s and 1990s.

6

Power in the city

After this he went down to Capernaum with his mother, his brothers, and his disciples, and they stayed there a few days. As it was near the time of the Jewish Passover, Jesus went up to Jerusalem. In the temple precincts he found the dealers in cattle, sheep, and pigeons, and the money-changers seated at their tables. He made a whip of chords and drove them out of the temple, sheep, cattle, and all. He upset the tables of the money-changers, scattering their coins. Then he turned on the dealers in pigeons: 'Take them out of here,' he said; 'do not turn my Father's house into a market.'

His disciples recalled the words of scripture: 'Zeal for your house will consume me.' The Jews challenged Jesus: 'What sign can you show to justify your action?' 'Destroy this temple,' Jesus replied, 'and in three days I will raise it up again.' The Jews said, 'It has taken forty-six years to build this temple. Are you going to raise it up again in three days?' But the temple he was speaking of was his body. After his resurrection his disciples recalled what he had said and they believed the scripture and the words that Jesus had spoken.

(John 2:12–22)

Faith in the City

Individual responsibility and self-reliance are excellent objectives. The nation cannot do without them. But pursuit of them must not damage a collective obligation and provision for those who have no choice, or whose choices are at best forced ones. We believe that at present too much emphasis is being given to individualism, and not enough to collective obligation. In the absence of a spirit of collective obligation, or the political will to foster it, there is no guarantee that the pursuit of innumerable individual self-interests will add up to an improvement of the common good. (9.46)

We must question whether, at a time when our economy is in transition to an uncertain future, a dogmatic and inflexible macro-economic stance is appropriate. We believe that a more open debate is needed about the type of society present economic policies are shaping. We recommend that the Church and its bishops should play a full part in such a debate, for the Christian Gospel sets values in relation to the dignity and worth of each individual, and in relation to human society, against which economic dogma must be judged. (9.52)

Introduction

In the Christian tradition political power is not seen as inherently or inevitably evil for the legitimacy of political sovereignty arises from the collective quest for the common good and public virtue, and the collective restraint of sin and selfishness (Wogoman). The modern democratic ideals of the universal franchise and the collective quest for the common good through the institutions of the state derive from Christian polity and Christian ethics. The location of sovereignty in the popular will of the people as well as in the authority of God was one of the central political insights of the charismatic leaders of the radical reformation (Rowland). The concept of the common good as the goal of the public and collective arrangements of human society is connected with the medieval and Christendom tradition of natural law. This tradition is recast in the modern idea of civil society. The institutions of education, culture, religion, and charity, partnered and supported by the institutions of governance, engage individual citizens in relationships of civic and private virtue which sustain the widest possible participation in the good life of all citizens. Civil society is not to be identified with the institutions of governance for in participating in the civic domain in local communities, citizens create intermediate institutions which are more reflexive and participative to the needs and choices of citizens than central governments elected at periodic intervals.

An alternative, and certainly sub-Christian, model of governance is that which presumes that citizens are fundamentally self-interested, that self-interest is the primary mode of social relationships and that the exchange system of commodities, labour and cash rewards — the free market — is the best institution for mediating most human interactions. The role of the state on this model is the *laissez-faire* one of minimizing constraints on the wealth-creating capacity of the exchange system, and of restraining harm rather than of promoting the common good (Wogoman).

The modern tradition of Christian socialism was developed in response to the emergence of such *laissez-faire* ideas in the nineteenth century and its leaders and ideals have played a significant role in British political life, and in providing a vision of a more just society for many clergy and lay people in inner city churches, particularly in the liberal catholic tradition. Christian socialists argue that the distribution of natural resources, especially land and the rewards for labour, should not be left to 'free' markets which tend to concentrate power and wealth in the hands of the few but rather that wealth distribution and wages should both be regulated by government so as to promote equality and the good of the whole community, and particularly of the poorest. Christian socialists also argue that ordinary people are best able to govern themselves and that the purpose of the state should not be to centralize the powers of governance (as in Marxist socialism) but to enable all persons to share power so they may participate effectively in the governance of their own communities and their own lives. Christian socialists are committed to the idea that the purpose of government is to contribute to the common good, conceived as a state of being in which all people find a measure of dignity and control over their own lives by having access to the necessities of life, and not just the rich or those in full employment (Bryant; Field).

The Christian socialist conception of society finds strong echoes in the developing tradition of twentieth-century Catholic social teaching (*The Common*

Good), and is fundamentally at variance with the currently fashionable idea that people are essentially self-interested individuals and the purpose of governance is simply to limit the potential harms of the expression of self-interest rather than actively to promote the common good. The judgement that persons are fundamentally self-interested has received some support from Christian realists as well as advocates of the priority of free markets. However, as feminists in particular point out, it does not accord with our earliest experiences of care and of personal formation in the family and in other relationships and networks of friendship and mutuality. People will act in ways which promote the common good in civil society as well as in the family or amongst close friends provided they can see that their efforts, and even sacrifices, do indeed promote the good, rather than being used by others for economic gain (Dorrien; *The Common Good*).

Many advocates of both free markets and of Christian socialism are agreed that where the state becomes too large and centralized, it is less likely to promote the common good and quite likely to foster dependency and domination. But, equally, where unrestrained markets create situations in which millions are excluded from mainstream society through unemployment and poverty, then many would agree that markets need more collective regulation and direction from the political and civil domains. At their best, markets, civil society and the institutions of governance represent in different ways the collective will of the people because they represent an aggregation of the relationships sustained and decisions made with respect to daily needs and aspirations. The danger, particularly in relation to markets and the institutions of the state, is that they are capable of creating and sustaining situations in which significant minorities of people are excluded from making creative decisions through which they can effect control over their own lives, and are hence also excluded from effective participation in civil society and political community. Markets and states, at their worst, can also be highly damaging to the networks of care, family, community and sociality through which civil society is sustained and the quest for the common good collectively pursued.

The resurgence of free market social models in the last twenty years in Britain and North America reflects a desire to release the creative capacities of individuals to order their own lives, families and communities. This freeing up of the creative or enterprising individual from institutional constraints has released new energies which have been mobilized in the regeneration of cities, not least in the range of new bottom-up structures such as tenant management of housing, or parent management of schools. This new mode of active citizenship has put more power in the hands of householders, parents, voluntary groups and local businesses, and has been an important corrective to the failures of local government in many cities in Britain to deliver responsive public services, not least in UPA public housing areas.

However, the shift towards the creative individual has also been accompanied by a redistribution of power and wealth from the poor to the rich, and by growth in private corporate power over workers and citizens. The institutions of civil society, the bonds of shared responsibility which protect children and vulnerable groups from the vicissitudes of markets or states, have been eroded by the deregulation of labour markets and reduced public services which have disproportionately affected the poor and the low paid. This collapse of civil society is evidenced in increasing public disorder, with riots a regular feature in many cities in Britain in the 1980s and early 1990s, rising crime, moral collapse, homelessness

and educational failure, and a collapse of the public service ethic. These social
consequences affect the quality of life and personal security of every citizen of
Britain's divided cities, and not just the poor. They have also produced growing
political alienation, as evidenced in the low participation of people who live in
UPA areas in the electoral process. The alienation of a significant minority of
people from the public life of the nation is directly connected to the failure of a
vision of the common good which links the interests of the rich and the poor, of
the suburb and the UPA (Jenkins).

But this failure also represents a spiritual crisis. It is the clearest evidence of
practical atheism in our secular culture for where we no longer worship a God
who is just and good, and who participates as Spirit in the struggle for justice and
goodness in creation and human life, we no longer find it possible to believe in a
conception of the common good as that end towards which all our endeavours
should be directed (Dorrien). The god of the market sustains belief in the law of
self-interest and a pessimism about the capacity of humans to care for one
another which is deeply damaging to democracy and community (Wogoman)
while belief in the God who is in Jesus and has not abandoned the world to sin
sustains a more hopeful and co-operative vision of society which fosters participation in civil society.

The story of Jesus overturning the tables of the money-changers and traders
provides one of the clearest indications in the Gospels that our Lord associated
spirituality with political involvement, and in particular with challenges to the
structures of money and religion which deny people creative control over their
own lives (Rowland). In this action Jesus 'turns the tables' on the powerful, using
the symbols of their own power, and the symbolic space of the temple, to
denounce the powers that be. The story of the closing of a dangerous battery-
breaking factory in the midst of a UPA housing estate in Wolverhampton is an
example of this linkage between faith community and civic action (**Walsh**). Like
Jesus in the Temple, the residents of Heathtown identify the source of power
which is oppressing them and symbolically challenge this power at its source,
calling, chairing and controlling meetings in city conference rooms with councillors. They present expert evidence which subverts the expertise of the powerful,
and they adopt partnerships with all power-holders whose interests coincide
with the good of this community.

The great danger of political involvement for Christians is the tendency to
identify particular political projects or social structures as inherently Christian
and redemptive. Alongside a hope that effective participation in civil society can
advance human flourishing, Christians have traditionally retained a realistic
estimate of the possibilities for evil as well as good in collective economic and
political arrangements of whatever ideological hue. In parts of Jesus' teaching,
and in the writings of Paul, we encounter the language of the powers, as those
fallen forces which tend to dominate and oppress human life (**Wink**). Paul, like
his Jewish contemporaries, sees these powers at times as fallen supernatural
beings or forces whose actions determine the outcomes of human existence. But
at other times he sees the powers as those tendencies which are operative within
the structures and systems of the world order, and particularly in political
systems where one group comes to dominate and exclude another. Paul's account
of Christian community as the body of Christ in 1 Corinthians 12–14 indicates
that these kinds of oppressive polities are not to be copied by churches (**Yoder**).
Christian communities are supposed to manifest a counter-politics in which the

weak are heard alongside the strong, and in which every member is an active participant.

This political concern for the weak is also evident in Paul's argument that Jesus turns the tables on the powers, supernatural and social, not by a show of force and violence, but on the contrary by the non-violent weakness and foolishness of the cross. Jesus allows the powers to put him to death even as he is shown to have reminded the political power in the person of Pilate that his power ultimately comes from God (John 19:11). But in the resurrection of Jesus the authority of God over the powers is re-established, the cosmic powers are disarmed and 'captivity is led captive' (Colossians 2:16). The cross is the ultimate symbol of the turning of the tables where the powerless and vulnerable Messiah is put to death and yet overcomes through this very powerlessness. The powers which do the deed are ultimately trounced by the power of the Spirit of the risen Christ who through the Apostles turns the world and its powers upside down.

The cross has been an archetype for symbolic acts of non-violent resistance to the powers throughout Christian history. Symbolic action against the powerful authorities of the city — whether a political party or heads of private corporations — can have an effect way beyond the size of the action itself. And this kind of symbolic action is particularly significant for oppressed and marginal groups who do not have access to the substantial resources of a national political party or private or public corporation.

The identification of God with the excluded in the crucifixion of Jesus, and the emphasis of Paul on the weakest members of the body of Christ, both undergird the tradition that Christians should judge the economic and political arrangements of secular society on the basis of whether they exclude or incorporate the poor and the vulnerable from participation in the good life (*The Common Good*). But this represents an equal and perhaps even sharper challenge to the churches which claim to follow Jesus and Paul. The Church at various times in its history has embraced patterns of leadership, management and power which are as hierarchical, centralized and exclusive as any which may be fostered by secular political ideologies and practices. Churches must reform their own political and organizational structures so as to exemplify the political and social values, and the models of leadership, sustained in the teachings of Jesus and Paul.

Churches in UPA areas in particular should foster patterns of leadership, organization and ministry with high levels of participation by local people, the voiceless and powerless in secular society, rather than relying on imported clergy and even imported lay members. Some would argue that the churches are already successful in this, for example voicing the grievances of striking miners, single parents or impoverished refugees against government and media representations of such groups as scapegoats for society's ills (Habgood). However, many ecclesiastical structures from parish to Synod or Diocese are still unrepresentative of the poor and the marginalized and there is need for fundamental reform if they are to find a place and a voice in the mainstream churches. Few who minister in UPA areas doubt the deep spiritual yearning of people in these areas. The problem for established churches is that their patterns of organization, like their patterns of worship, often mirror the social practices of dominant middle-class groups in society at large and are therefore thoroughly alienating to people who live in UPAs.

Dioceses and national churches must also find mechanisms for giving a voice to the voiceless in the wider communion of the Church, to the powerless people who are excluded from a fair hearing in the media or in national political debate. Networks of local churches (denominations) witness through the organizational and spiritual connections of congregations in different areas to the communion of the poor and the non-poor as the children of God, and to the graced potential of human communities to express reconciliation between persons and classes of persons. The Church at national level cannot acquiesce to political or economic arrangements which systematically exclude millions of children and adults in contemporary Britain from effective participation in the political, social, economic and cultural life of the city. The churches have a spiritual duty to seek to ensure that social divisions and exclusions are not replicated but challenged and overcome within church structures and practices.

The Church is not the kingdom and many Christians believe God as Spirit is active wherever the voiceless are given a voice, wherever oppression is challenged, and wherever people regain creativity and dignity in the living out of their own lives in communities of hopefulness rather than despair. But at the same time the churches represent a polity, a polity which is supposed to anticipate the feast of the kingdom where all are invited to the banquet table and where the first shall be last and the last first. The political role of the Church is then both symbolic and societal, communitarian and engaged. While fostering those human and moral bonds and values which promote human flourishing and participation in and through the practices of just institutions in the wider society, the churches must also, and even more importantly, exemplify the bonds and values of vulnerable love, servant leadership and participative ministry in local worshipping communities.

Organizing for action

Margaret Walsh

We went to live and work in the inner city with great dreams to empower and to liberate! Local people began to discover the benevolent Hope Community, knowing that we had that extra tin of beans and a blanket or two. We soon were battling with a dependency mentality, born from ever increasing hardship and a hopeless lack of self-esteem. The temptation was great. It gave us the opportunity to play 'Ladies Bountiful' and to be in control over peoples' lives at a very basic level. Soon, however, we also came to know the looks of resentment. Added to this was a growing fear of 'burn out' as we attempted to be all things to all people.

Still, the empowerment dream beckoned. We got involved in local projects, designed to give people a say over their environment. In the early days, it was difficult to understand why so few people availed themselves of this opportunity. Those who did, were at every meeting and were mainly white and middle-aged. As the time went on, we coaxed and cajoled and managed to bring some local friends along. Often they left, feeling let down by us and by the 'powers that be'. They complained bitterly about the official jargon and decided that such meetings were a waste of time. Decisions were made long before they could understand what was going on and the agenda rarely addressed their real concerns. This was no fault of the professionals who were working to a time scale and within very limited parameters. The meetings tended to be very boring and went on and on! Little was achieved. We felt that we could make better use of our time and were finding more and more excuses for sending our apologies.

We went to the estate, well equipped with counselling skills and how to do a social analysis. Now, I cringe at how patronizing we can be and marvel at the patience of the people. Mercifully, it wasn't yet too late when we began to realize that we needed to listen more carefully to the hopes and fears of our neighbours, while at the same time sharing our own lives, rather than imposing an agenda for their empowerment and liberation! We felt that our time would be far better spent by going out and having focused conversations with the people rather than our usual 'chit chat'.

We still went along to the occasional meeting. During one 'AOB', I began to tune into a local issue which I had heard mentioned several times but dismissed because there was always some official who assured us that the Authority was 'doing all in its power to resolve the situation'. We were also reminded that it was the role of our local representatives to put the pressure on and that they were already well aware of the problem. That was good enough for me but some locals would not be silenced. 'It's all about ducking, diving and back-handers', they explained. The following day, I met Jim and some others who had worked tirelessly on the problem, despite being fobbed off by all quarters. During that conversation, I began to understand something of the issue.

In 1989, G. & P. Batteries began operating in what used to be a quiet cul de sac on the estate. The process used involved smashing open batteries, releasing the acid and allowing the reclamation of lead. The firm claimed to have 20 per cent of the UK market and their customers included the Ministry of Defence, British Airways, British Rail and the Local Authority. Battery-breaking is a process that is banned in Hong Kong and so strictly regulated in Holland that it does not happen there. In fact, Dutch and European lorries were often seen delivering to the site. Local people, concerned at the process and the increasing traffic levels in the quiet street at all hours, sent a petition to Wolverhampton Borough Council. In June 1993, a Council report said that dust samples from G. & P. Batteries revealed very high lead content. A further report stated, 'there are fundamental problems that can only be fully resolved by the company moving its operations to another location'. However, there seemed to be no will on the part of the Local Authority to take action.

I am ashamed to say, that I was unaware of the existence of the factory which had already been operating on the estate for a few years! As I listened to Jim and the others who had not given up despite numerous setbacks, I began to recognize the tremendous potential these people had to take control and to bring about change. I also knew of others on the estate who had the same passion for justice. But all their efforts seemed in vain. It was clear that people needed to get together, to be better informed, organized and strategic.

Around about this time I had been introduced to Broad Based Community Organising later known as 'Citizens' in the Black Country. It was a life-line, at a time when we were more and more retreating back to our flats and giving in to the temptation to hand out the 'goodies'. We already knew many with leadership potential and hundreds of others who would offer support. Like myself, most didn't know that G. & P. operated on the estate. 'I take my children for a walk up that way regularly but I never realized the risks,' said Sonia. When people were informed, they were incensed and were ready to do something for the sake of themselves and their children. Some pointed out that environmental action groups should be contacted. Greenpeace was mentioned. We realized that this issue gave an opportunity for local people to do things for themselves and resisted the temptation to pass the problem on.

We decided to put our BBO [Broad Based Organising] training into action and called a meeting, bringing together those who wanted to do something about the issue. At our first planning meeting, attended by about twelve residents plus members of the Hope Community, we spent time discussing potential allies and opponents. People were tired of the 'buck passing' and decided to target the Chair of Environmental Services and Consumer Affairs. We knew that this person was in a position to bring together all the relevant parties. The potential allies whom we contacted included: the local doctor, the head teacher, 'Kwik Save' and an engineering firm which operated close to G. & P. employing a large workforce.

With encouragement and support, members of our group took responsibility to set up the meetings. 'I have never before spoken to a posh person! What do I say?' said a very nervous Sue. Soon she became an expert!

Though we had good enough reason to be angry and aggressive, it was agreed that we should behave with courtesy and respect. In the course of our planning meetings the values which we held in common came to the surface and directed how we wanted to proceed and we knew that together we could behave with dignity and self-confidence no matter what the provocation. Many meetings followed. On one occasion nearly one hundred people turned out, at very short notice, to stage a protest at the Civic Centre. I had never seen such a gathering from the estate, in terms of numbers, age range and ethnic mix.

We rehearsed our meetings carefully. We were taught how to keep to an agreed agenda, how to chair, how to keep to time, etc. After one such meeting, a Company Chair commented: 'If only our meetings were like that!' Afterwards, there was a careful evaluation and we were taught a basic tenet of BBO, i.e. that all action is in the reaction. This enabled us to plan the next step. We involved an independent chemical engineer in the analysis of dust samples and the shocking results were a field day for the media! Fortunately they were sympathetic and reported in great detail. The Local Authority wasn't very happy and accused Citizens of being alarmist and irresponsible!

We steadily grew in self-confidence, mainly because we worked together, were well informed and strategic and we experienced a newfound recognition and respect from those in 'high places'. Among the many meetings we organized was one which included the factory owners, the Chair of Environmental Services, Council Officials, the Director of Public Health and a number of other key players. I will never forget it! Neighbours, who would not be seen dead at a public meeting, took the chair and controlled the agenda and the timing. We were all nervous but, because we had carefully rehearsed, we knew what to expect and had one another's support. When it finished, the first-time Chairperson said: 'Fancy we, the little people, being able to do something like that!' Obviously we also had our enemies but were immediately suspicious when attempts were made to divide us. Sustained action by local residents and considerable media attention brought more and more momentum to the issue. Local cats, seriously ill with lead poisoning, made it into the national press.

During the course of this action, I began to realize more and more that our most important achievements were when local people began to grow in self-esteem and realize their own power and potential. The Good News which Jesus promised the Poor, was happening before my eyes; captives were being liberated and the oppressed set free. As events unfolded and finally the date was set for the relocation of the factory, I could only marvel at the amazing grace of the One who came to live among us and be with us always. The dream to empower and to liberate was becoming a reality.

Unmasking the domination system

Walter Wink

Some elements of socialization are universal, shared by all societies and persons: concepts of space, time, number, measurement, causality, classification. Likewise, people are not merely passive recipients of tradition. They not only take in their socialization, but take it over, leaving out what they dislike.[1] But that freedom is exercised within a highly circumscribed space, and as long as the delusional assumptions remain unconscious, they are seldom effectively transcended.

Christians have docilely sided with their governments, and justified the slaughter of millions of other Christians who, for their part, supported the other side, without any recognition that *both* sides were serving the values of the kingdom of death. Political elections are not a contest to see which party is capable of the greater compassion, but to see which will be truer to the delusional assumptions (increased military budgets, more prisons, stiffer sentencing for criminals). *The church has no more important task than to expose these delusionary assumptions as the Dragon's game.*

The perception that the delusional system runs deeper than propaganda leads to a further important insight: those who are victims of the delusional system are nevertheless responsible for how they have been shaped. And if they are responsible, then they can choose to be liberated from it.

People are socialized into their roles by means of the delusional assumptions from the earliest age — and this includes oppressors as well as the oppressed. They will further have learned to deny to themselves and others the fact that this misinformation causes them pain. We can hold out hope for the transformation of oppressors because to some degree they too are victims of the system and at some level have felt conflict, as in the case of white boys in South Africa when they discover that they must kill the love they had for the black maids that have cared for them since birth. (Some of those who have refused conscription have actually given this as the reason: they could not go into black townships and shoot at those who had nursed them.)

Both oppressors and oppressed have often attempted to resist the system that malformed them into their roles and assumptions, and have only given in because of the material rewards offered by the system and the terrible penalties attached to resistance. Society continually reinforces and justifies the mistreatment of the oppressed group, so that the oppressed tend to 'misbelieve' the same misinformation about itself that the social system as a whole teaches.[2]

The rulers of the earth do not know that they too are held in thrall by the Domination System. They do not know whom they serve. They probably believe that the delusional assumptions are true. They are being 'played with' (*delusi*) every bit as much as their victims, though they are, of course, highly rewarded for playing. They may even be good fathers and mothers, contributors to charities, attenders of churches, and upholders of 'traditional morality'.

And yet, for almost fifty years now these rulers of East and West have kept the Damoclean sword of nuclear omnicide poised over the heads of all humanity, rationalized under the theory of Mutually Assured Destruction (MAD — though what the United States really had was a policy of first strike). That they were quite prepared to destroy virtually all sentient life on the planet, possibly for ever, is an index of the degree to which humanity has been irrationally captive to the delusional system. And both sides were *agreed* on these values. Neither side had sufficient confidence in its own people's commitment to their national identity and ideology to consider non-violent national defence as an option. Folly on such a colossal scale is almost supranatural. Credit it to the Dragon.

It was fine men who tortured the woman we spoke to in Argentina. One insisted to her, 'But I go to Mass every morning too.' Another proposed marriage (they had tortured her husband to death two years before). These men were not sadists. They had merely surrendered themselves to the idol of the state. Once they had crossed that line, any evil was good if it served the idol. So their position was coldly rational and logical on their own premises. There is a form of madness, Chesterton remarked, that comes upon those who have lost everything else but reason. The Beast creates an atmosphere that blinds people to higher human values and turns perfectly nice people into beasts. These men were in thrall to the Dragon, to serve the Beast. *But they gave themselves to be captured.*

This is the paradox of moral maturity: we are responsible for what we do with what has been done to us. We are answerable for what we make of what has been made of us. Our capitulation to the delusional system may have been involuntary, but in some deep recess of the self we knew it was wrong. We are so fashioned that no Power on earth can finally drum out of us the capacity to recognize truth. However long it must lie buried, or however severely it has been betrayed, truth will out.

The Czech playwright (and later state president) Václav Havel wrote, while the communist regime was still in power:

> Because the regime is captive to its own lies, it must falsify everything. It falsifies the past. It falsifies the present, and it falsifies the future. It falsifies statistics. It pretends not to possess an omnipotent and unprincipled police apparatus. It pretends to respect human rights. It pretends to persecute no one. It pretends to fear nothing. It pretends to pretend nothing.
>
> Individuals need not believe all these mystifications, but they must behave as though they did, or they must at least tolerate them in silence, or get along well with those who work with them. For this reason, however, they must *live within a lie*. They need not accept the lie. It is enough for them to have accepted their life with it and in it. For by this very fact, individuals confirm the system, fulfil the system, make the system, *are* the system.

When anyone steps out of the system and tells the truth, lives the truth, that person enables *everyone else* to peer behind the curtain too. That person has shown everyone that it is possible to live within the truth, despite the repercussions. 'Living within the lie can constitute the system only if it is universal.' Anyone who steps out of line therefore '*denies it in principle and threatens it in its entirety.* ... If the main pillar of the system is living a lie, then it is not surprising that the fundamental threat to it is living the truth.' That is why it must be suppressed more severely than anything else.

> For the crust presented by the life of lies is made of strange stuff. As long as it seals off hermetically the entire society, it appears to be made of stone. But the moment someone breaks through in one place — a Solzhenitsyn — when a single person cries out, 'The emperor is naked' — when a single person breaks the rules of the game, thus exposing it as a game [*delusio!*] – then the whole crust is exposed as a tissue on the point of tearing and disintegrating uncontrollably.[3]

The delusory web spun around us can be broken. Everyone is capable of liberation. Most people are not deliberately unjust. Even our current enemies are in some sense victims. Jesus can command us to pray for our enemies, not because it is pious to do so, but because they are potentially capable of recognizing the wrongness of the present system. We must love our enemies because they too have been deceived by the Dragon's delusional game.

Often, even the liberator is locked into oppressive conditioning and behaviour. The Book of Revelation is a case in point. Never has a more withering political and economic criticism of empire been penned. The author sees with clairvoyant exactitude the bestiality of Rome, and behind it to the satanic spirit undergirding it. But he fails to relate this revelation to other aspects of androcracy. As Tina Pippin notes, he sees powerful, autonomous women as evil (Jezebel, the Whore); the good woman clothed with the sun is valued solely for giving birth to a male messiah, and then dismissed. Women are seductive; their bodies are capable of defiling men. Hence the 144,000 'virgins' who are the first fruits of the redeemed are men 'who have not defiled themselves with women' (Revelation 14:4). All three of the female figures in Revelation are dealt with violently. The Great Mother is pursued by the Dragon; the Whore is brutally murdered; and Jezebel will be stricken with disease and her 'children' killed.[4]

The Book of Revelation contemplates a transformation of power relations in which everyone will be able to enjoy the beauty of gold and gems that the rich had hoarded for themselves (21:18–21). The revolution begun by Jesus is continued and even extended politically and economically by John, but abandoned in reference to Jesus' teaching on love of enemies and the liberation of women. Hence male domination of women remains intact, and it is not even clear that women will be permitted in the New Jerusalem — so deep is this author's misogyny. Concern for justice is never enough; each social struggle must be seen in its relationship to the larger perspective of the inbreaking of God's domination-free order.

The Dragon's strategy is to eviscerate opposition by a sense of *induced powerlessness*. To accept its delusional assumptions is, in effect, to worship the Dragon, to hold its values as ultimate, to stake one's life on the permanence of its sway. 'The whole earth followed the [First] Beast, spellbound. They worshipped the Dragon, for he had given his authority to the Beast, and they worshipped the Beast, saying, "Who is like the Beast, and who can fight against it?"' (Revelation 13:3–4). Obeisance to the Beast requires as its gesture a continuous shrug. 'Who is like the Beast, and who can fight against it?' (shrug). 'I just carried out my orders. If I hadn't done so, someone else would have' (shrug). 'I don't enjoy the violence depicted in my company's films, but this is what the public wants' (shrug). 'I didn't want to get on drugs, but I was afraid the other kids would say I was square' (shrug). As R. D. Laing put it,

> Each person claims his own inessentiality. . . . In this collection of reciprocal indifference, of reciprocal inessentiality and solitude, there appears to exist no freedom. There is conformity to a *presence* that is everywhere elsewhere. . . . Mind and body are torn, ripped, shredded, ravaged, exhausted by these Powers and Principalities in their cosmic conflict.[5]

'Who is like the Beast, and who can fight against it?' is the mantra whose chanting by the masses guarantees compliance. That melancholy refrain echoes in the minds of citizens in totalitarian societies. The state apparatus is ubiquitous: Who is like the Beast? Anyone could be an informant: Who can fight against it? Soon one begins acting as censor to one's own mind, in terror of the single slip of tongue that could reveal one's thoughts, afraid even of night for fear of babbling sedition in one's sleep.[6]

It is significant that the Satan we see in Job who wanders up and down the earth and to and fro upon it, spying out people's faults, was probably inspired by the model of the Persian secret intelligence agency.[7] Like Freud's superego, Satan represents the harsh internalized voice of one's socialization, not yet lifted to consciousness and therefore to the possibility of being contradicted. Satan 'tempts' us, not just with moral indiscretions, but with obedience to oppressive values that the society itself declares to be holy and right. Satan provides mind surveillance for the internalized system, and tattles to God, who is actually betting on people's capacity to be authentic (Job 1–2).

In Chile, during the rule of the military dictator Pinochet, I asked a churchman about repression there. Public censorship of the press and media is not nearly so severe, he replied, as the self-censorship people exercise, out of fear. 'In our country,' mused an Eastern European, 'people are rarely imprisoned for their ideas ... because we're already imprisoned *by* our ideas.'[8] A government does not itself have this power; people must voluntarily surrender this power to the state.[9]

Those in power *want* us to be awed by their power, to act deferentially towards them. The European conquest of the colonies was made possible by vastly superior technology for warfare and communication, but by themselves these advantages could not have secured continued domination once the indigenous peoples had mastered these technologies (running them, indeed, for the masters). Lewis Mumford remarks on the sense of superiority, the arrogant swagger and easy assumption of being better, that characterized colonial administrators and unnerved any opposition. The subjects became convinced of their inferiority in the presence of such men. Britain ruled by teatimes, dress codes, and the flag; only occasionally were weapons needed. *It is not overt force but the symbols of power that rule the hearts of people.*[10] When hundreds of Indians nonviolently submitted themselves to the blows of police in Bombay on 21 June 1930, the men who clubbed them to the ground hour after hour were not British, but several hundred of their fellow Indian countrymen, under the command of only six British sergeants.[11]

Domination is always more than a power relation, notes Joel Kovel. It is a *spiritual state of being*. The dominator exerts power by extracting being from the dominated. Capitalists often get more than the labour power and surplus value of their workers; they also degrade the workers' being and puff up their own being. Thus the unmistakable narcissism of class superiority. White racists do more than materially exploit blacks; they make themselves members of a superior race and regard blacks as less than human, even animalistic. Sexually exploitative males do more than control the labour and bodies of women; they make themselves into the bearers of rationality and history, while the woman is made into dumb nature.[12] Thus domination always entails more than injustice. It wounds — and it intends to wound — the very soul itself.

Domination is all the more potent when it is not perceived at all. In his book *Authority*, Richard Sennett comments on the way many doctors treat their clients as bodies rather than persons, or how bureaucrats can ignore the difficulty their welfare clients have in filling out complicated forms: these very acts of indifference serve to maintain dominance. When one is needed by others more than one needs them, one can afford to be indifferent to them. 'Someone who is indifferent arouses our desire to be recognized,' Sennett writes; 'we want this person to feel we matter enough to be noticed.' Afraid of the indifference of persons in authority, not understanding what it is that keeps them aloof, we come to be emotionally dependent. This indifference to ordinary people carries as its coercion a shaming effect: it makes them feel insignificant.[13] For life is not just an encounter between human beings, but a struggle to the death for recognition. One does not merely desire the other, but desires to be desired by the other.[14] And it is this desire to be desired that leaves us so vulnerable to the Powers.

Poor people feel non-existent, valueless, humiliated. No one takes notice of them, unless their votes are needed by the rich — in which case, likely as not, they even vote against their own self-interest. They often have little confidence in themselves, and actually believe that the rich know what they need better than they themselves. When Jack Nelson-Pallmeyer interviewed Honduran *campesinos*, their answers would often be prefaced with degrading phrases such as 'We are stupid, ignorant people who know nothing', or 'We are like oxen who know nothing.'[15]

People not only choose to be where they have been detained, but they conclude that because of God, the fates, or their own inadequacies, they deserve it. As a Bolivian Indian woman put it after her eyes had been opened by Bible study in a Christian base community, 'Do you mean that *nowhere* in that Book does it say we have to *starve*?'[16]

So deep is this internalized oppression that Gustavo Gutiérrez has based a wholly new task for theology upon it: not helping the bourgeois discover the 'meaning of life,' but assisting the dehumanized to recover their humanity.[17]

Powerlessness is not simply a problem of attitude, however. There are structures — economic, political, religious, and only *then* psychological — that oppress people and resist all attempts to end their oppression. Psychotherapy has often taken the dominator personality and dominator family as normative, and has tried to adjust the client to the Domination Society. As the family systems therapist Thelma Jean Goodrich puts it, 'We need to stop trying to fix up people so that the system works better, and start fixing up the system so that people work better.'[18]

Systemic injustice is to a high degree invisible to its perpetrators. The man who uses sexist language is generally unaware of the pain of exclusion experienced by conscientized women. A person may be remarkably free of racial prejudice, having as friends people of disadvantaged races, and yet still support structures that perpetuate the systematic control of one racial group by another. 'Racism acts as a spiritual force within our social structure even when the people causing it have no intention of acting from prejudice and are unaware of doing so.'[19]

This deeply internalized oppression is the reason that *unmasking* the Powers is seldom enough by itself. As Reinhold Niebuhr observed, people in power generally do not capitulate simply because the ideologies by which they justify their policies have been discredited. 'When power is robbed of the shining armor of political, moral and philosophical theories, by which it defends itself, it will fight on without armor; but it will be more vulnerable, and the strength of its enemies increased.'[20] Indeed, it fights all the more desperately, because it knows that its time is short (Revelation 12:12).

So besides an unmasking of the oppressors, there must also be a *healing of the servile will* in their victims. Along with revolutionary analysis and praxis, there must be therapies.[21] The task of exposing the delusional system requires the development of a social psychology of domination. Simply criticizing the illegitimacy of the masters can lead to two results, both of them negative. The oppressed may decide to beat the oppressors at their own game, rather than changing the game (hence the espousal of redemptive violence by some early liberation theologians). Or the oppressed may be driven to even deeper alienation. For now, as Richard Sennett points out, the oppressed can no longer respect themselves for having allowed themselves to be pillaged and yet they are still not free from their masters. Rather than strengthening them to revolt, the recognition of their weakness may foster self-doubt: if I have been so cowardly and stupid as to put up with such treatment, I *deserve* what I get. It is my own fault that I am weak.

Furthermore, Sennett continues, if all are created equal, if we all leave from the same starting gate of life, and you are way ahead and I am far behind, then I have no one to blame but myself for not having made more of my life. Thus workers are entangled in a dragnet that systematically prevents their perceiving the faults of the system (not everyone does start from the same gate; some are far ahead at birth due to family wealth, education, race, gender, and station in life; the gospel does not teach that we are born equally, but born incomparably, each utterly unique, utterly beloved by God).[22] The victims blame themselves, and the system gets off unscathed.[23]

Powerlessness is never an empirical fact, however. It is not the outcome of a realistic analysis. *A sense of powerlessness is always a spiritual disease deliberately induced by the Powers to keep us complicit.* Any time we feel powerless, we need to step back and ask, What Principality or Power has me in its spell? *No one is ever completely powerless.* Even if it is only a matter of choosing the attitude with which we die, we are never fully in the control of the Powers unless we grant them that power. 'Christ has left the devil only whatever power unbelief allows him,' asserts Heinrich Schlier.[24] The victory of faith over the Powers lies, not in immunity to their wrath, but in emancipation from their delusions. And as to their wrath, even there we do not know the limits of God's redeeming grace. So it is always appropriate to pray for miracles. What seems to us impossible is usually another's limited vision or faithlessness in which we have let ourselves become trapped. Faith is the confidence that possibility transcends compulsion; freedom, necessity; life, death; eternity, time.

> The Impossible is standing in front of me
>   and looking me in the face.
> The Incredible is credible.[25]

Those who have internalized their oppression, who are awed by the Beast and its powers into passive obedience, and who worship its show of might, provide it all the permission it needs continually to extend its power. What is so exhilarating about the revelations that came to John is their capacity to disenthrall, to awaken, to unlock what William Blake called 'the mind-forg'd manacles'[26] and set people free.

Vision heals. Mere awareness of the state from which we are fallen is not enough to effect systemic change, but it is its indispensable precondition. Apocalyptic (unveiling) is always a protest against domination. Liberation from negative socialization and internalized oppression is a never-completed task in the discernment of spirits. To exercise this discernment, we need eyes that see the invisible. To break the spell of delusion, we need a vision of God's domination-free order, and a way to implement it. For that, we look to God's new charter for reality, as declared by Jesus.

NOTES

1. C.R. Hallpike, *The Foundation of Primitive Thought* (Oxford: Clarendon Press, 1979), p. 55. Erich Fromm defined socialization as the process of 'learning to like to do what we have to do' (*The Sane Society* [New York: Fawcett Premier Books, 1977], p. 77).
2. Ricky Sherover-Marcuse, 'Unlearning Racism Workshops' and 'Toward a Perspective on Unlearning Racism: 12 Working Assumptions', 6501 Dana, Oakland, CA 94609. I cannot agree with her social determinism, however; people are not just victims — otherwise they would cease to be moral agents responsible for their acts. They are seduced, but they are culpable for letting themselves be seduced.
3. *Václav Havel or Living in Truth*, ed. Jan Vladislav (Boston: Faber & Faber, 1987), pp. 45, 56, 59.
4. Tina Pippin, 'The Heroine and the Whore: Fantasy and the Female in the Apocalypse of John,' unpublished paper, courtesy of the author.
5. R.D. Laing, *The Politics of Experience* (New York: Pantheon Books, 1967), pp. 13, 132.
6. Danilo Kis, 'The State, the Imagination, and the Censored I', *New York Times Book Review*, 3 November 1985, 3.
7. A. Lods, 'Les Origines de la figure de Satan, ses fonctions à la cour céleste', in *Mélanges syriens offerts à R. Dussaud*, vol. 2, *Bibliothèque archéologique et historique* 30 (Paris: P. Geuthner, 1939), pp. 649–60; C. Colpe, 'Geister (Dämonen)', *Reallexikon für Antike und Christentum*, ed. Theodore Klauser (Stuttgart: Anton Hiersemann, 1976), 9:569–70.
8. Csaba Polony, quoted by Charles Upton, 'Who are the Archons?', *Gnosis* 2 (Spring/ Summer 1986), 5.
9. Elizabeth Janeway, *Powers of the Weak* (New York: Alfred A. Knopf, 1980), p. 169. See also Gene Sharp, *The Politics of Nonviolent Action* (Boston: Porter Sargent, 1973), 1:7–62.
10. Lewis Mumford, *The Myth of the Machine: The Pentagon of Power* (New York: Harcourt Brace Jovanovich, 1970), p. 7.
11. Richard B. Gregg, *Power of Nonviolence* (New York: Shocken, 1966), pp. 26–8.
12. Joel Kovel, *History and Spirit* (Boston: Beacon Press, 1991), p. 102.
13. Richard Sennett, *Authority* (New York: Vintage, 1981), pp. 86, 92.
14. Joel Kovel, *History and Spirit*, p. 125.
15. Jack Nelson-Pallmeyer, *War against the Poor* (Maryknoll, NY: Orbis Books, 1989), p. 21.
16. Charles Upton, 'Contemplation as a Revolutionary Act: Response to Simone Weil's *Waiting for God*,' unpublished manuscript, courtesy of the author.
17. Gustavo Gutiérrez, *A Theology of Liberation* (Maryknoll, NY: Orbis Books, [1973] 1988).
18. Thelma Jean Goodrich, 'Women, power, and family therapy: what's wrong with this picture?', in *Women and Power: Perspectives for Family Therapy*, ed. Goodrich (New York: W.W. Norton, 1991), pp. 23, 31.

19. Ward Ewing, *The Power of the Lamb* (Cambridge, MA: Cowley Publications, 1990), p. 47.

20. Reinhold Niebuhr, *Moral Man and Immoral Society* (New York: Charles Scribner's Sons, 1932), p. 33.

21. J.B. Libánio notes that every social system needs three elements to maintain itself: legitimacy, therapies, and social control; and this is as true for countercultural or revolutionary groups as for any others ('A community with a new image', *WCC Exchange* 2 [May 1979], 37, 40).

22. See G. Tinder, *Political Meaning of Christianity* (Baton Rouge: Louisiana State University Press, 1989), p. 32.

23. Sennett, *Authority*, 28, 33, 41, 46; and Sennett and Jonathan Cobb, *The Hidden Injuries of Class* (New York: Vintage, 1973).

24. Heinrich Schlier, *Principalities and Powers in the New Testament* (New York: Herder and Herder, 1961), p. 58.

25. Steve Shelstad, in a workshop at the Ecumenical Theological Center, Detroit, December 1990.

26. William Blake, 'London', in *The Complete Poetry and Prose of William Blake*, ed. David V. Erdman, rev. edn (Berkeley: University of California Press, 1982), p. 27.

The parish and politics

Gerald Wheale

The parish of St James' with St Clement's, Moss Side, is an inner-city parish in Manchester. In the last 20 years, half of the Moss Side area has seen its housing cleared and redevelopment take place. The remaining half has been subject to considerable activity in the field of housing improvement and rehabilitation. A new district centre has been built, complete with shopping precinct, indoor market and leisure centre. In the years before the redevelopment process got under way in Moss Side, every indicator of social decline was already high. ... They included a substantial proportion of housing falling below minimum standards, a disproportionately high degree of mobility, a disproportionately young population (30 per cent under 15) and a disproportionately high immigrant population.[1]

*   *   *

Although redevelopment is complete and the rehabilitation of property well under way by the 1980s, problems still remain. 1981 Census material revealed that 26.4 per cent of the population were under 15; Moss Side residents tended to be poorer and overcrowding tended to be worse than in other areas of the city; 650 households still lacked a WC; 24.9 per cent of residents were born outside the UK (this figure does not include second- or third-generation immigrants); the overall unemployment rate was 24 per cent and youth employment (16–19) was 39.4 per cent.[2] On the basis of information drawn from unemployment figures for Moss Side, a local community worker observed in January 1982 that the local unemployment register had increased by 80 per cent over the last two years and that youth employment had increased by 90 per cent in the same period. On 10 November 1983, there was still a minimum of 6,906 persons unemployed in Moss Side. Vacancies unfilled at the Moss Side Job Centre totalled 185. Riots took place in Moss Side on 8 and 9 July 1981.

This picture of Moss Side has formed the context of my ministry for the last twenty years. My initial understanding of the situation when I came to the area in 1962 led me to the belief that such conditions were an affront to the God-given dignity and integrity of Moss Siders as human beings and as a community. My commitment as a priest required me to preach the gospel and administer the sacraments but also carried a moral imperative to identify with and to struggle alongside my parishioners in their search for true humanity. Attempts to grapple with the implications of impending redevelopment of the area quickly led our church council and congregation to ask fundamental questions about the nature of the parochial system and the role of the Church. Requests to the City Planning Officers and to Diocesan officials for information on strategic planning for the future, revealed the powerful influence of the institutions of our society upon the quality of life of individual citizens. The failure of both institutions to engage in a dialogue to plan for the future, resulted in frustration, disillusionment, aggression and even conflict between local congregations and the Diocese and the Moss Side community and the Town Hall.

This powerful institutional dimension and the relationship of the Church to it, was discussed into the early hours of many mornings with a long-standing friend, Brian Cordingley of the Manchester Industrial Mission team. The kingdom of God became a more important concept in my theology and was strengthened, developed and related to community involvement in a fruitful relationship with the William Temple Foundation.[3]

* * *

A particular style of ministry has evolved in relation to a particular situation. I believe it to be a ministry based upon word and sacraments. It has also been, and still is, a ministry which has attempted a reconstruction of community in Moss Side as part of God's purpose to bring in His kingdom. Ministry for the ordained must be the living out of faith in the place where they find themselves just as it must be for the laity. A worshipping and supportive base is essential for the people of God. The base, in my case the parish, is an observation post on society; here we pick up and test the attitudes of society to the poor. At this margin of society we are more than a church unit with an internal self-contained and self-interested life; we are in the forefront 'doing theology' by working out our faith in the realities of a disadvantaged and poor community. Our witness is at many levels; proclaiming the gospel and celebrating the sacraments and expressing the power of Christian love in our community. By these means we seek to enable man to discover his true humanity.

To put it another way, the parish is the testing ground for true humanity and the arena for the living out of faith. Man cannot be fully man in church alone. Church should not simply be the vehicle of receiving man's gifts of time, money and talent to sustain and enhance its own structure and life, but a means whereby mankind is enabled to discover its salvation and fulfilment in God in daily living. Neither is the parish an end in itself, it is an integral part of the process of living out the faith in the universal brotherhood of man. Every parish is set in a world context within the eternal purposes of God, so the ways in which it lives out faith are relevant to, and significant in, that wider context.

I see this style of ministry for both priest and laity as theologically justifiable and necessary in practice, but it has drawn a wide range of responses from both the Church and the secular world. In the Church, there are a few kindred spirits, and more, who wish this style of ministry could be accepted, but who speak of the 'dead weight' of many of the laity or the 'diocesan establishment'. There are many others who would find this style 'too radical' and compare it to 'a proper ministry'. From the secular world there has been a variety of response. Within the local community many have said that it is 'good to see someone standing up for Moss Side' and that our Church and particularly our Church-sponsored Housing Association, has shown that 'things can be made better in Moss Side!'

Some of our more radical leaders in Moss Side would see my efforts as typical 'sloppy liberal' establishment, conscience-salving, activities which only reinforce an already repressive system. After many years of building relationships and establishing credibility, there is a good deal of evidence to show that politicians and officers at both city and national level regard our efforts, particularly in housing, with approval and support.

Since its formation in the 1960s, the Housing Association sponsored by the churches in Moss Side (Mosscare Housing Limited) has grown steadily to its present holding of nearly 1,000 properties. Its main efforts have been concentrated into areas of housing need and physical decline. There are strong indications that regeneration is occurring in some sub-areas where private buying had collapsed some years ago. Families in housing need have been given rehabilitated homes with a further 30-year life span and, more importantly, confidence in the future has been regenerated as near-derelict and denuded communities have been reconstructed. The 'tenant-intensive' style of management and the community base of the Association have led a number of community organizations to Mosscare's door with requests for housing projects to help those in special need, for example Polish Catholic elderly, single West Indian homeless and families with mentally handicapped members. The Deputy Director of Mosscare is Chairman of the North West Regional Council of the National Federation of Housing Associations and the Association had two representatives at the Department of the Environment consultations held during 1983 on inner-city regeneration through Housing Association involvement.

The community base of the Housing Association has been symbolized by the staff of the Association working from the Moss Side Pastoral Centre. This Centre, opened in 1973, replaced the old St James' church hall in Moss Side and was designed by, and is still managed by, a group drawn from the local Council of Churches. Its purpose was to provide an accessible point at which the Church could be seen to have a working base from which to show its commitment to the community of Moss Side. It was designed to be an open and accepting building into which people could come with confidence and without embarrassment to share in the various activities of the Centre or simply to seek help with any problems. Happily, the experiment has worked and the building provides a home for parish functions (including worship during the winter), church council meetings, the Housing Association, a community project, residents' group meetings, the local carnival committee, advice bureaux for the MP and local councillors, a dancing school, the Methodist Brownies and many other activities.

Because it is a 'multi-use' centre, all files and the records of daytime users are stored away at night and all furniture is multi-purpose. As parish priest, I am at my desk by 8.00 a.m. so that 'the church' may be seen at work as people go about their daily business. The Centre gives Moss Siders ready access to the Church and its ministry and to other caring agencies. It also gives to the Church, and to me as parish priest, a most significant point of entry into many community activities as well as an enormous number of contacts with local people.

Three workers of the Longsight/Moss Side Community Project work from the Pastoral Centre. This project was founded by the local churches in the late 1960s and two major aspects of its work in Moss Side deserve mention here. The first concerns its work with residents' groups. This has been a long-term piece of work which began with resident response to the redevelopment process. Response in the early 1960s and early 1970s was particularly volatile as larger areas of Moss Side were cleared and new housing was built. Participation in planning for the future was very much a live issue and the Moss Side Social Council (later the Moss Side Peoples' Association) enjoyed a quite spectacular career as it confronted the City Council with the undesirable consequences of its housing policy, which many felt was leading to 'the destruction of the Moss Side community'.

The Community Project committee felt that a professional community worker could be of service to the community in expressing this kind of concern and resources were allocated to this work. The lessons learned in the work on redevelopment issues were then used in ongoing work with residents' groups in the area who tried to encourage a change in City Council policy towards the rehabilitation of housing. When such a change did take place and improvement, rather than demolition, was adopted as a Council policy, one of the most significant factors in the choice of areas for improvement in Moss Side was the high degree of resident commitment to the new policy. I believe that that confidence was well founded as there has been a considerable improvement in the physical fabric of the Moss Side area. Many houses have been improved by the City Council and by the Housing Associations active in the area. The confidence generated by this activity has led in recent years to one or two of the major financial institutions, as well as the City Council, funding the improvement work of owner-occupiers. Central Government policy on 'New Initiatives in Housing' was also intended to encourage regeneration of this kind, but the experience of our Housing Association, formed for this purpose, seems to suggest that the exercise is not financially viable in Moss Side. This view was expressed to Sir George Young at the Pastoral Centre during his visit to Moss Side in October 1983.[4]

The work with the residents' groups still continues and currently covers issues such as street cleaning, the continuing problem of prostitution, the use of vacant buildings and land in the area and road widening proposals for a major road into the City through Moss Side. These and other issues are also taken up through the Inner City Partnership Committee.

At a wider level, the Parish Church, the Housing Association and the Community Project are all represented on the Moss Side Consultative Committee set up by the City Council. Strong local councillor representation on this body makes it a significant vehicle through which the community can make its voice heard on Moss Side issues. This body, with City Council backing, mounted extensive consultations with the community through the Moss Side Conference after the riots of 1981. Following a large conference with many community representatives present, a series of smaller conferences was held on specific issues and an encouraging number of initiatives have been mounted as a result.

In the present economic climate, two factors stand out as major stumbling blocks to progress; the first is the time taken to put together the proposals and to get them through the various levels of the decision-making process and the second is the availability of funds to finance any initiatives. There is often a package of resources to put together which may be compromised if any one supporting agency fails to deliver.

* * *

The second major aspect of the work of the Longsight/Moss Side Community Project which deserves mention here is its work with co-operatives. An Asian community worker with the project team drew attention to the exploitation and isolation felt by Asian women who were involved in the 'outwork' system in the textile trade. So that they could supplement their family income, many women spent long lonely hours at home producing garments on hired industrial sewing machines. With children at school, they were cut off from social contact, with little chance to learn the language of the host community in which they lived. An action/research team of two workers was appointed. It took years to investigate and put together the elements of a co-operative venture. The workers' reports to the Project Management Committee amply demonstrated the incredible complexity and frustration involved in trying to secure premises, machines, funding for supervisors, designers, cutters and the co-operative worker members in the training period as well as the difficulties of ensuring a constant flow of work from suppliers and guaranteed market outlets. It is a tribute to their tenacity as well as to their skill that they succeeded at all and that they sustained the interest of a nucleus of women during the many months of preparations.

* * *

Have I been involved in politics? The way in which I have described the context of my ministry, the development of my theological understanding and some of the work undertaken by myself and others in the name of ministry, could well raise that question. The question also implies a further question as to whether it is appropriate for a priest to be so engaged.

It is difficult to answer these questions directly but my mind goes back to theological college days when Mervyn Stockwood, who was then Vicar of Great St Mary's in Cambridge, gave a series of talks on ministry. One of these talks was about whether the parish priest should be involved in politics. I remember very clearly two of the points which he made. One of these was that the exercise of ministry in itself generated a personal political stance on the part of the priest, and the other was that the activities undertaken in the parish are themselves a commentary upon the outworkings of the political system as expressed in the life of the local community. In his opinion, this meant that every priest ought to work out an explicit political stance and should be sensitive to the political implications of parish activities.

At the time I did not understand the implications of what he was saying, but now, with twenty-five years of experience, twenty-one of them spent in a disadvantaged community, I can bear witness to the force of his argument. The exercise of power and the control of resources by the institutions of our society have a very powerful effect upon my life and the lives of those I minister to. Decisions made by such bodies as Central or Local Government either enhance my dignity and integrity as a human being and a child of God or they impair and restrict it. So, too, they enhance or impair the life of the local community of which I am a part. In short, these institutional activities either enable or block the coming of the kingdom of God. A very large part of the exercise in power and the control of resources is, in fact, the political process of the society and world in which we live. It seems to be that, whether I like it or not, both I and my parishioners are bound up in a political process which we cannot avoid. We cannot ignore it; although in my experience, many try to by compartmentalizing 'faith' and the other dimensions of life. Grappling with the political dimension presents us with untold difficulties and dilemmas but must be undertaken if we are to be fully Christian and if I am to exercise my ministry to the full.

At this point I would wish to enter a rider on behalf of those of us who would plead that the Church should take the structural/institutional dimension of life more seriously than it does at the moment. We are often attacked as somehow lacking compassion in the exercise of our ministry to the individual. The criticism seems to be that the pastoral ministry is neglected so that political activity can be pursued. I would wish to respond by saying that in my experience compassion is a quality which is strongly exhibited by those of us who share this standpoint and that a significant proportion of our ministry is expressed in pastoral care. I would also raise the question of whether, in some areas, the view that the priest is constantly in demand for pastoral care is a myth in these days. During the last three years I have come across an increasingly large number of clergy who have talked of a running down in demand for traditional pastoral care. I am sure that there is no less need but perhaps it is now being met by social workers, community workers or advice bureaux workers, who are all particularly active in areas of disadvantage.

* * *

The ethos of my life, training and ministry, is Western, liberal democratic and Protestant. My theology supposes that love as found in Jesus is capable of bringing reconciliation between God and man and between man and his fellow man. Reconciliation is the key-stone of faith and I celebrate the death of Jesus on the Cross as the 'full, perfect and sufficient sacrifice, oblation, and satisfaction for the sins of the whole world'.[5] I am, however, faced with a world in which there are many examples of those in positions of power exercising their power and controlling the associated resources in a way which is both obdurate and repressive. Criticism by the disadvantaged is interpreted as disloyal or as expressing unhealthy anti-Establishment feeling and solidarity with the disadvantaged and repressed is treated as subversive. Reconciliation between the disadvantaged and the oppressor does not seem possible and some Christians respond by opting for confrontation, conflict and revolution.

I have spoken to Christians from abroad who speak of suspending their theology until the revolution is over. I do not find that an acceptable solution, although I must also face the fact that I am not in the same situation! Archbishop Runcie accurately describes the position for me as a priest working in England when he writes:

> I believe, however, that the Christian seriousness brought to government by an establishment in which laity as well as clergy have always held positions of responsible leadership, has contributed greatly to the growth of a corporate sense of obligation towards the needy and a respect for justice which has softened conflict and enhanced the life of every citizen. It is, of course, easy to detail what still needs to be corrected and where welfare provision is not sufficiently generous, or not applied with enough compassion, but it would be foolish to let proper indignation blind us to the achievements of our society in recent centuries or cause us to forget what a rare and fleeting experience in the history of the world it is to live in a society which is secure, reasonably just and moderately prosperous.[6]

Even though I accept the position adopted by Archbishop Runcie, I am conscious that I do not suffer the harsh realities of the life of the disadvantaged as they do themselves. Commitment to, and identification with, the disadvantaged is not the same as being disadvantaged oneself. A Moss Sider expressed it to me in the following terms — 'You say "we this" and "we that" and "we the other", but you are not the same as us; you can walk out at any time, we are stuck with it!' It is easy for the liberal Christian to overlook the urgency in the plight of the disadvantaged. When the liberal Christian neglects the urgency for reform, the militant in society responds by adopting the view that almost any tactics are legitimate in attempting to alter an intolerable *status quo*. To pontificate that two wrongs do not make a right may result in being accused by the radical of making a facile moral judgement from the comfort of a middle-class armchair.

I remain critical of the Church as an institution because of its failure to recognize and significantly engage the political dimension of life but I also believe that the Church of England can no longer be labelled the Tory party at prayer! There are now many parish priests for whom a life spent in ministry to the disadvantaged is the living out of a faith which has in it a more 'left-wing' political stance than hitherto. They live close to the realities of disadvantage as they are experienced in their own parish. They are often politically to the left of their laity, although not to the left of many of their parishioners! The professional job of living out the imperatives of faith means that they have to work out a faith stance in the context of disadvantage in which they work. It is not difficult for them to recognize the paternalistic authoritarianism of our own democratic society for the Church itself has been, and still is, guilty of this style of management in its affairs.

Notes

1. G.A. Wheale, *Citizen Participation in the Rehabilitation of Housing in Moss Side East, Manchester*, unpublished PhD Thesis, University of Manchester, 1979, pp. 91–2.
2. R. Morris, *A Social Survey of Moss Side Based on the 1981 Census*, unpublished project whilst on placement from the Northern Ordination Course, July 1983.
3. *Involvement in Community, A Christian Contribution*, a Report by the Community Development Group of the William Temple Foundation in collaboration with the Community Work Advisory Group (London: British Council of Churches, 1980).
4. G.A. Wheale, Memo of visit of Sir George Young, Resumé of points made (Under Secretary of State, Department of the Environment), Mosscare Housing Ltd., Development File, Programme July 1982 to November 1983, 4 October 1983.
5. *The Prayer of Consecration*, Book of Common Prayer, 1662.
6. Robert Runcie, *Windows onto God* (London: SPCK, 1983), p. 63.

The Church and powerlessness: an exploration in spirituality

Austin Smith

One Friday night, in the summer of 1981, a young man was stopped by the police on Granby Street in Liverpool. He was riding a motorcycle. Some say the police knocked him off it, others say he was just stopped. A crowd gathered. Everyone agrees the crowd got angry. The anger built up into skirmishes with the police. Was this incident, so caught in the predictable rumours of inner city communication, the cause of Toxteth's midsummer rioting madness? I do not think so. Police/community tension is but a symptom, though a vital one, of inner city decay.

Unemployment, outright vandalism, bad education, lack of communal facilities, failure of parental control, left-wing outside trouble-makers — these were just some of the reasons given, and often fiercely defended, for the whole problem.

* * *

It is true that each human being is born for infinity. It is equally true that I can make fundamental and radical choices which determine my life. I am also conscious of the reality of my own richness, in that I believe God has called me into a participation with him in a wonderful and inspiring task of creative power. All this is further enriched by my belief in the God who became part of my own human condition. Social, economic and political theories, along with the structures and institutions which they spawn, cannot change such profound and breath-taking truths. Nevertheless they can bring about, existentially, a helplessness and hopelessness which bar and bolt the human spirit into a prison of living futility. Faith may well have victory in an imperfect world. But faith would be mocked if those who have the power to make the world more perfect selfishly agree to live with the imperfections to the detriment of the less powerful and the perpetuation of the totally powerless. It is for this reason that ideological and institutional criticism and change are part and parcel of the Church's mission. And it is equally important that the Church remains reflective at all times when it comes to its own institutional alliances. If inherited institutions are challenged, one needs to be careful not to give the benefit of the doubt to the institutions. It has been pointed out that Catholics in authority remained blind during most of the nineteenth century to the need for great social change, 'due, it may be remarked, not so much to lack of generosity or ignorance of the wretched condition of the workers as to sheer incomprehension of the new problems posed by the industrial revolution'.[1]

* * *

The fact of the matter is: rumouring and riot-torn cities, decaying dockland and puzzled tears in the face of human 'brokenness' are intrinsically caught up in the process of institutional and structural failure.

* * *

It is very right for the Church to express its concern, and follow this up with action and collaboration, in matters relating to the problem of unemployment. But caution is called for. The statement, 'unemployment is evil' is only valid within the context of the kind of society we have. For, I would suggest, the statement, 'employment is good' is not necessarily acceptable. The social, economic and political game we play, if one may lean on the thought of Wittgenstein, begets the rules and therefore the language of employment and unemployment. Such a game implies that some will have 'power', socially and economically, to hire others. Now this may well be the world we are forced to live in. But the Church must have an eye for deeper concerns. Above all it must have an eye for the matters which lead to fundamental and radical equality.

In the present situation this implies two levels, simultaneously in existence, of criticism. One which reaches out into the world of the unemployed and condemns the alienation implied in that status in the contemporary patterns of society; the other must present a vision of life which demands an ever evolving process towards equality. Both are based upon the creative right, God given, which belongs to man and woman in the development of this world. To develop creation is not a sociological task. It is a theological task.

The final tragedy of our world, with its inherited institutions, is the exclusion of too many from truly participating in the development of the fulness of life.

> To be free is no longer a matter of removal of restraints in individual initiative. To be free means being empowered by society to participate. This is the significance of the new preoccupation with participation. . . .[2]

It is the exclusion of low income people (from the broader social and

economic participation which is open to others), when this is not voluntary on
their part, which we define as being the essence of poverty.[3]

Any of us living, working and attempting to reflect in the inner city today
would readily affirm this opinion. I may have difficulty with describing such
a lack of participation as the essence of poverty, but as a working description
I will accept it. The problem rests for the most part with the inherited
institutions as described by Toynbee. They control our imaginations. And
they abort, too often, our critique and action.

* * *

There seems to be a terrible fear of anything which begins to move outside
the acceptable norms of social, economic and political life set by our
institutions. Community development work (and there is a great deal wanting in this area of influence), has given birth to imaginative work in the inner
city. But at the end of the day it too often comes face to face in a state of
confrontation with acceptable institutions. Or, worse still, institutions play
one group off against the other. In essence it is about participation. Community development, liberation movements of women and blacks, Greenham
Common, anti-racism, to mention but a few areas, are prophetic voices,
which herald the death agony of our tired social, economic and political
institutions. More and more people are refusing spiritual and mental colonization.[4] That such a voice goes unheard is reason for sadness; that such a
voice is being articulated is reason for hope. That the Church has become
part of the voice in certain areas of the world is reason for joy; that such
participation by the Church is not seen as an essential aspect of its mission is
reason for regret. Such regret is not for any vague social reason. The regret,
and the sadness, strike very deep spiritual chords in the spirit of Christian
humanity and humanity in general.

* * *

Spirituality must realistically emerge from and with the times. By spirituality
itself I understand: 'that basic or existential attitude ... which is the consequence and expression of the way in which (we) understand (our) religious,
or more generically (our) ethically committed, existence'.[5] I would stress that
submission to historical reality. This historical reality today is two sides of
the one coin. On one side is the phenomenon of powerlessness; on the other
is the reality of institutions which I have understood as preventing or not
fulfilling the desire for total participation in the development of life. Thus my
personal pilgrimage to God, and union with the God of all mercies and
justice through Jesus, is made or articulated against the backdrop of institutional oppression.

* * *

I would stress here that I am not making any kind of false distinction, still less
separation, between the moral, the dogmatic and the spiritual. Thus there is
a distinctive task to be done in the moral sphere when it comes to facing the
institutional confusion and failures of our day in matters social, economic
and political. But what I am suggesting is that such commitments must give

birth to an existential attitude in terms of faith and in terms of union with Christ. In a word, I believe that if the Church is to be part defined, in the words of Metz, as a 'place and institution for socio-critical freedom' and socio-economic and political action, there is a deep spiritual challenge to be faced.

I do not make such remarks lightly. And I do not make them in an abstract manner. I make them as a priest and religious, who has lived for the past twelve years in the inner city of Liverpool, now popularly known as Toxteth.

For authentic inner city ministry one must cross a prepositional bridge. One must move from ministering 'for' to ministering 'with' the powerless of this world. Such prepositional preoccupation may seem no more than playing the community development game. And, indeed, this is often the case. But if it is real, then it is anything but a gimmicky game. For as soon as one seriously takes up this prepositional change in life one is forced to change the game of life itself. One has to face this not by way of methodology but by way of understanding the worst level of sinfulness which people of the inner city have suffered. 'Withness' highlights the presence or absence of participation in their lives. It comes across in residents' meetings, in community groupings, in educational projects and in co-operatives. The fundamental struggle is to make 'withness' real and authentic. Therefore one is called to be not only as close as possible to their action, but above all things to attempt to share the suffering. In my own case there will always be a measure of simulation in this regard. But a warning light is forever flashing, especially when quicker methods seem called for. That light says, 'Do not resort to past patterns'. What especially it calls to in my own soul is a renewed understanding of the meaning of purgation to find a deeper union with God. This deeper union is looked for, and sometimes found, in a union with the suffering of a powerless people. It is a union which means enriching compassion with collaboration. And because it is a question of collaboration it has about it all the agony and the ecstasy of creation. It means attempting to seek a 'nothingness' within oneself, that 'nothingness' which is hidden under all the layers of a 'somethingness' that is superficial in its very meaning because it is given by the world of status and position and, indeed, power. One is asked to find the very nakedness of one's existence, held in the hand of God, until one finds a namelessness in terms of this world. But in terms of God it is the namelessness of sheer existence. It brings one face to face with the fact of the God who could only stammer that his name was 'I am, who am'. This name brings suffering in that one is reminded of the total equality of human existence in the sight of God. It is a terrible sin that thousands, indeed millions, who share that common existence have been denied by the structures and the institutions of this world the opportunity to live up to their name.

One night of the riots I came home and read the following notes which I had taken the night before. 'The trials described by John of the Cross — the "Dark Night". In this state, 1) the mind can no longer exercise itself in discursive reasoning as it did before. 2) The light of contemplation it receives is so faint and crucifying that the soul believes itself plunged into a night of darkness'. Of course, I am making analogies. I had come in from burning streets and the screams and all the sirens. But is the analogy to be made too much of, or should we be brave enough to say, 'that is the revelation of the Crucified', found in the terrible and terrifying world which ultimately leads us to such situations . . . ? Is there a mystic brokenness here in this city? I remember that night reading that poem of John:

How well I know the spring that brims and flows,
Although by night
This eternal spring is hidden deep,
How well I know the course its water keep,
Although by night . . .[6]

Is the ghetto, perhaps, to give birth to the same spirit as a cubby-hole in a Spanish Carmel produced? Is there a song of belief and contemplation still to be sung in the horror of our man-made madness — inner cities? Sometimes I have advised religious, community workers, teachers, social workers, of all denominations and none, to take a rest when it all seemed too much. But not always now. For they must be led, we all must be led, through a spiritual darkness to participate at a deeper level in the suffering of the powerless. And having suffered and having agreed to continue to suffer, stand side by side with them against the institutions which have oppressed them. God flows on in the depths of the sacredness of human existence. We all need to reach for it. And there will be no new day without that suffering. We find it so difficult to live in the midst of antithesis. We either wish to return to old and well worn theses or rush to temporary new syntheses of reconciliation. It is of no avail. We need to bear the horror and alienation and rejection of the antithesis. The Church cannot 'do differently' without 'being differently'.

I have watched the fatigue and depression of many friends and my own community as they struggled day by day with the task in hand. That task is that of living and working where they are. It is the struggle for that 'withness'. It can only be purchased by suffering supported by faith. But it is also something which participates in the paradox of Christianity. It is the paradox of having to live simultaneously in joy and sorrow, ease and pain. It is 'the simultaneous' which was dramatically offered to humankind by wounds on a glorified body.

The Church, I believe, is being called to understand this task throughout the world. It is a profound spiritual task. Let not those who will not attempt to understand it accuse those who suffer to understand it of a vague humanism, salted with a still more vague political theology! Christians like Martin Luther King and Oscar Romero have been witnesses in our age of a new ground of Christian commitment. It is a commitment which is not within the category of specialization. It is the commitment which will have none of a world, ideological and institutional, which oppresses. It is a commitment which leads us to look at all our stupidities, and at perhaps one of the greatest: to live in a world which can transport moon-rock to earth for the curiosity of the scientist and cannot move grain around the world for the feeding of the hungry. The whole Church must make up its mind.

Near the cross of Jesus stood his mother. . . . After this Jesus knew that everything had now been completed, and to fulfil scripture perfectly he said: 'I am thirsty'. . . . After Jesus had tasted the vinegar he said, 'It is accomplished' and bowing his head he gave up his Spirit. . . . As soon as they came ashore they saw that there was some bread there. ... Jesus said, 'bring some of the fish you have just caught. ... Come and have breakfast'.

In his suffering was to be found his rising. And in his suffering is to be found our suffering, and in our suffering his rising.

NOTES

1. Roger Aubert, *The Christian Centuries: A New History of the Catholic Church*, Vol. 5: *The Church in a Secularised Society* (London: Darton, Longman & Todd, 1978), p. 144.
2. Gibson Winter, *Being Free* (New York: Doubleday, 1970), p. 27.
3. *Proceedings of the Special Senate Committee on Poverty, no. 21* (Ottawa: Ottawa Information, 1971), p. 44.
4. Patrick Kerans, *Sinful Social Structures* (New York: Paulist Press, 1974). Both quotations under notes 2 and 3 are quoted in this little book, on pp. 87–8. But I think the separate references are worthwhile.
5. Hans Urs von Balthasar, 'Meeting God in today's world', *Concilium*, 9 (1) (London, 1965), p. 5.
6. G. Brenan, *St John of the Cross: His Life and Poetry* (Cambridge: Cambridge University Press, 1973), p. 165.

Further reading

John Atherton, *Faith in the Nation: A Christian Vision for Britain* (London: SPCK, 1988). Examines the common good and the body of Christ as Christian resources for a reciprocal and participative society which balances free markets and democratic institutions.

Chris Bryant, *Possible Dreams: A Personal Account of Christian Socialism in Britain* (London: Hodder and Stoughton, 1997). An engaging account of the personalities and movements which created the Christian socialist tradition in Britain and its continuing influence in the contemporary Labour Party.

Manuel Castells, *The Urban Question: A Marxist Approach* (London: Edward Arnold, 1977). Argues that grassroots community groups and co-operatives may provide the answers to the contradictions of capitalist-led urban development between human life quality and planning for profit and the maximum mobility of goods, labour and natural resources.

The Common Good and the Catholic Church's Social Teaching: A Statement of the Catholic Bishops' Conference of England and Wales (London: Catholic Bishops' Conference, 1996). Clear and concise account of the option for the poor and the concept of the Common Good in Catholic Social Teaching. Critiques the exclusion of the poor from proper participation in civil society and in democratic and economic life in contemporary urban Britain.

Gary J. Dorrien, *Reconstructing the Common Good: Theology and Social Order* (Maryknoll, NY: Orbis, 1990). Comparative exploration of different models of the kingdom of God and the common good in the social ethics of a range of contemporary theologians from Rauschenbusch to Bonino. Argues for a more decentralized vision of democracy.

Faith in the City of Birmingham (Exeter: Paternoster Press, 1988). There is much in this report on the partnership of the Church with politicians and local government agencies in efforts to regenerate local communities in urban priority areas.

Frank Field, *The Politics of Paradise: A Christian Approach to the Kingdom* (London: Collins, 1987). Criticizes *Faith in the City* for failing to link poverty with wealth, or to identify specific ways in which resources could be redistributed from rich to poor. Argues that the Christian contribution to politics should focus on the formation of individual conscience and character, and shared values, through education in the way of the Kingdom and through the sharing of a theological vision of society grounded in the Bible.

Laurie Green, *Power to the Powerless* (London: Marshall Pickering, 1986). Explores the spiritual and theological significance of power and powerlessness. Argues that the crucified God is not only in solidarity with the powerless but, through the Cross, the power which is distorted by domination is returned to the poor and the powerless have power restored to them.

Laurie Green, 'The body: physicality in the UPA', in Peter Sedgwick (ed.), *God in the City* (London: Mowbray, 1995), pp. 105–18. Working people experience powerlessness in their bodies and physical environment: through the control of their bodies in manual labour; in the post-industrial demise of working-class manual jobs; and in the physical decay and ugliness of many UPA environments. People in the inner city also regain power over their lives through bodily expression in sexuality, boxing, body-building, and other forms of physical display and assertion. The emphasis on embodiment in the UPA resonates with the story of the God who is at home in the body of Jesus Christ.

John de Grucy, *Christianity and Democracy: A Theology for a Just World Order* (Cambridge: Cambridge University Press, 1995). Powerful exposition of the constitutive links between Christianity and democracy and of the contribution of the Christian understanding of justice to a continuing and prophetic critique of democratic practice with first-hand case study material from the transition to democracy in South Africa.

John Habgood, *Confessions of a Conservative Liberal* (London: SPCK, 1988). Part One in particular on public faith in which the former Archbishop of York argues that the churches often speak for those whom the British establishment oppresses, reflecting an option for the powerless which has biblical warrant.

Michael Jacobs and the Real World Coalition, *The Politics of the Real World* (London: Earthscan, 1996). Surveys the global connections between growing poverty and unemployment and the deregulation of global as well as national markets. Argues for the recovery of democratic control of economic resources and processes to prevent a drift into further and more extreme inequality, and poverty, with associated rises in crime and insecurity, and reductions in quality of life.

David E. Jenkins, *God, Politics and the Future* (London: SCM Press, 1988). Essays and reflections on the threats to democracy and citizenship which extreme social divisions encouraged by monetarist economism represent: includes two valuable essays on urban issues and the Church in the city.

Chris Rowland, 'Reflections on the politics of the Gospels', in Robin Barbour (ed.), *Kingdom of God and Human Society* (Edinburgh: T & T Clark, 1993), pp. 230–41. Argues that although Jesus did not talk in political terms, none the less his teaching presents the contours of an alternative polity which was so subversive to the Jewish subalterns of Roman imperialism that it ultimately led to his death.

Jim Wallis, *The Soul of Politics* (London: HarperCollins, 1995). Argues that a Christian approach to politics will emphasize both personal responsibility and the collective quest for social justice. It also involves a process of spiritual conversion to a 'prophetic spirituality' and a 'politics of community', a process illustrated with a fund of stories linking spiritual and social transformation.

J. Philip Wogoman, *Christian Perspectives on Politics* (Philadelphia: Fortress Press, 1988). Excellent clear textbook survey of Christian approaches to politics: good critiques of isolationalist, sectarian and Christian realist positions.

John Howard Yoder, *The Politics of Jesus: Vicit Agnus Noster* (Grand Rapids, Michigan: Eerdmans, 1972). Paradigmatic exposition of the politics of Jesus as a politics of non-violent resistance, given effect in contemporary society in a politics of the church as a distinct community of value and love which resists the seductions of power.

7

Generations and gender in the city

These are the words of the Lord of Hosts: I have been very jealous for Zion, fiercely jealous for her. Now, says the Lord, I shall come back to Zion and dwell in Jerusalem. Jerusalem will be called the City of Faithfulness, and the mountain of the Lord of Hosts:

Once again old men and women will sit in the streets of Jerusalem, each leaning on a stick because of great age; and the streets of the city will be full of boys and girls at play.

(Zechariah 8:2–5)

Faith in the City

Many of the elderly owner-occupiers in decaying terraces are widows, unused to handling housing maintenance and afraid of being swindled by 'cowboy' builders. Their children have moved away from the area and they are unable to join them. They feel deserted and alone. (10.29)

When families become homeless it is usually the women who have to try to look after children in the squalid conditions of bed and breakfast hotels or homeless family accommodation, just as they have to cope with the family in a tower block flat, with nowhere safe for the children to play. Single parents, usually women, get offered the worst accommodation ('they wouldn't be able to manage a garden'). (10.32)

There are sizeable groups of young people who are trapped in UPAs, who only gain attention when they become a threat, who are denied equality of opportunity and life chances, and with whom the Churches have little or no contact. (13.94)

Introduction

The growing incidence of delinquency and crime amongst the children who live in Britain's inner cities and peripheral housing estates, and the growing fear of crime — mugging, burglary, even rape — which old people in these areas experience is one of the tragic evidences of the increasing poverty of UPAs in the last twenty years. Poverty is one of the surest factors leading to family breakdown and the multiplication of single parent families (**Holman**). Poverty and long-term unemployment in the family, and to a lesser extent lone-parent households in poor areas, are clearly associated with delinquency in a significant proportion of children from UPAs, and if unchecked, of subsequent criminal behaviour.

The fracturing of relations between old and young evidenced in the frequent victimization of one generation by the other is also a consequence of the breakdown of extended family networks so young people may have little regular contact with their own grandparents. The breakdown of kinship networks and community spirit of the kind which sustained the urban poor in difficult circumstances in earlier generations (Young and Wilmott) is partly a consequence of the destruction of the spirit of place by insensitive and often inhuman housing redevelopment in the 1960s and 1970s. But it is also a consequence of the dual advancement of increased prosperity, and consumerism for the majority, and cuts in welfare payments and social service provision for the unemployed or under-employed minority in the 1980s and 1990s (Mays). The dramatic rise in burglary and car theft in most UPA areas, and the increasing incidence of public order disturbances on many UPA estates, with riots a relatively common happening particularly in the summer months, are both functions of the increasingly divided nature of post-industrial Britain.

Family breakdown amongst the urban poor, related partly to the strain poverty and long-term unemployment place on marriage (**Holman**), contributes to the feminization of poverty, whereby those who primarily experience the vicissitudes of poverty in child-rearing — making small amounts of money stretch to buy clothes, shoes, food and provide warmth for children — are women. On many estates children have no stable relationships with fathers, but instead male figures come and go, increasingly detached from family life as they have lost the capacity in a machine-driven manufacturing economy to find regular work and hence to support a family (Dennis and Erdos; **Harrison**).

Male under-achievement in schools, the demise of traditional working-class heavy engineering and manufacturing jobs, and the increasing inability or unwillingness of young males to stay in stable family networks have all contributed to rising male crime and suicide rates. The displacement of males from secure jobs and permanent relationships has been accompanied by changing attitudes to marriage and sexuality which have made it more socially acceptable for women to raise children entirely outside of marriage. This tendency is enhanced when already inadequate welfare payments are greater for two adults living at separate addresses than when they live under the same roof. The feminization of poverty in Britain and North America is also a function of limited provision of state-funded child care and nursery education for under-fives, so that divorced or single women who bring up their children alone are mostly denied the opportunity to find work and escape the economic and social poverty of welfare dependency. Even when they do find work, lone mothers are likely to receive much lower rates of pay for the part-time work which is most compatible with child-care because of the casualization and deregulation of the labour market, and the continuing gender bias in levels of pay.

In addition to cuts in the relative value of welfare payments and child-care resources, public-funded youth work and specialist youth programmes such as

Intermediate Treatment and detached youth workers have also been dramatically cut back in recent years. These programmes for young people on housing estates with few amenities and distant from the cultural hub of city centres are a cost-effective way of resolving delinquent tendencies in disaffected poor young people. The increased resources currently being devoted to young offender institutions, and the growing number of young males in Britain's prisons, may be seen at least partly as a consequence of reduced public investment in play areas and sports pitches, youth clubs and community centres, child care facilities and youth workers in UPAs. These facilities are available to dual income families in suburbs or city centres who can afford to pay for private facilities and who often enjoy better public provision than the residents of UPAs. The unequal provision of social facilities for the children of the poor is not only evidence of a collective failure of morality, but also of ineffective budgeting as the long-term costs of increased crime and delinquency will far outweigh the short-term savings to the Exchequer and the taxpayer.

The problems of poverty, and reductions in public resources for community building and caring, also impact on older people in UPAs, many of whom live alone, and the majority of whom are women (*Ageing*). The contemporary feminization of poverty is also apparent in relation to the elderly, for women over the age of 60 are more than twice as likely as men to be impoverished. Again, this is partly a function of economic gender bias and the traditional dependency of women on men both as wage-earners and pensioners, as well as the tendency of women to outlive their male partners.

More than a quarter of Britain's children are now living in conditions of real poverty, poverty so bad that in 1996 health workers reported a growing incidence of rickets in children from poor families, a bone disease associated with malnutrition, and of tuberculosis, associated with poor damp housing. Parents living on supplementary benefit can frequently not afford fresh fruit and vegetables for themselves or their children. The only food available locally, and the only food they can afford, is mostly tinned or frozen processed food. With reductions in spending on social housing in the 1980s and 1990s, more than a million children in Britain live in damp sub-standard and often multi-occupancy flats, houses and hostels while homelessness amongst young people forced out of the parental home, or more often leaving local authority 'care' with no skills and no jobs, has grown rapidly (*Something to Celebrate*). Old people in UPAs are also suffering from the effects of reductions in public investment in social housing and in the value of pensions relative to earnings, and of increases in indirect taxes on fuel, clothing, household repairs and other essentials which have shifted the tax burden from those in work to the unemployed and retired population.

The reduction in resources which our society is prepared to devote to the nurture of children and the care of older people in UPAs contrasts markedly with the increasing resources devoted to private consumption by the comfortable (**Young and Halsey**). The burden of income and corporation taxes is lower in Britain than in any other European country while the costs associated with social breakdown in UPAs (crime, family break-up, vandalism, ill health) are growing faster in Britain than in any other developed country except the USA, whose New Right policies of reductions in resources devoted to poor children, lone parents and the elderly poor we have been shadowing (**Holman**).

The breakdown in relations between young and old and the failure of the rich and powerful to respect the poor and vulnerable, the widow and the elderly, is viewed by the Hebrew prophets as the consequence of the failure of the Israelites to worship God in truth, and to follow God's law which enjoins respect for elders and care for children, widows and the weak as fundamental features of the justice the Lord requires. Micah identifies alienation between the generations as the direct consequence of the idolatry and greed of the wealthy and Israel's rulers. The text from Zechariah sees this alienation being reversed as the worship of the true God is restored in Zion. In an evocative image of social harmony and justice in the city, the prophet envisions the old sitting, and the young playing freely, in the streets of Jerusalem.

These prophecies point to the task of the Church in the UPA and in the nation as a whole to challenge the economic and moral pressures on the family, and the social and spiritual forces which have broken down relations between the generations and substituted the idolatry and morality of private consumption for the worship and ethics of the God of love and justice. The primary form of this challenge will be the fostering of worshipping and caring communities in which children, parents and old people enjoy worship, education and fellowship together. The active participation of children in worship, in music or banner making, through dance or drama, and in the Eucharistic meal, needs to be fostered by churches as a counter-sign to the generational alienation of the wider society.

Education in the Christian story is also an essential means of challenging the values and alienation of contemporary culture, connecting the stories of suffering and struggle in the UPA with the struggles for justice of the people of Israel and the promise of healing and redemption in the stories of Jesus. Education for productive work has become the primary focus of the secular educational system, and in communities where there is little productive work the educational rationale is consequently socially weak. The churches' commitment to education in the new urban industrial cities in the nineteenth century, from which the secular education system emerged in the twentieth, reflected an alternative religious grounding for education exemplified in the Jewish tradition which requires of the youngest child at the Passover meal to ask his father to explain 'why we do this'. The diaspora Jews of second-century Europe were the first people to develop systematic schooling because they believed that only through educating their children in the stories of their ancestors could they give them a sense of identity and purpose even when they were exiled from their land.

Education is of vital importance for children who are exiled in the UPAs of modern Britain, in housing estates and inner city housing which few parents would positively choose for their children to be brought up in. Effort and success in education remain the surest determinant of upward mobility and provide the only outward route from the UPA for most young people. But too often UPA children are disadvantaged by poor parenting and housing, and by under-achieving schools. Equally, however, the education system still tends to judge success and giftedness entirely in academic terms, terms which are inappropriate for many children whose gifts may be located more in personal, artistic or musical skills than in academic performance. Recent curricula and budgetary changes in tandem with the new heavily academic league tables have reduced time for and spending on sports, music, art and drama.

Church involvement in education and child care, through church schools and Sunday Schools, can act as a counter-sign both to inequality in education, and to

an overly academic or productionist approach to education and child development. However, the Church's traditional commitment to education needs to take
supplementary or alternative forms to its sponsoring of church primary schools,
and traditional Sunday School, if it is to begin to address the needs of children
and parents in UPAs. In parts of inner city North America and Southeast Asia,
where state child care is inadequate, many churches use their premises to run
professional day-care and nursery facilities for young families. In some UPAs in
Britain churches are using their church halls for congregational members to run
after-school clubs for children. Parenting classes for adults are also an important
means by which the local church can address and seek to reverse the decline in
standards of parenting associated with family breakdown (Utting *et al.*; *Something to Celebrate*).

When Jesus speaks about the family he says on a number of occasions that his
family is no longer exclusively his biological relatives but all those who take up
the call, and the values of the kingdom of God (Barton). The Christian vision of
the Church as the family of God may provide resources for new approaches to
the generation gap, and to the breakdown of traditional family and kinship
structures in UPAs (*Something to Celebrate*; **Harrison**). The life experience and
parenting skills of older retired neighbours might be a resource for struggling
young parents whose own parents may live many miles away. Young children
benefit immensely from contact with old people who have both the wisdom of
their years and at the same time can identify with children who have not entered
into the heavier responsibilities of adult life which old people have begun to leave
behind. The advancing health of many old people, even those living in poverty,
means they may have energy and strength to give to the wider community. But
because of the decline of social networks and fear of crime in UPAs old people are
bunkered at home for much of their time in front of television sets. Again, the
Church may be able to help mobilize some of these hidden gifts of older people,
and equally to encourage the young to use their spare time in service of those
older people who can no longer tend their gardens or shop for food, encouraging
and enabling young and old alike into new relationships of reciprocity and
care.

Poverty and parenting

Bob Holman

Parenting is hard work in the best of circumstances. For parents on low incomes, even well-intentioned parents who want the very best for their children, the task is made more difficult both in the short term and also in the long term. Sometimes poverty leads to a crisis which then upsets the upbringing of the children.

A single parent I knew was offered cash by a loan shark just before Christmas. 'Here you are, hen, take it, give the kids something nice on Christmas Day.' She took the money. The children enjoyed the presents. Then by January she was due to pay back £45 a week, with the total increasing each time she failed to pay. The shark's thugs banged on her door while the tearful children cowered inside. Then they smashed all the windows of the flat with the threat that she would be next to be smashed unless she paid. The petrified mother gathered her children, borrowed the coach fares, and fled to another town, where they finished up in a Homeless Families Unit. I lost touch but I know the children had been subjected to fear, violence and insecurity which may well have harmed their development.

Crises brought about by lack of money can lead to family conflict. One family kept an alsatian dog for protection. One day it broke a leg in the street and one son, with some presence of mind, nipped into a call box and summoned a vet. Fine. The vet came promptly, removed and treated the dog. But the fee was £50 and the family could not pay, for £50 was half their weekly income. The smaller children kept badgering the mother and the teenage youngsters to get back their beloved dog. One of the teenagers suggested that they saved the £50 by cutting down on food but the mother angrily objected that it was impossible to reduce their food budget by any more. Tempers flared. Meanwhile, every day the dog remained with the vet he charged extra boarding fees. Then he threatened legal action to get his money. The children blamed the mother for not having enough money, the mother blamed the son for calling a private vet instead of the PDSA: a family uproar brought about by £50 — or lack of it.

Eventually the family asked me to help, and I negotiated with the vet to get him to halve his fee and then took the dog to the PDSA. This incident is almost a farce, yet it has a serious side, for it exposed the children to family arguments and conflict. The experience is not unusual. Shortage of money does bring worries, tensions and disputes.

A study by Professor Jonathan Bradshaw and Hilary Holmes of families living long-term on welfare benefits found that 59 per cent admitted to strong disagreements over money. Rudolph Schaffer, professor of psychology at the University of Strathclyde, concludes that family conflict is almost always damaging to children. He writes, 'There is now overwhelming evidence that conflict produces all sorts of undesirable effects on children, and is probably the single most pernicious cause of maladjustment.' All families, including affluent ones, have some conflicts. But there is little doubt that poverty can lead to crises which increase the likelihood of family arguments. After all, a vet's fee is unlikely to disrupt the lives of most families.

In the long term, poverty means not just a disturbing crisis but also a relentless, grinding struggle to survive. It entails a daily material pressure which is unknown to the majority of people.

Families and social policy

From *Something to Celebrate: Valuing Families in Church and Society. The Report of a Working Party of the Church of England Board for Social Responsibility*

What do families need in social and economic terms to survive, to thrive and to be able to fulfil their caring roles?

Perhaps the first requirement is an ordered society which determines, in the public interest and with due recognition of the rights of all, what is and is not lawful behaviour. Society needs a framework of laws which regulate citizenship and/or the right of abode; record births, marriages, divorces and deaths; and provide for the ownership of property. Other responsibilities include taking steps when families are falling short in ensuring the well-being of their members. The most obvious example of this is the duty of local authorities to investigate where children are believed to be at risk of significant harm. Families need a safe environment, so provisions for dealing with crime, including racial attacks, must be in place and enforced.

The second requirement relates to the essential material needs of families. Families need:

- a sufficient and reliable income either from employment or from social security or from private means, in order to keep themselves fed, clothed and warm, and to meet other household expenses;
- secure housing;
- access to schools for their children, day care when they need it and help and support when looking after the children is difficult;
- access to preventive health services and to health care in times of illness;
- special help when it is required, for example after the birth of a baby, or when someone is chronically ill, disabled or mentally ill;
- support during times of family tension and difficulty and, when necessary, access to arrangements for dealing with separation, divorce and responsibility for the children, including child maintenance;
- a secure environment in which spiritual, mental and imaginative growth can take place and relationships be fostered through sport and through play.

While the private market has a part to play in providing for these needs, many of them have to be met through collective arrangements, organized and administered by national or local government on behalf of society. In turn, families help to finance these provisions through taxes, national insurance contributions and other charges. How these needs are to be met is the subject of vigorous debate in an open society. But if they are not adequately addressed, then families will suffer and so will society. If the resulting strains on the family are too great, relationships within the family may be badly affected, sometimes to the point of a break-up of the family unit.

* * *

For most people of working age, the most satisfactory way of acquiring a sufficient and reliable income is through secure employment with adequate payment.

Until the late 1970s and early 1980s most men thought in terms of finding a steady full-time job, often expecting to spend their whole working lives with a single employer. This has changed. There has been an escalating trend towards planned redundancies, lay-offs, short-term contracts and part-time jobs. Employees have to be much more flexible, to reckon to change their employment, and even their occupations, much more frequently, and to work irregular hours. There has been an erosion of job security across the social spectrum, though its impact has been felt in different ways.

The number of manual jobs, particularly in traditionally labour-intensive heavy industries, has diminished. Many high-wage jobs for manual workers such as miners have gone, often to be replaced, if at all, by low-wage employment. Many unskilled workers now have to live with the anxiety that they may never find work again. Many young people who leave school without qualifications or skills have to face the real probability that they may never find secure employment at all. This changes the way the traditional male role of family breadwinner is perceived. It also alters the balance within many families since much of the growth in employment has been in employment for women. Moreover, great stress can be experienced by husbands and wives who have different patterns of shiftwork and cannot spend much time together.

Amongst skilled and professional workers, the reduction in job security has often been accompanied by an increase in working hours. Employers often want their employees to work very long hours, and this has created a new work ethic which can conflict with family life. Time spent travelling to work also means less time for the family. Employers may require workers to move often, which can cause strains in families, particularly where there is a conflict between the careers of husbands and wives. Constant moving can disrupt children's education and makes it more difficult for families to make friends and put down roots in their local communities.

The increasing number of mothers in the labour market in part reflects the changing role of women in society, but the primary motivation has been the need to bring more income into the family. Over the last decade there has been a dramatic increase in the number of women who are combining motherhood and employment.

• By 1992, 63 per cent of married mothers were in paid work, 21 per cent full time and 41 per cent part time.

- Some 42 per cent of lone mothers were employed in 1992, 17 per cent full time and 24 per cent part time.
- Among married mothers with a child under five years, the proportion in employment has increased from 27 per cent in 1977 to 47 per cent in 1992, 14 per cent full time, 33 per cent part time.
- Three-quarters of all married mothers with a child over five years are in paid work, 27 per cent full time, 47 per cent part time.[1]

Part-time employment has many advantages for women with children because it allows them more scope to combine paid work and family responsibilities. But it also has disadvantages. Low pay is particularly common among part-time women workers. This is because many of the jobs are in the service industries where wages are typically low and because the hourly rates of pay for part-time workers are often set at a lower level than those of full-time workers in equivalent jobs. Promotion opportunities are more limited and the extent to which part-time workers receive employment protection through the labour laws is restricted by rules related to hours of work and years of service.[2]

Official policies in this country see the changed and more flexible labour market as highly desirable because it will create more jobs. But the other side of the coin is more insecurity for many of those in work who are trying to earn their living and support their families. The majority of European Union countries have decided that the pursuit of greater flexibility must be qualified by measures to protect the wages and working conditions of those in employment — hence the Social Chapter adopted by the other 11 EU members and in all probability in the future by the new EU member states. The UK has opted out of the Social Chapter, has abolished most of the Wages Councils which set minimum wages for some of the lowest paid occupations, has reduced employment protection rights, and has experienced — and indeed encouraged — an increase in low-wage employment.[3]

There has been some recognition among major employers of the need to develop more 'family-friendly' policies in the workplace, in particular policies which allow more time for the demands of parenthood, for both fathers and mothers.[4] We would wish to encourage this trend and see it extended to a wider range of workplaces.

* * *

All families experience variations both in their income and in their expenditure. In our view it is right that the state should intervene to sustain family incomes by providing Family Credit for low-paid families, Unemployment Benefit for people who are temporarily unemployed, Income Support for those who are unable to work, Child Benefit for dependent children, disability benefits for people whose prospects of work are inhibited by disability, and pensions for elderly people.

In recent years there have been a number of changes to the social security system that have affected families. These have often been small changes designed to save public expenditure but in their cumulative effect quite important for families. Perhaps the most important of these was the decision taken in 1980 to break the link between benefits and earnings. Since 1980 most benefits have been uprated by inflation only. Thus as earnings have moved ahead of prices, the living standards of those who must rely on benefits have declined relative to the living standards of those who work. In our view this drift in the comparative value of social security benefits cannot be allowed to continue without isolating those on benefit from the rest of society and destabilizing the inter-generational contract implied in a 'pay as you go' scheme. The social security system reinforces social cohesion and helps to protect the vulnerable. If it is allowed to diminish in relative value it will undermine social solidarity in this country — a point emphasized by the report of the Joseph Rowntree Foundation *Inquiry into Income and Wealth*.[5]

Another change has been the drift from reliance on contributory benefits to selective and income-related benefits. The latter benefits are not claimed by all those entitled to them and create poverty traps in combination with the tax system when they are withdrawn as earnings rise. The increase in real housing costs in recent years has tended to work against the Government's attempts to reduce the impact of the poverty and unemployment trap.

There have been constant incremental changes for unemployed people, among which have been the abolition of earnings-related Unemployment Benefit, the abolition of child additions to Unemployment Benefit, culminating now in the proposal to replace Unemployment Benefit by a Job Seekers Allowance. There has been a massive increase in the numbers of people, including unemployed people, dependent on Income Support. The majority of lone parents were certainly worse off as a result of the introduction of Income Support,[6] but other claimant groups also suffered from the replacement of additions for special needs by the cash-limited and mainly loan-based Social Fund and by the fact that they had to pay water charges and, now, 8.5 per cent VAT on fuel for the first time.

One of the most dramatic changes in the Income Support scheme was the ending of entitlement for most 16 to 18-year-olds. The idea was that young people of this age should be supported and subsidized by their parents. They should either stay on at school or enter the Youth Training Scheme (YTS) where there was an intention that places should be guaranteed for the whole age-group who needed them. However, there is evidence that YTS has not succeeded in delivering either the quality or the quantity of training that is required and young people have had to fall back on the resources of their parents. Young people who have been in care, or are unable to live with their families, perhaps because they have been thrown out, seem to be falling through the net. Although a severe hardship scheme was eventually established, it has proved cumbersome and far less effective than a straightforward right to Income Support, even with work-related safeguards. One result has been a large increase in youth homelessness in the last decade or so.[7]

* * *

Having a good place to live is one of the most important bases for family life. Housing provides security and stability, and a familiar environment that is particularly important for young children.

At the beginning of the First World War, nine-tenths of all accommodation was privately rented; now the proportion is only 8 per cent. Between the two dates, slum clearance, the sale of better standard properties into owner-occupation, and the lack of incentives to develop new privately rented homes all contributed to this steep decline. Efforts by successive governments since the 1970s to reverse this trend have had only limited effects.

Although all local authorities were able to build houses for rent from 1900, the biggest expansion in this sector came after the Second World War. Council housing represented over one-quarter of the housing stock in 1961. By 1990, this had declined to one-fifth. An alternative provision of low-rent housing by housing associations was stimulated in 1974 by legislation which enabled the associations to receive up to 90 per cent of the costs of developing accommodation.

Changes in legislation have reduced subsidies for building low-rent accommodation both in the local authority and housing association sectors. Measures have also been taken which have allowed rents to approach 'market' levels in both the public and private sector. The Government decided that these increased rent levels would be met through Housing Benefit for people on low incomes. The 'burden' of housing costs was transferred from the Department of the Environment to the Department of Social Security. The Department of Social Security has plans, however, to cap its Housing Benefit bill, which has escalated in recent years.

It is very difficult for young people starting work for the first time to find rented accommodation at a price which they can afford, particularly in rural areas.[8] This often forces them to continue living in their parents' home at a time when they might do better learning to fend for themselves. These difficulties are compounded when two young people are ready to start life on their own, because learning to be a couple in the inhibiting atmosphere of a parental home can be stressful.

The major form of housing tenure has become owner-occupation, which stands at just under 70 per cent. Traditionally owner-occupation has offered security of tenure and freedom from harassment. There has been a degree of choice about location and style of accommodation. In addition, there have also been considerable financial benefits through tax relief on mortgage interest payments and the acquisition of a capital asset. Owner-occupation was given a further boost by the Right-to-Buy policy in 1980 for people in local authority accommodation. Great difficulty has, however, been experienced by many families in maintaining mortgage repayments during times of unemployment. A stagnant housing market has made it difficult for people to move to take up work, and for others the capital value of their property is less than the outstanding mortgage loan. Many families cannot meet their mortgage obligations from a single salary and this has put pressure on families for both partners to find work. Further pressures will arise if proposed new measures to restrict severely the payment of mortgage interest for those on Income Support are implemented.

The chances of families having accommodation which is secure have decreased markedly in recent years. The ultimate manifestation of such insecurity is homelessness. Between 1981 and 1991 the number of households accepted by the local authorities as homeless and in priority need doubled. Some 78 per cent of these were families with dependent children or households including a pregnant woman.[9] It was estimated that in 1990 alone a quarter of a million children were among those accepted as homeless.[10] Local authorities have statutory duties towards homeless people.

Families accepted as unintentionally homeless by the local authorities have a right to permanent accommodation, probably after a period in temporary accommodation. In 1993, of over 58,000 households in temporary accommodation, 41,000 were in short-life housing, 12,000 in hostels and 5,500 in bed and breakfast hotels.[11]

The Churches' National Housing Coalition — along with many other organizations in the field of housing and homelessness — believe that the relative neglect of affordable rented housing must be reversed. All available resources should be used — council housing, housing associations and private landlords, and through new home building for rent and by bringing empty property back into use. Given that families need stability in order to flourish, we recommend that the Government reviews its housing policies in order to achieve a clearer and fairer strategy.

* * *

We conclude this chapter with one of the most disturbing aspects of family life today: the number of households living on very low incomes. This includes those households where the wage-earners are on low pay and those families which receive Income Support. It can include people at all stages of life: children, unemployed people, people with disabilities and long-term illnesses, and elderly people.

There is no doubt that the period from 1940 to 1980 was one of unprecedented improvement in the living standards of most British families. One of the 'Five Giants' that Beveridge identified in his 1942 report as standing in the way of social reconstruction was Want. His recommendations for social security were largely implemented in the spate of legislation of the 1940s that led to the introduction of Family Allowances (now Child Benefit), National Assistance, and a national insurance scheme covering the major contingencies of unemployment, widowhood, sickness and retirement. These benefits, together with a National Health Service free at the point of demand, fiscal and economic policies which ensured extraordinarily low levels of unemployment, and growth in dual-earner families, led to a major assault on want. Real Gross Domestic Product increased nearly threefold between 1945 and 1980; real disposable income nearly doubled; average working hours fell; and most social security benefits more than doubled in real terms. If a statistical series existed that traced poverty consistently over those 40 years, it would show that while there was always a minority of families living on low incomes due to unemployment, low wages, disablement, or family disruption, in general the proportion in poverty had fallen.

Since 1979 there has been an unprecedentedly sharp increase in income inequality and in poverty. Whilst average incomes have continued to rise (by 36 per cent between 1979 and 1991/92), income inequalities have increased. More children now live in families with low relative incomes and the least well-off families are poorer than the least well-off families were in 1979.[12]

* * *

In this chapter, we have discussed a series of policy areas as they affect families and indicated some directions which we believe policy should take.

We need now to look at some broader issues of family policy and the principles which underlie them.

First, we want to emphasize again that families and society depend on one another. The family has the prime responsibility for the care and upbringing of children and for the care of its own sick, disabled and frail members. In the main, families shoulder these responsibilities willingly and lovingly, and in so doing they make a major contribution to the well-being of the whole of society. But there is reciprocal responsibility on the part of society to give the family practical support through the collective arrangements already discussed. Moreover, society should refrain from making more and more extra demands on the family, often beyond its capacity to bear. We have been through a period when support for the family has been weakened while more demands were made of parents. This was implicitly acknowledged by Norman Lamont, Chancellor of the Exchequer in 1991 when he spoke of the 'widespread view in the House and in the country that more should be done to help families with children'.[13]

Second, we have to consider what the policy response should be to the fact that the family in the UK, now more than ever, takes many forms: single parents, divorced and separated parents, cohabiting unions, step-families as well as the two-parent, married couple who marry once only and stay together. Should a 'family policy' operated by Government seek to favour one family form rather than another? Should it go further and seek to disadvantage other family forms — by reducing benefits, for example — to discourage the formation of such families in the future? Such a policy implies sacrificing today's children in order that tomorrow's children will be born only into favoured family forms. We do not find this acceptable.

Family policy has to deal with families as they are today. There is a strong case for policies which teach young people about the responsibilities of parenthood and policies which have the effect of preventing family breakdown, either by reducing unnecessary stress (caused by job insecurity or homelessness, for example) or by offering help in times of stress, through a range of family and marriage support services. But once a new family is formed, the principal task of a family policy is to support the new unit to enable it to carry out its caring role.

Third, we are aware that many people and families in our society are faced with the threat of poverty, either for long periods, or for a series of short periods. Inequality has increased so much that the standard of living of a large minority is now falling further and further behind the majority. . . . We see this as a very serious development, both for the individuals and families who are suffering from this disadvantage and for society as a whole. We seek a society which:

- rejects social division and aims to promote social cohesion;
- seeks greater equality in life chances for all its people, particularly for children and young people;
- seeks a balance between personal responsibility and family autonomy on the one hand, and, on the other, a sense of community and solidarity with one another.

Such a society is best suited to the well-being of families and is one to which families can make a worthwhile contribution.

NOTES

1. *The General Household Survey* (London: HMSO, 1992).
2. J.C. Brown, *Escaping from Dependence. Part-time Workers and the Self-employed: The Role of Social Security* (London: Institute of Public Policy Research, 1994).
3. A Bryson, 'The 80s: decade of poverty', *Low Pay Unit New Review* (National Association of Citizens Advice Bureaux (NACAB), December 1989/January 1990); NACAB, *Hard Labour: Citizens Advice Bureaux' Experience on Low Pay and Poor Working Conditions* (NACAB, 1990); NACAB, *Job Security: CAB Evidence on Employment Problems in the Recession* (NACAB, 1993).
4. *Parents at Work: UK Employer Initiatives* (Wainwright Trust, 1994), gives many examples of this.
5. *Joseph Rowntree Foundation Inquiry into Income and Wealth* (York: Joseph Rowntree Foundation, 1995).
6. M. Evans, D. Piachaud and H. Sutherland, *Effects of the 1986 Social Security Act on Family Incomes: The Welfare State Programme* (London: London School of Economics, 1994).
7. National Association of Citizens Advice Bureaux, *Severe Hardships: CAB Evidence on Young People and Benefits* (NACAB, 1992); I. McLagan, *Four Years Severe Hardship* (London: COYPSS/Youthaid/Barnardo's, 1993); J. Greve, *Homelessness in Britain* (York: Joseph Rowntree Foundation, 1991).
8. *Faith in the Countryside: Report of the Archbishops' Commission on Rural Areas* (London: Churchman Publishing, 1990).
9. Table 8.12, *Social Trends* (London: HMSO, 1994).
10. Greve, *Homelessness in Britain*.
11. Table 10.26, *Social Trends*.
12. *Joseph Rowntree Foundation Inquiry into Income and Wealth*.
13. *Hansard*, 19 March 1991, col. 179.

Family and community socialism

Michael Young and A. H. Halsey

It is not too far-fetched to compare the first half of the last century with the last half of this. Children are not having their bodies crippled but too many of them are having their spirits maimed. There is still joy and achievement. But there is also growing distress and pain. This is brought home periodically by the train of tragic children thrust into momentary prominence by the media. They come like so many others from families which have broken down, families which have been plunged into poverty, schools which are in disarray, an economy which has left so many young people without jobs — more young people out of work than there were and more young men than young women.

Neglect has taken a multiple toll:

• The number of drug offenders between the ages of 17 and 29 doubled between 1979 and 1989;

- Reading standards among 7–8-year-olds declined during the 1980s;
- Expulsion of children from school became more common. Between 1986 and 1991 there were dramatic increases in the use of 'all types of exclusion for children in all age groups';
- The number of children in care under the age of 10 increased from 1985 onwards;
- The proportion of children on Child Protection Registers almost quadrupled during the 1980s;
- Total reported crime, including juvenile crime, increased by almost 80 per cent and violent crime by 90 per cent during the ten years 1981–1991;
- The suicide rate among young men aged 15–24 increased by 75 per cent from 1983 to reach a peak in 1990;
- The number of deaths from solvent abuse increased between four- and five-fold between 1980 and 1990.

Richard Wilkinson brought together these facts in a report published by Barnardo's[1] after the Commission on Social Justice had completed its task. He traced the decline of children's quality of life to the wrong-way-round redistribution there has been under Mrs Thatcher and Mr Major, from the poor to the rich, from children to adults, and generally to the increasing gap between richer and poorer. The Commission summed it up too: 'Today, the gap between the earnings of the highest-paid and those of the lowest-paid workers is greater than at any time since records were first kept in 1886'.[2] We live in a country in which homeless families can be moved on to a new housing estate with no furniture and only the belongings they can carry. 'As a result, families with children were sleeping on mattresses on the floorboards of brand new three-bedroomed houses with no other furniture whatsoever. An experienced housing manager commented that he had never seen such poverty except in third world countries.'[3]

Inequality has been growing and so has the fragility of the family. Some of the most telling evidence about the changes comes from the longitudinal studies which have followed samples of children born in 1946 (the Douglas study), in 1958 (the National Child Development Study) and in 1970. All three sets of children have now grown up and some of them have children themselves so that some of the long-term effects of disruption in one generation can be brought out. The broad effects were the same in all three samples and the outcomes were not just the result of poverty. The same consequences were found cross-cutting all social classes and income groups. In the 1946 sample, the children who experienced their parents' divorce before they reached 15 had lower levels of attainment at school as well as more emotional disturbance and more delinquency, and were themselves more prone to divorce or separation than those whose parents had remained married.

The 1958 sample has been examined in the same way and the outcome is, if anything, more dire. The people whose parents' marriages broke down are more likely to finish school at the minimum age and to leave home before they are 18; they are much more likely to suffer from psychological problems; and the men are much more likely to be regular smokers. For children with a divorced parent and a step-father or step-mother the differences from families with two natural parents are even more striking. Girls in step-families run twice the risk of pregnancy outside marriage while teenagers, and we know from other evidence that they run more risk of sexual abuse too, sometimes from step-fathers. Girls and boys in step-families are twice as likely to leave school at age 16. David Willetts summed up the evidence by saying 'better death than divorce, better single parent than step-parent'.[4] There is also a link with juvenile delinquency. Another smaller longitudinal study found that 'Up to the tenth birthday, the future juvenile delinquents were more likely to have experienced broken homes or separations from their parents'.[5]

In the three main samples the children of divorced and separated parents were in a minority. This continues to be so but to a lessening extent. In 1985 80 per cent of children in general under 16 were living with both their natural parents. This is an absolutely key indicator for the state of child nurturing. But the statistic has been moving rapidly the wrong way. The 80 per cent of 1985 became 70 per cent by 1991[6] and may be no more than 60 per cent now. Increasing proportions of children are being born and brought up without a committed father, or with several. One five-year-old said: 'I've got three daddies which is nice at birthdays but not at other times.'[7] Britain is on the way to becoming a new kind of matrilineal society. More and more children are being brought up by their mothers with fathers being most noticeable either by their absence or by their plurality.[8] It is unlike most of the matrilineal societies described by anthropologists which give men an important role. Fewer couples are the joint guardians of domestic security and serenity for their offspring. It can, of course, come out well with only one parent, or in any kind of family. Hewitt and Leach put forward a proposition which is incontestable: 'Individual children thrive in any kind of family where they are well cared for by loving parents or parent-figures.'[9] But increasing numbers of children are not well cared for.

Things have been made worse by education's subservience to the economy. Against this background, children are seen not in their own right for their gifts as children but as potential adults who will one day repay the efforts of the teachers and the support of the taxpayers by starting to earn and pay taxes themselves. In every class in every primary and secondary school in the country some pupils are clearly going to make the grade. They are going to continue in education beyond the minimum age. They are going to get jobs. And then below them, and below the doubtfuls whom no teacher can be sure about, are the children who may never be capable of jobs — often because they come from disturbed families and because they have no adults in their lives who take an informed interest in what happens to them at school.

Teachers unwittingly, or if wittingly unwillingly, have become recruiting sergeants for the economy. Pupils who are unlikely to pass muster are put into the lower streams. When a consistently unfavourable view is taken of their 'ability', children can become thoroughly disheartened. Without motivation, they do not succeed. Pupils made to look foolish become foolish. If it is thought (or even feared) that they will become unemployable, they are all the more liable to. The prophesy becomes self-fulfilling. The invasive economy has invaded education. If the economy is believed to be a meritocracy, whatever the human losses, the school has to be a meritocracy too. In class there has to be an underclass.

One of the great hopes of the last half century was that comprehensive schools would avoid stigmatizing children in the way that the 11+ had done. But that hope has not been realized. Instead of the 11+ we have schools being graded, with much encouragement from the government, so that forceful parents can scramble to get their children into the best while other schools slide back. Instead of the 11+, we have streaming which divides the sheep from the goats and can be more humiliating than the 11+. This elitist policy needs to be challenged on many fronts by a new government. Better training when pupils leave schools will not be enough; the problem has to be tackled in the schools as well.

Unless some steps are taken, those who are condemned early will end up having lost confidence in themselves. They may not even get any noticeably useful skills out of school.

> A major survey into the attainment of a representative group of 21-year-olds has revealed that almost 15 per cent have limited literacy skills and 20 per cent have only very limited competence with basic maths. ... We have also demonstrated the major effect that poor basic skills have on job prospects, unemployment, housing and health and the inter-generational transfer of reading difficulties. Screening of 10,000 students in further education colleges revealed that almost 4 in 10 would need some additional help with basic skills if they were to get a qualification at NVQ level 2 (i.e. a National Vocational Qualification at craft level).[10]

There has also been continuous pressure on school finances, which has been made more grievous by the endlessly repeated criticism of the teaching profession and of local education authorities by successive ministers who have become the leading critics of the education they are responsible for. We don't say that some reforms were not needed. But the government has tried to do it in the wrong way. They have certainly succeeded in one thing — undermining the confidence of a whole profession. Yet throughout a long-drawn-out confrontation the government has always presented itself as the reformer. There have been nineteen Educational Reform Acts since 1979 — Reform Acts with a sense of desperation about them, each seeking to cope with the problems created by its predecessors — and almost all failing in their purpose because the government has been unable to gain the co-operation of the teaching force who are supposed to act on the Acts. A government in power for sixteen years repeatedly laments the poor school performance of young children and yet never accepts that it has any share in the blame for it.

The perceived failure of an earlier generation of progressive school reforms has led to a reaction, promoted by the present government, which we consider wholly misguided. 'Child-centred education' may have become a sneer or a term of abuse but what are we to think — that education should not be child-centred? More effective teaching methods and means of maintaining order are needed but we do not believe this should entail a return to premature selection and grading. And even those who see education merely as a preparation for economic activity now acknowledge that the nation cannot afford the neglect and failure of its academically less successful children.

If we have given the impression that the fragmentation of families and the undermining of education have been injurious only (or largely) to the children of poorer families, we should say that this has not been our intention. Neglect is not a problem of poverty alone, but a much more general problem for the whole of society, including the well-off. Families are fragile right across the social spectrum. But within the whole there has been a new kind of polarization between richer and poorer.

Alongside the endless variations between increasingly complex types of family, a twofold social division has opened up. On the one hand are the people who are unemployed or in constant danger of it. They are short on money and relatively long on time. On the other hand are the people who can be thought of as the overemployed. They are short on time and relatively long on money. One class is caught out by so much week being left at the end of the money; the other by so little time being left at the end of the week.

The first group have been multiplying as unemployment has continued, with more of them than before in the trough of each successive depression and also at the peak of each successive boom. There are over a million long-term unemployed and many more 'economically inactive' and, after being out of work for months or years, many are unemployable. Many young people, of the kind pre-judged failures at school, have never been in work, especially the low-skilled, and especially men. The rising incidence of male unemployment is a grave matter, especially for the sons of fathers who are out of work and who are taught in primary schools where they have almost no compensatory male models amongst their teachers. Many of the men who have no place in the economy have no place in the family either. The problem could be due in part to the decline of manufacturing and in part to the greater difficulty unemployed people have in bringing up children who will not be unemployed in their turn. They have the time for it, and that is certainly a boon, but if they are very much depressed and impoverished by their unemployment that will certainly not make it easier for them in their role as parents.

The worst-off people are those without any wages coming in who are wholly dependent on social security. Along with them, but often still on the margins of unemployment, without any secure job, are the single-parent families in which the mother has been compelled to go out to work in order to make ends meet.

Towards the other extreme are those who are too busy rather than not busy enough. One of the parents (usually the father) may be working at a demanding job which keeps him out of the home for much of the time in which the children are in it and returns him to it fatigued. His income may be so high that his wife (or partner) does not need to work for financial reasons. But the great majority of better-off families are better off because they are 'dual-career' families where the mother is working as well as the father. While at one extreme neither parent can find any work, at the other, not one but both parents have too much of it.

Their children are liable to suffer not from money-poverty but time-poverty, when they get too little of the time of either parent and much too little of both parents together. Time-poverty can be almost as grievous for children as the more ordinary kind. The people who succeed in holding their own best in a modern economy are those who make themselves the slaves of the clock. This applies with special force to single working parents and to couples who combine two jobs with the care of children and a home. They need an acute sense of time and of how to ration it out even when they are with their children. Creatures of the clock can be abstracted, always aware of what they are missing, of what they are not doing, even while they are doing whatever they have to; the children can be restricted to contact only with part of a person, the whole person being not quite there. The adults can be so taken up with what they are going to do next that they have no time for the moment in which children live.

Even within families the adults can be driven by their own individual timetables and sometimes this has gone so far that the members of a family do not even eat together. The commensality — the eating together — which Max Weber regarded as so necessary to human solidarity — will hardly survive the microwave. The tendency, after so many other social groups have been fragmented, is for the immediate family to become beset by a hurry sickness which is out of kilter with the rhythms of childhood, most obvious with the most affluent but spreading down the social scale with the rise in the standard of life, as it is so misleadingly called.

All this raises the question whether husbands and wives (or partners) should so often both go out to work full-time or even part-time. As Kiernan has said, 'The key and long-term trend which is having a fundamental effect on the roles of men and women is the marked increase in the level of women's participation in the labour market.'[11] This is accompanied by a well-documented failure of men to take a larger domestic or nurturing role. Where children are young, and jobs do not match neatly with nursery or school, the absence of both parents can hardly fail to be a disadvantage to their children. Why should there be any debate on whether the needs of industry or of children should come first? It is clear to us that as far as public policy goes, the children should come first. This is not to say that there should be any slackening in the move towards more flexible working hours and part-time jobs generally but that the financial pressures to take paid work should not be as intense as at present. If it were relieved there would still be time-harassed parents but there would not be so many, and there would then be fewer time-harassed children.

In a family in which the parents suffer from so many demands on them, the danger (we are saying) is that they will not have enough time for their children when the children need so much of it, in fact need almost all the time there is at the early and also at some other stages of their development. If they do not get enough of the time, attention and love of one or both of their parents, and of course still more if they are deprived of one or both of them, the children may not build up enough trust, enough of a sense of security about their attachments, to be able to strike out when the moment comes into independence and self-reliance, and reach maturity with enough of the capacity to love which is generated by the love and affection that they once received. If their childhood is serene as well as stimulating, later on they will be able to combine self-reliance, and the self-interest which will give brio to life, with that ability to transcend self-interest and regard the interests of others as in some way their own which is the sinew of any society. If that does not happen, without necessarily being aware of the origins of their destructiveness they may become determined to make society suffer in reprisal for what they have suffered. Britain and many other countries are on the way to becoming moral wildernesses filled with children seeking revenge against older generations who seem to have turned their backs on them. 'Sorrow concealed, like an oven stopp'd, Doth burn the heart to cinders where it is.' One can see what Shakespeare meant. Even when it does not go as far as that, lack of self-respect can rebound on others. It can only be destructive to love thy neighbour as thyself if you do not love yourself at least a little; worse still if you hate yourself.

* * *

The balance between the material and moral economies has been upset. In the material economy driven by hedonism people are valued for the contribution they make to production and for the incomes they extract from it. In the moral economy, people are valued not so much for what they do as for who they are. They are mothers and fathers, they are grandmothers and grandfathers, they are children, and they are friends. The ties of kinship and friendship create moral obligations which can override the 'cash nexus'. The sad fact is that for 25 years and above all since 1979, and the amoral Thatcherite counter-revolution against the welfare state, the primacy given to the material economy has undermined the moral economy. Politicians have talked about the need to introduce more personal responsibility instead of 'dependency'. But fine words do not butter any parsnips. Families have had no moral lead from a government which has not been altruistic in its own behaviour: it put such complete faith in the market and in things which are sold on it. Without a foothold in the productive domain, the children have been the losers and even their numbers are declining. Fertility is falling away.

The values to which modern electorates have subscribed with such single-minded intensity are all to do with things, not people. On this vital matter Karl Marx who got so much wrong got it very much right when he wrote about the 'fetishism of commodities',[12] a fetish which he thought, even when he was writing, was on the way to capturing the minds of his contemporaries. Commodities, as he saw them, were accorded an inflated significance as though they had human qualities.

The value put on commodities has even shaped (and misshaped) the forms taken by altruism. Mothers who go out to work to earn money often have to do so in order to keep their children in necessities. But at some notch above that it does not mean quite the same thing if they say 'It's all for the kiddies.' Such behaviour is altruistic in intent. But it is curious that people should exert themselves in order to get money for all manner of toys and other paraphernalia of a child's life which can, after a while, do little more than clutter up the house to which they are dutifully motored back. The commodities are tokens of love when what the children need is not a token but love itself and the time in which to give and receive it. Here is fetishism in its family form. In richer families the fully kitted-out youngster who sees rather little of his or her dutiful but misguided mother and father and is no longer a poor forked creature: he or she is festooned with the products of up-to-date technology. But not necessarily to be envied on that account. The bounty is tainted.

In so far as the modern economy makes people lust after things, it is subtracting value and energy from personal relationships and adding value and energy to objects. A television set is not the brother to a vacuum cleaner, and no personal attachments are ordinarily allowed to stand in the way of ever increasing production. It is perfectly justifiable to sack people, to hire people, to promote people, to demote people, to do almost anything to them if it is in aid of mammon or rather techno-mammon. It is perfectly justifiable to require people to move all over the place in the interests of industry even if the consequence is that children also have to move school at the formative stages of their lives.

The situation will not change unless there is a calming of the economy. To push all the time for maximum possible growth is wrong-headed and equally so to encourage the competitiveness which is held to be necessary for it. The personal harm is the awful cost we have to pay. We should be able to congratulate ourselves not on higher growth but on lower growth in the economy if it reduces time-poverty and if it supports higher growth in the quality of human relations and a betterment of the social as well as the physical ecology.

NOTES

1. R.G. Wilkinson, *Unfair Shares: The Effects of Widening Income Differences on the Welfare of the Young* (Barnardo's Publications, 1994).
2. Report of the Commission on Social Justice, *Social Justice, Strategies for National Renewal*, (New York: Vintage, 1994), p. 28.
3. David Page, *Building for Communities* (York: Joseph Rowntree Foundation, 1993).
4. The Family Contemporary Papers No. 14 (1993), p. 16.
5. D.P. Farrington and D.J. West, 'The Cambridge Study in Delinquent Development: a long-term follow-up of 411 London males', essay in *Kriminalität* (Springer-Verlag, 1990).
6. According to a special rerun of the General Household Survey made for this pamphlet.
7. *Lots of Love*, Compiled by Nanette Newman (London: Collins, 1974).
8. See G. Dench, *The Frog, the Prince and the Problem of Men* (London: Neanderthal Books, 1994).
9. P. Hewitt and P. Leach, 'Social justice, children and families' (London: IPPR, 1993).
10. R. Dearing, July 1993, 'The national curriculum and its assessment: an interim report', quoted in Report of the Paul Hamlyn Foundation National Commission on Education, *Learning to Succeed* (London: Heinemann, 1993), p. 5.
11. K. Kiernan, 'The Respective Roles of Men and Women in Tomorrow's Europe', paper given at the International Conference on Human Resources in Europe at the Dawn of the 21st Century.
12. K. Marx, *Capital: A Critical Analysis of Capitalist Production* (London: George Allen & Unwin, 1938).

Women of the Manor — ministry on an Urban Priority-Area council estate

Barbara A. Harrison

In a sense, the Manor is in a time warp. Extended families, living within a small geographical area, may have disappeared in other areas of the country: in this part of Sheffield they are still numerous. At their heart is Nan-Nan (grandmother) or Great Nan-Nan. She has no economic power, but her influence is immense. Her home is always full of visiting family — they come over for meals, especially Sunday lunch, childminding, company, advice. She knows all the birthdays and wedding anniversaries by heart; there is always a greeting card waiting to be posted. Her family often spans four generations — women commonly become great-grandmothers in their mid-fifties — and is usually large. As she grows older, the balance of care begins to tip: housebound and infirm, she never lacks someone to shop and make her meals and keep her company. But she never loses the right to speak her mind. At her funeral there will be no lack of tears, and a real sense that someone of importance has been lost.

Within the family, there will almost certainly be women who are bringing up other people's children. Babies of young teenage girls are often brought up by the grandmother or aunt: when relationships break up and the burden of caring for several small children becomes too much for the lone mother, or when a mother dies or goes into hospital or prison, the children will be taken on by other members of the family. This simply seems the natural thing to do, and there is irritation at the need to justify it to the DSS, or cope with formal adoption procedures.

For 'family' women, everything is relational. Their exact position within the extended family is complex: they are bound by many interwoven ties of affection and concern, of love and hatred. A succession of partners may mesh them in with several family networks. There is a keen sense of belonging, but often in times of crisis, the women are under intense strain as they try to care for their children, siblings, parents or grandparents. Any pastoral care which is to be effective for them must take on board the whole complicated pattern of relationships that give meaning to their lives.

Of course, this picture of busy, supportive/demanding family life is not universal. On the Manor, as elsewhere, there are women struggling, alone or with children, not only to make ends meet but also to make some sense of a lonely and isolated existence. Particularly poignant is the situation of girls under eighteen, who are usually ineligible for state benefit. If their own family turns them out or is unable to give them any financial help, they may find themselves classed as homeless and housed in poor accommodation with little or no furniture, and dependent on friends for meals and emotional support. On the other hand, childlessness can bring its own problems of loneliness and lack of support: women who have children who have 'got on' and 'bettered themselves' often share this sense of isolation when the family moves away to other parts of the country or the world.

This situation is common in more affluent parts of the country, but there strategies are available for coping — visits to stay with children, coffee mornings, WIs, long-distance telephone calls, voluntary work. On the Manor, women living alone are seen as not conforming to the normal pattern of family life; they often lack the money and confidence to make and keep contact with others. If they are elderly, they often feel they are the only one left of their generation.

The struggle against poverty dominates the lives of many of these women, young or old. A crisis is always around the corner — when the cooker suffers an irretrievable breakdown, or the TV licence is due, or the children need new shoes. Without the resources of the wider family to help out, there is often little choice but to take on a loan from the Social Fund or from a private loan company. It can take a superhuman effort to pay off one debt before the need arises to incur another. Not only is physical energy dissipated in the search for cheap goods and in journeys on foot to housing and benefit offices, but emotional energy is channelled into the constant struggle to survive. No wonder their horizons are narrow and there is little energy left to make connections between their own sufferings and wider political issues. The kind of pastoral care welcomed by these women is supportive, and directed to individual care and concern.

For some women on the estate, however, new and exciting roles have developed. Under pressure of the need to speak out for the rights of tenants caught up in the massive rebuilding programme, women have emerged as leaders in tenants' associations and other community groups. In some cases, training in a trade union context has provided the necessary skills; others have learned them on the job.

Alongside this political development is an educational one. Because of low attainment at school, there is a reluctance to attend formal adult education classes held in school buildings. Much more accessible, both in location and ethos, is the Manor Training and Resources Centre. This is a thriving project with a local management committee, offering courses in a wide range of skills in friendly surroundings and, more often than not, taught by Manor people. An increasing number of women are taking up these opportunities for adult learning — not only in subjects traditionally within their sphere like sewing, machine knitting and basic office skills, but also in word processing and woodwork. Despite the high local rate of male unemployment and the accessibility of the courses, there has been a low uptake by men; but provision of good child care has encouraged even women with young families to come back into education. At the time of writing, only women have enrolled for a new course designed to give access to higher education.

The discovery of unsuspected talents, and the acquisition of officially recognized skills, have brought new confidence and, in some cases, paid employment. There has also been a challenge to the woman's role in the family, especially where the woman's partner is out of work. There has been conflict and a need to adjust traditional expectations of one another. In the face of opposition from the man, the self-doubt which had originally to be overcome before educational or political opportunities could be taken, sur-faces regularly. 'Yes, I know I managed to do A, but I can't see myself doing B.' To avoid conflicts at home, efforts to develop skills may be abandoned.

There is a need here for a pastoral ministry of recognition and encourage-ment. Imagination is called for when trying to understand the effort involved in the struggle against inhibiting factors, both external and internal, as women from the estate begin to explore their own potential. They have come a long way in a short time. Many live with partners whose self-esteem has been smashed by long periods of unemployment, or, in a growing number of cases, the experience of never having been employed at all. It turns the knife in the wound when their womenfolk acquire skills — especially where these lead to paid work. Women need support in facing up to conflict situations, and in exploring new patterns of family relationships.

* * *

The local church is finding that the more traditional forms of individual care may still be appropriate for women who lack family support. It can be valuable simply to have another adult person to take time to listen to the anxieties that weigh so heavily. The majority of a local Anglican congregation is made up of women who have no families or no close relatives in the locality: asked what they thought was good about the Church, they replied almost without exception, 'The fellowship and friendship it provides.' But emotional support and encouragement often need to be supplemented by down-to-earth practical help. In a community where family networks are so normative, there is a need to promote other networks where relationships can be formed and support given and received. Local luncheon clubs are a good way of providing interest, company, and caring for senior citizens.

There is a lot of informal sharing within families — for example, the passing on of baby equipment from one young mother to another. A fund set up by the local churches tries to provide grants or goods to those for whom the help of a family is not available. In a sense this fund acts as a kind of makeshift family in time of need. But great sensitivity is needed. Volunteers who humped a heavy wardrobe and chest of drawers to an upstairs flat in response to a request through a social worker for 'Anything at all to keep the family's clothes in' were taken aback by the firm response, 'Take them away! They are brown — and I don't like brown furniture!' Personal dignity and the right to choose can be more valuable than much needed material possessions. Sadly, it is much easier to persuade the local congregation to be involved with 'ambulance work' of this kind than in joining local protest groups for a more just system.

There are other respects in which Church attitudes, as well as the nature of Church activities, prove unacceptable. Some clergy assume that they do a service to local people by encouraging them to get on and get out. This is often totally unrealistic. A senior Church leader, on a visit to a Manor church, advised a young never-employed woman who had completed an employment training scheme in the use of industrial sewing machines to 'Think big! You could go in for fashion designing and work as a couturier in Paris.' More practicable advice, if it involves moving out of the community, fails to grasp the deep-seated loyalty that exists towards the estate. One day a woman was found crying on the pavement; asked if she needed any help, she replied, indicating the rubble of a demolished house, 'That was my home for fifty years, and look what they have done to it.' More than half the tenants who were forced to move out of their homes in the massive demolition programme chose to be rehoused elsewhere on the estate rather than in another part of the city. There is little response to an approach which tries to encourage people to better themselves so that they can move out.

Ministers serving on the Manor over the years have been committed to working alongside the community. But great tact and discernment are required here also to do this in a way acceptable to local people. Co-operation is cautiously welcomed, but there is a great fear of clerical domination: clergy are thought to be at an unfair advantage derived from their education, the resources at their disposal, and their perception by people in power. Experience has shown that they have a tendency to take over local groups. A local woman activist began a sentence with 'I'm afraid ...'. Teased by a minister present that she always gave the impression that she was afraid of nothing, she became deadly serious. 'There is one thing I'm afraid of,' she said. 'It's you and X [another local minister]. You pretend to be with us, but you're only biding your time till you can take us over.' It is not yet clear whether women ministers are seen as less likely to dominate, and whether in fact they are more able to resist the temptation to 'take over'.

'As we have visited the UPAs, we have been very aware of the contribution made by women to local life, and yet the under-valuing and under-utilization by the Church of the talents and skills they have to offer' (*Faith in the City* report: 6,21). On the Manor there is little sign that women who are becoming aware of their own dignity and worth, and who want to work for change in their community, see the local churches as places appropriate for these endeavours.

In the first place, Manor women challenge the notion that pastoral ministry is in the main to individuals. Women whose whole lives are defined by their position in the family network or networks need to be understood in that context. Sitting for half an hour in a woman's home may be more revealing of the competing claims upon her time and energy than a series of interviews in the vicarage study. Building up such knowledge can be time-consuming and long-term: it involves a low-key, easy approach which makes home visits acceptable to the family. Ministry to those who lack family networks may involve working alongside lone women to create other net-works. The congregation is beginning to twin one of its members with each person who receives Communion at home. It is hoped that a friendship will begin which will result in more frequent visits that will effectively link the housebound with the active worshippers. There is a lot of imaginative work still to be done in the encouragement of new networks, where women without an extended family can be valued and where they can make a contribution.

There is a challenge too to any aggressive, up-front style of ministerial leadership. It is the constant complaint of local people that they are treated as 'all fools' by council officials and 'all rogues' by the local press. However exaggerated this perception may be, it is widely believed and deeply resented. There needs therefore to be great sensitivity in the way people are treated by the Church. In the context of local community groups, a minister needs to learn the skills of listening, of not talking too much, and of respecting the experience and knowledge of those who have spent a lifetime in the area. It can be especially difficult, I believe, for male clergy to value the contribution of local women, since it takes a huge imaginative leap for them to value the things that women value.

Manor women also demand of the Church a recognition of their own dignity and desire for autonomy. Younger women experience a degree of independence within the family of which their grandmothers would never have dreamed. They are increasingly becoming persons in their own right. They chafe at their dependency on the arrival of the giro cheque with their benefit, or the council workman to repair a long-broken window. They will not be moved by a Church that offers yet another form of dependency — on the vicar, or even on God.

Finally, women on council estates present a challenge as yet only dimly perceived to traditional understandings of the nature of God. These women have only recently begun to explore their own strengths and to move away from total economic and emotional dependence on their menfolk. A growing number are getting involved in the struggle against official attitudes that imply that those who live on benefit deserve less choice, less respect, and should exhibit greater deference and a greater acknowledgement of their indebtedness to the rest of society. It is not good news for them to be presented with an image of God as an old-style head of the household encouraging or even demanding dependency. The work of feminist theologians in search of appropriate images of God could be extended here. For it is not only a challenge from women in general, but from women and men together in a dependency culture. Perhaps in a community still rich in extended family relationships there is an opportunity to explore images of mutuality: a special contribution from the women of the Manor might be God as Nan-Nan.

Further reading

Ageing: Report of the Social Policy Committee of the Board for Social Responsibility (London: Church House Publishing, 1990). Thorough Church of England report on ageing in contemporary Britain including the particular problems of older people in poverty and in inner cities. Also includes effective theological reflection on ageing.

Stephen C. Barton, *The Family in Theological Perspective* (Edinburgh: T. & T. Clark, 1995). Valuable collection of essays drawing on biblical, doctrinal and ethical reflection on the status of the family in the Christian tradition and in modern society.

Neville Cryer, *Michel Quoist: A Biography* (London: Hodder and Stoughton, 1977). Inspiring life story of the author of *Prayers of Life* and his work with young people in the Young Christian Workers movement in post-war industrial France.

Norman Dennis and George Erdos, *Families Without Fatherhood* (London: Institute for Economic Affairs, 1993). Argues that the prevalence of family breakdown, and the related growth of lone parent households, are the principal causes of increases in reported crime since the 1950s, and that children who live in families without fathers are not only more prone to delinquency but are also disadvantaged educationally, economically and socially.

General Synod Board of Education, *Children in the Way: New Directions for the Church's Children* (London: National Society and Church House Publishing, 1988). Argues the Church should give greater priority to the needs of children, and to the support of family life through such endeavours as the uniformed organizations, marriage and parenting classes. Also proposes greater use of all-age worship and joint learning opportunities for children and adults.

Caroline Glendinning and Jane Millar (eds), *Women and Poverty in Britain* (New York: Harvester Weatsheaf, 1992). Papers which chart the deleterious effects of changes in social security payments combined with the redistribution of wealth from poor to rich represented by the 1980s' shift from income to sales taxes on the health and welfare of children in poor families.

John B. Mays, *Growing Up in the City: A Study of Juvenile Delinquency in an Urban Neighbourhood* (Liverpool: University Press of Liverpool, 1954). The first major study to argue that delinquency amongst children of the long-term poor is not so much evidence of maladjustment as of sub-cultural resistance to a dominant culture which condemns them and their parents to underemployment, bad housing and poverty.

Michael S. Northcott, 'Children', in Peter Sedgwick (ed.), *God in the City* (London: Mowbray, 1995), pp. 139–52. One-quarter of British children live in households with below half average income. The children of the poor are again suffering from the diseases of poverty such as tuberculosis and rickets in 1990s' Britain. The positive focus on children in the teaching of Jesus, and his more general concern for the vulnerable is contrasted with the poor life chances and prospects for the children of the poor in Britain.

Susanne S. Paul and James A. Paul, *Humanity Comes of Age: The New Context for Ministry with the Elderly* (Geneva: WCC, 1994). Examines the implications of extended life expectancy, and of privatization and free market economics, for the quality of life of older people and for the Christian affirmation of life from birth to death. Explores problems and solutions mostly in third-world contexts, including hopeful stories of old people taking to the streets to demand, and organize for, a better deal.

David Utting, Jon Bright and Clem Henricson, *Crime and the Family: Improving Child-Rearing and Preventing Delinquency* (London: Family Policy Studies Centre, 1993). Argues for a greater commitment of state and voluntary resources to the dissemination of parenting skills as a cost-effective way of reducing delinquency.

Harriett Wilson and G.W. Herbert, *Parents and Children in the Inner City* (London: Routledge and Kegan Paul, 1978). Seminal empirical study demonstrating clear links between poor performance in school, delinquency, and poverty and deprivation in inner city families.

Michael Young and Peter Wilmott, *Family and Kinship in East London* (Harmondsworth: Penguin, 1962). Classic study of the rich and sustaining extended family patterns which prevailed in the East End of London throughout much of this century and which are only now beginning to break down.

8

Work in the city

The kingdom of Heaven is like this. There was once a landowner who went out early in the morning to hire labourers for his vineyard; and after agreeing to pay them the usual day's wage he sent them off to work. Three hours later he went out again and saw some more men standing idle in the market-place.

'Go and join the others in the vineyard', he said, 'and I will pay you a fair wage'; so off they went. At midday he went out again, and at three in the afternoon, and made the same arrangement as before. An hour before sunset he went out and found another group standing there; so he said to them, 'Why are you standing here all day doing nothing?' 'Because no one has hired us', they replied; so he told them, 'Go and join the others in the vineyard.' When evening fell, the owner of the vineyard said to the overseer, 'Call the labourers and give them their pay, beginning with those who came last and ending with the first.'

Those who had started work an hour before sunset came forward, and were paid the full day's wage. When it was the turn of the men who had come first, they expected something extra, but were paid the same as the others. As they took it, they grumbled at their employer: 'These latecomers did only one hour's work, yet you have treated them on a level with us, who have sweated the whole day long in the blazing sun!' The owner turned to one of them and said, 'My friend, I am not being unfair to you. You agreed to the usual wage for the day, did you not? Take your pay and go home. I choose to give the last man the same as you. Surely I am free to do what I like with my own money? Why be jealous because I am generous?' So the last will be first, and the first last.

(Matthew 20:1–16)

Faith in the City

We have been confronted time and time again with the deep human misery — coupled in some cases with resentment, in others with apathy and hopelessness — that is its result. The absence of regular paid work has eroded self-respect. 'Give me back my dignity' was the heartfelt plea from one man — made redundant with no prospect of a job — at one of our public meetings in the North-West. (9.38)

We must make it perfectly clear that we believe there is no instant, dogmatic or potent solution to the problem of unemployment. Certainly the Church of England cannot 'solve' the problem of unemployment. It possesses neither the mandate nor the competence to do so. Yet as it is in the position of being the national Church, it has a particular duty to act as the conscience of the nation. It must question all economic philosophies, not least those which, when put into practice, have contributed to the blighting of whole districts, which do not offer the hope of amelioration, and which perpetuate the human misery and despair to which we have referred. The situation requires the Church to question from its own particular standpoint the *morality* of these economic philosophies. (9.41)

Introduction

Comparative studies of poverty rates amongst adults and especially children indicate that Britain and the USA have seen very dramatic increases in income inequality and poverty since the governments of Thatcher, Reagan and their successors in these countries embraced the principles of New Right economics: reductions in the relative value of welfare payments as compared with real incomes, reduced income taxes for high earners as incentive to entrepreneurialism and wealth creation, the privatization of public services and natural resources such as water, reductions in public spending on social housing and housing improvement, and the deregulation of the labour and financial markets. These changes resulted in dramatic rises in income inequality in the 1980s and 1990s. But their most significant impacts on poverty arose from their effects on the labour market for they hastened the demise of full-time unskilled and semi-skilled work in manufacturing industry, much of which was relocated to third-world countries with low tax regimens and anti-union laws (Sassen). Much of the semi-skilled manufacturing and service work that remained in Britain and the USA was casualized, with a dramatic shift of the employed population from full- to part-time working, and real increases in long-term and short-term unemployment. In the UK the rise in unemployment in the Thatcher era was fivefold. In the mid-1990s there were signs of the rise in unemployment slowing, mainly through the increase in part-time and casual work, though caution is needed in interpreting UK unemployment figures which, at the time of writing, exclude significant proportions of those who are actually available for work, including those under 25 and those over 55.

Unemployment, under-employment and wages below the official poverty level of half average wages are closely correlated with the conditions of relative and absolute poverty which we have seen afflict many who reside in Britain's inner cities and peripheral housing estates. Unemployed people have a higher mortality rate than those in work because of suicide and health problems, they are more likely to experience some kind of mental illness, and often have problems with self-esteem, living as they do in a society which defines personhood and even citizenship very largely in relation to productive work and wealth (**Ballard**).

The changes in employment patterns in Western cities are not, however, limited to countries which have embraced the principles of deregulation and free markets, though they have been more rapid and deleterious in their effects on inner cities in these countries. The other central factors in the restructuring of the capitalist city are the changing nature of work and the globalization of systems of production (Sassen). New technology means that much of the manual labour which was formerly performed by people is now performed by machines and computers. This generates a requirement for unskilled people to undertake retraining if they are to find secure formal employment in the changing labour market where quasi-professional skills such as the ability to manipulate information, or multiple skills such as the ability to diagnose and fix a fault in an automated production line are the dominant forms of formal work in industrial organizations (Ormiston and Ross).

However, information-based work is not simply displacing manual work. While it is enabling companies to strip out layers of formal unskilled production-line work, other forms of unskilled work remain, and may even increase, in the cities of the new global and informational economy, as the growing army of casually employed hotel porters, bouncers, nannies, security guards, waiters and cleaners in British cities testifies (Sassen). Industrial organizations are shaking down their employment base, out-sourcing service functions and only retaining full-time employees in certain key areas. Manual workers and even professional workers may be rehired once new technology is introduced, but often only on a part-time or self-employment basis.

The factory production line system in many ways gave rise to the pattern of working-class life in the new industrial cities of the twentieth century (Bookchin; **Hopkins**). It produced repetitive work designed to maximize efficiency by minimizing input and changes in movement from the worker on the line. The work was boring but through union power it became increasingly well paid and sustained increases in living standards amongst largely unskilled working-class communities into the 1960s. The gradual replacement of robots for humans in boring repetitive work is in principle a good thing for few would choose to participate in boring meaningless machine-minding if they were not forced to it by economic necessity. However, long-term dependence on unskilled labour fostered communities in which brawn was more important than brain. These communities provide the obvious source of the new non-unionized and informal style of labour favoured by the deregulated and increasingly service-oriented labour market. They also provide a large pool of residual unemployed which acts as a suppressant of wage levels, and a deterrent to new casual workers seeking employment rights or improved levels of pay.

The growing emphasis on information, high-technology, financial and services sectors produces a new tendency to hierarchy and peripheralization. Cities where industrial and port premises were concentrated, such as Liverpool or Sunderland, are left with a large pool of unskilled people and these cities increasingly lose out in the new global economy as their residents lose control over their working lives. Much higher rewards are, however, available to successful entrepreneurs and information handlers in the globalized informational economy, and the financial and information centres, such as London, Leeds or Edinburgh, which the new economy favours (Sassen). The rapid shift which has taken place in Britain from formal to casual employment, and from organization employed to self-employed or under-employed creates new classes of winners and losers in society, and radically reshapes the urban environment, with winners in gentrified terraces or refurbished industrial premises often living cheek by jowl with losers in decrepit multi-occupancy or unsaleable social housing.

The radical economic restructuring which has had such deleterious effects on British cities, and particularly on formerly working-class, manual, low-skill communities in UPAs, finds surprising resonance with the economic context which is hinted at in the parable of the labourers in the vineyard. The Gallilean economy in the time of Jesus was undergoing economic restructuring. The growth of international trade through ports such as Tyre led to increasing marketization of the production of cereal crops and of fishing. The crops were taxed in kind in order to feed the growing cities of the centre of the Empire, such as Rome, and the demands of the growing Roman army. Recent archaeological evidence of large wine and olive presses, and of bunk housing around large farm buildings for tenured labourers, suggests that big farms were increasingly common in the time of Jesus, brought about by the failure of many small farms under harsh trading conditions. The fishing industry was also increasingly internationalized, facilitated by food processing techniques including salted fish and bottled fish sauces and fish tail soup favoured by the Romans.

Consequently, two economies existed side by side: traditional small-holder farmers supporting their own families, and a growing market economy involving large landholdings, processed food for export and the trading and manufacture of luxury goods for the wealthy. In the time of Jesus the province of Galilee was moving from one economy to the other. The Herodians and other wealthy Jews were doing particularly well out of the new economy, while many peasants and landless labourers were doing badly as they lost their small-holdings through high taxes and became hired men who worked on a daily basis when they were picked up in the market place, as in the parable.

The new market economy led to fragmentation of the traditional Jewish kinship and landholding structure, to social division and fragmentation. This is why there are so many condemnations of luxurious living in the Gospels: wealth is seen not just as an obstacle to the kingdom but also as an obstacle to the Jewish practice of social justice. For the Jews the economic ideal was still that of the self-sufficient small-holder farmer having his own vines, fig or olive trees, and grain fields. Each household traditionally had a right to live off a portion of the land of Israel, a right enshrined in law. To become a hired hand, a day labourer, was to have fallen from this ideal, to be marginalized and excluded from the vision of the good life as defined by Jewish religion and social traditions, and to know hunger on a daily basis.

The parable indicates that the inability to perform an honest day's work and receive the means to live is a fundamental wrong. The landowner goes out into the market a number of times and when he finds workers at the last hour of the day still without work he is shocked and concerned and offers them work. The parable also teaches that equality of wages in a monetarized economy is preferable to a system of rewards and incentives which gives some a tenth or even a twentieth of the wages of another.

However, the parable is ambiguous in relation to the social changes of the last twenty years, for it points to the value of independence in employment and the potential limitations of being a hired labourer or organizational employee, precisely the values affirmed by the new 'enterprise culture' (Sedgwick). If the restructuring of the labour market means that more people return to the ancient Jewish ideal of the economic self-reliance of the household, with large numbers of home-based self-employed, this may be no bad thing. The values of self-reliance, self-help and creative entrepreneurialism have not been limited to the growing small business culture of Britain in the 1980s but may also be found in many UPA areas, and not least in those community enterprises, charities and voluntary initiatives which churches in particular have often fostered in UPA areas as means of generating local employment, creating and recycling wealth within UPA communities, and subverting their dependence on outside agencies, whether private banks or public landlords (**Lean**). The shrinking of the state has opened up opportunities for an expansion of the voluntary sector which can be glimpsed in many UPAs with the growth of housing associations instead of faceless local authority housing departments, the involvement of churches and local charities in Manpower Services Commission job creation and training projects and, more recently, Community Care contracts in relation to care for the aged and the mentally ill (**Ballard**; Kane). Church initiatives in relation to local wealth creation and community action include credit unions, community farms, workshops, food and furniture co-operatives, arts and cultural groups and Local Exchange Trading Schemes (**Lean**). Many such projects have benefited from start-up grants from the Church Urban Fund (**Grundy**). Many others have attracted government or local authority funding. The involvement of the churches in these projects reflects a spirituality and a theology of social change which encourages individuals and communities to respond creatively to the larger economic restructuring which cities are experiencing and to attempt to take charge of their own future (**Lean**).

In addition to the many courageous attempts to respond to change and economic restructuring at local level, the churches nationally in the last two decades have also become increasingly critical of government policies which have exacerbated the shake-out of organization employment, and at the same time reduced the value and availability of unemployment benefit, now renamed Job Seekers Allowance, to those without work as a consequence of social and economic change. Since *Faith in the City* the churches have become the single most prominent non-governmental force in critiquing the negative effects of economic restructuring on the flourishing of human families and communities (**Ballard**). Industrial chaplains and UPA parishes have been prominent in this critique, and in the development of palliatives to unemployment at local level. Industrial chaplains have also been particularly prominent in efforts to develop a revised theology of work in the light of economic restructuring and the reduced availability of work in the late capitalist city.

In the industrial city human life for the working classes was shaped by relatively uncreative work in the service of machines which never stopped. The shift system, the male culture of the factory floor and the deep mine, the working men's club and the pub, represented an ambiguous culture of working-class solidarity which none the less demonstrated the wondrous capacity of people in the face of meaningless and often oppressive working conditions to find purpose and to shape communities of care. But this culture was also a culture of oppression, especially for women. It stunted human possibilities for creative work and spirituality, and fostered a secularism which was ultimately corrosive of faith in God and of Christian worship. The churches made many pioneering attempts to engage this culture in the worker priest movement, in industrial mission and through the urban–industrial priest or minister who embraced the institutions of work, and the people who worked in them, as a vital part of his parish (**Hopkins**).

However, the church as a whole responded to the all-embracing power of productive work in the industrial city with mixed voices. The prayers and liturgies of the Church of England's Alternative Service Book written as late as

1980 contain no references to working life in urban industrial cities, though they retain many agricultural images of work (**Ballard**). Most Sunday services and sermons are performed or uttered without reference to the dominance of industrial work, and the pain of its denial, in the modern city. The gap between the worlds of work and worship is enhanced by the historical failure of the churches to reverse the secularizing drift of urban industrial and popular culture in twentieth-century cities, despite the efforts of industrial chaplains and socially aware parish clergy in urban–industrial parishes to bridge the gap between the world of industrial work and the local church.

Industrial chaplains, and some theologians, have sought to develop a new theology of work in the light of this continuing gap between work and worship, as well as the changing nature of work, and the tragedy of mass unemployment in the late capitalist city (Sedgwick; Ormiston and Ross; Fox). They argue that we need to revalue work itself, seeing it not as the essence of what it is to be human, as Marx proposed, but as having value only inasmuch as it gives expression to human creativity and enables the formation of relationships and networks of solidarity and care. They propose a reduced emphasis on paid work and an increased valuation of all kinds of human creativity, and especially those which industrial society has tended to undervalue, including the making and sustaining of stable and compassionate relationships in families and local communities, and the nurture of children who are so often pushed to the margins of neglect in a work-obsessed culture and of poverty in a culture which denies adequate living standards to those out of work (Fox).

This approach tends to critique the traditional Protestant work ethic and instead to seek to recover the balance between work and rest, weekday and Sabbath, creativity and contemplation, money and life quality which is to be found in the Old Testament. The ancient Hebrews saw work and rest as a reflection of the originating pattern of divine creativity in the six days of creation, and the day of divine rest and enjoyment of that which had been created (Moltmann). This pattern was also an ethical pattern, setting limits on the exploitation of worker by landowner and proscribing debt slavery. The ancient Jewish ideal of household independence and self-reliance seems to reflect a bias towards the small organization and the local community which may find an echo in the attempts of individuals and voluntary groups in the late capitalist city to remake an economy from below when the organizational economy of formal work has failed them.

The consummate work of the people of God in the Old Testament is the work of worship, with which were associated most of the great cultural and ethical achievements of ancient Israel. Only when productive work is ordered and balanced by the spiritual work of worship will it bear the creative moral and aesthetic fruits of truth, justice and beauty in human relationships and cultural production. This Old Testament vision of work argues for the crucial importance of the reconnection of work and worship in the modern late capitalist city, in the UPA and in the city centre or suburb. Work addiction, boring mindless repetitive machine-minding, demeaning unskilled and low paid work, and the denial of work and the associated poverty and loss of freedom and dignity, are all manifestations of a malaise with respect to work culture in the late twentieth century which the move to self-employment, voluntary work and community self-reliance is still not adequately addressing. The poverty and welfare dependency of the UPA are more the product of this malaise than of any other single factor.

A new theology of work will involve an emphasis on creativity and service in which work is seen as essentially to do with the fostering of relationships; between rich and poor, between the sick and the healthy, between children and parents, between people and the land, and between sustainable technologies and genuine human needs. The inner and spiritual work of meditation, and the community work of worship, which build the deeper relationship between ourselves and God, and which liberate us from the heresy that we are what we produce, will also play a central role in the recovery of a genuinely Christian understanding of work in a post-industrial age (Fox).

Light in the city: stories of the Church Urban Fund

Malcolm Grundy

THE ADVENT PROJECT, BIRKENHEAD

The Advent project is an employment initiative of the Society of St Vincent de Paul, an international charity largely supported by lay members of the Roman Catholic and some Anglican churches.

The Advent project helps in areas where the unemployment rate is three times the national average. As well as money from the St Vincent de Paul [SVP] Society, the Catholic newspaper, *The Universe*, has given its support. The idea was launched at the annual meeting of the Society in Scarborough in the autumn of 1988. The appeal was launched in the Advent of 1988 — hence its name — with the slogan that 'All the unemployed want for Christmas is a job'. It is now a fully registered charity. The Urban Fund was at first cautious in its support of this principally Catholic charity but has decided to go ahead as a strong measure of inter-denominational support. The first piece of work is based in Birkenhead and Mike Kennedy, the Project Director, says:

> Our aim is simple. We believe the statutory bodies are not coping sufficiently with the unemployment problem. We believe that our Churches have the local community involvement, commitment and trust to be able to directly help the most disadvantaged.
>
> Being in a deprived community where unemployment runs at two or three times the national average, up to 30 per cent or more, usually means your personal confidence is sapped, you shun 'officialdom', you need motivating, you need to have your horizons opened to enable you to help yourself.

The Advent Project helps unemployed individuals set themselves up in business under the Government's Enterprise Allowance scheme.

Tom Elcock was 58 when he was made redundant from the printing firm where he had worked for 27 years. He was unemployed for twelve months before the SVP contacted him. 'I kept looking for jobs, but unfortunately my age seemed to be against me. The help offered by the Advent Project was "a godsend".'

'Going down the dole office, I used to feel "This is wrong", ' he says. 'The sad thing, the thing that hurt me most, was seeing so many young people down there.'

Tom Elcock now has his own business, Chameleon Art, which he runs from the front room of his home in Birkenhead. He trained as a Commercial Artist after leaving school, and is now putting his training to good use, producing designs, displays, illustrations and paintings.

His most recent commission was from the Mowlem construction company who asked Tom to design the company Christmas card. He has also produced some of the designs for the Advent Project literature.

Paul Kelly and Mark Richards represent the other end of the unemployment spectrum in Birkenhead. Both 20, they have known each other since they were five and neither of them has had a full-time paid job since they left Bishop Challoner High School in 1985.

They, too, now have their own company, Advent Electronics. Based in a room above a shop, they assemble electronic circuit boards for burglar and fire alarms.

Their latest project is the research and development of a Biocide Dosing Unit, for use in cooling towers, to stop the spread of Legionnaire's Disease.

Their love of electronic gadgetry dates back to their schooldays, and their knowledge and experience come from the various Youth Training Schemes in which they have been involved.

'There was no hope of me getting a job in electronics,' says Paul who heard about the Advent Project when he met the manager, Mike Kennedy after helping out at the SVP summer camp.

The project has been particularly helpful, they say, in providing advice about grants and business contacts. 'Large companies wouldn't be interested in helping people like us,' says Mark.

Being on the Enterprise Allowance scheme, and having the support and advice of the Advent Project, has meant that they will be masters of their own destiny. 'We'll be able to plan our future,' says Mark, 'instead of living from day to day like you do on the dole.'

Peter Voice, 31, had been unemployed for eighteen months before he became involved with the Advent Project. 'It was absolutely soul-destroying,' he says.

Now, with Wayne Humphries, 25, and John Lovett, 21, he is the co-owner of Leisurekraft, a workers' co-operative manufacturing fibreglass canoes. Since setting up business in an out-building of a friend's house, they have made seven canoes. The three met on a Community Programme scheme where they were taught how to make the canoes. Peter realized he couldn't face going back on the dole. 'I had to do something,' he says. 'There was no way that I was going to go back on the dole.'

Their canoes sell for £130, which they hope is within the reach of people on low budgets and groups such as youth clubs and scout groups. 'We like to feel we're putting something back into the community,' says Peter.

For the three budding businessmen, the help of Mike Kennedy and the Advent Project has been vital to the success of their enterprise, particularly the marketing advice.

The three are slowly getting used to the idea of being their own boss. 'We're loving it because no matter how hard it gets for us, the rewards are basically our own,' says Peter.

They are confident about the future. Leisurekraft is set to expand with plans to manufacture fibreglass trailer bodies, and weather protection shields for motorcycles.

For John, the youngest of the partners: 'This is a chance in a million to work for ourselves, instead of working for someone else and getting exploited.'

Money for the Birkenhead Advent Project, £24,000 over three years from the Church Urban Fund, will be matched by an equal sum from the Catholic Church.

The parish church and the industrial worker[1]

Gordon Hopkins

The parish of Pallion is a mile and a half up-stream from the mouth of the river Wear. It is in the centre of an enormous concentration of industry, and from the Alexandra bridge there is a panoramic view of industrial life, which must be unequalled in extent and character: six shipyards, six engine works, two large collieries, the enormous Pyrex glass works, and the works of the largest cranebuilding corporation in the world. Beyond lies the large Pallion Trading Estate, with a variety of factories, the biggest of which include the Bristol Siddeley aero-engine works, and David Brown's engineering works, along with the Thorn AEI Electrical Industries. Some of the factories on the Trading Estate, and especially the clothing factory, employ a very large number of girls and women.

In the early days of the war it was not difficult to make contact with the shipbuilding and marine engineering industries in the parish, especially since the Vicar's previous seven years had been in a shipbuilding parish on Merseyside. During a long number of years in Pallion, it had been possible, gradually, to get to know a very large number of people engaged in varying kinds of work in local industrial life. At no time has life for most of them been plain sailing or easy for very long, and people are glad of the chance to talk informally about a great many different facets of industrial life, with its problems and difficulties. Basically, of course, most of these problems are essentially human in nature and origin, and there is no difficulty whatever in describing the relationship that is gradually built up between the parish priest and the people he has met as being 'pastoral' in character.

During the war, a great deal of work was set on foot in the parish amongst adolescent boys and girls. At that time nearly all the boys in the parish became apprentices in one of the shipyards or forges. The men in the works and the yards, along with the foremen and management, seemed to be quite genuinely interested in all this club work that was going on amongst these lads in industry. So here was a valuable additional point of contact.

In the early 1940s, the Dean of Chester (G. W. O. Addleshaw), along with the Bishop of Accra (Richard Roseveare SSM), were deeply concerned to discover whether something similar to continental Jocism could be made to work amongst young industrial workers who were members of the Church in this country. Quite a considerable number of young workers were trained in Pallion along these lines, and they are the people who have since been most effective and faithful in Church life, and have, in almost every case, pursued extremely interesting and worthwhile careers in industrial life. It seemed that here was an effective instrument ready to hand, and it was very widely agreed in Church life that this movement was a 'good thing'. Yet it was only put into action in half a dozen parishes up and down the country. However, perhaps it is only fair to add that the essential point of Jocism and kindred movements is that the whole structure of a man's working and domestic life must be spread out before God, and caught up into the action of the Eucharist. This was seized upon, and emphasized, by 'Parish and People' and the liturgical movements in England and on the Continent.

In the shipyards, engine works, and factories in Pallion, the vast majority of the working people live in Sunderland, and up to comparatively recently it was possible for a great many Pallion people to walk to and from work, and even get back home to dinner. Although Sunderland will shortly have a population of nearly a quarter of a million, it is still a fairly tightly knit community, in which people know one another very well, and is not a merely loosely knit conurbation, as the boroughs are on Tyneside. This makes it possible for the parochial clergy to make ready contact with the works, and to be accepted as such within the local set-up. It may be that, in some respects, North-East England is not as starkly secularized as some other parts of the country, so that the vicar of the parish is still accepted in this kind of way.

The ecumenical issue has not been directly raised, but within the works there have been extremely friendly relations with people of the various Christian communions, and this has been especially true of a number of extremely able and thoughtful Roman Catholic shop stewards.

Within a shipyard or factory the parish priest will be doing work that is essentially pastoral in character and in intention, yet, as with the full-time industrial chaplain, he will, of course, exercise exactly the same kind of care to avoid any kind of proselytizing.

The parish priest, like the industrial missioner, if he remains in the same place over a good long period of time, is able to get together groups of people who are prepared to meet and discuss, outside of working hours. These will not be large groups, but they can be very interesting, and, whether they are largely active trades unionists, or whether they are groups of personnel managers, it can provide a meeting place between those who have been working all their lives in the old industries, and those who have recently come into the area in the new industries on the Trading Estates. The parish priest ought to make a point of getting to know those who work in the Youth Employment Service.

It emerges very often during the discussions with those who are concerned that only a small minority of industrial workers are prepared, on behalf of their fellow men, to persist in the kind of sustained effort that is involved in the work of a shop steward, or other such official. They are often genuinely devoted people, and in need of encouragement in face of frustration and disappointment at being let down so often by their fellow men. Their work involves a ministry by the minority, *vis-à-vis* the majority, who appear to them to be quite irresponsible, and interested only in 'money, pools, and pints'. The clergy are not the only people to indulge in lamentations. Perhaps some mutual encouragement may ensue!

It has constantly been asserted by those engaged in industrial mission that the parish church ought to exercise the kind of self-denying ordinance that refuses to tether the more intelligent and responsible sort of church-going industrial worker to the parish pump. He must be free to give of his best, as a responsible person, to the Trades Union movement, to the Town Council, or to his professional association, and the parish priest ought very readily to agree. The truth of this kind of assertion is more generally recognized today than it used to be. At this point, however, it is important to state that, if the influence to be exercised by the responsible worker in the secular world is to be effective and sustained, it is essential that he be rooted and grounded in a firm apprehension of the Christian faith, and in a deep knowledge and love of God and of his fellow men. Experience suggests that, although a man ought not to be tethered to the parish pump, yet, if he is to survive effectively as a focus of Christian influence, he will need a strong sacramental life as the background to his existence. It looks as though the Roman Catholics do much more for the spiritual life of the industrial worker than we do in the Church of England.

The parish priest who has worked for a long number of years amongst people in industry becomes hesitant about accepting some current generalizations. It is not true, here in Sunderland, that there are very few church-going Anglicans who work in our local industries. In the largest of our shipyards and marine engineering works there are a substantial number of people who play a leading part in church life, and are exercising some kind of responsibility of a worthwhile sort in industrial life, at very varying levels.

It is often said that the clergy must be willing to learn when they enter into industrial life. What use can be made of this learning? If it leads to a real understanding in some depth, then a parish priest is better equipped for training and guiding young people who are about to become apprentices. The Church today is weak in the kind of moral theology which enables apt advice to be given, spiritually, to an industrial worker, and a sound working knowledge of industrial life is a great help here, as it is in teaching and preaching where a man's ministry is in an industrial setting. He must use his knowledge responsibly and with integrity especially in any situation where he can be of use in a work of reconciliation. This will not often involve him in any overt negotiations within industrial disputes. In these days suspicion and misunderstanding go very deep; this has worsened in recent years. Any work that is of a healing sort needs to be done at a pretty deep level. It is only viable where the priest is selfless in doing it and where any sort of publicity is avoided.

In the early days of industrial mission it was assumed that the bulk of the work would be directed towards encounters with manual workers on the shop floor. In these days manual workers are a much smaller proportion of the total labour force employed in a large factory, and there is no doubt about the fact that men who work in many different kinds of supervisory grades, along with technicians, and middle management in general, are very deeply perplexed, sometimes driven almost to despair, by the apparently insoluble nature of the problems which they meet almost every day. Awareness of this, of course, does not suggest that the need could be readily, or quickly, met by the parochial clergy, but it does suggest that the parochial clergy need to be more fully aware of the kind of strains to which men and women are subjected today, in their working lives, and, at the same time, to realize how radical a change has come over the pattern of working life, at almost every level, during the last twenty-five years.

It may be that the parish priest is able to visualize a good deal of what goes on in industrial life, without being too closely involved in it. He is aware of the immense importance of their working lives to industrial men; yet, in many ways, work means far less to industrial men today than it did twenty years ago. He is able to see the same man both at work and in his domestic setting, and this will prevent him from arguing too hotly about the real work of the Church being *either* in the parish *or* in the factory.

Of course, there are dangers and drawbacks, as full-time practitioners know only too well. There is a sense in which a parish priest can do only a mere fraction of the work that cries out to be tackled. There is the appalling problem of the rapid mobility of the parish clergy in these days; and the parish priest knows that a great deal of this kind of work is intimate, intangible, and personal in character. He knows that his successor may not be at all at home in this kind of field, or he may be succeeded by someone who will rush in and make blunders.

The parochial clergy in the Rural Deanery are interested and appreciative of the fact that work is on foot which they value; and yet it is true to say that, over the years, very few have made the kind of contacts in industrial life locally that are open to a parish priest. The shyness and the hesitancy persist, and there is curiously little available in the nature of training offered to the young clergy for this work in most large industrial towns. An outstanding exception is in the thorough training given to the younger clergy who are associated with the training schemes for young miners provided by the National Coal Board in County Durham.

The shyness may persist, up and down the country, partly because of the very widespread impression that there was a wedge driven in between industrial mission and the parochial clergy. There was, earlier, resentment over this, and particularly about the implied suggestion that the parochial clergy were tinkering about with an outworn institution, while the specialist practitioners in the field were getting to grips with the secular world, or with the 'real' world. The parochial clergy have tended to identify industrial mission with 'South Bank attitudes', and to sheer away from this whole field. This is not the moment to embark on words about 'busyness' or priorities. Equally it would not do to indulge in a tirade about the liability of so many parochial clergy to be hamstrung by keeping in being their 'organizations'. Instead it can briefly be said that a parish priest who is prepared to learn and to listen will find that the work which lies open to him in an industrial setting can, and should, make valid demands on his time. Because the work is done in a field in which the priest is there on sufferance, rather than by 'right', it is specially salutary for him. He has to earn acceptance and to maintain this in proving his integrity. This fact alone makes the work worthwhile for the priest. The work is exacting, but it is both interesting and rewarding. Its direct results cannot be easily assessed or measured; yet, when faithfully maintained, it is essentially fruitful.

NOTE

1. Reprinted, with the Editor's permission, from *Theology*, **69**, 549–53 (December 1966), where it was the fifth in a symposium of six essays on *Industrial Mission*.

Prophetic action: the churches' involvement

Paul H. Ballard

To many people's surprise the issues of work and unemployment, alongside the cognate concern for the inner city, have stimulated more active involvement over social issues within the Church than has been seen for many decades. Every level of Church life has been affected, from the national councils of the denomination and ecumenical bodies to parishes and congregations in city and country, from the industrial heartlands to the middle-class suburbs. The main reason is surely very simple. As the recession bit and unemployment rocketed skyward, it was clear that everyone was being affected. There cannot be many congregations in which no one is unemployed, or is connected to a family in which someone is unemployed, or in which there are no youngsters struggling to get a job. Work has become a major personal and communal pastoral concern. Out of this has emerged some signs of those reserves of Christian compassion and responsibility which are more often dormant and untapped.

Of course not every Christian is committed, involved or comprehending. As always, there is a concerned minority that makes the running, but they have been increasingly heard and responded to. This surely is the way things work. The burden or responsibility of those who feel drawn into certain commitments and concerns is a prophetic voice in the wider community of faith. When events and circumstances change, then appropriate and relevant groups find themselves at the centre of the stage. This has happened in this instance with Industrial Mission and others with similar concerns. Suddenly their representative, but often marginalized, role has become important. The Church needs and is grateful for the wisdom and expertise of men and women who over many years have worked the urban and industrial patch. Here is the basis for operating on a wider scale not only within the churches and through the churches but in the wider community. It is frequently the urban or industrial chaplains who find themselves as the Christian representative presence, in local, regional or even national projects and organizations.

* * *

Bonhoeffer, in the *Letters and Papers from Prison*, talks about meeting God in man's strengths, not his weakness.[1] We need to recognize more firmly that, alongside the ministry to the poor, there is a continuing task of critical, prophetic and radical acceptance of the gifts of those who are part of the riches of society, its strengths and resources. At the same time there has to be an affirmation of the solidarity of mankind. The reality of sin, the need for renewal and the gifts of grace are for us all. We are all God's poor and we all have gifts to bring to the common wealth. If these are acted upon then pastoral action, however limited it may necessarily be in any given situation, will be part of the fabric of our response to the wholeness of God's care and concern for and in his world.

It is not easy to characterise the Church's involvement in work and unemployment over the past few years. This is because, by the nature of the case, it is bound to be varied, diffuse and largely uncoordinated. It would be possible to try to bring it to some order in a number of different ways. For instance, we could look at what is happening at different levels: national, regional and local, or again by listing projects set up by each main Church, or through ecumenical co-operation, or by auxiliary groups, whether as part of a wider agenda or as a specialist concern. However, it is suggested that the most useful methodology will be to take four kinds of activity: (a) involvement by word and deed in influencing policy or events; (b) raising the levels of debate and information in and beyond the Churches; (c) practical involvement in the immediate dilemmas that face the unemployed; and (d) the creation of a spirituality that is a resource for those in and out of work. These categories are never wholly separate. Each affects and depends on the other. Nevertheless, they seem to provide a reasonably clear framework for discussion.

* * *

The *first* kind of activity is perhaps the most controversial. By what right does the Church enter into the complex and specialized fields of social and economic policy? Is it possible to point to one line of action or series of conclusions as being the gospel response? These matters cannot be argued here. That is the task of theological ethical theory. All that can be done is to make a basic affirmation that it is the responsibility of the Church and of every Christian to play a full and informed part in social and political life. This will involve coming to and pressing for conclusions that are held, in part at least, on the basis of an understanding of the Christian faith. But that does not endow all or any of these conclusions with an absolute authority that lifts them above controversy or question.

Debate, even radical disagreement, perhaps conflict, is part of the search for truth and the way to test ideas, structures and policies. Prophetic activity is not immune from public debate, as the biblical prophets knew, but it is an act of obedient witness, both within the plurality of the Church and within the diversity of the world, reviewing our lives by the gospel imperative. Of course there is authority, within the Church as well as beyond it, but it is necessary to recognize that authority carries weight in proportion to its authenticity as much as its source. Both within and beyond the Church, authority has to accept critical evaluation. Nevertheless, it is important that Christians are free to become involved, not least because they too are part of our pluralistic society and have a right to be heard.

At the national level there are several ways in which the churches address issues of national importance. Church leaders can make statements or preach sermons. They are also, in varying degrees, able to enter into the political processes, formally through the bishops in the House of Lords; most often, however, informally by meeting and conversing with people in different walks of life or members of different national or regional bodies. Church bodies also take up particular issues and often make submissions to government enquiries or other important bodies. From time to time a working party will include in its report specific recommendations on public policy. The recent Archbishop's report — *Faith in the City* — included a study of employment in the inner city.[2] Meetings between representatives of the Churches and other key groups are organized from time to time at places like St George's House, Windsor. The Industrial Mission Association has a continuous series of meetings with significant groups, such as officials of the Department of Employment, the Manpower Services Commission and senior management of key industries.

Similar activity can go on at a more local level. Submissions have been made in the formation of county structure plans. This has happened, for instance, in the Sheffield Ecumenical Mission to South Yorkshire,[3] and in the Tŷ Toronto — the Call to the Valleys Project — to the Glamorgan Counties.[4] Industrial Mission teams are in dialogue with key industrial and local government groups.

Such activity can, from time to time, spill over into more direct action. A large redundancy programme or new industrial development can trigger off not only union action but community action. Church groups or clergy have frequently been involved. Even if there is no official Church support, some members of a congregation can often be part of such action. In any case the issues will be very much alive and probably divisive. Everyone in the district will be caught up in the situation. Local churches or Councils of Churches will be challenged as to how and by what means they should become involved. Whatever the decision by the ministers or congregations, the following guidelines are important:

1. Be fully and realistically informed. It is easy to get swept along by local feeling or press reports. Understand the issues. Find out where the power lies and who is pulling the strings. Find out where different groups and elements want to go, why and with whom. What are the consequences of closure or remaining open? What options are available? Who is wooing the Church and why?

2. Discover what roles the Church would be expected to play both among its members and the community. This may suggest real constructive possibilities. It will certainly indicate the points of resistance and misunderstanding.

3. Decide on the appropriate stance but recognize that it will be difficult to sustain and will be opposed. It is a commitment that will demand time and strain. It is no good if one is not prepared to pay the cost.

4. Decide what the specific Christian contribution is. This may not be proclaimed overtly, but if there is no conscious theological reason for involvement it will quickly get forgotten, eroded or overturned.

5. Be aware that circumstances and attitudes change. Monitor what is going on and adjust action in relation to commitment and reality. The resolution of a conflict always demands some give and take. What is non-negotiable? What are the demands of prudence?

6. Recognize that, after it is all over, people have to learn to live together again. However just a cause, there can be no absolute enemies. The aim is justice and peace. The hope is to effect change in people as well as in the pursuit of a specific goal.

7. Use good resources for advice and support both from the Church and beyond.

The *second* kind of activity is closely allied to the *first*. Any involvement in practical action or advocacy is bound to be a learning process both for those involved and for others who are drawn into the discussions. But there is also a legitimate task in purely trying to raise public awareness of the issues involved and to open up the debate to considered and informed Christian opinion. Therefore national reports of working parties both advocate lines of practical action and offer information, discussion and conclusions for a wider public to read and talk about. Other documents — from substantial books by Christian commentators and symposia or reports of conferences or working parties, to substantial booklets on topical issues from study groups and articles in journals and features in the religious and secular press — are all intended to keep the pot of ideas and reflections boiling.

There is, at a national level, a resource (which is often neglected) for the wider public in the reports and publications of such bodies as the Board for Social Responsibility of the Church of England, the British Council of Churches and the William Temple Foundation. ... There is also a growing number of locally based publications designed to stimulate discussion in house groups, youth groups and elsewhere. For example, the Teeside Industrial Mission have produced a series of booklets called *Respond*, written by a group set up by the mission as a forum for sharing concerns about the region. The booklets, among many topics, look at the future of Cleveland, the nature of work, unemployment and Christian responsibility. And the Council for Christian Care in Exeter has a series of discussion starters called *Unemployment Concerns*, as well as an occasional series of booklets on related topics. The Exeter Council, the Cardiff Adult Christian Education Centre, the Ammerdown Study Centre and other Church-related groups, run study days and short courses on current socio-economic themes. At a national level, the William Temple Foundation, Scottish Churches House, St George's House, Windsor, the Iona Community, the Luton Industrial College, and many others, bring together groups of concerned people for study and exchange, or provide courses and training for those engaged in different kinds of Christian social ministry and action.

Two central concerns will come together in most of these publications or meetings. There is, on one hand, a desire to tease out a theological understanding of the nature of work in society. Christians need to have a framework within which to set particular questions and challenges. This will be a framework which will offer not direct answers but a sense of direction and purpose, a panorama of God's grace and calling. And, on the other hand, there has to be a real appreciation of the actualities of the present, of how things work and the human possibilities. Christian action emerges from the continuous interweaving of these two strands.

The *third* level of activity is that of finding things to do, small and large, that can be seen as a practical expression of concern for those who are caught up in the difficulties of the recession. This, of course, will relate to both political action and becoming informed. Any project or scheme, however slight, is symbolic of Christian prophetic commitment. To become engaged with the issues of work or unemployment must involve a process of learning.

At a national level this is embodied most clearly in Church Action with the Unemployed (CAWTU). 'CAWTU creates', in the words of some publicity, 'a resource of information and experience which enables local churches of all denominations to respond more effectively to the social tragedy of unemployment.' This is done through a London office and a network of regional contact people, mostly related to Industrial Mission. A series of leaflets offers guidance on how to set up projects. Local experts can be called upon to advise. Local projects and action groups can affiliate and be given help and advice. There is a Launch-pad scheme that disburses small grants and loans to individuals or groups to provide a start up for schemes to help the unemployed, to provide assistance for small businesses, for tools to enable a person to earn, or for course fees. There are also resources like videos for use in conferences or on courses. Other organizations, like Church Action On Poverty, are also involved in these issues, although often with a much higher political profile.

Throughout the country there are literally hundreds of local and regional Church-related projects. CAWTU has published a directory of 100 such projects.[5] This, however, represents but a fraction of what is going on, much of which will not be known beyond the immediate locality. This does not even begin to include all that is done for and with the unemployed through the growing networks of social and pastoral care, or in the normal activities of a congregation, from youth clubs to house groups. These CAWTU projects or schemes may be based on a congregation or a council of churches, or very frequently through the local Industrial Mission in cooperation with others. Some are explicitly church-based; others are part of cooperative enterprise with local authorities, government agencies, voluntary bodies, the unions or the CBI. They vary in size from providing a base on the premises to large-scale enterprises with workshops, from drop-in clubs to advice and education centres.

In the CAWTU directory we find six schemes in Scotland which can be taken as fairly typical of the smaller projects to be found almost anywhere in the country. In Grangemouth there is a Community Project workshop started by the local clergy and supported by the local Council of Churches and the Community Council, in which 27 people are engaged in renovating furniture and other work. A local congregation in Kirkcaldy is supporting a YTS off-the-job training programme in 'Life and Social Skills'. The Gilmerton Parish in Edinburgh incorporated a workshop into its youth activity to help young people to find jobs more easily. The Anderston Parish in Glasgow was instrumental in setting up a resource centre and library to link the unemployed to local needs. In Glasgow, too, industrial chaplains provide courses and seminars to help the redundant adapt to their new circumstances. And industrial chaplains in Dundee are also involved, with the support of the churches, the Social Services and the Trades Council, in providing a resource centre to sponsor initiatives taken together by the unemployed and the employed.

On a much larger scale we can turn to 'Impasse' in Cleveland. This is funded by Urban Aid and the MSC in four centres. The main idea is to stimulate practical interest in alternative lifestyles without paid employment, and to encourage personal independence on low level incomes, often as self-employed people. In the Middlesborough centre there is a series of workshops and craft rooms and a fully equipped garage. Skilled persons give advice, there is opportunity for training, but the facilities can be used to do one's own do-it-yourself jobs or to take on occasional work for others. A tool library allows people to work at home. The restaurant specializes in and advises on low budget cooking. There are facilities for drama, photography and sport. 'Camps' are held in school holidays for parents and children to learn new skills.

In Newport, Gwent, the Industrial Mission sponsored the 'People and Work Unit', which is 'an independent action-research organization to encourage local economic and social enterprise'. It thus advertises jobs, stimulates new economic activity, does research, holds seminars, provides a library and publishes a regular review.

St John's Urban Ministry, based on the Parish of Penydarrcn, Merthyr Tydfil, is an agency of the MSC, offering short-term employment to hundreds of people in Mid Glamorgan and Cardiff, mostly seconded to organizations or the churches to provide a wide range of social services. There are hopes that the scheme can expand to other centres.

In Buckhaven, in Fife, local churches have formed a Church Agency which has been recognized by the MSC. In a town with 40 per cent unemployment, over 500 people are engaged in a series of community projects such as creating an arts and crafts centre and offering restoration work on such things as staincd glass windows and furniture.

Nor is all this only for industrialized towns and cities. Truro Diocese has a mobile centre in a double-decker bus that can take an advice centre to different villages. In Lincolnshire, a village church school, now closed, provides premises for youth training courses for a whole district.

Almost all these schemes, however, depend on funding from government or other sources, and most of them are also dependent on co-operation with other bodies. This raises four important questions that have to be faced. Although such action is generally less controversial than political or industrial protest, because it appears not to challenge in any radical way the normal criteria for Christian pastoral activity, it nevertheless cannot be entered into 'inadvisedly or lightly'. It is just as important to ensure that the implications of any such project are thoroughly appreciated and accepted.

1. It cannot be avoided that 'he who pays the piper calls the tune'. Monies will only be given to meet certain set criteria and any project has to operate within those criteria. It may be that these severely limit the vision and purpose intended. Sometimes there are ways of putting together a package that fulfils the original intention through different bodies financing different parts separately, each fitted to the criterion of different agencies. It is essential, therefore, to recognize that accepting such grants can skew the project out of its intended direction or tie a project down restrictively.

2. Involvement with the funds available from different government schemes, in particular the MSC, raises another sharp controversy. There are those who would argue, with some justification, that all these schemes have fatal flaws. They are short-term and increasingly fail in their aim to be stepping stones to jobs. They do not in any sense tackle the underlying problems of economic recovery and social justice. At their best they are palliatives. To accept such money is to collaborate in what is really a 'con trick'. To recognize the force of such an argument need

not be — although it may be — associated with a strongly critical stance against the present economic system. On the other side it can be argued that such schemes do provide some benefits which it would be foolish to turn down: those who enter a scheme do have a better chance of a job, and there are personal spin-offs in terms of greater self-confidence. Moreover it is possible to use the schemes to start the shift to an alternative lifestyle. In any case is it not better to do something than nothing? If 'the system' offers resources that can be appropriated then ought that not to happen?

Such a debate has been going on within Industrial Mission and elsewhere. The British Council of Churches had to clarify its mind before accepting the position as an agent for Opportunities for Volunteering, handling over £200,000 a year. Such a decision was not easy, and there should always be a clear awareness of why and under what conditions any grant can be accepted.

3.   A co-operative project presents similar problems. The churches are often the weaker partner so that their distinctive reasons for wanting to participate are often lost sight of. In any case an overt Christian label is not always thought desirable and may even be impossible under certain terms of reference. Social forms of witness with people in the community have more usually to be implicit, while more explicit acts of witness have to be expressed elsewhere. Too often the Church merely becomes a convenient base and there is little connection between a worshipping congregation and the project. Is it, therefore, still worth it or is there a Christian reason to go ahead? This implies the need for a carefully thought out doctrine of mission. Does it matter if the Christian presence is only implicit or indirect? If it does matter, what is the appropriate way of making it explicit? If it does not matter, then in what sense is this action gospel? However, there are three aspects of the gospel that such projects affirm, each of which being central to the nature of mission. These should not be set aside as being irrelevant when discussing the form of Christian involvement.

First, and most crucial, is the affirmation of the future. These schemes and projects we have mentioned state that people are worth time and trouble, that their futures are important and that society has to find creative and positive ways forward. For all their limitations, they are real and prophetic actions and are thereby significant. Fundamentally, they affirm belief in the Kingdom of God.

Second, the churches will be seen, however obscurely, to be caught up in the real affairs of the community. The gospel is about the world, its quality of life and relationships. Gospel meanings are found in the everyday experience of people as they work out their daily lives.

Third, Christian action is for the sake of the other. To treat people as people means that they have to be given space and time and attention in order that they may discern and appropriate their own self-understanding and responsibilities. This is why CAWTU insists on working 'with the unemployed', not doing things for them or providing services; certainly not so that the churches can claim the allegiance of people in return. It is the unemployed who 'set the agenda' and whose story is being written. Christians witness to the God who seeks the good of his creatures that they may enter into the fullness of his purposes, the God of infinite patience and utmost constancy, who is willing to be with his creation in the weakness of love, faith and hope.

4. In practical terms to take on a scheme requires commitment; yet it can be 'the stone of stumbling' that raises all the fundamental issues. People are needed to run it. Time and space are needed to provide for it. Rooms will be taken over. New people will be in and out. There may be damage or nuisance. In a congregation which is used to a community centre this may not be a problem. In a traditional context, however, it may mean breaking down old habits and prejudices, working with new schedules and accepting new demands. Moreover it is easy to start something off only to find that it is much more burdensome than expected. Whatever the proposals, there has to be thorough research into the costs and demands. There will also be legal responsibilities that have to be covered. Even a small internally promoted scheme has to be properly prepared for and accepted responsibly.

Two specific warnings have to be given. MSC-funded activity, even run by other agencies, is not the answer to a failing situation. Nor should such schemes be regarded as cheap ways of getting work done, often on the buildings, without recognizing that there is also a responsibility to provide training and worthwhile experience. At least the congregation should be satisfied that any task force engaged to do some work is indeed fulfilling the fundamental purposes of the scheme, which is of benefit to the employees.

Fourth, and finally, concern over work and employment in our society has to inform the spirituality of the people of God. In the last resort the specifically Christian action on behalf of the world is worship and prayer. If, in our culture, work is in crisis and yet is so crucial to our well-being and self-understanding then, in offering the world to God, this must be a clear and constant concern.

Unfortunately, the evidence suggests that, despite some improvement in recent years, the world of work and industry is not widely acknowledged in worship. This is in line with our divided and truncated view of religion as being related to our private and inward life. It is true that Harvest Festivals have frequently been widened out to include the fruits of manufacture and human skills, and that Industrial Sundays are urged on the churches. But prayer for commerce, industry and labour is comparatively rare. In the Alternative Service Book of the Church of England, the only mention is hidden within Rogationtide prayers. Other service books and most new hymn books are just as tentative. Certainly, this all-consuming aspect of life is not at the heart of our common and eucharistic prayer, that central act of any tradition that both proclaims and creates the attitudes of those who take part. This seems strange when the Liturgical Movement of the 1930s onwards stressed the material and communal nature of sacramental worship. The production of a resource book, *Work in Worship*, by the Industrial Christian Fellowship and the Oxford Institute of Church and Society is therefore to be welcomed all the more.[6]

It goes further than that, however, for Christian worship is potentially social action. It has always been recognized that the proclamation of the Gospel is subversive to all human achievement. It is a public statement that 'the world is the Lord's'. Those who so believe cannot but accept that this puts into radical perspective all our assumptions. Work, therefore, becomes part of our offering to God, to be done as our service to his Kingdom. True work is that which contributes to human welfare and will include much that the world sets to one side as of no consequence. The Christian should, also, sit lightly to those things, like status and reward, that seem to be the marks of greatness in society. Status comes from service. Moreover there are other kinds of work than labour: contemplation, creativity, fellowship, joy and peace — these suggest that we must include all that makes life worthwhile. At the heart of Christian worship there is bread and wine, 'fruit of the earth and work of human hands'. This is the mystery of human work. At its best it reflects God's purposes, and mediates God's creative grace, for he comes to us through what we do; and at the same time we offer to God our work that he may take it up into his very own work which is the Kingdom of God.

This does not provide a programme of action or prescribe a political or personal decision. What it does is open up our perspectives and widen our sympathies to recognize the creative excitement of exploring tomorrow's world. Yet there is work to do, for it is around the Bible and in the intimacy of prayer that Christians can work out for themselves and together in groups what their obedience in the gospel is. For many it may not appear that there is much overt change. But new attitudes, new expectations, new sympathies for the situation of others will inform and transform the routines of normality. Others may hear a dramatic call to explore on the frontiers of emerging social lifestyles — co-operatives, simple living, and ecological economics. Many will find themselves trapped by circumstances into painful decisions and transitions. Together we can find spiritual strength to work through both personal problems and anxieties, to support each other in times of crisis and above all to have a lively sympathy and a caring spirit.

NOTES

1. Dietrich Bonhoeffer, *Letters and Papers from Prison* (Letters for 20 May, 16 and 18 July 1944, and poem 'Christians and Pagans') (London: SCM Press, 1981).
2. *Faith in the City* (Report of the Archbishop's Commission on Urban Priority Areas) (London: Church House Publishing, 1985).
3. *New City: South Yorkshire in Search of a Soul* (Sheffield: Sheffield Ecumenical Mission to South Yorkshire, 1979).
4. Specifically through personal representation and short papers, but based on *A Socio-economic Strategy for the South Wales Valleys*, a project sponsored by Tŷ Toronto, Aberfan. See also P.H. Ballard and Erastus Jones, *The Valleys Call* (1985) (Ferndale: Ron Jones, 1975).
5. Bob Nind, *Action on Employment* (London: Church Action with the Unemployed, 1985).
6. Cameron Butland (ed.), *Work in Worship* (Industrial Christian Fellowship and the Oxford Institute for Church and Society, London: Hodder and Stoughton, 1985).

London: new life in the inner city

Mary Lean

Leonard Johnson, Lawrence Fearon, Delaney Brown, and Errol Williams grew up close to one another in Harlesden (an area of Brent that includes Stonebridge), running with gangs and getting into trouble with the police. Peer pressures were strong and incentives to go straight weak. Williams, who learned brick-laying in Borstal (a youth custody facility), describes starting work on a building site: 'A friend I used to get into trouble with came by and asked what I was doing. He went into his pocket and pulled out a lot of money and said, "This is what I just earned." I walked straight off the site.'

As young men, they each came to a turning point that led them away from crime into community action. All four are now evangelical Christians and say that it is their faith that inspired and sustained them.

Delaney Brown's parents sent him to Sunday school, but he started stealing when he was fourteen. It was a form of business: he knew what people wanted, where to steal it, and where to sell it. 'Ninety per cent of my life was crime,' he says. At the same time, he knew that he would one day become a Christian, 'but in my time'.

When he was eighteen, he and two friends were arrested for picking pockets. Although on this occasion they were innocent, they were found guilty. Brown was sentenced to three months at a detention centre. Right after his hearing, the doctor ruled him unfit to serve his sentence on the grounds of a leg injury (sustained during a burglary six months earlier). He was sent back to the magistrates, who, to his astonishment, released him on bail. Waiting outside the court for his friends to be driven away, he had a 'dialogue with God': 'OK God, I understand that you don't want me to go to prison for stealing. OK, no more stealing.'

He stopped stealing but went on selling dope. Two years later, he decided to stop that too when he saw some girls smoking cocaine in a club and realized that they were bringing up the next generation. It hit him that if things went on this way, in a generation's time, 'we would still be at the bottom of the pile as black people'.

Meanwhile, Brown's closest friends, Johnson and Fearon, had been in Borstal and prison. Johnson had been thrown out of school at the age of fifteen, ran his own gang, and ended up serving a four-year sentence for burglary. In prison, he began reading books by Martin Luther King, Malcolm X, and Stokely Carmichael and was intrigued by how often the Bible was quoted. He went to the source and was hooked. 'The Bible was like a magnet,' he says. 'It began to convert me.' Eventually, he broke down, alone in his cell, and told God, 'If you can change me, I'll spend the rest of my life helping other people, to pay back for what I've done.'

Johnson started to avoid some of his friends and stopped smoking and getting visitors to bring him 'illegal' items. 'I felt I had to do these things to let God come into my life,' he says. To his surprise, he was granted parole after only nineteen months, in spite of the fact that he had another case outstanding against him.

Adapting to life outside was tough. Johnson was embarrassed by his conversion and tried to keep it quiet, but his friends noticed a change. 'Most of them didn't accept it,' he says. 'Some stopped talking to me. My car tyres were getting slashed, my life was being threatened. I was told to leave the street.'

One night he ran into Lawrence Fearon at a party. Fearon had also just left prison, determined to go straight. Two things had made him reconsider his life: a fire at his apartment, in which he and his girlfriend lost all their possessions, and a stretch in Ford open prison, where he met long-term prisoners whose families had grown up while they were inside. 'I realized that this wasn't where I wanted my life to lead,' he says. Back on the streets, Fearon felt uncomfortable with his old lifestyle: 'I was beginning to wonder if there was something wrong with me.'

The two men talked about their dilemma. Johnson compared it to being caught in a whirlpool, jumping from one boat to another: parties, fighting, women, clothes, crime. 'The whirlpool was dragging us under and we weren't noticing it. I told Lawrence that I had jumped out and was swimming to the shore.' They left the party and began to talk about what they could do for their community.

Their first attempts were erratic. Johnson went out on the streets at night, looking for muggers and trying to talk them out of it. He'd march into pubs, bang the table for silence, and harangue the drinkers and gamblers: 'I was trying to tell them we could do better with our lives.' They called meetings, and eventually large numbers began to turn up to talk about what was needed in the community. One of the prime movers at this stage was Juliet Simpson, a young woman who lived in the Stonebridge Estate.

In the spring of 1981, Johnson, Fearon, and Simpson, along with four other friends, set up the Harlesden People's Community Council (HPCC). They took over the Annexe, an underused youth club, and started running drama, dancing, and other classes; a Sunday school; and mother and toddler groups. To give the young people an alternative to petty crime, Johnson got hold of cheap watches and clothes for them to sell. Fearon called him a 'legitimate hustler'. With the money they raised, they gave out small loans. They began to build a relationship with the police, which meant that they could liaise with them when people got arrested and confront them on issues of police harassment.

The atmosphere in Stonebridge was highly charged. In April 1981, there were riots in Brixton, in south London. In July, a wave of rioting engulfed twenty-two inner-city areas, with the worst outbreaks in Liverpool and Manchester and in Southall and Brixton in London. Johnson went around Stonebridge telling people, 'We're not going to riot here.' One Friday night, things came to a head. Youths gathered outside the Annexe, where there was a disco, and the police lined up with riot shields. Johnson and Simpson came out of the Annexe and shouted to the crowds, urging them not to destroy everything they had just begun to build in the community. 'If you're determined to riot, go and do it somewhere else. This area is depressed enough already.' People began to drop their weapons and drift away.

The riots focused national and local concern on the inner cities. The HPCC's role in averting a riot in Stonebridge brought them to the attention of the local government, the Brent Council, which arranged for its policy coordinator, Richard Gutch, to help the HPCC articulate what should be done. One of their recommendations was the creation of a major facility for the community. When a local bus depot came on to the market, Johnson and Fearon saw its potential. At a meeting in September, the owners of the depot agreed to give the HPCC six months to raise the £1.8 million (US$2.8 million) to buy it. At a noisy session packed with members of the community, the council agreed to help find the money. Gutch and the HPCC set to work on a feasibility study.

Delaney Brown was sceptical when he first discovered what was going on. 'I was trying to rebuild my life,' he says. 'When Leonard and Lawrence talked about getting grants from the council, my impression was that they were going to rip the council off, so I wasn't interested. It was only when I discovered that they were reading the Bible that I knew they'd changed. They used to be blasphemous to the point that I'd walk away because I thought lightning was going to strike them.'

Errol Williams also started to work with the HPCC toward the end of 1981. He and his gambling friends in the pubs used to call Johnson the 'mad preacher'. What changed his mind was the prospect of working in an office. 'At school I'd always wanted to be my own boss, have a desk and chair and telephone and put my feet up.' He took over running the HPCC classes, living off his unemployment benefit and $19 expenses a week — a big drop from the $300 or more he could make gambling. He says that he had become fed up with the cheating — and the physical danger if one got caught — and was looking for a way to give it up. The HPCC provided the alternative he needed.

Johnson, a natural leader and visionary, was convinced the £1.8 million would come through. Fearon had his doubts. At midnight that Christmas Eve, he stopped on his way home through a park near the bus depot and prayed for a sign. 'I felt a warmth come over me,' he remembers. 'I felt very calm, as if God was present. When I looked up, I could see the bus garage in the distance, and it was all lit up. There were people moving about in it and it was like the place was already up and running. I knew the thing was going to work.'

After six months of negotiation, and just ahead of deadline, grants came in from the national, metropolitan, and local governments to meet the bill. Mike Wilson, who took part in the early meetings with the Brent Council, sees the council's decision to back the project as good economics. 'You either spend £20 million [US$30 million], which is what the Brixton riots cost in terms of the damage done, or you invest in the community.' In February 1994, with the bailiffs at the door, he still reckoned that Brent had gotten a bargain. 'They've spent or mobilized about £13 million [US$20 million] over a number of years instead of what they could have spent in one,' he said. The creation of Bridge Park, with facilities requested by the community, eased the frustration that could have erupted in further trouble.

The HPCC moved into its new offices on 5 May 1982, and set about raising the money for the centre. A local firm gave them old office furniture, which they renovated and sold. 'We were very strong on doing things for ourselves and very critical of others,' says Fearon. But the sums required were so great that they found themselves depending more and more on grants.

Grants came from the European Social Fund, the Department of the Environment, the Urban Programme, and Brent Council. They used the European money to raise the wages of people employed through the Manpower Services Commission, a government training scheme attacked by the Left as 'slave labour'. In the years up to 1988, over 400 people were trained through this and other schemes while working on the site. Among them were the HPCC members themselves; they understudied professionals who were employed to teach themselves out of their jobs. HPCC also set up its own building company to do some of the building work.

The first phase of the scheme — including the Information Technology Centre (ITEC) and a pre-school centre — was completed by March 1983. The ITEC went on to become the Middlesex ITEC, which now trains over 250 people a year. The second phase was dogged by conflicts with unsatisfactory architects, control struggles with the council, and troubles with some of the professional staff. In July 1985, the project's finance manager and his assistant made off with £50,000 from the project's bank account. As the years dragged on and the HPCC got more tied up in red tape, the community itself got impatient, and some of the founders, including Juliet Simpson, moved on.

Finally, in October 1987, the complex was completed. It boasted a 1,250-seat gymnasium, squash courts, a sauna, and physiotherapy rooms; thirty-two units for starter businesses; training and seminar rooms; a recording studio; and a bar, restaurant, and hall for 400 people. Bridge Park was becoming famous as a symbol of inner-city hope: its founders were invited to meet the Royal Family; they attended conferences overseas and were taken up by the Conservative government. Celebrities flocked to see Bridge Park. On 20 December 1988, the centre was officially opened by Prince Charles.

Interviewed on television that year, Leonard Johnson summed up what Bridge Park meant for Stonebridge: 'It's a way of showing people on the streets, people without academic qualifications, people who don't think they are able to make headway in life, that they have skills to offer, that they are not written off, that determination and belief can also carry them forward.'

In 1989, its first year of full operation, Bridge Park earned 52 per cent of its total income, and Brent Council promised an annual grant of £365,000 (US$569,000) for the next five years. A consultants' report urged expansion, with the inclusion of private-sector representatives on the board. Three years later, at the end of March 1992, the council withdrew its funding. Since then, the centre has been run by volunteers and has lived off its rents. By February 1994, it had debts of £1 million (US$1.5 million) and was being taken to court by Brent. What went wrong?

Both sides agree that the skills needed to manage a multi-million-dollar building are different from those required to get it off the ground, though opinions differ as to whether the HPCC could have swung it with more support and training. It's clear, too, that Britain's dive into recession in the late 1980s came at just the wrong time for Bridge Park. As the recession deepened, the private sector had less money to spend, and the central government stepped up pressure on local governments to cut back on services. 'Bridge Park came to us for money three times a year for four years,' says Charles Wood, the chief executive of Brent (a non-political post). 'The council began to feel that at a time when we were having to close down old people's homes and schools in an already deprived area, it was difficult to be putting half a million pounds into a hole.'

There was a political factor too. The project had been launched with the help of a Labour council, which believed in subsidy, at a time when the Conservative national government was trying to force local governments to economize. Initially, according to Richard Gutch, the HPCC tended more toward the Conservative rhetoric of 'individual entrepreneurship, getting up and doing for themselves rather than relying on the welfare state'. The HPCC thought that it would not need public money once Bridge Park was up and running. This made the HPCC popular with the national government but was unrealistic.

In 1991, control of the council passed into the hands of the Conservatives, who urged commercial viability. By then, the HPCC knew that Bridge Park could not break even on its own and depended on council grants. 'If we set commercial prices, then the community couldn't afford to use Bridge Park, even though it was built for them,' says Errol Williams, who took over from Johnson as chairman in 1992. 'If we charged community rates, we wouldn't be able to make funds to run Bridge Park.'

The trigger for Brent's withdrawal was a critical report by its auditors, which revealed the extent of Bridge Park's debts and suggested financial irregularities. The audit was forwarded to the Fraud Squad, amidst adverse publicity, but has not led to any action. 'I'm not going to say no stealing has gone on in Bridge Park,' says Williams. 'But my conscience bears me witness that there's been no fraudulent dealings by its founders or the board. Do you think if Brent could have found any fraud we would still be here?' Gutch, who worked closely with the HPCC until he left Brent town hall in 1985, is inclined to agree. But he thinks that some employees may have exploited a lax regime.

Gutch attributes many of Bridge Park's problems to a lack of people with the professional expertise to handle the bureaucratic and management side. Of the core group, only Mike Wilson started out with the report-writing and budget-making skills required for a large-scale project. From the outset, town hall officials expressed concern about handing public money over to inexperienced people — particularly ones with criminal records. Some would have been happier if the project had been under direct council control, though Gutch is convinced that this would not have worked.

The danger in such circumstances, he says, is that outsiders try to take over. 'The issue is how to help in a way that is enabling and empowering.' This is no academic question for Gutch. He recalls an early disastrous attempt to draft a document *for* the HPCC rather than working it through *with* the members. 'They were really critical that they hadn't been involved. We started again. I talked with them about each chapter, wrote it up, gave them each a copy, revised it — and in the end we had a document that they felt reflected what they wanted. It was very labour-intensive. After I left, I don't think there was anyone who tried to perform that role — keeping a watchful eye, advising, helping the group to take more responsibility and control.' Without someone to interpret them to each other, relations between the council and the HPCC spun into a downward spiral.

Maurice Forsyth, principal field officer for Britain's Commission for

Racial Equality, sees this as a classic case of an imaginative programme whose initiators were not given enough support. Mike Wilson, general manager from 1985 to 1990 and now acting company secretary, agrees. 'There tends to be a lot of underinvestment in people who are working in front-line situations, where, if nothing is done, people will suffer,' he says. The HPCC was torn in two trying to run the development and placate the officials, on the one hand, and trying to keep the community happy, on the other.

The divorce between Brent and Bridge Park has been bitter, with accusations of dishonesty and incompetence from one side, and of racism and ingratitude from the other. 'We're being told we're good enough to have initiated this, to have brought Prince Charles here, to have attracted millions of pounds, to have stopped two riots, but we are not good enough to stay and run it,' says Williams.

For the HPCC, the issue of whether Bridge Park remains in black hands has been vital. 'We don't want it to be, "We gave them the money and they screwed up. Blacks are incompetent,"' explained Brown early in 1994. The creation of the centre gave a tremendous boost to the black community; the discouraging effect of its loss would be just as great, he believed.

The core group at the heart of the HPCC shares a strong evangelical Christian faith. For Johnson, Fearon, Brown, and Wilson, it is what brought them into community work in the first place; for Williams, it developed in the process. Fearon maintains that only a spiritual encounter could have liberated him from his sense of inferiority and given him the courage to embark on the bus garage project. 'It was incredibly ambitious,' says Richard Gutch. 'They needed something to make them believe it was all going to happen — either religious faith or a pretty strong commitment to the idea. They had both.'

Every morning since 1984, the members of the HPCC have met to study the Bible and pray together. 'If we hadn't had that spiritual fellowship, our relationships would have gone out the window,' says Fearon. They pray for the council as well as for themselves. 'We have faced every situation with prayer and determination, and in every situation so far we've found a solution,' says Mike Wilson. Their catchprase is, 'God, we can't wait to see how you're going to get us out of this one!'

The downside of this faith in God's provision, according to Gutch, has been a tendency toward over-optimism, particularly in the early days. There was a feeling that God was with them and that it would always be that way. The convictions of the inner core may also have alienated people of different views who wanted to work with the HPCC. They certainly contributed to the reservations of some at the town hall. 'They were passing over public money in the form of Urban Aid Grants,' explains Gutch. 'Usually that can't be given for specifically religious initiatives.'

Faith has enabled the members of the HPCC to hang on long after pure obstinacy would have run out. It helps them to look at success and failure in a different way. 'When I look at Bridge Park with the natural eye I feel depressed, angry, hurt, used, weak; I feel I've had enough,' says Williams. 'When I look at it from God's perspective, I feel completely different. I see the fulfilment of the dream we once had; I see people being educated, trained, feeling fulfilled in their lives, being successful, being able to unleash their unlimited potential. And then I say to myself, I'm going on.'

In spite of the present difficulties, there have been real achievements. Where there were two black businesses in Harlesden High Street when they began, there are now at least twenty, according to Brown. The area is now a major development area, drawing millions of pounds, and the HPCC helped put it on the map. And although Bridge Park itself is struggling, some of its offshoots are thriving. SCoLAR, set up by Williams, runs training programmes for the long-term unemployed and in schools and prisons; it also contributes to the training of civil servants and prison governors. The HPCC has played a part in setting up numerous enterprises.

Individually, each of the men is involved in helping other communities, at home and abroad, to launch their own projects. Wilson and Fearon both work for Christian organizations involved in social issues; Brown works with the London Enterprise Board, helping young people set up businesses; Johnson is an international consultant. The future, says Wilson, 'has got to be about how the principles we have acquired here are replicated elsewhere'.

They miss the early days, before the hassles of administration and grant raising took them away from the hands-on work with the community. Was Bridge Park a mistake?

'I would not say I wish I had not done it,' reflects Fearon. 'We had the experience of working through a vision and seeing something of it come to fruition. We can point to it as an example. There are people who wouldn't have had a job or a home without Bridge Park, and that makes it all worthwhile.' He believes that the HPCC made mistakes in allowing itself to become a political football and in failing to organize local support. 'If I did it again,' he says, 'I'd be a lot more astute.'

Further reading

Murray Bookchin, *The Limits of the City* (Buffalo, NY: Black Rose Books, 1984). Argues for the recovery of community and face-to-face relations as key to the recovery of human and ecological harmony in urban production and exchange systems and city governance.

Anne Borrowdale, *A Woman's Work: Changing Christian Attitudes* (London: SPCK, 1989). Charts the continuing influence of gender stereotypes in attitudes to work and child-rearing, and in particular amongst Christians, despite the majority experience of women in work.

Church of England Board for Social Responsibility, *Industrial Mission, An Appraisal: The Church's Response to the Changing Industrial and Economic Order* (London: Church House Publishing, 1988). An insider's review of industrial mission which identified the strengths of industrial chaplains in identifying with the world of work, and in generating imaginative responses to unemployment, but also the major gulf between industrial mission and local churches.

Matthew Fox, *The Reinvention of Work: A New Vision of Livelihood for Our Time* (San Francisco: HarperCollins, 1994). The dysfunctional nature of work in modern society is seen by Fox as a consequence of a narrow conception of productive, paid work. He argues that the experience of work will be rebalanced with the needs of children or the planet when output is measured in terms of the sustaining of communities and relationships of care, and not just profit.

Margaret Kane, *Theology in an Industrial Society*; *Gospel in Industrial Society*; *What Kind of God?* (London: SCM Press, 1975, 1980, 1986). Kane's trilogy of books on the people and churches of industrial and post-industrial Northeast England represent a sustained form of 'bare-foot' urban theology outside the university, seminary or deanery. Kane identifies a series of theological models and discourses for interpreting and engaging the problems and possibilities of changing work patterns, new technologies, and urban-industrial decay and regeneration.

Jürgen Moltmann, *On Human Dignity: Political Theology and Ethics* (London: SCM Press, 1984). Sees work as a sharing in God's creativity, as means for community building and service, as a vital form of individual fulfilment and expression, and the denial of work as a fundamental affront to human dignity.

Michael S. Northcott, 'A place of our own', in Peter Sedgwick (ed.), *God in the City* (London: Mowbray, 1995), pp. 119–38. The struggle for a livelihood and decent housing in deprived neighbourhoods experiencing the downside of globalization is manifest in a range of local community enterprises and projects involving job creation, housing renewal, city farms. Such projects are often sponsored by faith communities and churches who are able to build on their deep roots as communities of place in UPAs.

Hugh Ormiston and Donald M. Ross (eds), *New Patterns of Work* (Edinburgh: St Andrews Press, 1990). Essays which reflect on changing work patterns and especially on down-sizing and out-sourcing, the consequent growth in sub-contracting, temporary and part-time working, reduced employment security and access to occupational pensions and other forms of work-based welfare.

John Rogerson (ed.), *Industrial Mission in a Changing World* (Sheffield: Sheffield University Press, 1996). Includes first-rate accounts of the history and current condition of the industrial mission movement, and essays on changing work patterns, new technology and the future of work.

Saskia Sassen, *Cities in a World Economy* (Thousand Oaks, CA; London: Pine Forge Press, 1994). An excellent survey of the implications of globalization, and in particular of the global markets in finance and employment, for the economic vitality and social welfare of post-industrial urban communities.

Peter Sedgwick, *The Enterprise Culture* (London: SPCK, 1992). A fascinating account of the self-employed and small business culture fostered in the Thatcher era and its implications for traditional theologies of work, employment and wealth.

9

Worship in the city

So come to him, the living stone which was rejected by men and women but chosen by God and of great worth to him. You also, as living stones, must be built up into a spiritual temple, and form a holy priesthood to offer spiritual sacrifices acceptable to God through Jesus Christ. For you will find in scripture: 'I am laying in Zion a chosen corner-stone of great worth. Whoever has faith in it will not be put to shame.' So for you who have faith it has great worth; but for those who have no faith, 'the stone which the builders rejected has become the corner-stone, and also a stone to trip over, a rock to stumble against'.

They trip because they refuse to believe the word: this is the fate appointed for them. But you are a chosen race, a royal priesthood, a dedicated nation, a people claimed by God for his own, to proclaim the glorious deeds of him who has called you out of darkness into his marvellous light. Once you were not a people at all; but now you are God's people. Once you were outside his mercy; but now you are outside no longer.

(1 Peter 2:4–10)

Faith in the City

Worship in the UPAs must emerge out of and reflect local cultures: it will always be the worship of Him who is totally Other and yet is to be found, worshipped and served through the realities of UPA life. The worship of the Church that is part of the UPA will be the worship of a Church that is present in celebration, confession, compassion and judgement. (6.101)

To understand worship in this way means that certain aspects of UPA life will necessarily greatly affect the formation of the worshipping life of the UPA Church. The main contribution of the Church to our cities is to be itself, and true to its vocation. It will gather up and inform local life. (6.102)

Introduction

In this passage Peter, the Apostle of the Jewish Christians, is writing to the Gentiles. He argues that, though they were not the people of God, none the less

worship and faith make them a living community who experience divine grace in
their gathering together, and who proclaim the works of God in the midst of the
struggles of life. Worship of the true God is the essence of what it is to be the
people of God in the UPA, as in every place (Ford and McFadyen). The Church
can never be satisfied with becoming just another social work or community
development agency. The Church exists first and foremost not to change the
world but to worship the God who is in the rejected Jesus (Hauerwas and
Willimon).

The worship of the one who is rejected, a stumbling block, has particular
significance in the UPA, for people in inner city areas and peripheral housing
estates experience a great deal of rejection and blame from the wider society,
whether as scapegoats for society's ills or as people who are not considered
creditworthy. The paradox is that the UPA is both stumbling block and corner-
stone in relation to the prosperity the rest of society enjoys, for that prosperity
was built on the sacrifices and commitment of the forebears of people living in
UPAs to unskilled, heavy manual work which for much of this century was the
engine of economic and social progress. But in a society where new investment
creates more work for machines than persons, and where more manufactured
goods are imported than made in Britain, the cornerstone has become a stumbling block. The under-skilled who for more than two centuries were the engine
house of collective prosperity are marginalized and stigmatized in post-industrial
Britain as irresponsible single parents or feckless unemployed. The life stories of
people in UPAs consequently include many experiences of rejection, despair,
violence and dejection (Green).

The God who is in Jesus, as Peter reminds us in this passage, is a God who
identifies with rejection and suffering, who does not pretend it is not real, or seek
to avoid it. Rather this God comes to earth as a person who embraces the
suffering of the poor, the sick and the marginalized, who seeks to bring salvation
through suffering, both in his ministry of wholeness and in his redeeming death
on the cross. Jesus comes to people who are excluded from the temple, from
respectable society and from economic security, and proclaims to them the good
news that they are accepted not rejected any more, that their way of life on the
margins brings them closer to God than the respectable securities and exclusions
of religious and wealthy people.

In the Gospels we frequently see Jesus eating and drinking with tax collectors,
publicans, sinners and the poor. In his earthly life he treated those whom society
despised as 'no people' as the people of God. He celebrated with them in
anticipation of their inclusion in the coming reign of God and he praised their
faith, perseverance, spontaneity and neighbourliness in his parables and teaching. This connection between joyful celebration, exclusion and poverty is part of
the offence of the Gospel to the materially wealthy and worldly wise. It points to
the profound truth that those who have less of the world's goods travel more
lightly, and consequently their lives are more often focused on relationships with
people than on possessing things. They have a capacity for joyful response to
God and to the gift of life which is often lacking amongst the wealthy, as Jesus
points out many times in his ministry from the story of the widow's mite to the
story of the rich man and his store houses (**Pearce**).

Celebration, affirmation and praise are truly redemptive experiences for those
who often experience criticism, exclusion and blame (Ford and McFadyen).
Praise of God creates self-belief and shared trust, it establishes that God is

dependable and loving, and that we are the people of this God, who relies on us to be vessels of divine love (Wallis). Celebration frees us from the poverty of production and consumption as our main life purposes because it connects us with God who is the only ultimate end. In celebrating God we affirm that it is not work or its absence, money or its absence, which determine our existence but the free grace of the God which we experience in praise (Suurmond). But too often church is not seen or experienced as a place of affirmation or free grace in the inner city but as a place of judgement and exclusion, a place of 'them' and not 'us' just like all the other institutions and agencies which determine the lives of the poor. And so, like the stone the builders reject, many urban church buildings are shunned by their neighbours on Sundays, though they may still come to them for christenings or funerals.

Urban churches have sometimes been reborn once they cast aside their redundant stone buildings. The temple of this passage is a living temple, not made of stones but of people. Contemporary 'house' churches, and many black-led churches, often meet in school halls, hotels or conference centres, reflecting the belief that it is the enthusiastic praises of the people of God who make the space holy, and not the gothic arch or the tabernacle of the reserved sacrament (Cox). Their emphasis on spontaneous praise and joy meshes better with the experience of the marginalized than the formal rites and ceremonies of more established churches.

For many, however, the traditional church or sanctuary, inherited from previous generations, is the symbolic still centre which provides continuity with the past amidst the threats of rapid urban change and upheaval. The parish priest or minister who disturbs the old symbols of the urban church — the eagle lectern, the commemorative plaque, the altar rails — or the Dean or Bishop who declares a parish surplus to requirements may find communities angrily resistant to their passing. The church is a symbol of transcendence in the midst of pain. In the nineteenth century the often miserable slum areas of the new industrial cities provided a fertile ground for the revival of ritual and ceremony in many Anglo-Catholic parishes. The profound witness of these churches to the Incarnation of Jesus as human victim and priest, and of divine and saving power in Christ the victor, was expressed in a range of ritual engagements with the life of working-class communities from the Sunday High Mass to festivals and Holy Days which sought to recreate the rural echoes of the liturgical year around the new working patterns of urban industrial cities (Kendrick). Colourful vestments, high cere-mony, incense, candles, confession and processions around the parish were reintroduced in slum parishes to provide an aesthetic and a spiritual haven in the midst of the oppression of factory work and of fetid overcrowded slums. Sunday Schools, youth organizations, guilds of altar servers, surpliced choirs were also developed to provide education and spiritual and aesthetic discipline in the midst of squalor.

However, in the contemporary inner city or outer estate many parishes find the old formulas and organizations harder to sustain in the face not so much of squalor or real hunger as of secularism and apathy. The resonances between this style of parish and traditional working-class communities have been lost as traditional working-class life has also disappeared in the face of rising affluence amongst those in secure employment, and the breakdown of social cohesion and family structure amongst the unemployed and low waged. The acquiescence to the social order that the haven of the Mass seemed to imply also played a part in its diminishing appeal. Part of the attraction of Pentecostalism, and the new house churches which have emerged in places such as the East End of London and in outer estates in many English cities, is that they seem to offer a more active style of praise and celebration which encourages people to find spiritual power in the gifts of the Holy Spirit and collective affirmation in loud joyful music, and thereby to challenge the forces which oppress them (Cox). Testimony and story-telling are a feature of the black-led churches, and of many of the new urban Pentecostal and house churches: in this way people share their experiences of redemption in their struggles for life in the city and against its powers and idols. Even in the most traditional setting, contemporary worship needs to be earthed in urban life if it is to attract the people of the city, and cannot be so transcendent that it fails to reflect their struggles or to evoke hope in the midst of them (Church of England Liturgical Commission).

Praise and celebration may seem to represent a triumphalist short-cut where shared stories are more often of the apparent triumph of evil, pain and rejection than of grace and humanness. But the God who is in Jesus does not only respond to the predicament of suffering and sin with an invitation to celebrate. In Jesus we encounter a God who knows and embraces rejection and suffering, drawing them into the heart of divinity. On the cross Jesus demonstrates that the God whom Christians worship is a God who redeems pain not by pretending it is not real, nor by identifying it with fate or poor karma, but by entering into the pain, by embracing suffering, redeeming rejection by becoming rejected.

There is a wide recognition of the need to remake ritual in UPAs so as to reflect this divine embrace of our brokenness (**Ward and Wild; Bradbury; Morisy;** Church of England Liturgical Commission). Ritual is vital to the rebuilding of broken lives, relationships and communities. Shared rituals have this magical capacity to make things appear different, to transform sadness into joy, tears into laughter, and to inspire us to believe that our deep longings for affirmation and wholeness are not the result of some kind of cosmic or divine joke but the imprint of God in all of us, reminding us that we are made to be whole, to know love, and to be accepted not rejected (Driver; **Ward and Wild**).

The strength of Islam and of Pentecostalism amongst ethnic minorities in the inner city, and the resurgence of various forms of paganism in many UPA communities, provide evidence of the continuing need for ritual in our society. Islam's strength lies in its ordered times for worship, the deep adoration in body as well as mind which Islamic ritual represents, and the fundamental connections between a vision for society and worship which Islam has always sustained. Islam in Britain is also a religion of an oppressed minority. It provides a sense of empowerment, and resistance to oppression, which the Christianity of the colonizer and of racist white society does not seem to offer. Pentecostalism's strength resides in its exaltation of praise as the determinative action of the church, and in the capacity of Pentecostal praise to lift people out of their struggles and give them hope (Cox). Like Islam it is also an embodied form of worship expressed in the physicality of its praise and music, and in its emphasis on spiritual empowerment Pentecostalism gives power to the powerless.

Worship is a vital source of resistance and of energy in facing the social evils of violent conflict and rejection which are the daily reality of life at local parish level (**Morisy**). But the liturgies and official rites of the church rarely relate to these evils, or provide resources for resistance (Leech). Good ritual and liturgy provide a real encounter between Christian tradition and daily experience in the conflicts of urban life. But in order to bridge the gap, people need to own worship and to be full participants in it, coming as they are with their pain and hopes, and with their traditions and gifts (**Bradbury; Morisy**). Creative and experimental liturgy will have a particularly central place in the UPA church for the shared and participative work of shaping and performing ritual will enable people to overcome the alienating strangeness of imported liturgies and ancient hymns which so often disempower the marginalized (Walsh).

There are many excellent examples in the history of urban and industrial mission of the ability of imaginative pastors, preachers and worship leaders to reconnect worship, liturgy and life in the urban environment. The prayers of Michel Quoist encapsulated and yet redeemed the alienation and deprivation of the young people of Le Havre in Northern France in the 1950s (Cryer). Horst Symanowski wrote his sermons with the help of a weekly meeting of working men from the factory where he ministered who would interpret the weekly lectionary through the stories and struggles of their lives (Symanowski). Some have found new uses for their stone temples making them live during the week as centres for the community rather than as cold worship space for Sundays only (**Morisy**). The worship space of the sanctuary thereby reaches out into the other parts of peoples' lives. Margaret Walsh describes how her community developed a liturgical style in interaction with the people of Heathtown which centred on the sharing of stories, the singing of songs and the making of prayers by the people themselves (Walsh). It was not the Eucharist or the mass which parish priests wanted the people to attend, but it was a ritual bridge between the formal and public liturgical culture and the informal and marginalized culture of the UPA.

The authors of *Faith in the City* drew attention to the significance of the boundary rituals of the rites of passage as modes of ministry and mission in the UPA, for it is in these rites that the majority of people in UPAs still have contact with church. Rituals of naming and baptism involve the affirmation of children in the context of a society which consigns more than a quarter of all children to distressing poverty, decrepit housing and decaying school buildings. They also involve in the baptismal vows affirmations of the importance of resisting evil as the means of human flourishing. Rituals of resistance to evil have a symbolic significance in communities where evil confronts people fiercely in their streets and their homes (Leech). Stories of domestic violence, racial hatred, child abuse, muggings and abusive behaviour are more often the daily testimony of magistrates' courts than church meetings. Worship in the UPA needs to incorporate these stories into a narrative of resistance and of hopefulness even in the midst of evil, reminding participants that in identifying with Christ crucified and risen they may find the moral and spiritual power to resist evil and turn it away (**Morisy**).

The determinative ritual of the Christian Church is the Eucharistic celebration. The earliest urban house churches met every Sunday to perform this rite of eating and drinking, remembrance and celebration, atonement and reconciliation — it was the determinative feature of their pattern of worship. But the earliest house churches shared this meal in ways very different to our own formalized Eucharistic styles. We know from the abuses Paul condemns at Corinth that they shared a full meal together as part of the Eucharist, and not just the sacramental elements we traditionally share. We know that their Eucharistic songs and prayers were mostly not written down in books but shared orally and spontaneously by the celebrants. We know that while a few elders may have presided, all the members were regarded as celebrants, sharing in the rite of celebration their own particular gifts of prophecy, healing, teaching, music or hospitality.

The problem of the Eucharistic shape of Christian worship for many churches in UPAs is not the centrality of the Eucharist but the form the Eucharist has taken in the late twentieth century, a form which seems to exclude so much of that which is the common life of people in the UPA, and which seems to rely on the strange texts and traditions of alien cultures and histories. However, some UPA churches have responded to these problems by the development of a principal Sunday service focused on the ministry of the Word, a form which is provided for in *Patterns for Worship*.

The key to recovering the Eucharistic shape of ritual in the urban priority church is to see the Eucharist as the sacramental sign of the reign of God in the midst of the denials of God which are the daily reality of the UPA (Balasuriya). The Eucharist is the ultimate symbol of the redemption of the marginalized but in its co-option by the church of the powerful it has come to symbolize the power of administration rather than the calling of the powerless (Balasuriya). The robes of the traditional Catholic Eucharistic celebrant are the robes of a fourth-century higher civil servant, robes which represent ministry as the power of the Christianized empire. We may need to divest the Eucharist of the accretions of power which are so alienating to many in the UPA. Recovering the Eucharist as symbol of resistance and liberation will also involve recovering some of the spontaneity of the early Eucharistic prayers before their codification as written texts designed to impose centralized orthodoxy on heterodox local worshipping communities. It will involve recovering the significance of the Eucharist as a shared meal in communities where evidence of genuine malnutrition in the form of rickets is re-emerging in the children of the poor. It will involve energizing the Eucharistic celebration as an act of collective praise which encapsulates the power of the Spirit, and of shared performance, to make real a new order of reality in which freedom and dignity are restored to the oppressed (Leech; Driver).

The Church exists to worship God. Worship, ritual, celebration have the power to change us and transform society because they involve the evocation of the Spirit of God who is active in our struggles to resist evil and affirm the good, and because they draw on and focus the power of human groups which is so much greater than the power of individuals on their own. The determinative work of the UPA church and the UPA pastor is in this sense no different to the work of the church in every place, but the obstacles to, and opportunities for, liberative worship which changes lives and brings salvation near are so much greater in the inner city and the peripheral housing estate. The Church at national level devotes considerable resources to the construction of liturgies which are intended to be universal in design and performance. But language or rituals which may give transforming expression to the praise of God in the suburb or the city centre may be irrelevant or even oppressive in the UPA (Leech). The task of worship leadership in the UPA is therefore all the more exciting and challenging for we cannot simply run the pattern of worship which the church issues from above (**Bradbury**). Authentic praise will engage, connect and empower us in the midst of our daily struggles and conflicts in the city. It will also enable us to transcend the divided city, enabling us to see the God who is in the crucified Christ who wept over the city before it killed him, who offers liberation and hope in the midst of sin and despair, and who promises that the poor will see God.

Human rites: worship resources for an age of change

Hannah Ward and Jennifer Wild

A SERVICE OF HEALING FOR A HURTING WORLD

Silent meditation

As the mountains are round about Jerusalem, so the Lord is round about his people, from this time forth and for evermore.

(Psalm 125:2)

Be ye transformed by the renewing of your mind. God hath not given us the spirit of fear; but of power and of love and of a sound mind.

(Romans 12:2; 2 Timothy 1:7)

Responsive praise

LEADER How manifold are your works, O Lord!

MEN AND BOYS
    In wisdom you have wrought them all — the earth is full of your creatures.

WOMEN AND GIRLS
    The sea also, great and wide, schools without number, living things both small and great.

LEADER God looked at all creation, and found it very good.

ALL   May the glory of the Lord endure for ever.

(Genesis 1:31; Psalm 104:24–5)

Hymn (Select a hymn of creation and praise)

Prophetic challenge

LEADER Listen, people of Israel, to this funeral song which I sing over you;
    Virgin Israel has fallen,
    Never to rise again!
    She lies abandoned on the ground,
    And no one helps her up.

MEN AND BOYS
    You people hate anyone who challenges injustice and speaks the whole truth in court.

WOMEN AND GIRLS
    You have oppressed the poor and robbed them of their gain.

MEN AND BOYS
    And so you will not live in the fine stone houses you build or drink wine from the vineyards you plant.

LEADER I know how terrible your sins are and how many crimes you have
        committed. You persecute good people, take bribes and prevent the
        poor from getting justice in the courts.

MEN AND BOYS
        The Sovereign Lord says, 'A city in Israel sends out a thousand
        soldiers,

WOMEN AND GIRLS
        but only a hundred return;

MEN AND BOYS
        Another city sends out a hundred,

WOMEN AND GIRLS
        but only ten come back.'

ALL   The Lord says to the people of Israel, 'Come to me and you will
        live.'

                                                      (Amos 5:14, 10–12)

Dialogue

*Begin by having eight to ten worshippers stand one at a time to read
a current news headline. These headlines should identify suffering
in the world in need of God's healing. Ask all to reflect on these
headlines and similar ones they themselves have read. Encourage
worshippers to write on a 3 × 5 index card provided for them one
or two sentences that reflect their thoughts and concerns. Allow
time for participants to share aloud what they have written.*

Corporate confession

Lord, we listen to your prophets' words, knowing they are for us. We have
misused your world, so perfect at Creation. Land meant to provide for all,
provides for only a few. Young men dream of ploughs and corn, but find
instead guns and warplanes. Women who want homes for their children and
soup for their pots, pitch refugee tents and boil grass for dinner. Babies born
with your promise, die from disease and starvation. In your world of plenty,
millions face impossible choices — food or heat, shoes or a coat, electricity or
rent.

Lord of Creation, move us from hardness to compassion, from guilt to
forgiveness, from apathy to action, from complicity to justice. Heal our
brokenness and the wounds of your creation. Amen.

Words of assurance and forgiveness

'Comfort my people,' says our God. 'Comfort them! Tell them they have
suffered long enough and their sins are now forgiven. Come to me and you
will live.'

                                             (Isaiah 40:1–2; Amos 5:12)

Homily or sermon

Eucharist, Holy Communion, Lord's Supper

After partaking of the bread and cup according to your tradition, invite worshippers to the altar for special prayers of intercession and healing for our world.

Period of intercession
(Gathered at the altar)

LEADER We are together here as members of the Body of Christ, called to do his healing work on earth. Let us claim his healing power and know with certainty that that power will flow through us, his channels, to those in need. Let us be assured, too, of the promise made to all intercessors: '... whatever you ask in prayer, believe that you receive it, and you will.'

(Mark 11:24)

Anointing with oil and laying-on-of-hands

The rituals of anointing with oil and laying-on-of-hands should be incorporated according to your own religious tradition or as you feel appropriate. The following format is but one alternative.
    As part of the period of intercession, have a bowl of olive oil available. Those who wish may kneel, prayerfully lifting up both the concern written on their cards and their own personal requests for healing that in their lives which prevents them from being fully open channels for God's healing power. The pastor or a team of clergy and lay persons can move from worshipper to worshipper for laying-on-of-hands and anointing with oil. Some worshippers may wish to verbalize their petitions for healing while hands are laid on their heads and the oil is touched to their foreheads. But whether or not petitions are verbalized, repeat together these words for each individual: 'Lord of Creation, Lord of Mercy, bring your healing touch.'

The Good News of deliverance
(Read in unison)

ALL The Sovereign Lord has filled me with the spirit.
God has chosen me and sent me to bring good news to the poor,
To heal the broken-hearted,
To announce release to captives
And freedom to those in prison.
God has sent me to proclaim

That the time has come
When the Lord will save all people,
And defeat their enemies.
God has sent me to comfort all who mourn,
To give to those who mourn in Zion
Joy and gladness instead of grief,
A song of praise instead of sorrow.
They will be like trees
That the Lord has planted.
They will do what is right,
And God will be praised for what is done.
They will rebuild cities that have long been in ruins.

(Isaiah 61:1–4)

Hymn of praise and victory

Benediction

Bread for the World

* * *

A RITUAL TO INVITE LIGHT INTO AREAS OF DARKNESS

This can be used in large or small acts of worship. I first used this with several friends as we invited people to name political and ecological concerns at the beginning of Advent. It can be used on any occasion when people sharing worship will feel helpless at the size of the issue, and have to wait speaking, acting only a little at a time.

A speaker raises consciousness on an issue.
A representative of the worshippers comes forward, lights a candle, says:

I light this candle as a sign of the Light of Christ that will be with us as we commit ourselves to hear, wait and in time act upon what we have heard.

This is repeated after each speaker.

For example, issues we spoke about were:

Poverty in the world, and world banking.
Seduction to over-spend, by the media and materialism.
Justice for women.
Recession: who pays the price?

Mary Robins

* * *

We are not alone

Introduction

This service is prepared to encourage people who are involved in the struggle for justice, peace and truth.

Opening sentences

Let us remember who we are:

LEADER   We are the people of dignity.
Down the ages we have been the people of God,
the people who know themselves to be called
to freedom, courage and truth.

PEOPLE   We light a white candle for that dignity
and the power of God in us.

LEADER   We are the people who weep
for the suffering of the world.
We are the people who walk with the Christ
towards all who grieve,
who are oppressed and exploited.

PEOPLE   We light a purple candle
for those who suffer with the people
and the power of Christ is in us.

LEADER   We are the people of hope and faith.
In the Spirit we celebrate our energy
and strength, our power to heal
and our calling to work with God
in the recreating of the world.

PEOPLE   We light a green candle
for our hope in the Spirit.
We are not alone.

Naming our weeping

LEADER   Where is the pain in our lives?
The people name their fears, angers, areas of pain.

LEADER   You are not alone.

PEOPLE   Your tears are our tears.

Affirming our hope

LEADER   Who are the people who have given us strength
and courage, who have created models for us?
The people name the people.

LEADER   These people walk with us.

PEOPLE   We have company on the journey.

The Word (Reading from the Bible)

Affirmation of faith

LEADER Let us affirm our faith in God:

ALL   We believe in God
          who created and is creating the earth,
          who so loved the world that Christ was sent
          to live life with us
          and the Spirit to be our strength.
          God has favoured us and appointed us
          to be a light to the peoples
          and a beacon for the nations;
          to open eyes that are blind,
          and release captives from the prisons,
          out of the dungeons where they live in darkness.
          In solidarity with the people of God
              around the world,
          and in company with the other churches
              in this city,
          we name ourselves as those who, in Jesus Christ,
          are enough to do the task
          in this time and this place.
          We have heard the call of Christ
          to follow in the way of the cross.
          In faith we lay down our fear,
          our weakness and our lack of worth
          and announce again
          with those who have gone before us that,
          'Where the Spirit of the Lord is, there is liberty'.

Intercession

LEADER Let us ask God for help along the way;
RESPONSE
          'Jesus, remember us' (*Taizé – sung*)

The commitment to each other

          A symbol of common humanness is shared.
LEADER In the face of all our realities:
ALL   We are the people who heal each other,
          who grow strong together,
          who name the truth,
          who know what it means
          to live in community,

moving towards a common dream
for a new heaven and a new earth
in the power of the love of God,
the company of Jesus Christ
and the leading of the Holy Spirit.

Blessing (sung)

Dorothy McRae-McMahon

Inner city spirituality

John Pearce

Perhaps because of the unwelcoming environment which pertains so widely in the inner city, it seems that God shows his hand more clearly and (dare we say it?) more crudely in these places.

The evil one is certainly at work in his most obvious guises and many inner city congregations are constantly in touch with people living in houses which are 'possessed' or oppressed by demonic manifestations. It is almost a routine for the pastor and some of his people to go out to 'exorcise a house' from noises or smells or sounds which appear to come from the evil one. All too often the Devil has been invited in by the use of the occult. Sharon and Jim came to the vicarage one day. She was nearly hysterical; he was white as a sheet. They had been playing with a ouija board and he had been forcibly thrown right across the room by an unseen force.

No less evident is the power of the Living God and frequently there are stories of visions, dreams and the like. Rosie told the story of how she was uncertain what job to do, when the Lord appeared to her in a great brightness and told her specifically what she must do. Many people find that their Bibles fall open at precisely the right text to guide them in their current circumstances. The voice of God is often heard as plainly as he was heard by Elijah. This is presumably because, where people have not been used to logical thinking, God deals with people in a way more suited to them. The intuitive and the experiential is often of greater importance than the usual methods of guidance, laborious as these often are. When people cry out in desperation for instant miraculous answers, God sometimes meets that need instantly and the world of the Old Testament somehow seems incredibly close and Samuel's experience as a child in the temple becomes as natural as going to the fish-and-chip shop.

For this reason those who advise and counsel in the inner city (and no doubt deep-country situations) need to recognize that the more acceptable cerebral ways in which God deals with men may not be usual in these areas. For, in a sense, God walks in the city in the cool of the day and men and women have the intimacy of his friendship and conversation in ways which they can understand.

* * *

Whereas middle-class society is largely based on the individual, in inner city areas the basic element of life tends to be corporate, whether that be the family or the group at work. Men go out together to the pub or the club or football. Women go out shopping with a friend. Decisions at work are taken by the local union grouping and the individual sinks his responsibility in that of the whole. And of course in many ways a corporate philosophy of life is far superior to the rank individualism which has produced appalling loneliness and isolation in Western society. There is far more in common with the Christian ethic in life in a body than in the fierce independence of the individualist.

If the church is to develop the life of its members and to enable them to grow in maturity, it must enable the evolution of groups and teams within the church. An inner city church will not so much be a congregation as a series of small groups, who are deeply commited to each other, coming together for common worship on Sunday. The home group will therefore either be based on natural friendships or will quickly evolve into such if it is to be successful at all. It will also be a far more all-embracing organism than the mainly cerebral group of the suburb.

For example the group will probably have a good number of parties (remember the pancake party when one of them stuck on the ceiling!), trips out and the like. There will also be a high degree of personal and practical caring for the sick and those in difficulties. Ivy once had her purse stolen in the market. Within twenty-four hours she had made a handsome profit from gifts! Often a group will 'take on' a seriously ill person and enable them to stay in their own home. Bill, with multiple sclerosis, was able to stay in his own home almost until the last because the home group visited him every single night to settle him down for the night.

Unless an inner city church develops these groups (formal or informal) it will fail to become a church of the neighbourhood and will attract mainly only the misfits and the upwardly mobile (the 'private' people). Such groups do not need to be based as a house group. Gatherings of peer groups and interest groups can be deeply supportive and enable people to live in community in the hostile environment of the urban desert. A group of elderly people used to meet weekly. As they grew older and more infirm they continued to care for each other and became a kind of 'family' to each other, as the more active called on the house-bound almost every day.

There is a real place for Christian communities and Communes in the inner city. Communities such as the Little Brothers and Sisters of Jesus or the Franciscans have pioneered a way of life which involves living in ordinary small terrace houses or flats and sharing the life of the community fully, while retaining an ordered life of prayer. One of the most interesting examples of this is to be seen in the Community of the Word of God which has now been in existence for fifteen years and whose centre is in Hackney, East London. It is exciting how many people come to that terrace house. The chapel (which is really only a passage on the way to the bathroom!) is a place full of a sense of God as three times a day local people gather with the community for prayer and praise using the Anglican daily office, or the Taizé form, or informal extemporary prayer. It is helpful for folk to be supported in their own prayer by the constant prayer and worship of the community which, incidentally, consists partly of local people and partly of 'incomers'. There is a need for many more experiments such as CWG.

Another support has been found in the 'sharing group' where two, three or four people meet regularly to share their lives, confessing their sins to each other, confiding their problems and praying for one another. The sense that one is no longer alone provides a parallel to the sense of group loyalty which is a characteristic of the workplace and, instead of being inimical to one's Christian faith and ethic, it strengthens the arm.

Since people so often feel insecure and inadequate both as Christians and as leaders, there is everything to be said for appointing people to posts in pairs which is, after all, what our Lord did. Decisions can be shared, guidance can be checked and (most important of all) it is possible to pray together about the matters which are being faced.

The common view of the Bible study group involves a leader who is highly prepared, having read all the necessary commentaries. He or she will control the group carefully, if with subtlety, and will ensure that the required passage is more or less adequately treated and completed within the hour set for it. The exercise is essentially cerebral and the members will go away having learned a good deal more intellectually. They will have become more 'instructed' Christians.

In the inner city the group will outwardly look much the same except that it will be important not to 'read round' because not everyone present will be able to read and certainly some could not face reading out aloud. But there the similarity ends. Of course the Bible will be opened and, after a few explanations by the leader to explain difficult sections, there will be a 'free for all'. This may be a period which will last all evening when the members share what the passage means to them. Inevitably, this may seem at first sight to be a very long way indeed from the most obvious applications of the passage but God uses his scriptures in most remarkable ways and very quickly the group will move away from 'what the scripture says' to 'what the scripture means to me' often with a very deep sharing of personal problems, deep hurts and painful concerns. And as each ministers to each from the Word, there is a deep sense of the presence of the Holy Spirit and an exciting awareness of the immediacy of the Word of God to present situations. One evening Peter was leading the Bible study. He had only recently learned to read but was deeply soaked in God's Word. Sharon came full of sorrow and mourning on the anniversary of her mother's death. Most of the hour was given to listening to her as she recounted her pain and her distress and as the others shared their own experiences as far as they could in order to bring balm to a painful situation. The passage chosen for the night, was left far behind. At the end of the hour, Peter spoke firmly, 'Now we will read 1 Corinthians 15'. And so as the group ended with free prayer, everyone felt that God had spoken today to Sharon's situation and to theirs.

Just as the individualistic spirituality will not suffice to nurture the perso-nal life of the Christian, nor will it prove adequate to nourish the life of the congregation. To work alone is a contradiction in terms for the Christian and so there will be group decision-making in the church. 'It seemed good to the Holy Spirit and to *us*.' Of course sometimes a particular individual will have a prophecy or word from the Lord but, more often, as the group prays together informally and discusses a problem they will be led to a common mind which will give the strength to move forward. For example a Warden or Youth Leader will rarely take solitary decisions but will take counsel with others and fast and pray as a group before major — and even minor — decisions are taken. Again and again the meeting with the eternal and numinous God comes as the group waits together on the Lord — and less frequently as the individual prays alone. This is not to say that the 'private' Quiet Time is unimportant but that it feeds the group rather than *vice versa*.

'Who should be the new youth leader?' was the question. One person was the 'obvious' choice. Two others were possible. The fourth was an 'also ran'. The group went away for a long time of prayer together followed by quiet waiting upon God. At the end of the day all came back together with a name. All four produced the name of the 'also ran', given by God to the group after deep prayer. That person went on to be an outstandingly successful and professional youth and community worker.

To take another example, one local church began to feel burdened and concerned about an estate of 4000 people. Rats were often seen on the roof five floors up and human effluence frequently surged up through the drains. Conditions were deplorable. The Church Council gave an evening to discussion and prayer. As a result the church in co-operation with social workers, Communists and Conservatives leafleted the estate and founded an independent Tenant's Association which quickly achieved a great deal to improve the quality of life on the estate. This happened because of a corporate life of extempore prayer together with the opportunity to wait in silence on the Lord to receive his guidance.

The Holy Communion is at the heart of the life of many inner city churches. Family Services and Guest Services will be arranged for evangelistic purposes but it is at the Lord's table that Christians renew their strength and feel part of the body of Christ. At the Lord's Supper Christians find the equivalent to the solidarity of the Working Men's Club or the public house. They belong and they belong to Christ, strengthened by *doing* something and not merely sitting in pews hearing words for, at the Communion, they come forward together and receive that Bread and that Wine which is their spiritual food.

It is significant that people who leave the inner city churches by moving out often feel bereft of fellowship and especially of the sense of belonging to each other which is expressed not just in the 'Peace' but in the hand-shaking and hugging which is to be found at the church door. It is important that membership of the Body of Christ feels a reality.

In many situations and not least in the privatized pastures of the outer suburb the Christian life has to be lived largely alone as the individual battles out his problems alone and without any deep fellowship. One of the greatest of all benefits of inner city life is the rich sense of community which is engendered when people feel the need to be close to each other in a hostile environment. Out of this experience there comes a deep sense that we belong together and this is found to a most pronounced degree in the inner-city church as people spend much time with each other, dropping into each others' homes without ceremony. The sharing of one's needs and problems and joys is a natural result of this closeness and many are the informal times of prayer that go on in homes after the sharing is done. It therefore becomes more natural to join in shared extempore prayer and there is a richness and an immediacy about these prayer meetings which are unique and precious.

There is a sense that 'when one member suffers all the members suffer' and this leads to a very high degree of pastoral care being shown to those who are going through periods of distress or weakness. There was one occasion when a certain man had had a fall and was lying in bed recovering. He had to get up fourteen times that day to open the door to Christians who had called to care!

Another result of the high degree of community life is the way in which the healing ministry goes on outside doctors' surgeries and church buildings. It becomes natural to gather round a sick or sad brother or sister and, with the laying on of hands all together, to pray informally that the needy person may be healed.

Of course all this cannot happen if the Christian Way is taught as a formal thing which essentially belongs in church and requires proper liturgical forms. One of the sad developments in modern liturgy has been the desire of some to provide services for all occasions. We must at all costs preserve the informal side of Christian worship and ministry.

There is nothing which tones up the muscles of an athlete like the need to put out his best against able and perhaps even stronger opponents. It is this sense of challenge which is especially to be met with in the inner city. The environment is hostile. Even some of the people one meets may be violent and menacing and certainly there is an increasing sense of insecurity with the prevalence of mugging on the streets and the amount of burglaries. But the battle is more accurately seen as a spiritual one when the individual Christian is alone in his factory, office and school in a setting where everyone else has quite different values. The local church, however lively it may be, is often comparatively small and few people come to it unless they are already committed Christians or at least considering the faith in an active way. When folk go out visiting from the church, they may frequently find the door slammed in their face and there may be real opprobrium to be borne from neighbours and family.

However, in the majority of cases the very opposition produces a stronger and more virile faith which enables a greater courage to be displayed and also produces a more serious attitude to prayer. If one's friends and neighbours are really so opposed to the faith or are at the very least totally apathetic, this leads to a greater enthusiasm in devotion and in sacrifice. Christianity is not an easy option or an interesting activity for one's spare time. It has become a matter of life and death, an issue where one's own integrity is 'on the line'. It is for this reason that the spirituality of the inner city dweller is often much more vigorous and committed than may be found elsewhere.

Where the lines often appear to be clearly defined between Christian and non-Christian, there is inevitably a high incidence of sudden and definite conversions. There are two consequences of this phenomenon. First of all, where the person has a deeply emotional new birth, there will frequently be a reaction which is very like what St John of the Cross calls 'the dark night of the senses' and the new convert needs to be prepared for this as, otherwise, he will too quickly assume that this newfound Lord has promptly left him and will be tempted to abandon his recently established discipline of prayer and Quiet Time.

But the consequence (of seeing many definite conversions) upon other Christians is to strengthen their faith. When a person such as a well-known drug user suddenly turns to Christ and is delivered from the habit, church members are shown (in a very dramatic form) the power of their Lord and, as a result of their prayers become very definite and full of expectancy. It is by no means easy to teach believing and receiving prayer in those parts of England where people live lives which are essentially private but, where everyone knows what is happening down the street or in a block of flats, prayer is seen as more effective and more urgent than it often seems in other areas except in the true village. In such areas therefore priority will be given to petitionary prayer, and the church prayer meeting as well as the private intercessions of local Christians are likely to be dominated by very specific and clear-cut petitions of the kind that Jesus clearly envisaged in his teaching when he said 'Ask and you shall receive'.

Praxis, prayer and liturgy in a secular world

Ann Morisy

Liturgy, if it is to be described as 'apt', needs to express people's deepest fears and hopes. Apt liturgy should also enable people to put their fears and hopes into a wider context by sensing the resonances between their own situation and humankind as a whole. One of the costs of the low level of religious literacy in our society is that people are deprived of conceptual tools which could help them locate their circumstances, both positive and negative, in a more universal framework. Apt liturgy is a way of providing a framework of understanding which helps people to move beyond self-centred and narrow horizons. The language of both modern and traditional liturgy can denote links with our forebears, as well as help us understand our relationship to the struggles being acted out in today's world. Far from being a psychological disaster area, as many secularists hypothesize, liturgy is one of the most profound, as well as most convivial, activities known to humankind. Involvement in some form of liturgy, regardless of how short or simple, enables people to understand themselves better and to appreciate their place in the world. To quote Peter Shaffer in his play *Equus*, 'Without worship you shrink, it's as brutal as that.' Robin Green writes that 'Liturgy, which is the vehicle through which worship is expressed, creates an environment in which human beings confront those sides of themselves which under normal circumstances they dare not face.'[1]

I was invited to the celebrations to mark the third birthday of the Jubilee Centre run by a Baptist church in London. Anyone who had any contact with the centre from its outset had received an invitation. That included the many people who had approached the centre for help in rescheduling their debts and getting some order into the financial aspects of their life. The evening celebration began with a summary of how the centre began, and how it had developed. Mention was made of the name of the centre, chosen because of the Old Testament injunction in Leviticus 25 that every fifty years God wanted the Children of Israel to wipe out the debts which had accumulated between people, and give everyone a fresh start. For people both outside and inside the Church, this kind of revolutionary talk makes socialism look tame. It certainly encourages many to see the Bible in a new light.

As might happen at any annual meeting of a voluntary organization, due acknowledgement was given to the trusts that had made grants and the volunteers who had given their time and expertise, but then a time of prayer was held. For the volunteers and the people who had availed themselves of the advisory service, this seemed a natural thing to do; after all, it was a church-run project. In reality, few people object to five minutes sitting on a chair with their eyes closed.

The minister began by acknowledging everyone's debt to God for his gift of his Son. He asked God to forgive our society's preoccupation with material gain. He moved on to pray for those people who find themselves harassed by debt. He then prayed for the plight of nations in Africa and South America cast into debt through the world's system of commodity trading. One of the volunteers then read from chapter 7 of Luke's Gospel about the time Jesus dined with Simon the Pharisee. As often happens with Jesus, the good guys in the story turn out to be a prostitute and the chap who owed the most money. Nobody preached; the short liturgy ended with the hymn 'The Servant King'. During the singing of the hymn there was scarcely a dry eye in the house.

This short liturgy provided an extraordinarily powerful combination of insights and experiences for those who were up to their eyes in debt as well as for the volunteers who had seen the destruction which debt can cause. People were able to locate their situation in a wider context, both through time and within the world today. It raised awareness and enabled people to link personal or local struggles with more global ones.

Those present at the birthday celebration were also introduced to the potency of the Bible. An insight was provided about the earthy and radical nature of Jesus, in contrast to the image of a meek and mild Jesus which litters uninformed thinking. This radical Jesus could upturn the prevailing values on behalf of the poor and put- upon. This image provides a foundation on which people can begin to understand the need for God to be incarnate in this world, and how Jesus is an expression of God's involvement in, and commitment to, our world. It is only when this relationship is understood that people can start to appreciate why Jesus is so significant to Christians.

The birthday liturgy at the Jubilee Centre also moved people to tears. This is an important phenomenon indicative of people moving from an inability to worship because of the limitations of their beliefs, to a capacity to sense the intimate yet awesome aspect of a God who invites us to call him Father.

The quiver of a chin as emotions are engaged carries a real transformational quality for people who previously have had little contact with formal religion. A number of people experienced a new way of seeing at that birthday liturgy. Perhaps the experience was not sufficient to bring about what is traditionally described as a conversion, with the often unspoken expectation that the person then becomes committed not just to the Gospel of Jesus but also to the institutional Church. However, the experience of the evening provided very rich themes which people could ponder in their hearts and, at a later date and possibly in combination with other triggers, draw on in a life-transforming manner.

I remember an experience I had at a weekly prayer meeting for users and volunteers at that same drop-in centre for homeless people in which Pat was involved. About a dozen people had gathered, mainly users of the centre. Between them they faced chronic problems of alcohol and drug abuse, mental illness and social inadequacy. We sang the well-known chorus 'Bind Us Together, Lord'. It was never my favourite; in fact I find its sentimental longing for cosy fellowship nauseous. The final verse, which suggests that 'We are God's chosen', usually implying a fresh-faced gathering of worthy people, I find particularly off-putting. However, this time as I sang those words I found myself wondering whether the motley group of homeless and mentally distressed could be God's chosen. The answer came without hesitation: yes, they were most certainly God's chosen, and for the first time in my life I had a clue about the vastness of God's grace.

Bruce Reed would describe my experience as an example of regression. He, and others concerned with group dynamics, stress that regression is not a negative process. Rather, 'Regression in service of the ego, or the relaxation of ego control, does not imply infantile or pathological behaviour, but rather it is essential for the creative process, not least because it allows the emotions to be engaged.'[2] Bruce Reed suggests that by introducing liturgy into the place where people's struggles are focused — for example, within a community ministry project — an opportunity for regression is introduced. For some it may seem sufficient that the experience brought me an insight into the nature of God. Bruce Reed, however, would look for more, because regression is such an important precursor of creativity.

The experience did go on to yield more insight. It became clear that if the disparate group which gathered to pray each week were God's chosen, then it followed that they had the capacity — the right, in fact — to structure and lead the prayer meeting. From then on, the afternoon prior to the prayer meeting was used to help people prepare and assemble their ideas and, if they felt they needed it, rehearse their contribution. This in turn led to another, even more significant, insight. As a Christian drop-in centre, it had become the natural base for a number of people whose mental illness, usually schizophrenia, seemed to take the form of religious mania. They were often preoccupied with religious, often biblical, material, and normal functioning was relegated to insignificance. The weekly prayer meeting was, of course, a priority for them. What happened was this: for the first time they were invited to occupy a position of some authority in relation to all this 'God business'. They were encouraged to reflect on how they could use their awareness and commitment in a way that was helpful to others. And that cracked it. I am not going to say that the prayer meetings which resulted were earth shaking. Nor would I wish to claim that a key had been found to unlock people's chronic, as well as sometimes acute, mental illness. But certainly what happened was health giving. It enabled those who were usually absorbed in their intense internal world to look outward and consider the needs of others. It enabled them to respond to prompts and clues which normally would have gone unheeded. More than anything, it gave the simple but radical insight that psychiatry needs to resist the temptation to interpret the religious preoccupations of people experiencing mental illness as a symptom. It may be that by helping people engage with their religious preoccupations, and by taking such preoccupations seriously, they can be harnessed in the direction of health and wholeness.

Community ministry requires the involvement and commitment of lots of lay people drawn from both inside the Church and from the wider community. However, in order to maximize the creative insights to be derived from an upsurge of emotion such as that elicited by an apt liturgy, a degree of pastoring may be required. It needs the involvement of someone who can devise apt liturgy and share that skill with others; someone who can give effective public expression to that liturgy, and provide spiritual direction to help people move beyond sentimentality. The emotional response which is often prompted by apt liturgy is not in itself sufficient. A liturgy which has been designed to resonate with people's life experience may move them, but it is necessary to engage with minds as well as emotions.

In particular, those who, through their involvement in a community ministry project, begin to engage with the Christian faith are likely to need help in reconciling the notion of a God of love with a suffering world and suffering people. This means that an opportunity for reflection alongside someone with a confident understanding of the Christian faith is important. Too often the first step in the direction of a personal faith involves the shift in the person's view of God from a remote, powerful but impassive 'force' or power in the world, to an image of God as a soft, indulgent and kindly Father. However, such an image of God does not take account of the bitter pain and injustice of everyday life. It needs an understanding of the God who also suffers in the world's suffering if a faith is to develop which can sustain someone who is prepared to embrace burdens wider than their own. A sentimentalized fantasy, even if undergirded by a religious experience triggered by the apt liturgy, is not adequate to nourish someone who is prepared to exercise 'venturesome love'.

This kind of intimate religious education has to be promoted and overseen by someone who is proficient in theology and spiritual direction. These are usually the skills associated with ministers of religion. Ideally part of these skills includes the ability to pass them on to others. Therefore, one of the extraordinary features of community ministry is that instead of seducing clergy away from their priestly, or more spiritual, work, it requires them to undertake it in all earnest. Not only can a community ministry project extend the traditional pastoral ministry of the clergy, it also provides them with the opportunity to exercise spiritual direction and devise apt liturgy in a way which enables those with low levels of religious literacy to encounter concepts which they can meditate on in quiet and privacy.

This challenge would provide a very practical and appropriate module within clergy training. For example, students could be asked to design a liturgy for those who are affected by dementia and for those who care for them. What theological motifs would be appropriate in such a context? Perhaps the notion of pilgrimage? Perhaps the story of the widow's mite? When congregational leaders are able to link the Bible with people's current struggles, the Gospel can become as relevant today as it was when Jesus preached in Palestine.

How would the minister draw such a gathering of people together? How could they tap into the network of those affected by dementia? How would he or she consider being available if people felt they needed longer-term support? What would be the implications of hosting such a 'customized' liturgy twice a year? Trainee church leaders also need to learn about the impossibility of promoting such an initiative single-handed. More than anything, however, through such an exercise they start to see how the Gospel resonates with everyday issues and the struggles that people have.

The following example demonstrates how simple 'apt liturgy' can be. Often, the art is not so much in devising the liturgy, but in recognizing a moment when it would be significant:

> During the summer, members of an old people's day centre from the East End of London had a series of day trips. They chose to revisit the places where they or their children had been evacuated in the war. Most of the conversations during the journey focused on people's wartime experience. Although some lighthearted moments were recollected, for many there were stories of hardship and tragedy. A number of the people on the trips were Jewish, one part of the diverse nature of East London. What is more, Len, the volunteer who drove the minibus, not a church member as it happens, has a German wife, a fact Len anticipated most people would politely overlook and not allow to get in the way of their enjoyment of their day out.
>
> As the minibus arrived back, the minister was there to meet it. For two or three minutes she asked people about the sort of memories which had been rekindled. She then invited people to be quiet as she said a few words of prayer. In those prayers she was able to help people to acknowledge the range of emotions which had been evoked during the day: to acknowledge the hurts and tragedies which afflicted people of all nationalities; to pray for those who had died; and to give comfort to those who had been bereaved either in the war or more recently. She was able to speak of God who also grieves at the pain and suffering which afflicts the world; and to speak of a father who lost his son on a cross at Calvary. This short but apt liturgy helped people to put their individual experiences into a wider context. It went a little way towards healing people's memories, helping to soften hearts which might have become hardened, and in all it took ten minutes.

Those ten minutes marked out the day centre's trip as different from what might be organized by a secular organization. The words which were spoken and the thoughts and emotions which were evoked would otherwise have been hidden and isolating. It was the Church doing what only the Church can do. As for Len with his German wife, he took away with him a sense of acceptance rather than avoidance. He saw how faith was not about denying reality but rather about looking at the facts of our humanity in all our vulnerability as well as destructiveness. Those ten minutes provided him with powerful material to ponder in his heart. I know this because Len told me about it, and he told his wife about it as well.

One of the most important skills of the minister of religion is to contribute words which can express those moments and situations when others have found that words have failed them. The capacity to fashion a language for those private sorrows and unarticulated needs is particularly important in a culture in which people think they can live by bread alone. By enabling pent-up feelings to be acknowledged and located in a more universal framework, new channels of awareness are opened up for people.

Those responsible for training owe it to embryo church leaders to help them develop skills which enable them to connect with those who only 'half believe'. They need to become confident that they can provide people with concepts to ponder in their hearts as a result of just seven minutes of 'apt liturgy', for these are the demands which are made on ministers who get involved in community ministry.

There is a further contribution which the minister, with others, has to make in relation to community ministry. That is, to discern the optimal development of the community ministry project which is consistent with enabling people to do business with God. Whilst it is not the minister's task to organize and co-ordinate the work of the project, if the minister distances him or herself from the project it can have a profound effect on the project. The lack of involvement of key representatives of the local church increases the likelihood of the project adopting secular approaches, making the aim more and more narrow and focused simply on providing a range of services which address the needs of homeless people, or isolated parents, or those affected by dementia, or whatever group the project endeavours to help.

Countless projects perceive themselves as a Christian voluntary organization, whose priority is to continue to expand and diversify in response to the needs of the client group. In the process, paid workers take the place of volunteers, the project moves from its base in a local church, establishes new offices and operates under a new constitution which distances it, at first ever so slightly, from the local church which spawned it. This process can also [cause] some acrimony: the local church may be perceived as insufficiently committed to the issue, choosing to play it safe rather than wholeheartedly pursue the needs of the poor. Those who remain in the orbit of the local church can, in turn, see the project as having been a distraction to some of the congregation who have put the project's well-being ahead of the church's.

There is a genuine tension between the wider 'evangelistic' agenda which is facilitated by a community ministry project, and the more straightforward focus on service provision. The cost of retaining the evangelistic capacity of community ministry is that the project has to remain one that can be sustained through volunteer effort. The irony is that reputations in the Church, and in society as a whole, are not made through sustaining a modest volunteer-run community project. Enviable reputations are more likely to be achieved by building up a formidable voluntary organization which has an array of strategies for addressing the needs of its client group. In committing themselves to a community ministry approach, church leaders have to be alert to the tension within the model, and the possible tension within themselves. Community ministry requires people to achieve sufficient control over their ego needs to appreciate that the reward is in heaven or not at all.

One of the things which community ministry can do unintentionally is to cast regular Sunday worship in a negative light. The intimacy of the apt liturgy which takes place within a community ministry project, both in terms of relationships and sensitivity to context, as well as its emotional potency, can make the main Sunday service seem a cool and aloof affair. It is important that we do not lose confidence in public worship: it is the anchor which keeps innovative and 'customized' worship from taking on the characteristics of a sect.

The different dynamics offered by both a large group and a smaller group increase the scope of what can be offered in terms of liturgy. Robin Green suggests that, for people who have never been involved in worship, it is helpful for their early experience to be in a small group. Here the liturgy can reflect each person's experience, especially using the highly resonant contexts generated through community ministry. By contrast, Sunday worship, with the dynamics of the large group, is the medium which better expresses other aspects of our faith. For example, 'proclamation and prophecy, celebration and resurrection, offering and transcendence'.[3]

Those who only 'half believe', but are willing to express venturesome love, are likely to need a number of stepping-stones before they can *worship* the God of Jesus. To facilitate this, community ministry must be part of an overall mission strategy. It helps to see the apt liturgy which is possible within a community ministry project as akin to planting a church. However, instead of planting a Sunday by Sunday worshipping group, a satellite activity, i.e. the community ministry project, is created to provide the vital 'small group' experience of liturgy which is so important in helping people experience an awakening of faith. If community ministry ventures are viewed in this light, and not merely as expressions of the Church's social responsibility, there is a greater likelihood of the stepping-stones which enable a more explicit exploration of the Christian faith being put in place. These stepping-stones are often already available but, because we fall into the trap of thinking in compartments, we fail to see the significance of a timely invitation to consider joining a Confirmation class or an Alpha course. If there is to be an effective link between the project and involvement in Sunday worship, it is essential that the apt liturgy associated with community ministry is teamed with some method of enabling people to explore the Christian faith more systematically. The genuineness and intensity of needing God alongside can characterize many community ministry ventures, and this is a powerful evangelistic resource which needs to be located in an overall strategy if it is not to be squandered.

NOTES

1. Robin Green, *Only Connect* (London: Darton, Longman and Todd, 1987).
2. B. Reed, *The Dynamics of Religion* (London: Darton, Longman and Todd, 1978), p. 22.
3. Douglas Rhymes, *Time Past to Time Future* (London: Darton, Longman and Todd, 1993).

A worshipping community

Nicholas Bradbury

One evening I got into conversation with a young man named Dermot who lived next to the church. It was clear that he was in considerable need. He had just lost his job as a porter at Guys Hospital through persistent lateness on account of drinking. His personal relationships were in tatters, the relationship with his lover broken off. He was in trouble with the police. He had no money. He was on the slippery slope towards the alcoholism and vagrancy I was seeing all round me in the parish. And it suddenly became abundantly clear to me that though Dermot desperately needed the saving experience pointed to in worship, the service I was conscientiously planning for the next morning could do precisely *nothing* to meet Dermot where he was and nor could a thousand refinements of it. I saw then that no amount of tinkering with the churchy end of liturgical expression would reach Dermot. Any hope of Dermot experiencing the grace which for me came through the liturgy would begin by starting with *Dermot's* experience, with *his* feelings and convictions, and discovering what Christian worship meant within them. Otherwise Dermot was never going to make the journey from where he was to an understanding of the Church's concepts and symbols.

That evening I came to appreciate in a very practical way the pastoral futility of a good deal of the liturgy I had been trained to officiate at. Although I did not know what to put in its place I was forced to look at the emptiness of much of the Church's conventional liturgical apparatus when confronted with human need and suffering such as Dermot's. I suspected that the Church needed to make the journey from attachment to its own imagery and ceremony to Dermot's felt experience. Never since then have I thought of liturgy as something whose language the individual has to learn in advance, before being able to participate. During my years as a pastor I have come to learn that good liturgy is always an encounter between Christian tradition and ordinary experience.

Canon Eric James, a leading contributor to *Faith in the City*, has spoken of a similar experience in his own life. His upbringing had led him to music. He was a promising organist with permission to practise on the organ of Southwark Cathedral where he also had lessons. Naturally he enjoyed the beauty of the cathedral's musical tradition and manner of worship, thinking of it as something the church had to offer others. Then he took a job on the wharves of London docks. He met men whose language and whole social world seemed light years away from that of the cathedral. He found himself gazing into a ravine which divided these two worlds. And he was appalled. The Church which meant so much to him had built no bridges of communication between Cathedral-language and dock-talk. The gulf was deep and fixed. And Eric James went forward to ordination, his main desire being to help bridge the gap, to bring together those on either side.

The clear need, then, is to connect worship and ordinary feeling, and for liturgy to transcend the communication gap between different styles of language, barriers of social class and educational background. For this connection to be made, it seems that two conditions need to be met:

- People need to feel they *own* their worship;
- People need to be *full participants* in the worship.

To own your worship you must feel able to come as you are. You must be able to bring your feelings with you. This means that worship must be a safe place to bring anxiety, stress, depression, fear, loneliness, resentment, boredom, illiteracy, diffidence, bitterness, self-pity, grief, shame, anger, madness, guilt, despair, prejudice, hatred, or feelings of oppression. The words of the liturgy must not merely skim the surface of how you feel, leaving you essentially untouched. For example, the prayers of confession can be more than a ritual incantation. A good liturgy is able to confer an *experience of forgiveness*.

To reach people as they are in the inner city, worship must aim to blend tradition and liturgy with the living experience of the worshippers. I do not think it possible to offer a blueprint as to how this is to be achieved. Each congregation's own style of expression in worship is bound to be widely varied. However, the following illustrations taken from an inner city parish in London do show some instances in which worship was brought to life by the participants being able to own what they were doing.

According to Church of England rules you must have a licence to preach. But the Bishop had told me that in the inner city we should do whatever seemed right for the Kingdom. So, a month after becoming Vicar, I asked four mothers to give the Mothering Sunday sermon. The theme was to be the relation between the experience of mothering and faith. They were staggered. 'Give the sermon? Us?' 'Yes,' I said, 'Haven't you needed your faith in God since you became a mother?' 'Oh yes,' said Doris, 'when I had my Claire ...'. At once she started talking. 'That's perfect,' I said with genuine enthusiasm, 'Can you say that on Sunday?' Doris did in fact speak movingly of her experience of God in giving birth. Kate said that it was when she found out that her son David was going to be deaf that she first thought of God, and in different ways each mother was able to say how the experience of mothering had contributed to her faith. They were agreed that it was perhaps their deepest encounter with the mystery of God, as important as anything learned in religious instruction.

That Mothering Sunday sermon deepened the faith of those who gave it, but it also touched the whole congregation. In particular, people expressed surprise that religion, with its doctrines and creeds, could find room for something as ordinary as being a mother. I was pleased that the sermon was well received, but saddened that the religious expectations of habitual churchgoers should be so removed from their ordinary lives. I subsequently found that considerable imagination was needed to create liturgies around people's deepest personal experiences, but that it was well worth the effort to try. Repeatedly I have found that religion comes alive for people when they are encouraged to see God in experiences like falling in love, having a child, losing a job, or the illness or death of a loved one.

* * *

John, aged forty, was found to have cancer secondaries in his stomach and had only a few weeks to live. A short time before, in the first shock of learning the nature of his illness John and his family had begun a relationship with their parish church and had been coming on Sundays. John made friends quickly. He was a warm and attractive person and something of an extrovert (a talented singer and entertainer) with an easy and obviously genuine interest in others.

Before his illness John had been an enthusiastic sportsman. He had the build and strength of a rugby forward. As his massive weight loss occurred and his energy began to wane he and the family asked if there could be a service in church for him. They wanted to offer God their situation and ask for healing, and John himself wanted to be baptized. The family knew the seriousness of John's illness and felt God would be able to meet them in their plight, although wisely they did not attempt to prescribe how.

The family, with my help, prepared the shape of the service and chose suitable readings. After the rite of baptism John sang 'I'll walk with God from this day on'. It was deeply moving. Prayers followed and then the laying on of hands. First family, then friends and anyone from the congregation took part in this. They said prayers over John, and the family remained with him to hold and be present with him as others came up to lay on hands and to pray. John himself prayed that he would find God in what he was undergoing.

The striking thing about the service was the exceptional sense of fellowship it engendered. People seemed somehow united with John through the liturgy. It conferred a sense of peace and inner strength on John, his family and, it seemed, all who took part. John's situation and suffering did not prevent the growth of a love in which people gave and received from each other. It was that rare occasion when participants feel moved and softened by a sense of the surrounding presence of God. A fortnight later the Bishop came to confirm both John and his wife in a second service at which they both read and he again sang.

John remained at peace during the last weeks of his life. His final prayers were all thanksgiving and intercession for others. At his funeral his wife and four children gathered round the altar with the celebrants so as to surround John's coffin and face the rest of the congregation. Together they joined in part of a eucharistic prayer written for the occasion, and shared communion. They were too overwhelmed by grief to be able to disentangle feelings, faith and despair. But for many in the congregation it was a liturgy in which faith found itself and God became known in a new way.

Mary, John's wife, found her family extended by her involvement with the church. Some of her healing was certainly brought about as a result of the new friendships she made. But Mary has said that what she received from the church at that time went beyond friendship and must include the experience of God she recognized in the church's *worship*. Mary's discovery points to the intimate link between the quality of a congregation's worship and the quality of its pastoral care. The gospel's latent power of healing can be celebrated, made explicit and enjoyed in Christian worship, and indeed everything about Christian community is rooted in worship since its very existence is a response to God. This is what makes the Church's care distinctive in the inner city or elsewhere. It is the belief that the ultimate empowering force behind the universe is God's love, 'the love which moves the sun and the stars', as Dante put it, which sets Christian pastoral care apart from the other therapies offered by secular humanism. But it is in *worship* that this belief is celebrated in common. From this it follows that, from the viewpoint of pastoral care, there is something of the highest importance at stake in whether or not a congregation's worship realizes the latent healing power that lively worship offers.

The examples I have given so far each started with a strongly felt experience in the lives of particular individuals and described how an act of worship could be built out of that experience. But it is perhaps not surprising that the peak life events of birth, marriage and death, events which are central to all social and religious ritual, should lend themselves to this approach. It is much more problematic to achieve effective and compelling Sunday worship where the themes and readings are prescribed by the lectionary, and where there may often be, or appear to be, no intense or deeply felt communal experience round which a liturgical form can coalesce. How can worship connect with ordinary living and touch personal needs when so much of its content is given, prepackaged and ready to use, in the ASB? This is the key question. Most inner city people simply are not accustomed to liturgical worship and it is difficult for those who have been preparing these words for years to understand that they can seem alien and off-putting. I am moved by the Collect for Purity every time I say it. Yet from the viewpoint of someone like Dermot the liturgical jargon of Rite A blocks out its meaning. There was hardly anything he needed more than a sense of being forgiven. And he was quite ready to say he was sorry for what he felt was wrong in his life. But for him the pronouncement 'God gave his only Son Jesus Christ to save us from our sins, to be our advocate in heaven, and to bring us to eternal life', even delivered in one's best liturgical accents, cannot meet his need because its language does not connect with the language of his need.

It can come as a shock to inner city clergy when they discover how much of what they take for granted is in fact a stumbling block even to regular members of the congregation. Although for years they may continue meekly to mouth the words set before them people may say, when asked, that they think the confession is hypocrisy, the gloria gibberish (not to mention the creed) and much of the Eucharist a magical rite more to the glory of the priest than God.

Some styles of worship assume that the liturgy will meet people's needs simply by providing an ambience suitable for an encounter with the mystery of God: candles flickering in the Lady Chapel, the white lamp of the reserved sacrament, ikons and statues and coloured seasonal fittings may combine with the scent of incense to encourage a mood of prayer and a sense of the numinous, to raise up the congregation from the ordinariness of the workaday world. But this cannot replace the need for people to make more explicit connections between worship and their own experience. Neither can it be an adequate substitute to simply ignore whatever in Christian tradition is difficult or distasteful, as at St Jumbo's. Christians believe that God makes himself known in worship, which requires worshippers to draw on *all* that is included in the story of God's revelation to his people, not just those parts of the story they happen to like. If liturgy is reduced to being a vehicle of self-expression it cannot convey what lies at the heart of worship: the transcendent mystery of God.

Atmosphere is of course important and, for the necessary connections to be made, it must be an atmosphere of welcome. Newcomers need to be helped to feel they will be accepted as they are and that the worship is addressed to them as they are. This requires more than a bland announcement that the service begins on page 119 and that everyone is invited afterwards for tea. A convincing welcome then needs to be endorsed by the openness of attitudes in the congregation and by the general feel of things. The church interior, for example, will already have sent out a powerful signal to the newcomer. Churches which display a single poster, for the Diocesan Hassock-Making Guild, and put out a single collecting box for the church flowers, feel introverted and ecclesiastical. Churches awash with boldly coloured children's art displays, posters for Christian Aid and the Movement for the Ordination of Women, photographs of church office-holders or parish outings — or which have a well-stocked bookstall, an intercessions book, a suggestions box, and show evidence of action and involvement in the local community — inevitably feel more alive, more fun and more likely to mean what is said in the welcome. In an authentic worshipping community there is an almost tangible sense of liberation from narrow stereotyped views and expectations. Instead there is an atmosphere of exploration and discovery, a felt respect for the different faith of others. There is the quiet assumption that when each person prays in their own way, the faith of the whole congregation is enhanced. The priority of connecting liturgy to the personal experience of the individual should not be mistaken for an attempt to privatize the worship. It is essential for worship to be meaningful to each person privately but absolutely wrong ever to claim that Christian worship is capable of only private meaning. From the time Moses asked Pharoah to let the Hebrews go to worship their God in the desert for a day or two, worship of our God has been a corporate affair. Its meaning cannot be privatized. Christian worship has something of the community atmosphere of the upper room at Pentecost about it. It is inseparable from proclamation of, and gathering to celebrate, God's Kingdom. The Peace during the Sunday Eucharist, for example, is often something of a climax in a UPA church. It can be a poignant gesture of reconciliation after a row, a time to hug the bereaved, to greet unfamiliar people or a time for a moment of humour with a friend. Barchester congregations, who squirm at the very thought of such an unbuttoned interruption of Divine Service, are sadly deprived of this capacity to share human warmth, and inner city churches here have an advantage over them in being able to express their corporateness with less inhibition.

The manner and lead of the celebrant are obviously important in establishing the mood and vitality of the liturgy. Clerical sing-song or prayers recited parrot-fashion, for example, instantly destroy it. The sensitive addition of free prayer or leaving a space for silence can assist it. For example, in the opening penitential rite the celebrant can explicitly acknowledge that people are bringing their needs to church and invite members of the congregation to recollect their feelings — whatever they are — and use them as a basis for their worship. Such an introduction can enable people to tune in to their *whole* selves and to the liturgy itself. But a decisive way forward to achieve the sought-for connections between liturgy and experience is for the congregation to prepare its own Sunday Eucharist. The sense of involvement that this confers generates new life like spring after winter. You need only participate in this process once for there to be a kindling effect with enduring results. I have found that for a congregation to do this, for it to experience owning its worship, is a watershed. It results in the discovery of fresh meaning, powerful fellowship and renewed worship of God as the source of grace.

Any group of any age can participate in preparing the worship or, at a 'parish weekend', for example, the whole congregation can do it. Clearly it is important to plan how the preparation is going to be done. People will need space at the start to say how they feel at the prospect of preparing worship, especially if it is not something they have done before. It will no doubt be a relief to them to discover that others feel as diffident and hesitant as they do. If more than a small number of people are involved it will be practical to share the task by dividing into small groups. Depending on the number of people available groups might be given the choice of preparing either the penitential rite, the ministry of the Word, the intercessions or the eucharistic prayer, being responsible for co-ordination or choosing the music.

Those who opt to prepare the *ministry of the Word* face the task of imaginatively communicating the theme of the day, as illustrated in the readings. They may use drama, movement, drawing, music or spoken explanation. They will of course have to study the readings and will no doubt wish to draw on what they themselves have learned while doing the preparation. They do not need to present a common view. Differences can reinforce the vitality of the presentation as long as it is cogent, carefully rehearsed and sufficiently short. Those preparing *the intercessions* need to keep in touch with any other group in order to blend their themes, feelings and hopes into the prayers and offer up the action or change of heart which might arise from the service. They also need to be flexible: Someone may ask for the laying on of hands. People may want time to contribute their own biddings. A long silence may seem appropriate or, on the contrary, a speedy ending if, for example, the chorus of wailing infants is becoming too painful. However well they prepare, the intercessions group need to read the signals coming from the congregation at the time. The group preparing the *eucharistic prayer* should combine its traditional shape and content (preface, *epiclesis*, institution narrative, *anamnesis* and *doxology*) with the freshness of what this particular worship has celebrated. Since the eucharistic prayer is central in maintaining Christian continuity it must be in this sense conservative and theologically well-earthed. But this doesn't mean sticking punctiliously to some specified form of words. The preface, for example, can succinctly incorporate images or phrases from what has gone before, summarizing, but in a eucharistic context. In this way it becomes a thanksgiving in which *today's* themes and intentions can be built onto the recital of the great acts of God in the history of faith — a sign of this congregation's being one with the pilgrim people of God whose story they have just read in the Bible.

The corporate preparation of worship will result in more than lively liturgy on Sundays, it will nurture the prayer of the congregation. An almost imperceptible growth of spiritual confidence seems to be gained by belonging to a fellowship in which you experience the faltering attempts of other people just like you trying to say their prayers. Shared prayer assists in learning to pray. And shared preparation of Sunday worship enhances the church's response to liturgical celebration in general so that a youth group, a group of women, or elderly or unemployed people might prepare and lead a service where this would have been unthinkable before. Similarly the events and seasons of the calendar such as Advent, Christmas, even Harvest Festival, can find a significance they lacked while the church's liturgy remained over against the ordinary experience of people rather than in conversation with it. But it is during Lent, Holy Week and Easter that the liturgical year provides the greatest opportunity to interiorize what it means to be a Christian. And by preparing for Holy Week and Easter as a congregation inner city people can come to experience how the climax of the Christian story — the suffering, death and resurrection of Christ — connects with their own story.

One way to achieve this connection is by using one's imagination. Each member of a group might be asked to identify with one person involved in the passion drama: Peter, for example, or Judas or Mary Magdalene. After time for preparation each person can be asked to describe the story as they have experienced it in the role of their chosen character. Exercises like this can bring the story of Christ's Passion alive. But there is also the need for people to connect their story with the Easter symbolism of new life through death. In Tottenham one year we attempted to do this by organizing such a wide variety of Lenten activities that everyone would (we hoped) find a suitable means of preparing for Easter. There was dancing, painting, handicrafts, singing and making an Easter garden in the churchyard as well as prayer and discussion groups. Each activity was designed to help prepare for Easter. The dancers, for example, prepared a dance to convey in movement the passion and resurrection of Christ which they danced during the Easter services.

The liturgical drama of Holy Week speaks loud in a UPA because it is something done rather than conceptualized. Provided that inner city people participate fully in it and feel they own it, their worship can be lifted out of imprisonment in prayer book texts and kissed into life.

Further reading

Tissa Balasuriya, *The Eucharist and Human Liberation* (London: SCM Press, 1979). Examines the association between the Eucharist and oppression in the history of the Church, particularly in the colonial era. Explores the liberative potential of the Eucharist for the poor and oppressed when it is released from the social conditioning of the institutional church.

Church of England Liturgical Commission, *Patterns for Worship* (second edition, London: Church House Publishing, 1995). Addressing the needs of worship in UPAs was one of the stated aims of the Liturgical Commission in this volume and it includes liturgies designed to address the needs of different civic and social contexts, and accounts of the development of alternative patterns of worship in inner city and suburban parishes.

Harvey Cox, *Fire From Heaven: The Rise of Pentecostal Spirituality and the Reshaping of Religion in the Twenty-First Century* (London: Cassell, 1996). The fastest growing form of worship on earth began in cities and spread from city to city. The author of *The Secular City* shows how this movement has spread around the world, and how the radical orientation to praise and spiritual experience of Pentecostals has energized struggles for personal and social transformation.

Neville B. Cryer, *Michel Quoist: A Biography*. (London: Hodder and Stoughton, 1977). An informative account of Quoist's ministry with young Christian workers in northern France.

John G. Davies, *New Perspectives on Worship Today* (London: SCM Press, 1978). Explores the resources which new forms of worship provide to people experiencing the ups and downs of rapid social change.

Tom Driver, *The Magic of Ritual: Our Need for Liberating Rites that Transform Our Lives and Communities* (San Francisco: HarperCollins, 1991). Explores the human need and longing for ritual found in every human culture, the performative and transformative potential of ritual. Argues that the regularization and control of ritual 'from above' have diminished its potential, particularly for the poor, as a means of social and personal transformation.

David Ford and Alistair McFadyen, 'Praise', in Peter Sedgwick (ed.), *God in the City* (London: Mowbray, 1995), pp. 95–104. The central task of the church in the UPA is divine praise and worship, not least because the struggles with that which is against God — sin, idols, addiction, economic and cultural exclusion — are so visible in UPAs. At the same time praise gives confidence and respect to those who participate in it and therefore empowers people in the midst of these struggles to find dignity, love and self-respect: 'Praise opens up the horizon within which present conditions can be seen to contradict the life and will of God; it energizes commitment to a new and different future; and it helps set an agenda for change.'

Robin Green, *Only Connect: Worship and Liturgy from the Perspective of Pastoral Care* (London: Darton, Longman and Todd, 1987). Explores the potential of ritual to create order and meaning for damaged people and damaged communities.

Daniel Hardy and David Ford, *Jubilate: Theology in Praise* (London: SCM Press, 1984). Powerful theological exploration of the centrality of praise as recognition and respect both for the human and the divine.

Stanley Hauerwas and Will Willimon, *Resident Aliens: Life in the Christian Colony* (Nashville: Abingdon, 1989). The first responsibility of the Church is the formation of worshipping communities and of individuals who share Christian values and commitments and who apply these commitments in their daily lives, sustained in this by the proclamation and celebration of the stories of God amongst the people of God.

Susan Hope, 'Sanctuary', in Peter Sedgwick (ed.), *God in the City* (London: Mowbray, 1995), pp. 191–8. Sue Hope combines two key spiritual insights in this essay: 'Those of us who live and work in the inner city recognize, and are humbled by, the presence of the Holy Spirit in the ordinary lives of those among whom we live and work.' 'The life of the authentic Christian community is one in which transcendence and the numinous, including in all likelihood the pentecostal gifts and charisms, and the incarnate "ordinariness" of love and relationships and commitment and joy and pain sharing are woven together into one fabric — a tapestry which proclaims in many colours the good news of the gospel.'

Bruce Kendrick, *Come Out the Wilderness: The Story of the East Harlem Protestant Parish* (New York: Harper, 1962). A classic portrait of a famous inner city parish which experimented with a range of new styles of ministry including Bible Study groups for factory workers, programmes for drug addicts, rural retreats on a farm for inner city dwellers, innovative youth programmes and campaigns for housing and other improvements in the densest and poorest housing area of New York City.

Kenneth Leech, *Struggle in Babylon: Racism in the Cities and Churches of Britain* (London: Sheldon Press, 1988). Includes a powerful reflection on the role of liturgy and ritual in challenging the evil of racism and prejudice, including prayers and processions on streets most marked by racial conflict or racist attacks.

Jean-Jacques Suurmond, *Word and Spirit at Play* (London: SCM Press, 1994). In the midst of a utilitarian urban culture Suurmond proposes that the playful and joyful celebration of God is an end in itself which is also participation in the Kingdom of God. Similarly, the struggle for justice or a healthy environment is not an end but is important in itself whether or not it achieves results.

Horst Symanowski, *The Christian Witness in an Industrial Society* (London: Collins, 1961). Account of the imaginative preaching and worship ministry of a Lutheran pastor in an urban industrial context in post-war Germany.

Jim Wallis, *Call to Conversion* (London: Lion, 1981). The founder of the Sojourners Community argues that Christian community focused on the experience of celebration and shared living needs to become more central to the lives of urban Christians struggling with the social realities of oppression and domination.

Margaret Walsh, 'Here's coping: the Hope Community, Wolverhampton', in Peter Sedgwick (ed.), *God in the City* (London: Mowbray, 1995), pp. 52–71. The religious community of sisters of the Infant Jesus which Margaret Walsh led devoted considerable energies to social and community issues, and the alleviation of individual suffering, but all of their work with the poor was set in the midst of daily worship which included members of the local community as well as the sisters. The community adopted a pattern of monthly celebrations in which local liturgies were developed by people of the estate who had become friends of the Hope Community, many of whom had never had a formal connection with the churches.

Gibson Winter, *Community and Spiritual Transformation* (New York: Crossroad, 1989). Another influential urban theologian explores the potential of worshipping communities to transform society and to fill the moral and spiritual vacuum experienced in much modern urban culture.

10

Ministry in the city

The folly of God is wiser than human wisdom, and the weakness of God stronger than human strength. My friends, think what sort of people you are, whom God has called. Few of you are wise by any human standard, few powerful or of noble birth. Yet, to shame the wise, God has chosen what the world counts folly, and to shame what is strong, God has chosen what the world counts weakness.

He has chosen things without rank or standing in the world, mere nothings, to overthrow the existing order. So no place is left for any human pride in the presence of God. By God's act you are in Christ Jesus; God has made him our wisdom, and in him we have our righteousness, our holiness, our liberation. Therefore in the words of scripture, 'If anyone must boast, let him boast of the Lord.'

(1 Corinthians 1:25–31)

Faith in the City

For the parochial system to be made more effective will require a development of varieties of sector ministries: to where people work, are educated, pursue their leisure activities and are treated when sick or infirm. In the UPAs ministry to specific groups — such as young people, the homeless, and drug addicts and their families — may be needed. There will also be a need for ministry to particular institutions — prisons, hospitals, schools and other educational institutions, and the social services. As well as the need to relate to places of employment, an outward-looking ministry in the UPAs should relate to unemployed people. (5.50)

Introduction

One of the most influential books on the development of ministry in the city in the 1960s was Ted Wickham's *Church and People in an Industrial City*. His core thesis was that the churches had failed to develop an adequate response of buildings and manpower to the urban areas of Britain, that there was a consequent rural–urban imbalance in the provision of resources for ministry and this was the main reason for the failure of the mission of the Church amongst the working people of Britain's cities. This failure was of profound importance to Wickham and others who saw an offensive contrast between the early Church, described in the first chapter of 1 Corinthians as a community composed mostly of those who were not wealthy or high in status, and the Church of England, which in Britain's cities was increasingly the church of the comfortable. Wickham argued that the way to bridge the gap which had opened up between urban industrial communities and the church was not so much to build new churches — there were hundreds of half-empty Victorian churches in Northern industrial towns and cities — as to develop a mode of mission which reflected the secular structures of the city, and especially of the industrial character of the city.

Leslie Hunter, Ted Wickham and other pioneers began a ministry to industry which emerged out of chaplaincy work in the armaments factories during the Second World War. After the war industrial missions were established in London and Sheffield and subsequently in a number of industrial centres throughout Britain (Hewitt). Priests and pastors in France, Germany and other parts of Europe were also seeking to bridge the gap between the churches and working people (Perrin). But the European approach involved efforts to reach the industrial worker at the factory gate or in his home or club through educational or study groups, or through the more radical solidarity of the worker-priest movement where priests took up jobs on the shop floor. However, neither the British model of industrial chaplaincy nor the European model of ministry outside the gate effectively reversed the secularizing effects of working-class culture, and the alienation of working people from the church.

Industrial mission was one of a variety of responses of the churches to the declining significance of organized religion in urban industrial Britain which included team ministries, the appointment of more specialist clergy or 'sector ministers', and the creation of church agencies for Social Responsibility. These moves were accompanied by a major programme of church closure and amalgamation in which the free churches led the way. Large numbers of free churches in inner urban areas were closed, while the Church of England with its territorially based parish system was, perhaps fortuitously, slower to respond to depopulation in inner urban areas, often retaining a presence in areas which other churches had abandoned.

What is most notable about the primary strategies of the church in response to secularization and urbanization is that the earlier historical phase involved an extension of the rural model of the parish system into urban areas, with subdivision of ancient parishes and the building of many new, unsuitably large, churches, while the modernist phase, from the 1940s to the 1960s, was characterized by a number of attempts to side-step the problems of the parish system and the local church and tackle secular urban industrial society in other ways.

These new styles of ministry were often motivated by a radical form of secular theology which celebrated the new autonomy of the secular world from religious values or institutions. The 'death of God' as traditionally conceived meant that 'the world set the agenda' for mission in this new era of the secular city (*The Church for Others*; Robinson). There was an attempt in effect to baptize the new secularity and autonomy of urban industrial society, led as it was by scientists and industrialists manipulating the 'white heat of technology', and by planners and developers who transformed the face of Britain's cities and urban housing areas in the 1960s and early 1970s. The transformations of modern urban industrial organization were said to be driven by the Spirit of God transforming human life for the good and therefore 'ordinary, competent participation' in the forces of technology, industry and social change was 'decidedly religious' (Phipps).

Harvey Cox argued that the secular city was the principal sphere in which God spoke to modern secular man for 'urban secular man experiences the transcendent in a radically different way than did his tribal and town forebears' (Cox). For Cox the Kingdom of God emerges in the optimistic view of the urban industrial world which he draws from selected social surveys of the city. It is the task of the church to engage the urban industrial character of secular life in the expectation of engaging with the God who is revealed in the social transformation of the secular city. Christian ministry is intended to bring lay people in industry and the urban world to a similar view of its possibilities, and of their missionary role within it. According to Gibson Winter the secularization of the world called forth the secularization of the church and its missionary structures: 'If secularisation is the true character of the world as free for responsibility before God, then we can understand the need for secularisation within the religious institutions, for they are the witnesses to this deliverance of man for responsibility' (Winter). Similarly, Margaret Kane argued that the purpose of Christian mission in industrial society is to help people in the secular world to identify the main issues, 'to break down the barriers between people so that they can face the questions together, and to give them hope and encouragement that will inspire them to expect something to happen. This secular style of theology, which does not impose traditional Christian categories, but helps people to develop their own thinking in their own terms, is essential to this kind of exploration' (Kane).

Industrial mission represented this new style of mission to the secular, mission on the frontiers, but the problem was that it tended to lack a critical engagement with the ideologies and forces which were driving the secular city. This was precisely because this approach to urban mission devalued the Christian tradition and the role of the church as local worshipping community seeking and celebrating transcendence in the midst of the city. Instead these new secular missionaries argued for Christian self-effacement whereby the church would cease to retain its distinct sacramental and evangelical identity from the secular city (Northcott). This approach represented a deep theological belief in the capacity of new city structures, buildings, plans and complexes to progress the human condition, and to bring freedom and salvation to the urban masses.

This new theology of the secular also generated new styles of parish, community and group ministries in the inner city and in new housing areas (Beeson; Southcott). Experiments in house groups or house churches, house communions and new kinds of urban worship centre in schools, houses or community centres, and chaplaincies to local factories and schools as part of the outreach of the parish, involved the attempt to restructure the local parish and clerical ministry in inner urban and new housing areas. These new experiments in parish life and ministry sought to embrace the best of the modernist movement in the city as reflected in the modernist style of the many concrete churches which were erected in new housing areas. They also involved new forms of church-based social and community work, often modelled on the emergent styles of social and community work in the secular agencies (Lovell and Widdecombe; Finneron). Church-based community workers and projects sought to reverse the demise of community resources and solidarities in dealing with the opportunities and challenges of poverty, family break-up, unemployment, environmental and urban decay or blight, and racism. Instead of the uncritical adulation of social change and technology-led progress, churches and missionary efforts of this kind involved a more critical kind of solidarity which sought to challenge the negative effects of social change in the urban environment.

However, as the planning dreams of the secular city gave way to the human nightmare of living in damp, vandalized system-built housing, there was also the beginnings of a traditionalist back-lash in the 1970s to the secularization of the church and its structures, manifested in resistance to widespread parish reorganization of the kind proposed for many urban areas by radical bishops, theologians and church commissions or planners, and criticism of the secular styles of ministry from traditional parish clergy. New religious currents also emerged in the 1970s which decidedly rejected the secular drift of urban industrial Britain, such as the charismatic movement, albeit with its roots in the suburbs, but also the Black-led churches which are the fastest growing form of church in inner-city areas.

This backlash uncovered the fundamental theological weakness of much of the industrial and community ministry which the churches fostered in their attempts to come to terms with the new urban industrial world. Cox, Wickham and Robinson had sponsored a kind of supra-ecclesiology, the invisible church, not located in buildings, areas, congregations or Christian communities, but in the structures of specialist and sector ministry where the church was engaging with the world on its own terms. However, the adulation of the secular, and the embrace of social change as the movement of the Spirit, seemed to side-step the continuing harsh reality of social division in the inner city and on the factory floor. At the same time the secular 'death of God' was a denial of the God of love and justice whose presence is more likely to be found amongst the poor and the marginalized than in the human powers which drive towers and smoke-stacks into the sky, or toxic waste outflows into rivers and oceans. It was also a denial of the mission of the Church to speak the Word of Jesus Christ to the world, words of judgement as well as salvation, words of repentance and grace, which do not ignore the reality of evil, nor the need of all people in every culture, and not least the culture of the secular city, for liberation and transcendence.

Other urban theologians and missionaries began to express a much stronger sense of the calling of the church to *be* the church in the city. In *Built as a City* David Sheppard argued that the church's first duty in the city as in the suburb was 'to make Jesus Christ and His claims a serious adult proposition'. The church which intends to represent and proclaim the gospel in the inner city will be distinguished both from secular culture and from the rural or the suburban church. It will be a Church of and for the area, it will be a believing and worshipping Church, its common life will provide non-judgemental and thought-provoking fellowship, and it will raise up and train local leaders and decision-makers (Sheppard).

A significant impetus behind Sheppard's book was his involvement in the Mayflower Centre in the East End of London. This centre was part Christian community, part community centre, part local church. It anticipated a new trend in urban mission, one taken up by clergy and lay Christians, and by a number of monastic communities who left the confines of the monastery or convent and established new communities among the poor in the inner city (Smith). The Urban Theology Unit also reflected this approach with its combination of radical social action, educational and community work in inner city Sheffield, and its espousal of community living, shared incomes, and Eucharist-based worship centres in local churches and shop-front ministries (Vincent).

These new religious communities in and among the poor encountered the increasingly harsh realities of life in the inner city and the peripheral housing estate, and also discovered the genuine spiritual hunger which is more evident in such areas than in comfortable suburbs or rural villages and market towns (Smith). They also encountered the startling mismatch between the styles of ministry and mission which the church has pursued in inner-city areas and the actual patterns of belief and religious experience of the poor (Smith; Ahern and Davie). Clergy from middle-class backgrounds find the inner city culturally barren for the traditional style of ministry and church organization in which they have been trained.

Another key feature of Sheppard's book was the development of local leadership, and of styles of training and ordination which encouraged working-class leaders to come forward for ordination (Sheppard). One of the weaknesses of industrial mission was that it was primarily a clerically-led movement which, though it engaged with managers and workers in factories, rarely seemed to bridge the gap between the world of work, working-class culture, and the local church. Clergy as chaplains made these links and were able to share their accumulated knowledge with the churches, but they were not effectively helping lay Christians in local churches to make these same links for themselves.

The Christian movement began as an urban movement. Paul and the Jerusalem Apostles preached and persuaded Jews and Gentiles in the growing urban centres of Jerusalem, Rome and the Eastern Mediterranean. Those who were most responsive to their message were mostly people who through the vicissitudes of city life had in some way or another been pushed to the edge, marginalized as slaves, servants, ethnic minorities and the poor with none of the status of citizens and no say in their own future. In the text from Corinthians Paul argues that, socially disadvantaged as most Christians were, it was precisely because of their weak social position that God's presence and liberation are all the more evident in their lives, their worshipping communities and their struggles for holiness against the immorality which was all around them and even in the midst of their flawed community.

William Vanstone worked for over twenty years as a parish priest on a council estate in Northern England. When others were experimenting with new forms of ministry and trying to engage the structures and ideologies of the powerful, Vanstone practised a traditional Anglo-Catholic approach to parish ministry. He argues that the ministry of the church in the city is essentially the expression of the freedom of divine love (**Vanstone**). This freedom is not fundamentally about meeting human need, nor about providing social hope in communities which may be hopeful or may be despairing. The form the Gospel takes on the modern housing estate is not the form of the Christendom church meeting the needs of citizens for community and welfare. Much of this had been taken up by the welfare state and local authority social and community workers. Rather, the love of God finds expression in the weakness and vulnerability of worshipping and caring communities of faith whose very marginality to the economic and social structures of the modern city is their strength, the strength which in Paul's words is made perfect in weakness.

Vanstone's theological reflection on ministry in a new housing area, and on the nature of divine love, provides a deeply theological reading of the distinctive being of the church in the world, a church which exists *for* the world, in love for the world, but which does not seek to become the world, or to make the world into the church, because ultimately the church is for the world in order to express and discern the love of God hidden in the creativity of the modern city. Ministry in this sense is a ministry which respects the other and loves the other, not in order to control the other but in order to express the deep attraction of God which is hidden in every creative human act. Vanstone's theology encapsulates much that is most positive and profound in the incarnational and kenotic understanding of urban ministry reflected in the extracts which follow. And yet at the same time it seems to leave the question of the prophetic and evangelistic mission unanswered. How in the context of an urban world which is increasingly divided and fragmented, where the state no longer aspires to adequately meet the material and cultural needs of its poorer citizens, to say nothing of their spiritual needs, can the Church proclaim salvation and liberation from the powers and the structures of sin which oppress and divide? Is the traditional but vulnerable parish church the appropriate form for expressing divine solidarity with the poor and the marginalized in a culture which is deeply alienated from institutional religion but still spiritually questing (**Tiller**)? Is the weak, vulnerable but diminishing presence of outposts of the established church and the ministry of their clergy enough? Perhaps the model of church as a prophetic, disestablished and counter-society is actually the way ahead for ministry in our increasingly divided cities (Green; Leech and Russell).

Love's endeavour, love's expense

W. H. Vanstone

I have noticed over many years that the progress of quite serious thinking may be assisted by incidents of the most ordinary and even trivial kind. So it was in the present case. On a winter morning two schoolboys in their early teens asked me to suggest an occupation for their half-term holiday. I was unprepared and rather barren of ideas; but eventually, having once occupied myself in the same way, I suggested that they might make a model of a tract of countryside. I reminded them of an area around a waterfall in the West of Ireland which both they and I had recently visited: I explained how a model might be made out of stones and twigs and plaster and paint: I offered them a room in which to work, and I told them where they might find the necessary materials.

My suggestion made no great appeal, and it was taken up out of courtesy rather than enthusiasm. Enthusiasm was even less when the two had assembled their rather unattractive raw materials of stones from the street, dead twigs and old paint in dirty cans. Nevertheless, they began to work that same morning; returned in the afternoon and again in the evening; and by the end of the day they had something which they wanted to show me. Something was beginning to take shape. Next morning they came early; and thereafter, for three days, they worked with remarkable intensity and concentration, without thought of mealtimes or the lateness of the hour. From time to time I watched and listened. I observed how the placing of each stone and twig was a matter for careful discussion. Each was, as it were, surveyed and its possibilities assessed. One would be split or cut so that it would fit a certain place. It would be placed: and then came the moment of waiting to see if it was 'right'. It would be agreed that a certain stone should be painted to give the appearance of moss: and it would be agreed that a certain mixture of paint was right. But still one had to wait and see whether the stone would take the paint without distorting its colour; and again whether, when placed, the painted stone 'looked right'. Some stones and twigs and details of plaster-work proved 'difficult': they had possibilities but would not easily 'come right'. Again, a stone might appear 'right' until another was placed beside it: but then a difficulty appeared, and with it a new possibility: and the first stone must be repainted or replaced. The detail of the once unattractive and even contemptible material now became important: the dirt on a twig could prove 'just right' for shadow on the branch of a tree: spilled plaster could be made into rocks at the foot of the waterfall. In everything there was the possibility both of 'difficulty' and of 'coming right': and the full possibility of each fragment must be discovered and tried in relation to other fragments.

As the model grew and became of greater value, each step in its creation became of greater moment and was taken with greater intensity of care. Each item that was placed seemed to possess greater power to make or to mar. The two workers came to have, as it were, less room for manoeuvre: they worked less but watched and waited more. Having expended to the full their own power to make, they became the more attentive to what the model itself might disclose. They came to discover that which they were making, and to be affected by that which they discovered. The once contemptible sticks and stones now had a certain power over those who were using them — a power to effect or negate the completion of that which was being made, and so to satisfy or frustrate those who were making it. The two boys became vulnerable in and through that which, out of virtually nothing, they had brought into being. They became concerned for the safety of their model, anxious lest anyone coming into the room might touch and spoil it. They would permit the privilege of seeing it only to certain people who would have the discernment and sensitivity to appreciate it. When eventually the model was left in my care, I felt a quite serious responsibility for its safety.

As I watched this microcosm of creative activity, and as later I reflected upon it, three things gradually became evident to me. The first was that, in such activity, there was both working and waiting. One could say that the activity of creating included the passivity of waiting — of waiting upon one's workmanship to see what emerged from it, and to see if that which emerged was 'right'. The second, which followed from the first, was that, in such activity, the creator gave to, or built into, his workmanship a certain power over himself. He gave to his workmanship that which, if it were not his workmanship, it would not possess — a power to affect himself, to have value, significance or importance for himself. The third, which followed from the second, was that in such activity disproportion between creator and workmanship, or between creator and material, was overcome by the gift of value. That which in itself was nothing was transformed, in the creative process, into a thing of value: as the work of a creator, it received a new status in relation to the creator. The incongruity between the great and the small was overcome when the creativity of the great was expended in and upon the small.

The activity which I had watched involved no great skill, and its outcome was of no *aesthetic* value. It was not because skill had worked upon the sticks and stones, and beauty emerged from them, that they had become 'greater' in relation to the two human beings who had been engaged upon them. What had impressed me as observer was not the imaginative talent of the two workers, or the skill of their hands: it was the total concentration upon their work of such talent as they possessed, their obliviousness of mealtimes and of their own tiredness, their expenditure upon the one task of the whole of their energy and care. One might say that, for the creation of the model, the two had given themselves. If, through skill or practice, they had made the same model more easily, it would have lacked the particular value which it now possessed: there would not have been 'built into' it the self-giving of its creators. The same model, mass produced in a factory or casually constructed in the idle moments of a skilled workman, would have been of no importance; and for its safety I should have felt no sense of responsibility.

For the self-giving built into the model I could find no simple word or name but love. It was love which had overcome the disproportion between the creators and their workmanship, between human beings and sticks from the dustbin or stones from the gutter. It was love which had given importance to the sticks and stones, and, to myself, a sense of responsibility for them. I, the observer, perceived the importance of the model, and my own responsibility for it, because I knew it to be the work of love. I had actually seen the activity of love — the concentration, the effort and the unsparingness of self-giving that are involved in love. If I had simply been told that the model was the work of love, and if I had known little of what love involves, then my sense of the importance of the model, and of my own responsibility for it, would have been less strong. It was because I had seen what love involves that I knew that the model was no trivial thing.

Therefore, through this simple incident, I was helped to see that awareness of the importance of any aspect of material reality may be awareness not of its relevance to human well-being but simply of its being the work of love: and that a sense of responsibility for it may be a sense of responsibility for a work of love. My own awareness of the importance of that fragment of material reality which is the Church, and the naturalist's awareness of the importance of that fragment of material reality which is a particular marsh or pond or wood, might be awareness, however indistinct, of the whole of material reality as the work of love. I asked myself why I had needed several years and the adventitious help of a boys' holiday task to reach this simple and prosaic conclusion. I was compelled to answer that not until now had I realized what creative love is like. I had been told that material reality is the workmanship of the love of God: but when that love had been described to me it was different from that which I had seen built into the schoolboys' model. That which had been described to me as the love of God did not justify or explain the importance of that which it was alleged to have created. Therefore I knew that I must seek for a better description of the love of God — a description that might explain that conviction which, though unexplained and not yet unravelled, was still with me and still beyond doubt or question — the conviction of the importance of that small and simple fragment of material reality which is the Church.

If I could find such a description, it would make plain the importance not of the Church in particular but of material reality in general. Whether it would also point to some peculiar and distinctive importance in the Church was another matter. If it did not, my enquiry would prove in vain — or, at best, incomplete. But I knew the Church best in its concrete and material being — as a building to be cared for, as people in one place rather than another, as certain words said and certain actions performed: and it was of this concrete and material fragment that I was attempting to discover the importance. I thought it unlikely that I should do so unless I could first discover the generic importance of material reality: only by this way, it seemed, would it be possible to discover the specific importance of the Church.

The encounter of the Christian faith and modern technological society

E. R. Wickham

A major characteristic of the New Society is the plethora of new social structures, area and nation-wide, that cannot be tied down in territorial parishes, or encountered and influenced through territorial parochial structures of the Church.

In the pre-industrial society, certainly in England the Church's territorial structure was capable of bringing influence upon all the facets of human activity, including the power-points of society whose influence fell within the parish, in the person of land-owners, masters, farmers, magistrates, etc. And at the upper reaches of county and national life, the Church had her own hierarchical structure that met the 'powers of the world'. Social power was very largely concentrated in geographical areas, and the Church had her own territorial, geographical structure and her hierarchy of persons largely coincident with the social and political hierarchy of the nation. From Crown to village community, the Church was herself an integral part of a single social structure of the nation. It is precisely this church structure that has come down unchanged from the past, and which is now unable to impinge upon the new social structures of the New Society.

Those new social structures are consequent upon the industrial, technological, planned ordering of the new society. There are many of them — such as national and local government, and the political parties comprising them, the administration, the basic industries of a nation that run like arteries throughout the social body, with their highest projections probably in the capital, the larger industrial enterprises and works drawing labour from an immense catchment area and with their national projections, the trade unions with their area and national superstructure, the many new social agencies in the Welfare State etc., etc. There are many of them, and they are the new powers, 'principalities and powers' of the New Society, exercising an influence beyond that of the 'flesh and blood' administering them. They both create and express the 'feel' of the nation, form its public philosophy, colour society, create its 'angelic' or 'demonic' character, and can hold 'flesh and blood' as prey. This is no exaggeration, and the monolithic, totalitarian State is but an extreme expression of it.

Yet the new social structures are inherent in the New Society, and the Church, almost wholly expressed in static territorial shapes, lacks the agencies and instruments that can encounter and engage the principalities and powers of an industrial society. It is imperative to devise them.

In seeking to understand the widespread weakening of faith in nations that were once part of Christendom, we see many causes, that in turn are seen as effects of other causes, reaching far back into history. Some of these causes have been isolated and given ample study — the 'liberation' of the Renaissance, the philosophy of the Enlightenment, positivism, the impact of the empirical sciences, the atheism or agnosticism, practical or confessed, of working classes in revolt against the bourgeois institutions. Clearly too, the solidarity of men in their social pattern of life is a major determinant of religious habit, of their proneness or resistance to the Church. Once established, the culture-pattern tends to persist and in due course proves the immediate cause of social habit.

But below the sociological level of explanation, and created, nurtured and expressed by the historical reasons adduced, there is the deposit of new ideas, effective ideas, axioms, assumptions, attitudes to life, etc., which is the real public philosophy of an age, even if it rarely finds clear articulation. In fact we have little study as yet of the innate assumptions of modern men, typical men of the new industrialized society. But it would appear that within the confused thinking of the age, despite some things seemingly contradictory to it, a basic idea is that men have got 'to work out their own salvation'. It is implicit in the two most striking, dynamic factors that have made the modern age — the scientific and technological revolution, on the one hand, that has made modern industry and modern society possible — and, on the other, the social revolution with its implicit assumption that men can change the social order, make history rather than merely suffer it. Despite widespread frustration often leading men to admit an impotence and a sense of fatalism, this deposit remains a common factor in the New Society — whether in North America, the Communist State, or liberal–welfare–capitalist Western Europe.

It is disturbing to recollect that in general the churches of Europe resisted both the scientific conclusions in so far as they appeared to raise doubts about traditional teaching of religion, and also the social revolutions of the nineteenth and twentieth centuries. It is interesting to note that today both these factors, though emanating from such different quarters, find a common ground and meeting place in industry.

It is also important to consider that, in their different ways, both the 'scientific attitude' and the implicit ideas in social revolution can create and fortify the assumption that with knowledge and power men can make their own world — and that they alone must make it. And it is this assumption more than any other that appears to conflict with the traditional religious attitude, and in particular with the belief in God as Providence. Both factors have led men to secularism, which is not atheism, but a total preoccupation with their own affairs and the affairs of this world, and a massive indifference to the matter of religion. So 'the vertical dimension' has faded.

We should bear in mind that 'a return to faith' can be stimulated by many factors, some intrinsically good, but some questionable and dangerous; but whether such return should take place or not, there remains in the contemporary mind the deep contradiction between the new scientific axioms and assumptions, and the understanding of the Christian religious view as it has been traditionally received and presented. It is a good question to consider whether this contradiction is essentially biblical, or whether it may not be in part due to the 'slum-world' in which the Christian statement has historically been formulated, and in periods of history in which men were ignorant of their possibilities in mastering the world.

But if God is the Lord of history we are bound to look at the scientific and the social revolutions of our time in a providential and prophetic way. If the living God confronts men through the events of history, these two remarkable facts must take on profound religious significance, despite the confusion they seem to spell for traditional theological thinking. As yet the churches have in general failed to give prophetic articulation to these facts of our time. To do so would be to ask most radical and impossible questions, such as those posed by Dietrich Bonhoeffer.

> We are proceeding towards a time of no religion at all; men as they now are simply cannot be religious any more. Even those who describe themselves as 'religious' do not act upon it ... Our whole 1900-year-old Christian preaching and theology rests upon the 'religious premiss' of man ... if we reach the stage of being radically without religion (i.e. that religion was a historical and temporary form of human self-expression), what does that mean for 'Christianity'?
>
> How can Christ become Lord even of those without religion? if religion be no more than the garment of Christianity — and even that garment has had very different aspects at different periods — then what is a religionless Christianity?
>
> How can we speak of God without religion? How do we speak in secular terms of God?
>
> (Bonhoeffer, *Letters from Prison*)

These seem extravagant words indeed, but they suggest the magnitude of the task if the Christian faith is to make sense to the modern world. To face such questions would also be the beginning of the process of communicating the Christian faith to the modern world.

IMMEDIATE TASKS OF THE CHURCH IN HER ENCOUNTER WITH MODERN INDUSTRIAL SOCIETY

It is only out of deep analysis of the new industrial society that the real weaknesses of the contemporary Church — structural and theological — become clear. Such analysis is a most positive task helping us to understand the nature of the world and its institutions that we have to engage, its impact on society and human thinking, and indeed, its own peculiar and technical problems. Only so can we understand the proper role of the Church in that society, and the new areas of concern if that role is to be fulfilled.

There are, of course, no simple solutions to be neatly propounded to solve the Church's problems posed by the new society. Anyway, the problems of modern society, despite its promises, are new, dire and baffling, and they also are the problems of a Church called to minister to the world — beyond her own peculiar problems concerning engagement, encounter and communication. But the above analysis would seem to lay bare, certainly, four areas of concern, demanding new thinking and strategy on the part of the Church. Briefly we may list:

1. The Church needs to devise means whereby she can engage mammoth populations, and take root and grow within the indigenous fabric of society. This would seem to call for the deliberate breaking down of the congregation into natural working groups to engage the life of the parish within which they are set. It holds the promise of possibility, it also makes the concept of the laity meaningful and lifts it above the level of

idealistic exhortation. But with the high level of social mobility, and the rapid changes of ministers, it would need to be planned within areas larger than parishes, and made overall area or diocesan policy.

2. The Church needs new machinery for engaging the 'principalities and powers' of the technological society, notably, the structures of the basic industries and larger plants of a nation. In Britain in some places it has been proved that this is a possibility, opening up new areas of work and influence, that are normally the most intractable to the Church. It has called for work conceived in long terms, for trained manpower and money, and most important, for distinctive theological and sociological insights.

    The danger in the work — Industrial Mission — is that it should be conceived in narrowly evangelistic terms, as though the only criterion for the validity of the Church's work in the New Society is the incidence of return to the Church.

    Such work needs to go deep in the highly industrial localities, to be played from one area to another along the arterial lines of industry, and to be part of the national policy and planning of a Church.

    It too lays bare the true role of the laity in the world, and stimulates genuine 'frontier' thinking of the laity.

3. The Church needs a moral theology and moral scrutiny of the New Society and its institutions. Walter Lippmann has said, 'It is not enough to exhort men to be good; we must elucidate what goodness means.' We have failed to do this for our modern society. The Church — and its laity — is generally unable to evaluate and judge the trends and changes in the new society through lack of relevant social criteria. Moral, social and human questions lurk in what appear most highly technical problems of modern society, which far-sighted and sensitive men in industry are more aware of than churches. The Church cannot point men to the things that belong to their peace unless the real problems are understood.

    We need some corporate brains — theological and lay — focused on the technological society, at the service of both Church and society. It should not be beyond the power of the Church to produce this where she has machinery of engagement.

4. There is an immense theological 'task' to be done in communicating the Christian faith to modern men, imbued with the assumptions of typical modern men. It is no task merely of translation, but of reinterpretation, requiring an advance in theological thinking. Certainly we need to show the theological significance of science, technology and industry, and its relevance to the social revolution the world over. Only the right use of the one can meet the right demands of the other. This would seem to be the demand of God upon our epoch, the thing that belongs to our peace above all other, the demand of God's righteousness, belonging to the concrete content of faithful response.

    Once 'God' was manipulated by magic, and His actions wholly arbitrary; it was advance when He was understood as clothed by Nature. It was further advance when He was understood to act in history, responsive in grace or wrath to the obedience or disobedience of men. It is further advance when He is also understood to be providentially at

work through and in the web of human relationships and human
endeavour, of which industry is a supreme example. This is biblical; it is
one illustration of the re-interpretation of Providence that might convey
something of God's nature and purpose to modern men, at the point of
their strength.

The Church beyond the Church:
Sheffield Industrial Mission 1944–1994

Paul Bagshaw

Industrial mission is an agency of the Church, sent out by the Church into the
secular world of industry. Its missionary nature necessarily places it on the
boundary of the Church, a location captured in the key images of the 'gulf'
and the 'frontier'. The gulf is the divide between the Church and the world;
the frontier is the point where Church and world meet. The gulf has to be
bridged; the frontier explored. Sheffield Industrial Mission's changing understanding of the nature and purpose of its mission has been visible in the
kaleidoscope of ways in which the images of gulf and frontier have been
interpreted.

The particular boundary that the Mission straddles is the boundary
between the Church and the secular industrial and political order. The
Church experiences the paradox of faith in an institutional form. It accepts
the modern secular ordering as unquestionably legitimate, although, by
definition, its authority and legitimacy are grounded in human structures,
while the authority and legitimacy of the Church is God: numinous, infinite,
and transcendent. The way these incompatible positions are worked out in
practice constitutes the discipleship of the institutional Church in the midst
of the institutions of the secular world: the Church in politics. Historically it
may be that the Church has experienced this paradox most often as a
dilemma, and has sought to resolve it either by a desire to dominate society,
or by retreating from it into individualist piety. Yet neither position is tenable
for long. In practice there has been a wide variety of relationships, and the
border between the Church and the social order has been fluid, imprecise,
and unmapped.

This lack of clarity poses a particular problem for industrial chaplains.
Although SIM is an agency of the Church, authorized and commissioned by
the Church to undertake a particular piece of work in industrial society, in
practice chaplains have to a great extent determined their own priorities and
working methods. This has meant a constant danger that chaplains might
stray across the unmapped border into action unacceptable to the Church,
especially when they became involved in industrial conflict or politics.

Indeed, the border often only became clear when transgressed. The separation of authority and control constantly raised questions of accountability of SIM to the Church.

In the early 1940s these were distant problems. The initial motivation for the Mission was Bishop Leslie Hunter's perception of the gulf between the Church and the industrial working class, and the urgency of the challenge this posed the Church. To cross the gulf new techniques were needed which would be appropriate to the depth of the divide. Ted Wickham drew very little from the Churches' earlier approaches to industry because they all, including other examples of works visiting, failed to grasp how great the gulf was, and they glossed over the extent of the challenge to the Church. By contrast he rejected the French worker-priest model partly on the grounds that the gulf in Britain was not as wide as it was in France. Hunter characterized Wickham's approach as 'costly identification': to be with the workers on their territory, to drink in their pubs, and to talk about their concerns in their language. Wickham had stepped across the gulf, and showed it was possible for others to follow.

The presence and the depth of the gulf were a particular indictment of the Church of England and its relationship to the industrial order. It had patently failed to be the national Church that it claimed to be. Wickham charged the Church of England with refusing to acknowledge that it occupied merely a narrow niche in the social structure of the country, and that, as a consequence, it held no appeal to the working class. This was not a symptom of decline because the Church had never held the working class. The Church was in fact aligned with and financially dependent on the capitalist class. The depth of the alienation of the Church from the shop floor implied that if Christianity was to be established in the works it could only be done apart from the parochial ordering of the Church of England.

SIM was born at what was both the beginning and the peak of consensus politics, and the ideals of consensus became part of its genetic code. From the beginning SIM stood for justice in industry. But it did so from within a general framework of the affirmation of industry,[1] and only to the extent that it did not offend the sensibilities of management. Where chaplains breached this principle they could be excluded from the works, thus halting the mission.

The development of the Mission reflected the historical circumstances of the steel industry. The social disruption of the war, the sense of common purpose, and the lack of serious industrial conflict, allowed Wickham access to the works. The pattern of steel manufacture — of intense activity and longueurs — gave him opportunities to establish the snap-break meeting and the 'Sheffield model' of works visiting. The optimism of the post-war period, as well as his own undoubted charisma and skills, enabled Wickham to build up lay leadership in the works.

Wickham was guided by a classical approach to missions in foreign territory. He immersed himself in the culture and language of industry. The missionary task was to translate the Gospel into the vernacular, and to build up a worshipping church, with an indigenous leadership sufficiently deep rooted in faith to thrive without external oversight. This was a long-term goal, perhaps the work of several generations as other missionary enterprises had been.

By the time he moved to Manchester Wickham had created a new expression of the Church in the works. He had planted the Gospel in new soil so that faith might flourish outside the constricting structures of the dying Church of England. That his creation crumbled cannot be laid at Wickham's door. The missioners he left behind him were inexperienced, but all were committed to furthering the Mission as he had created it. Yet the new para-church was too fragile, its leaders too inexperienced, and the relationship between laity and chaplains too ambiguous, for it to withstand Jackson's unanticipated, and at first unrecognized, change of direction. Nor were there spiritual reserves elsewhere in the Church on which they could draw. Because Wickham had built an alternative to the structures and culture of the Church of England, lay leaders had only the slimmest contact with the hierarchy of the local Church, and Bishop Taylor would not support them. When trouble came the lay leaders turned back to Wickham because their own resources were inadequate and they had nowhere else to go. . . .

For Wickham's successors in 1961–1965 the gulf between the Church and the secular world, and the inability of lay Christians to be effective witnesses in the world, were accepted as an unquestioned fact of life. But SIM's very success, its widespread acceptance in industry and elsewhere, implied that chaplains and the Mission's laity did not themselves share that alienation. Working, as it were, on the other side of the gulf chaplains were able to stress the frontier, the common territory between the Church and the world. Their frontier task was to reconstruct Christian theology in such a way as to support the Mission as a lay enterprise, and to enable the wider Church to be faithful to its calling in the new circumstances of the secular world.

The desire to bridge the gulf between Christianity and secular culture lay at the heart of secular theology. 'Demythologizing' was the process of rooting out those elements of Christianity which, it seemed, separated modern people from faith. Chaplains both explored secular theology to the point of questioning Christianity's metaphysical base, and simultaneously reasserted a sacramental faith in which God's holiness was perceptible in the most mundane practicalities of ordinary life. However, although the intention may have been to restore the potential for belief and a sense of the holy amongst secularized people, the consequence was to threaten the numinous content and nature of the Christian message.[2]

* * *

Under Malcolm Grundy the theological gulf was all but eradicated. There was a single continuous frontier between secular analysis, theological under-standing, and the imperatives of Christian discipleship. This worked in both directions. Religious questions could be raised with those in industry through discussion of the underlying values and principles with which they worked. John Thompson's Society of Brother Lawrence promoted the ideal of a seamless continuity of employment and the mystical apprehension of God in the depths of the soul. Conversely, practical responses could be evoked from the Church in regard to unemployment by secular, even statistical, statements of the problem which were also descriptions of the evil, and prescriptions for a Christian response. In so far as there was a gulf for Grundy and for Draper it was the practical one which lay between the crying needs of the unemployed and the inertia of much of society including the Churches.

Throughout the 1970s SIM had given little prominence to political issues. Practical responses to unemployment were portrayed primarily as a Christian moral duty, although it was also direct intervention in a political issue. In the works chaplains continued to promote the central ideas of consensus. Notions of participation, reconciliation, and fairness at work remained constant themes, even when the political consensus that had nurtured these ideas had started to break down. On the one occasion, in 1977, when the Mission systematically asked its industrial contacts for their views on moral aspects of industry[3] it was clear that it was whistling a different tune to that of the industry it served. The general avoidance of political action did, however, keep SIM in line with the general tenor of the Church.

With the industrial convulsions of the 1980s the Mission embarked on a search for new methods appropriate to new circumstances. Works visiting remained important, but it became one method amongst a number. In particular, the Mission began to develop patterns of collaborative work with a variety of secular organizations. The gulf which gave the Mission a renewed motivation and new direction lay between the Gospel demands for justice and the apparent growth of injustice in secular society. Consequently the Mission became increasingly overtly political. Yet what dominated the Mission's image of itself was not the gulf, but the idea of the frontier, conveyed in the word 'links'. The Mission saw itself as weaving together many disparate threads into an integrated whole, rather than standing as a bridge over a chasm. The threads it drew together included theology, secular analysis, works visiting, parochial ministry, the institutional Church, the different denominations, secular organizations, and individuals' own experience of life.

The 1980s also saw a sea change in the relationship of the Church to social and industrial issues. This was particularly visible in the Church of England. It felt increasingly obligated to respond to social and political polarization, and sporadic friction with the Prime Minister, Mrs Thatcher, reinforced a long-term tendency towards greater independence from the State. At the same time there was a growing acceptance of the reality that active membership of the Church of England was confined to a small minority of people. The idea that the Church of England was the national Church, though still present, began to be supplanted by a sense that it was but one denomination amongst many. As such it began to see its interests as perhaps better served by co-operation with other denominations, than by too close an identification with the State.

There was no shortage of political issues which directly impinged on SIM's industrial work, but its capacity to respond in a political manner was steadily increased by the Church's greater acceptance of overtly political views and action. The movement in the Church's stance is revealed in its changing reaction to SIM's involvement in industrial conflict. After the steel strike of 1980 SIM was commended for treading the narrow line between opposing sides; during the 1993 campaign to keep collieries open SIM was commended for providing Church leaders with ammunition to lobby Conservative Members of Parliament to vote against their own government. SIM and the Church had moved together.

With the need for a political theology to underpin their growing involvement in political issues, chaplains turned to liberation theology, particularly as expressed through the World Council of Churches' Urban Rural Movement. Yet only on very rare occasions did SIM's growing emphasis on justice lead it into a straightforwardly confrontational approach to mission.[4] SIM drew from liberation theology the possibility of taking sides in a conflict as Christians, and rejected the requirement to side unreservedly and unambiguously with the oppressed against the powerful as an article of faith.

In fact, against the background of national political polarization and conflict in the 1980s, SIM remained wedded to the assumptions and values of consensus. It aligned itself with moves towards local political and economic partnerships which brought business and Labour leaders together. Where it became overtly involved in industrial conflict SIM stood 'on the side of the industry'; working alongside both management and workers locally in their common fight against a bigger external enemy, whether that be the Government or the recession. The other side of this consensual approach is that SIM has never raised the basic ethical questions of its continued involvement in, and thus its endorsement of, companies which are heavily committed to the armament and nuclear industries.[5] Nor has it raised the environmental consequences of products and processes in the firms it visits, with the one exception of endorsing clean coal technology. Again, this standpoint reflects that of the wider Church. Tension between Church and State in the 1980s partially reflected the fact that the Church remained wedded to the ideal of consensus while the State had rejected it.

After fifty years, has the Mission been a success? No objective answer is possible.[6] SIM's objectives have usually been formulated as ideal goals beyond practical expectation. It has always been dissatisfied with its work with lay people and, apart from some aspects of its first phase, SIM has not effectively been a lay movement. People have come into the Churches through each of the Mission's phases, though there is no way to count them; and the Church has been seen and heard in places from which it would otherwise have been excluded. There is no evidence that industrial culture has been modified by the presence of the Mission, but individuals in industry have consistently valued the chaplains' support and their, sometimes critical, contribution to both their working lives and their Christian discipleship. On occasions, such as at Hillsborough, the foundation that the Mission has laid down through its sustained visiting over many years enabled it to play a significant pastoral and public role.

The results of the 'extended seminar in applied theology' lie less in what change the Mission has been able to effect than in its ability to enrich the Church's understanding of discipleship. SIM has consistently grappled with the paradox of faith worked out in the world outside the Church. In doing so it has pieced together the jigsaw of faith, belief, practice, and secular reality. The result has not been a single picture, not even a sense of steady progression towards one normative picture, but a sequence of motifs, of different formulations and reformulations of the nature of contemporary discipleship, each of which has contributed unique insights and understandings.

The Mission also has knowledge, ethical reflection, insights, and experience of working with a wide range of secular organizations which can be placed at the service of the Church in its institutional discipleship. However, to the degree that the Church regards its boundaries as sources of threat and alien influence which demand ever vigilant policing, it is unable to accept or to value the insights of the Mission. Where faith is conceived in contrast to secular culture, to be protected against contamination by modernity, the Mission may not be welcome. But to the extent that the Church regards its boundaries as potential sources of strength and new life, the Mission has much to offer. Where faith is conceived as risk, as working out the paradox anew in the ever-changing world, struggling to keep the temporal and the transcendent together, the Mission may find a welcome.

Since 1944 Sheffield Industrial Mission has bridged the gulf and explored the frontier between the Church and the world. It has contributed to the potential for Christian discipleship in the industrial, commercial, and civic life of South Yorkshire. It has enriched the discipleship of the Church in society. It has sought to discover God at work in God's world and to further God's work in a godless world. It has struggled to perceive the holy in the unholy, to evoke faith in the midst of the secular, to realize the church beyond the Church.

NOTES

1. The Mission saw the development of industry as part of the providence of God. This was not, however, a simple or uncritical affirmation, and the relationship between industry, progress, and providence was complex. See 'Technology and providence', in E.R. Wickham, *Encounter with Modern Society* (London: Lutterworth Press, 1964), pp. 44–50.
2. It is probable that those who felt most threatened were defenders of traditional orthodoxy, not workers on the shop floor.
    The conflict of 1964–1966, and the revaluation of their predecessors' work by chaplains of a very different persuasion, have made an adequate evaluation of the secular theology approach almost impossible.
3. *Britain Today and Tomorrow — World Justice and British Economic Priorities*, A study by Sheffield Industrial Mission for the British Council of Churches and Christian Aid, September 1977. It is also probable that the managers the Mission talked to were likely to be amongst the more thoughtful and morally aware in industry.
4. Most notably over alleged racism in Cole Brothers.
5. Firms with which the Mission had contact were sometimes invited to bring a product symbolizing their industry to the Mission's annual Industry Service. On one occasion no fewer than three stainless steel hip joints were presented, no doubt also symbolizing the face which industry wished to turn to the Church.
6. As with the Church at large, there is no agreed yardstick against which SIM can be measured. The Church has seldom made explicit what it wanted the Mission to achieve. Its own stated goals have shifted markedly over 50 years, and have been formulated as ideals and statements of belief, not as benchmarks. Even if such a yardstick could be agreed, there is then no consistent stream of information which would allow one phase of the Mission to be assessed objectively over against another, nor which would allow the Mission to be compared against other patterns of ministry through the same period. Even an ostensibly objective test, the number of people brought into the worshipping Church through the work of the Mission (and there have been some throughout its history), evaporates on closer examination: there may be many influences on that decision, people come and go from the Church, and recruitment for the Church has not been the Mission's objective. Assessment of success is thus to a large degree coloured by the evaluator's own presuppositions. Calls to assess the Mission's success have often been perceived as no more than hostile strikes.

The associational Church and its communal mission

John Tiller

Unlike most town parishes the one I am describing had some sensible and realistic boundaries: the inner ring road of Bedford to the north and east; the river to the south; and at the inner end of the parish towards the town centre there was the borderland between residential family units and 'bedsit' land, where big Victorian houses had been converted into flats. The parish had its own local shopping centre, its own lower school and a middle school, a park for recreation near the river, and the basis of a very settled population which had received a very interesting mix in recent years.

The housing in the parish was divided into three distinct areas. First, there was the old terraced housing where some families had lived all their lives, and indeed one could still find two or three generations of the same family living in different houses in the same street. Since the 1960s the population in the area had become varied by the arrival of various ethnic groups including Italians, East Europeans, Asians and West Indians. Then in the 1970s, when the new housing estates in Bedford were getting further and further away from the town centre, these streets became very popular with young married couples buying their first homes, who found these solid and cosy little dwellings cheaper and more convenient than the new estates with their poor amenities and lack of a settled community. The second area contained pre-war semi-detached houses occupied by the original owners for the most part, now retired and having grown-up families who had mostly married and left home to live elsewhere: a middle-class, middle-aged and elderly district where the quiet streets contrasted with the life and noise of the previous area. Finally, on the opposite side of the main road going into town through the parish, there was a modern housing estate built on an old nursery where the Laxton apple had been developed. Some of the old apple trees had been left in the open spaces of this complex, which had won an architectural prize for its design and contained everything from sheltered accommodation for the elderly to starter homes and five-bedroomed detached houses.

So here was a neighbourhood which was very mixed, but at the same time had a definite sense of its own identity for reasons related to geography, to local amenities, and to the continuous life of the community which had always been changing but had never suffered serious disruption. And the parish church stood at the very centre, on the main road, where the three housing areas met.

Eighty per cent of the membership of this church was drawn from the parish. Its involvement in the community was quite extensive, and increased as time went on. We were able to build a new church hall complex attached to the church, and to begin community activities like a playgroup for youngsters in the area, a mothers and toddlers group to welcome new families moving in, a senior citizens' lunch club, and English classes for some of the non-English-speaking Asian immigrants. The extent to which this church was seen as a communal one was illustrated at the time of the Queen's

Jubilee, when one street opted to move into the church hall for its street party. Moreover, when parents at the lower school were worried about an education policy of moving their children to a different middle school, the parents' action group instinctively asked me as the parish priest to chair the meeting which they called.

I have described this particular situation because I now wish to recount four experiences which put a qualification against this whole concept of the communal church.

The first experience was when I visited a man who lived almost opposite the church in one of the terraced houses. He remarked: 'Of course, the church is not for the likes of us.' He expressed *the alienation of the working class* from the Church of England. One had to recognize that there was a Baptist church in the parish which had grown out of the desire of the working class *not* to be associated with the Church of England. It had for many years had a much more effective Sunday School in the neighbourhood than the parish church and it had its own historic place in the community. Of course that place was no longer distinctively working class, but the associational basis of the congregation remained and this in no way prevented it from having a communal role.

Next I recall the occasion when I visited someone from the modern housing estate, a man who drove past the church every day on his way to work. I introduced myself as the vicar from his parish church. 'Oh really, where's that?' was his response. He had never even noticed the building, nor had the thought that he belonged to a parish entered his head. He expressed *the rootlessness of the mobile class*. He did not expect to remain in the area long, and it would have been too painful for his family to get too involved in the community. He did not think in terms of belonging to a neighbourhood, but to a network of family and friends and the different worlds of business, leisure, and his home which was like a space capsule or a caravan temporarily parked in our parish. He was off most weekends, visiting his mother in a nursing home over a hundred miles away. We were irrelevant to him.

Then I went to see a bank manager who had just moved into one of the five-bedroomed, detached houses. I had received a letter from his previous vicar because his teenage children had been very keen members of the Pathfinder group in his church. As we also had a Pathfinder group there was an obvious point of contact. In this case I found that the man had opted to take his family elsewhere than to his parish church. The reason was fairly obvious. He was expressing *the discrimination of the rising class*: he, as a newly appointed bank manager, would meet much more important people, commanding much more important accounts, in the much more affluent parish next door. It has been correctly observed that the parochial system would have an opportunity of working only if it were compulsory. Once the possibility of obtaining all the rights and privileges of church membership by choice through electoral rolls had been introduced the parochial system, at least in the towns, was in effect destroyed. Possibly this did no more than adjust the church's structure to social realities, but it prompts us to question how far the communal model for the church is a hangover from the past.

This suggestion is reinforced by my final experience. One afternoon as I was walking down a street in the parish I found a friendly Italian at his front gate. He had no English, but we managed to converse in sign language with a bit of broken French. We were soon joined by another man who was the deacon in the local Ukrainian Uniat Church. We then went inside the house and had a splendid time drinking Stregas together, and communication got better as the afternoon wore on! In Bedford, the Roman Catholic Church has English, Italian, Polish, Slovenian and Ukrainian Uniat congregations. In that room we accepted one another as fellow Christians, but we represented *the plurality of ethnic groups* which was visible on the streets in that part of the parish at any time of day. Each group had a strong cultural identity and corporate outlook. It would be hard to pretend that this did not seriously affect, even if it did not demolish, the capacity of the Anglican vicar to be the focus of a communal church.

Now these observations are based on the experience of working in what was the most suitable parish in Bedford for the development of the communal model. The other parishes were in a much less favourable position, partly as a result of the way in which they had been divided up since Victorian times. The Church of England had gone through a process of having to put up new buildings to compete with the local chapels because people preferred to worship locally. But each of these daughter churches had aspired in time to become an independent parish. This was not just a matter of status: it was a way of securing continuity of ministry at a time when pastoral work was largely the preserve of the clergy; it was also perhaps seen as required by the communal model. As a result, the town-centre churches suffered. By the early 1970s, four of the seven Anglican church buildings in the centre were redundant. Their boundaries were in every case unworkable and they relied on eclectic congregations. It was not simply that the population had moved: one parish consisted of a council estate half a mile away from its town-centre church. The result of this approach, which has created weak parochial units, has been isolation and even competition among the separate parishes.

This has been a devastating factor in much of the urban ministry of the Church of England. The communal model does not relate to the different levels of community and the vagaries of parish boundaries when it is applied to the non-neighbourhood churches which constitute the majority of urban congregations today. Moreover few of the town-centre churches have been able to address themselves to some of the broader communal issues as effectively as they might, because the whole thing is organized on a system of separate, self-contained parish units. There are signs in some places that it might be better to link together a town-centre church with a particular residential hinterland.

The question which this reference to a particular urban situation poses for us is whether the communal model of the Church is a hangover from a now outdated experience of the parochial system, or whether the parochial system is just one expression of the communal model which might now be replaced by other more effective versions of the same thing.

In seeking to answer this question, I believe that we must take cognizance of the fact that membership of the Church is always on the basis of individual association through baptism. Baptism is the way of joining the Church, theologically speaking, liturgically speaking and pastorally speaking. And baptism is required for exercising the rights and duties of church membership, even in the Church of England, although this has of course been obscured by the widespread practice of indiscriminate infant baptism — and also by the legal oddity that in theory a minister could probably be compelled to celebrate the marriage of two unbaptized persons if one of them happened to live in his parish. However, the Church and State Report of 1970 regarded this situation as quite unacceptable to Anglican theology, and so already the assumptions of the associational model were being taken on board by working parties producing reports for the Church of England.

Where this individual association through baptism has been obscured, the Church has tended to be seen as in principle the religious aspect of the culture in which it exists. And where the culture is changing rapidly, in its moral and religious values (and I think we can claim from church statistics alone that that must be so in our society today), the Church that is without an associational basis of membership becomes much more marginalized than one that has (unless there is outright religious persecution). As Valerie Pitt commented in her minority report to that 1970 Church and State Report, we may find ourselves identifying faith not merely with culture, but with a dying culture. This, it seems to me, is the greatest danger offered in the communal model today. It really has more to do with our cultural past than with our religious present. With which particular culture are we identifying? Is it a culture that is in principle nostalgic, related to the small, close-knit communities of the past? Valerie Pitt went on to say that our culture itself, as it grows away from its Christian roots, increasingly compels us to choose an allegiance.

It therefore seemed necessary, in the parish in Bedford which I have described, to keep the associational aspect of church membership steadily in view. We required of those who came, or brought children, for baptism, attendance at a series of preparation classes, a minimum attendance on three occasions at our monthly family service, and sponsorship from within the congregation in addition to godparents of their own choice. In actual fact we had very many candidates for baptism, because there happened to be a baby clinic just down the road from the vicarage, and I had only to mow the front lawn on a day when the clinic was operating to collect three or four candidates! We did not have a sectarian approach; we were quite prepared to meet the expectations which existed within the community, but on terms which expressed the associational basis of the church's membership. And this was further emphasized by the fact that coming to church more than once a month meant attending the Eucharist. During my time there, we only had one person who wanted membership without commitment to this limited programme, and during the last two years the majority of confirmation candidates were young marrieds who had first come into the church's fellowship through this baptism policy.

It is possible to argue on the basis of this experience that a local church may have a fairly articulate associational basis for its membership while adopting a communal approach to its neighbourhood mission. In Bedford we had as our objective, what the discussion paper speaks of as 'the spiritual well-being of the entire community living within the parish', including the society and the environment as well as the needs of individuals. All the points made in that paper were reflected in our communal approach to mission. But there is no reason why that cannot coexist with a coherent and positive associational basis for membership of the local church.

Further reading

Trevor Beeson, *New Area Mission* (London: Mowbray, 1963). A well written portait of pioneering approaches to parish ministry in a new housing area in Stockton.

The Church for Others: A Report on the Missionary Structure of the Congregation (Geneva: World Council of Churches, 1968). This influential report argued for a radical shift of ministry resources from the maintenance of territorial and associational churches towards specialized ministries designed to address the social and spiritual needs of the city in the different sectors of urban life including city centre businesses and retail centres, factories, bureaucratic and non-governmental agencies and leisure and recreational facilities.

Harvey Cox, *The Secular City: Secularization and Urbanization in Theological Perspective* (London: SCM Press, 1967). Seminal text of urban theology, excerpted above, in which Cox uncritically attempts to baptize the socio-scientific account of life in modern cities as the new form of Christian living in a religionless age.

James D.G. Dunn (ed.), *The Kingdom of God and North-East England* (London: SCM Press, 1986). Though shaped by mining and heavy engineering for more than a century, the communities of post-industrial North East England are rural as well as urban, small town as well as large conurbation. This book presents stories of a range of community and church initiatives designed to address the social and spiritual conditions of the North East as signs of the Kingdom of God.

Doreen Finneron, *Faith in Community Development* (London: Church House Publishing, 1993). Argues from a series of case studies that attempts to use local churches as primary agents of community development have mostly failed because of a conflict between the primary aim of the church to maintain worshipping communities and of community development to organize around the needs of local communities. Proposes a collaborative model of ministry in which churches seek to establish community organizations which though not based on church structures are none the less resourced and partnered by church members.

Alan Green, Kenneth Leech and Hillary Russell, 'New Jerusalem or urban wilderness? Reflections on the urban Church of England', *Anglican Theological Review*, LXXVI, 4, 1994, pp. 465–82. Argues that Church of England inner city parishes often follow a chaplaincy or servant model of ministry, drawing on people who are not from UPAs to maintain the church buildings and services of the established church rather than creating grassroots churches which genuinely reflect the struggles and cultures of their local communities and the values of the Kingdom.

Laurie Green, 'Blowing bubbles: Poplar. Christian religious experience in the urban environment', in Peter Sedgwick (ed.), *God in the City* (London: Mowbray, 1995), pp. 72–92. Folk religion, rites of passage, a sense of place and of belonging to a particular community and territory are all elements which go to make up an incarnational and embedded understanding of the ministry of the parish church, its liturgies and sacraments, in the inner city. There is a longing for God and a spiritual sensitivity — to God and to evil — in the inner city which can be discerned when we listen 'with rapt attention' to the stories of the inner city, personal and communal, for in these stories we will find The Story of God Incarnate in Jesus Christ.

Gordon Hewitt (ed.), *Strategist for the Spirit* (Oxford: Beckett Publ., 1985) Biographical essays which describe the seminal role played by Leslie Hunter in the formation of the industrial mission movement in Britain as Bishop of Sheffield in the 1950s.

Margaret Kane, *Theology in an Industrial Society* (London: SCM Press, 1975). A classic statement of the theology of industrial mission by a theologian who was employed by Ian Ramsey, the Bishop of Durham, to be a consultant or 'barefoot' theologian outside the academy, working with people on the leading edge of ministry in the industrial North East.

Bruce Kendrick, *Come Out the Wilderness: The Story of the East Harlem Protestant Parish* (New York: Harper, 1962). A classic portrait of a famous inner city parish which experimented with a range of new styles of ministry including Bible Study groups for factory workers, programmes for drug addicts, rural retreats on a farm for inner city dwellers, innovative youth programmes and campaigns for housing and other improvements in the densest and poorest housing area of New York City.

George Lovell and Catherine Widdecombe, *Churches and Communities: An Approach to Development in the Local Church* (London: Search Press, 1978). Advances the case for the adoption by urban churches of the analytical tools and practices of community development as practised by community workers in secular agencies.

Michael S. Northcott, *Christianity and Secularisation: Urban Industrial Mission in North East England* (Frankfurt: Peter Lang, 1989). An ethnographic study of industrial mission and experiments in team and specialist ministry in the North East of England. Industrial chaplains, sector ministers, industrial workers, lay Christians and clergy speak of the achievements and failures of secular styles of ministry in their own words in this text. The study concludes with a sociological and theological critique of the secularization of the churches' theology and practice of ministry in the 1970s.

Henri Perrin, *The Autobiography of Henri Perrin* (London: Macmillan, 1965). The story of the French worker-priest movement told through the life of one of its pioneers.

Simon Phipps, *God on Monday* (London: Hodder and Stoughton, 1966). Gives a useful insight into the theological intentionality of industrial mission, and in particular the identification of secular social change with the transforming action of the Spirit of God which was commonly shared amongst industrial chaplains.

John Robinson, *The New Reformation* (London: SCM Press, 1966). Argues for a radical restructuring of the ministry of the church around the needs of lay people living and working in the secular city. The new reformation would allow new forms of ministry to be shaped around the needs and structures of the secular world.

David Sheppard, *Built as a City* (London: Hodder and Stoughton, 1974). This brilliant 1970s' survey of the condition of Britain's cities, and the role of the churches in them, includes a fine account of industrial mission (pp. 354 ff.).

Austin Smith, *Passion for the Inner City* (London: Sheed and Ward, 1983). Deeply felt account of the establishment of the Passionist Inner City Mission in Liverpool.

Ernie Southcott, *The Parish Comes Alive* (London: Mowbray, 1956). Drawing on the work of Abbé Michenneau in northern France and his own experience in urban parishes in England, Southcott charts the emergence of urban ministry at a time of rapid urban expansion and house building. He lays particular emphasis on the house group and on worship in the home.

John J. Vincent, *Into the City* (London: Epworth Press, 1982). Theological reflections on the church in the city which includes a number of stories and initiatives arising from the ministry of members of the core community of the Urban Theology Unit in Sheffield.

E.R. Wickham, *Church and People in an Industrial City* (London: Lutterworth Press, 1957). Argues that the church failed to reach the new working classes of the industrial cities because first it physically excluded them from worship by pew rents, and by not building enough churches, and proposes that the consequent gap between the churches and the working classes be addressed by the appointment of clergy as chaplains to factories and other places of work.

Gibson Winter, *New Creation as Metropolis* (New York: Doubleday, 1966). Key text in 1960s' urban theology which argued for the secularization of the institutions and practices of the churches in recognition that the secular metropolis is the new sphere of decisions of faith, and the deliverance of secular people from religious dependence to the responsible autonomy of the secular.

11

Mission in the city

While Paul was waiting for them at Athens, he was outraged to see the city so full of idols. He argued in the synagogue with the Jews and Gentile worshippers, and also in the city square every day with casual passers-by. Moreover, some of the Epicurean and Stoic philosophers joined issue with him. Some said, 'What can this charlatan be trying to say?' and others, 'He would appear to be a propagandist for foreign deities' — this because he was preaching about Jesus and the Resurrection. They brought him to the Council of the Areopagus and asked, 'May we know what this new doctrine is that you propound? You are introducing ideas that sound strange to us, and we should like to know what they mean.' Now, all the Athenians and the resident foreigners had time for nothing except talking or hearing about the latest novelty. Paul stood up before the Council of the Areopagus and began: 'Men of Athens, I see that in everything that concerns religion you are uncommonly scrupulous. As I was going round looking at the objects of your worship, I noticed among other things an altar bearing the inscription ''To an Unknown God''. What you worship but do not know — this is what I now proclaim. The God who created the world and everything in it, and who is Lord of heaven and earth, does not live in shrines made by human hands. It is not because he lacks anything that he accepts services at our hands, for he is himself the universal giver of life and breath — indeed of everything. He created from one stock every nation of men to inhabit the whole earth's surface. He determined their eras in history and the limits of their territory. They were to seek God in the hope that, groping after him, they might find him; though indeed he is not far from each one of us, for in him we live and move, in him we exist; as some of your own poets have said, ''We are also his offspring.'' Being God's offspring, then, we ought not to suppose that the deity is like an image in gold or silver or stone, shaped by human craftsmanship and design. God has overlooked the age of ignorance; but now he commands men and women everywhere to repent, because he has fixed the day on which he will have the world judged, and justly judged, by a man whom he has designated; of this he has given assurance to all by raising him from the dead.'

(Acts 17:16–31)

Faith in the City

An emphasis on the laity has been a strong theme to emerge in the written evidence submitted to us, and in our discussions in the UPAs. There was a particular stress on the need for a laity in the UPAs committed to making Christianity take shape in the local culture. We strongly affirm that lay people have an important role in developing the mission of the local UPA church. They can present the Gospel to others in a way that will make them feel 'this is for our sort of people'. Only those who are in, and of, the local area can say how God is speaking there. They can tell each other and the wider Church. (6.2)

Yet we have also had evidence that there are many obstacles in the way of developing an effective laity in the UPAs. They include the historical domination of leadership roles by those of other cultures, a concentration on words and books and equating intelligence and vocation with academic ability, a dependence on professionals, and a degree of conservatism among the laity. (6.3)

Introduction

The greatest movements of Christian revival in the twentieth century have begun amongst the poor and the working people of the new industrial cities of America, Europe, Africa and Asia. The first-century early Christian movement was an urban movement which began among the poor. Similarly, the twentieth-century Pentecostal revolution began in Azusa Street and has spread through the urban centres of the world from Santiago to Singapore, aided by the mobility of peoples and the free exchange of new ideas and religious practices which urban centres enable, in the twentieth as in the first century (Cox).

The Pentecostal urban revival of the late twentieth century has many parallels with earlier evangelical and Anglo-Catholic religious revivals in the new context of the nineteenth-century Victorian cities. Recent social histories of the mission of the church in the new urban industrial cities indicates that it was those churches which had a strong sense of religious identity and a strong commitment to the invention and revival of sacred traditions in the new urban context which thrived and grew (Cox). Parish clergy influenced by the Victorian evangelical or Anglo-Catholic revivals combined a strong emphasis on preaching, or ritual and sacraments, with a commitment to social justice often leading to political action. This combination of a spiritual and social programme proved highly effective as a missionary mechanism for the transcendent in the smoky and factory-dominated culture of London or Liverpool until at least the Second World War (Stockwood; Gorringe). Churches with a distinctive sense of their spiritual calling were also most successful and active in the sponsoring of Sunday Schools, uniformed youth organizations, women's organizations, working men's clubs and social welfare services which provided a range of points of entry for the new residents of the city and the spiritual life of the parish (Cox).

However, what worked in the Victorian and the pre-war period in the twentieth century is much less effective as a vehicle of mission in urban industrial or post-industrial communities. One of the reasons for this is the diminution in the social role of the parish in the secular city. Much of the social and educational work of the parish has been taken over by state-run social and welfare services which offer these services on the basis of need and right rather than charity. In the light of this progressive and caring urban government, modern liberal theologians in the mid-twentieth century proposed that instead of focusing on providing a sacred and ritual space for worship and preaching the church should merge its identity with the progressive forces of the city and seek to discern the sacred in the beneficent secularity of the city.

The liberal hope of social progress which many urban churches and theologians affirmed after the Second World War involved the co-ordination of the public and private goods of society for the welfare of all through progressive taxation, collective bargaining and contracts between capitalists and workers, and state intervention to transfer resources from rich to poor. This vision was in effect a secularized form of the Christian vision of the common good and of compassion, expressed in a society which still reflected and relied on Christian moral values. The liberal institutions of health care, education and social welfare contain within them people who are committed to the very highest ideals of compassion, caring and service, though the recent introduction into these institutions of unit-cost accounting methods, sub-contracting, casual labour and internal markets may well subvert these ideals.

There was a good deal which was 'good' about secular liberalism, hence the Christian liberal attempt to emulate and baptize its secular social vision. But this baptism of the dominant ideology of the twentieth century also had consequences for the proclamation of the Christian story. In particular it diverted the churches from their core spiritual mission of directing people to that ultimate and orienting goal which Christian tradition sets out for us all, namely the love and the worship of God.

The identity between the church's theology and patterns of urban ministry and the dominant ideology of secular society also presented an obstacle to mission amongst those who continued to experience the shadowside of secular progress. The irony was that in the secular city the church thrived in the suburb, in the places where the rewards and securities of the new order were greatest, while in the new housing areas the church struggled to establish and maintain strong churches, in a complete reversal of the mission of the early Church (**Vincent**).

The earliest Christian mission to the cities of the Mediterranean where Paul preached the gospel generated a series of 'people movements' amongst migrants, ethnic minorities and the poor. Early Christian evangelists were described by one pagan writer as 'wool workers, cobblers and laundry workers, and the most illiterate and bucolic yokels' who attracted 'children ... and stupid women' to come 'to the wooldresser's shop, or to the cobbler's or the washerwoman's shop, that they may learn perfection' (**Meeks**). Paul himself was a journeyman, making his living from working heavy cloth, albeit with an exceptional education. He founded churches which included members of the educated and elite of Roman society but which were primarily made up of members of the urban masses. The gospel which Paul preached, and the social forms the gospel took in the Gentile churches, reflected the cultural and social circumstances of their members. Paul preached Jesus Christ as the saviour, the divine Son, who could deliver his urban listeners from their subservience to gods, demons, magic and fate, all of which were very real to his audience (Green). The proclamation of Jesus as Lord involved the subordination of the gods, spirits and divinized kings which ruled the cultural imagination of the peoples of Rome and its satellite cities. To people who were depressed by the immorality and social oppression of these idolatrous cities Paul taught of the indwelling Spirit who could bring liberty and a new morality of love and mutual respect, and who could empower Christians to triumph over adversity. To people who were oppressed by fear of spirits and demons, and the sicknesses which they believed they brought, Paul announced release, redemption and healing through the Spirit of Jesus Christ. In other words, the spiritual teaching which Paul offered was directly relevant to the personal, moral and social problems which were the daily experience of city dwellers in the ancient world (Allen).

In preaching Jesus as Lord, Paul did not dismiss the reality of the world of fates and spirits in which his hearers lived. Neither did he simply denounce or blaspheme the idols which represented this imagined world in physical form. Rather, he made of this world of spirits and idols a series of cultural bridges to God, as in his address to the Athenians where he uses the altar to the unknown god as a vehicle for announcing the God who made himself known in the resurrection of Jesus from the dead. It is not that Paul approved of idolatry. On the contrary, he regarded idolatry as a great evil, for the worship of idols was associated with a range of ancient evils including ritual prostitution, slavery, bestiality, human sacrifice and nepotism. But in the churches which Paul founded he did not ask Gentile Christians to deny the continuing reality of the pagan context in which they continued to live. For example, meat offered to idols could be eaten, not least because otherwise Christians would be unable to have fellowship with non-Christians whom they might hope to convert. It is not that idolatry is not a significant source of oppression and evil, but that instead of aggressively denouncing the pagan culture, Christians could better witness to the reality of the Lordship of Christ over all spirits and demons, and the moral and spiritual power of the God who is in Christ, in the manner of their behaving and believing amongst idol worshippers, in their love for one another and their compassion to their neighbours (Green).

The style of Paul's evangelism involved the building of relational as well as cultural bridges between the gospel community and the urban communities which he visited. He networked first amongst his own people in the Jewish synagogues, and then in the houses of certain, mostly prominent, god-fearers — such as Lydia, Aquilla and Jason — preaching and arguing the gospel to small clusters of people who visited their homes (Allen). Despite the great size of the cities he visited, his strategy still began with personal evangelism, evangelism which drew on the networks of relationships, amongst Jews, god-fearers, educated citizens and journeymen to which Paul's providentially heterogeneous social status granted him access (**Bakke**).

Paul was a powerful and gifted teacher and apologist for the gospel. He was also an effective and strategic builder of communities of faith. His aim in every city he visited was to establish a group of converts who would rapidly acquire independence from his own skills and establish a community of Christians rooted in their own urban setting. All of Paul's fledgling churches were self-supporting financially, and self-sustaining in ministry from the very beginning. This meant that they were fully indigenous, fully contextualized and not dependent on outside authority which would have undermined or held back the development of local leadership and of patterns of worship, mission and ministry suited to the local cultural environment.

Modern inner city and housing estate churches by contrast tend to reflect the cultural and social circumstances of the traditional city centre or market town parish as many of these new churches began as extensions or sub-divisions of pre-existing parishes. Instead of planting financially independent churches drawing on locally ordained local leadership, the church has consistently imported money, ministry and missionaries from outside the city communities it attempts to reach. This has created a pattern of dependency and subsidy in much urban ministry and mission in which mission has been imposed from outside rather than grown within the dynamic of local networks of relationships drawing on the dominant interests, symbols, icons and values of inner city or new housing areas. One consequence of this has been that clergy moving into new areas complain they are unable to find local leaders. However, the recent devolution of tenancy control, or new forms of broad-based community organizing, which have become established in regeneration projects in inner city areas and public housing estates in recent years have demonstrated that local leaders are to be found. But their interests and voices need to be identified and listened to and their innate skills encouraged and mobilized in forms of leadership and community organization which are appropriate to their cultural context (Donnison; Lockwood).

Paul was an outsider and he learnt not to stay long, aware that his strengths as an evangelist and apologist for the faith were best used in a mobile ministry and would become weaknesses in the business of establishing independent churches. His continuing presence would suppress the emergence of spiritual gifts and ministries amongst the new Christians. Paul devoted considerable personal resources to building up a small group of god-fearers and converts into a dynamic and confident team which would learn mutual responsibility and communal self-reliance. Paul then relied on the Spirit of God and the spiritual creativity of his new converts to sustain and build up the small groups of converts he established into missionary communities, and communities of worship and loving fellowship (Allen).

Many new churches are being planted in inner city and new housing areas in Britain as in many other parts of the world. But these new churches are quite different in form and structure to the traditional parish. They are often focused initially on a small group of Christians and new converts who are built up into a strong worshipping fellowship where the power of praise to God builds up a sense of mutual affirmation and self-respect, qualities so often lacking in fractured inner city communities (**Bonnick; Bakke; Wallis**). The missionary task is to turn such small communities of praise and *koinonia* into 'people movements' drawing on the relational networks of the members — family, work, neighbours, tenancy groups — to attract and welcome new members, and outsiders, into the group so small group becomes church (Tonna).

Part of this missionary extension of the small group or housechurch will involve finding common cause with other groups in the local area in relation to issues of social action and personal need (**Bakke**). The missionary church will seek to identify the various networks of relationships and interests or 'people groups' that exist in the city and to mobilize different members of the church in personal evangelism to these different people groups (**Bakke**). Examples of such people groups in inner city Britain include single parents and their children, old people mostly living alone, gay people, ethnic groups, those suffering from some form of mental disease and being treated in the 'community', people with physical disabilities, the long-term unemployed, and school-leavers unable or unwilling to find work or training places. Some small group churches will perhaps be identified initially with one or other of these people groups. Other larger or more traditional parish churches may include people drawn from almost all of these people groups. Whichever is the case, it is vital for the urban Christian community that wishes to bring the Gospel of Jesus Christ to those who have not heard of or experienced its life-transforming potential to identify the people groups in its area and seek to shape and target particular mission or ministry events or strategies towards particular groups of people in order that their needs and concerns can shape the evangelistic opportunity which is created.

Above all, the missionary church is a church for whom outsiders matter as much as insiders. The danger of the small worshipping community is that it becomes a holy huddle existing for itself and defended from the social environment and from the stranger and the newcomer. The stories of new churches and traditional churches which are growing in contemporary inner city Britain are stories of a mutual inter-penetration between local environment and worshipping community, between insider and outsider. The church which is not shaped by its local environment to a considerable extent will be an alien church in a hostile environment. On the other hand, the church which ceases to exist as a distinct loving fellowship of salvation, worship and action is a church which has lost its vocation to be the visible body of Christ in the world (**Wallis**). Mission is a boundary activity, but for Christians to live effectively as missionaries on the boundary requires the supporting strength of a distinctive spiritual community where Jesus Christ is acknowledged as Lord and where the Holy Spirit inhabits the praises and the lives of God's people.

Plaistow Christian Fellowship

Helen Bonnick

Plaistow Christian Fellowship is one of a number of churches in Newham owing its origins to In Contact Ministries, which seeks to plant new inner city churches among the ethnic minorities and people of other faiths. From a handful of people meeting together in 1978 in a redundant Anglican church building, the fellowship had grown to about seventy by 1982. People were attracted through formal and informal evangelistic events: coffee mornings, Bible studies, services and missions, as well as by word of mouth. Perhaps the largest proportion of conversions was of friends or family of those already attending, and despite the original aspirations the church remained predominantly white.

By 1982 we had developed a distinctive pattern of worship and leadership and the request of the trustees for an alternative use for the buildings precipitated our move into independence. Leaving a group of In Contact workers to continue their task we came to the brighter, more accessible community buildings, taking our new name as we came. 'We shall go out with joy and be led forth in peace,' we sang as we moved, and that was to be our theme tune for some time, helping us through the problems of birth.

About sixty people made the move. Some of the original members have since moved away, for a number of reasons. Ten people are able to say that they have been involved from the start in one way or another. The others of the 100 (including children) currently on our membership list have either moved into the area, been born or born-again since. Only a handful have transferred membership locally. One hundred has seemed to be our maximum attainable number up till now, though it does not in any way represent our total number of contacts — more of that later!

Just as we came forth in joy, though also with difficulties, so during the last five and half years we have felt what might be described as growing pains. We have gone through periods of struggle, spiritually as well as physically, mentally and emotionally, but we have also been able to laugh and celebrate. We have often proved true the writer of Ecclesiastes as we experienced —

> a time to weep and a time to laugh,
> a time to mourn and a time to dance,
> a time to embrace and a time to refrain
> a time to search and a time to give up,
> a time to keep and a time to throw away.
>   (Ecclesiastes 3:4–6 NIV)

As we have grown and changed, the overriding consideration has always been to seek that which is good and pleasing to God; our purpose statement has provided a focus for thinking, for planning and for prayer.

Our Sunday morning service struggles into life soon after 10.30. The local laid-back attitude to timekeeping conspires with the requirements of non-Christian families, temperamental transport and last-minute dirty nappies to keep us for as long as possible from honouring God together! For some, too, there is a real battle of the mind and spirit each Sunday morning, and we try to help and encourage these people by collecting them. By 10.50 about sixty have usually gathered, though with a young congregation our numbers are considerably depleted during holidays.

There is no typical Sunday morning, though we follow a pattern of having a shorter family service on the first Sunday of each month, joining with another local fellowship for this every second month. A stranger standing outside in February would have wondered what on earth was going on as the hall rang out with football chants and people puffed and blew as we apparently took part in a keep-fit session. Paula the clown had lost her enthusiasm, but found it at last as she realized how much there was to thank God for. 'Not before time!' some people might have been heard to mutter as they lay slumped in exhaustion!

With a relatively high proportion of illiteracy in the area, considerable effort goes into presenting the message of Jesus in a clear, visual or physical way rather than relying solely on literature. So we use videos, music and movement (as one who takes part I would hesitate to call it dance) to help people understand and remember what is said. The leaders, spouses and those taking part in the service meet early for prayer. We have learned how important it is to claim God's protection on each of us as we join together, and also that each person should arrive already prepared before God. Inevitably this does not always happen; thus the service may be interrupted as we pray with someone who is struggling or respond to another person's worry.

Though we are relatively new as a fellowship and have people from many backgrounds, it would be foolish to pretend that we have no traditions or routines. Indeed, the morning service tends to be quite 'traditional': half an hour of praise, news, prayers, notices and a children's item, usually followed by a sermon lasting about twenty or thirty minutes and a time of open worship. All are encouraged to take part since all are 'ministers', though some do so more than others. It is exciting when new Christians take part, showing a vitality and a refreshing absence of spiritual jargon.

Albert is nearly ninety and only became a Christian in the last five years. He had not been inside a church building for over half his life but was persuaded by a friend to attend a harvest festival service, where he saw something different about the people that attracted him. He has been much sought after in past years as Father Christmas (we almost believe that he is the real one!) and he is valued, too, by us now for the wisdom he brings. When Albert stands up in a service we know that God has something to say to us.

At times the worship seems a real battle and we struggle to understand why this is. Leaving aside the physical distractions of people leaving for a cigarette, babies crying, guitar strings breaking and the fact that some come only as spectators, there is still a sizeable group that desires to meet with God, to enter into his presence, and to bless him. The gifts of the Spirit — tongues, prophecy and healing — are seen, but not always on a Sunday. The disappointment that some may feel perhaps serves as a reminder that we should seek to worship God each moment of our lives and not only on a Sunday morning. The introduction of a monthly evening praise time has proved more encouraging in this respect, as has our monthly prayer meeting, though whether this difference is because we meet in a smaller group of people, or have a greater expectation or different format, is hard to say.

We try to finish Sunday morning services by 12.15, at which time the children are becoming restless in their groups. But all is not finished and most of us then stay behind to share time, news and food together over a potluck lunch. This varies from week to week: roast chicken and salads or a nutritionist's nightmare of cakes and biscuits.

Mutual encouragement to know God better, for ourselves, takes place in many ways. Most belong to a cell group, meeting weekly. These groups might take up the theme of the Sunday morning sermon in order to develop further the teaching and ideas, but there is room for flexibility so that cell group members can get to know and serve one another better. Even in a fellowship the size of ours it is not possible to know everyone equally well, and cell groups are important for all, but particularly those who are stuck indoors, have few friends or see no one the rest of the week. There are also special teaching sessions from time to time on particular themes: the role of women, identifying and using spiritual gifts, worship; and groups of two or more often meet on their own initiative for discipleship, to study God's word together, or simply to go swimming. Other groups (e.g. men, young mothers) emerge and disappear as need dictates.

An important aspect of sharing together in the past has been a church weekend away, with a full programme of teaching, games and of course food. Some of the children in the fellowship have never been outside London and so for them it has been a very special experience. One memorable comment came from a four-year-old, breathing his first fresh air as we drove towards Sevenoaks: 'Yuck, it smells funny.'

The church weekend may come but once a year, but services in the park and days out in the summer come round more often. They provide a chance to forget the hole in the roof, the lack of a garden, the traffic fumes, the noisy neighbours, and to relax, throw someone in the boating lake, feed the squirrels and indulge in that most famous of local sports — football. (Whose turn is it to be West Ham this time?) Bruised and battered we queue later at casualty and give thanks in all things!

Jesus demands that his followers surrender their entire lives to him and we have as a fellowship spent time considering the implications for us. We can honour or dishonour God in the way we use our time, our money, possessions and talents as well as our bodies. To acknowledge Jesus as Lord of our homes and finances can be liberating. Though we cannot say that we have everything in common as did the first Christians of Acts, many have, however, opened their homes to others. Those with cars have insured them for any driver or offered a taxi service, and some have cooked meals for other families. Babysitting has been an invaluable service, and we have discovered the value of giving time just to visit and to listen.

We have enjoyed both God and one another as we have worked on each other's homes, decorating or even rebuilding. Some have learned new skills. Many have benefited from Terry's plumbing experience. In an area of poor housing but high prices we have worked wonders on a few homes through working parties, sometimes late into the night. Once, Kim's parents were due to arrive from America the next day and the hall was still unpapered, the

living-room unpainted and every room coated in dust. But we finished
everything and celebrated with drinks and photos before crawling home!

The spiritualist church down the road has a firm foothold in the area.
Terry estimates that 80 per cent of the local people have had some involvement in the occult. Those in the fellowship who have been involved in the
past have found daily obedience a struggle at times. We are very aware of the
spiritual battles going on around us and the need of God's protection.

On two or three Sundays over the last year we have sought to proclaim
God's victory, praising God as we marched and sang as a fellowship around
a particular estate. Others have prayed as they walked around on their own.
Far from being the great ordeal many expected, it has lifted our spirits as
people have come to their windows or gates to watch and wave, and as
children have joined us on their bikes. Through these marches and other
activities we have got to know the people on the estate and have had the
pleasure of seeing them join us on other occasions.

Some have found God's demands on their lives too painful and have
chosen the 'easier' way of their former lives, but they are few, and even some
of these remain in contact either by friendship or family ties. None of us is
perfect, and all of us are aware of the pull of old ways and old friendships. Pat
and Terry in particular have missed sleep in order to rescue people physically
or spiritually. Prison visiting, psychiatric appointments, drug and alcohol
counselling, support for those struggling in their marriages, attending case-
conferences for a child in care, providing a character witness, debt
counselling — at times these big responsibilities seem a daily demand, and
there is a danger that as we focus on the dramatic, others can feel left out, or
that we ignore the small, private problems. But we also learn not simply to
depend on the formal leadership to teach, correct and counsel. All of us can
hear God when we allow him to speak, and each of us can be used by God in
serving others.

Great contrast exists within the fellowship in terms of income — from a
family of four dependent on dad's dole money to married couples both
earning comfortable salaries. (We have no managing directors!) With the
distinction further drawn between the more well off young and the less well
off older people, a danger of division arises. So much depends on attitudes,
expectations or prejudices, but as we get to know one another better we hope
that these are overcome. Our giving as a fellowship is testimony to the way
God has worked in our pockets. Although we now pay only two full-time
workers (Terry and Pat and their family), rather than the original four, we do
so (we hope) in a more generous and realistic way. From our weekly offering,
averaging about £200, also comes rent and regular support for a number of
members and ex-members engaged in Christian ministries as well as the more
mundane stationery, printing and refreshment expenses. We just manage to
balance the books each year, but there is also much giving and sharing that
never appears in the accounts.

Is it the enjoyment of God which sets apart the new and renewed churches
from the more conventional? Many of us have experience of churches where
enjoyment was the last thing on people's minds. In Plaistow we have learned
that there may seem little in our daily lives to enjoy — friends, neighbours
and children suffer abuse, harassment and the stress of inner city life — but
God is good: he comforts us; he protects us; he never fails.

* * *

To be anything other than a select club we therefore need to present a God who is real and who is alive. We should not be simply superimposing our faith on to local, predominantly working-class culture, but presenting an honest and exciting way of living based on Christ's teaching and on our relationship of love and obedience to him. I use the words 'need' and 'should' intentionally — easy to say but much harder to do. Old ways of thinking and doing are hard to shake off. In doing what we believe to be God's will we can find ourselves at the receiving end of much criticism from inside as well as outside the church. We grow weary and are discouraged when we do not see 'results'. Some find the cost of commitment to the tough area of Plaistow too high and move away. In such a situation we have to trust God that we are being effective. Fortunately we are not alone. We have his Holy Spirit, and we also have one another.

Many churches within Newham have made a clear and determined effort over the last few years to shed the practice of each building its own little kingdom, so that there is now a series of overlapping networks of churches meeting regularly across denominations and across the borough. These are based, of course, on a shared knowledge and love of God, but also on the development of personal relationships among the leaders and increasingly among the congregations. PCF is involved particularly with a group of about ten fellowships which have taken the name of Newham Christian Fellowships.

Beginning from the leaders meeting regularly for prayer, there are now joint prayer meetings, celebrations, evangelistic events, teaching seminars and an annual march of witness, on some occasions linked with a float in the town show. Naturally enough, not all agree on every issue, but together we balance one another and have much to give and to learn. This unity is important since a greater number of people are able to present a message to the borough which is therefore less easily ignored. Together our numbers justify hiring the town hall for teaching, carol services and worship. In February 1986, on a memorable occasion, representatives of over thirty fellowships met across racial and denominational boundaries to repent of our past attitudes of mistrust and prejudice and to affirm our unity in Christ.

Being committed to the life of Newham has meant different things for different people. Staying put can be hard with old friends and haunts around or with the kids' education to consider. Many decide to do so, nevertheless, and others have moved in to live among the people for and with whom they work. As well as being involved with family, friends or neighbours, we support local organizations and activities, and some have sought to affect the decision-making of the council. With so many different interests involved — the unemployed, school governors, those engaged regularly in evangelism, mothers with young babies, and those committed to their careers, to name but a few — it is not possible to point in one direction and say, 'This is our priority.' Together, though, we are united in a desire to bring *shalom*, or wholeness, to the community, working for justice, peace and healing in whatever way we can.

PCF News has carried a series of articles under the general heading 'Salt of

the Earth' in which different individuals have written about ways in which
they are acting as an antiseptic, a preservative, a flavouring (a colouring? —
no artifical additives here!) to those with whom they mix daily. In her post in
a large local comprehensive, Jayne has tried to show respect to the pupils and
in so doing has gained the trust and friendship of many children. Recognizing
her Christian faith they often go to her for help in times of trouble, be it
academic, emotional or physical, seeking her advice, too, on issues such as
sex before marriage and family life. Other members of the fellowship also
count such lifestyle evangelism their main priority, while some are committed to a regular programme of door-knocking and literature distribution.
Their tireless efforts bring rewards when people come along to the fellowship. Rather more of us have been involved in following up contacts for
particular evangelistic events.

Being salt is not only for those in work. All have a valuable part to play in
community life whether informally through friendships and visiting people
or through involvement in more formal groups. A major project over the last
year has been a link with the local tenants' association. Some people have
asked when we hope to take over the running of the group and to make it
'Christian', but this is to misunderstand our intentions. We are open about
our faith, but our first role is to serve the community by being available for
advice, counselling or transport and by providing workers for their summer
play scheme and after-school club. It has been especially exciting when
children, parents and members of the committee have then come along to one
of our services. In an area where *social* church-going is certainly not the norm
and many people have been put off by conventional expressions of religion,
it is important that we are seen by others as practical people who genuinely
care, who can be trusted.

Social concern, social action or social change can be thankless tasks. A
group of eight people hoping to be salt through their involvement in the local
Labour party meet monthly to encourage one another, especially Steve — a
member of the council — throwing around ideas, considering the implications of various decisions or policies and providing emotional and prayer
support.

One part of living in God's kingdom which many desire and yet find so
difficult to take hold of is a sense of self-acceptance and self-worth. Past
experience for some, or ways of thinking for others, seem to place blocks all
along the route. Regardless of age, sex, race, education or background, God
loves each of us equally, but too often we do not treat each other accordingly.
Those involved in the children's work struggle with how to include them in
our worship other than in a token way. When is it right to laugh *with* the kids
as they sing (perform?) at the front and when are we laughing *at* them? Is it
OK to giggle when we sing 'He's got Vicky's goldfish in his hands'?

A growing number of us have children of our own, and there is often a
large group of children whose parents do not attend, some of whom it seems
are practically kicked out in the morning and expected to roam the streets. At
a recent count we had thirty under-twelves; services have to be relevant to
them. We need to provide more than just a baby-sitting service; rather
somewhere they can observe and be included in a different way of life, a
different set of values and worshipping the living God. In the past we have
failed to meet the needs of teenagers because of a lack of facilities and a need

for special skills and understanding. Soon we shall have to meet this challenge again.

Are we being effective in our involvement in the borough? We can look at our 'success' and encourage one another that we are, but when we look outwards at the people in need of so much, we can feel ineffective. We long to see God at work (even more than we do already), breaking into people's lives in a real, miraculous and healing way.

Evangelism

Raymond Bakke

I part company with those who say, 'Only do a social ministry', and with those who say, 'We only announce the Good News.' It is the News which transforms the climate and gives people hope. Only then can they find the energy to change things. The way some good news was received in a German prisoner-of-war camp illustrates this principle. Murdo McDonald spoke to his American colleagues through the fence in Gaelic, because English was not permitted. In 1945 they exchanged the news that the war was over — three days before the Germans heard it. During these three days they were still prisoners of war, with all the accustomed privations. Nothing had changed. But before the gates had been unlocked the good news had transformed their response to their situation. This is a parable of the way the Gospel can transform the lives of people who often remain in unemployment, poverty and other types of urban oppression.

The Gospel is news, not advice. The difference between Jesus Christ and the newspaper problem page is just at this point. Good advice is something to do, whether it be to repent, feel guilty, or whatever. I cannot go into the ghetto with integrity and tell people that they are bad and need to change, or to feel more guilty than they do. Jesus forgave people first. He did not ignore sin and he had a profound understanding of it, but he did not go to poor people and lay guilt and the law on them.

Christians cannot work in poor urban areas and not offer the Good News. If they do social work and all kinds of things and have failed to offer the Good News, they have failed to offer their best gift. Jesus offers something he has already done for you. Urban pastors like Peter and John in Acts 3 may have had few resources, but they always had News. There is no excuse for not sharing that News with all people every day, and in clear ways that give people the opportunity to accept or reject Jesus. How can we say we truly care for people if we do not care enough to confront them unambiguously with who Jesus Christ is and what he can do for them? Surely Carl Henry was right when he said, 'All ways of not evangelising are always wrong.' The late Paul Little was fond of saying, 'Scratch people where they itch in the name of Jesus Christ.' Caring about someone's personal needs is part of evangelism.

IMPERSONAL EVANGELISM

In my evangelism classes I use the Lausanne Covenant definition, that evangelism is the Good News of the Gospel about Jesus, which we proclaim by our words and our actions. The content of evangelism is who Jesus is, what he did, and what he continues to do. Jesus is the one who came into the world, lived and died and rose again, and now is the ascended, risen Lord who offers forgiveness to all who repent and believe. How then do we offer this Gospel?

[Elsewhere I have] described the 'overload' upon urban people resulting from their being swamped with 'secondary', or impersonal, casual relationships. They switch off from making these relationships. In lifts or underground trains they avoid looking at each other and stare blankly. I concluded that impersonal styles of evangelism — door-knocking, media or mailing, and giant crusades — do not take urban realities into account. The electronic media and the Billy Graham style of campaigns are probably regarded by most American and British evangelists as still the ideal ways to reach cities with the Gospel. Such campaigns have valid roles but they were not the primary means used by the early Church, nor are they the most effective means in our large, complex cities today.

Programmes for evangelism become additional layers of work for our already busy people, and are usually invitations for the public to come to our buildings. Pastors may prefer programmes for these reasons:

> They have not taken the time to identify the primary lines of communication which already exist for urban dwellers.
> The programmes may have been effective in their previous churches.
> They were taught these styles of evangelism in college.
> Their denominations expect or promote programmes.
> They have budgets set aside for programmes.
> Their own 'pastoral ego' requires them to be visible and productive in evangelism before their church members.

An example of inappropriate impersonal evangelism is the telephone evangelism attempted in Chicago by one Christian group. They called every number in the phone book and invited people to respond to Jesus. The programme was a disaster. It did not reach half our families, who are without telephones. Many of those with telephones did not speak English. Those who did speak English simply did not make this sort of decision on the telephone. You cannot call up an anonymous person in the city and deal with eternal issues. The method is incongruous and violates the whole psychology of urban people.

PERSONAL EVANGELISM

I would suggest that the only evangelism suitable in urban contexts is personal — church members ministering to their own 'worlds of relationships': family and extended family (biological); geographical; vocational. Each person draws a chart of his or her relationships in each of these worlds. The family chart includes the 'nuclear family' — the household — and the extended family, which may be scattered over the whole country. (My family, like most urban families, does not live in one locality. My parents live in Denver, Colorado, 1,000 miles from Chicago; my brother lives in Washington, DC, which is 750 miles in the opposite direction.) Church members then identify a basic need for each person, and select three or four of their family networks to minister to in practical ways.

The second network — the geographical — consists of people you have a primary relationship with, or could have, by virtue of where you live. They may be your neighbours, or occupy other flats in your building. They include your barber, the person you buy your food from, the mechanic who fixes your car, and the teacher of your child. The procedure is the same: select a few of these people and identify a need for each, and think how you plan to minister to them and share Jesus with them.

The third network is vocational. In order to help people minister in their workplaces I suggest that the pastor should make his second call — if not his first — where they work. Most urban pastors know very little about their members' worlds of work, unlike their rural colleagues who know everyone's work. In the city the congregation disappears during the week and the pastor has no idea what they do. His preaching becomes barren and irrelevant and he has no idea how to illustrate it. Some urban pastors may have created alternative congregational worlds for urban people, to compensate for their own loss of reality because they know so little about the urban world.

Many pastors have an anachronistic view of work. They communicate to their people that real work is 'church work' — by which they mean loyalty to church programmes. Luther put this idea out of date when he emptied the monasteries with the rediscovery that you could serve God in your vocation. Calvin affirmed that and went further, suggesting that you could serve God with your vocation. Pastors can help members to minister within their vocations. The results will be less visible in the sanctuary, perhaps, because the members will be occupied within their own worlds with counselling, Bible studies, and a whole range of mercy ministries. Pastors will encourage maturing members to assume union or management responsibilities, and will adopt a posture of listening and learning to accomplish this. The maturing Christians must describe their worlds for us, before we can help them to get involved effectively.

The 'come-all-ye' church structure, involving people in programmes within the church, is especially ineffective with men, whose primary identity is through their work. The pastor invites them to set aside this identity and enter a world in which the pastor is high and lifted up in the pulpit, and is the chief executive officer of the 'corporation' called 'church'. It is hardly fair or effective for pastors to ask lay people to leave their worlds of vocational identity all the time, and come into the church and be a vocational non-person among other worshippers, while the pastors parade their unique identity before them. This may explain why some male ministers have difficulty in reaching men, and why women come in such abundance. The pastor may be too vocationally over-powering for other males to feel comfortable.

Pastors should deliberately enter the several worlds of their members, and listen to their personal and corporate histories. Visits to their places of work affirm their members' identities and their call to mission in their vocations, which are areas where pastors have limited access. If the whole city is to be reached, members will have to do it in each of their worlds. The pastor can visit people in their factories and offices for lunch, ask them about their work, and help them to chart and think about the people with whom they work. In my ministry our church's evangelism was transformed by these visits to people at work; my encouragement of members to regard themselves as ministers opened up most of our opportunities. All this costs nothing because it takes advantage of the networks that already exist.

It is not an addition to people's crowded church programmes like most evangelism, inviting people to meetings, or calling door-to-door. These are really tiresome activities in the city — yet more duties for busy people. A congregation of 100 active members, where people are encouraged to identify ministry in all three networks, is no small church. It is the inability to see that the field really is the world that keeps urban pastors feeling insignificant. We must remember that our pastoral goal in the city is effective ministry, not the efficiency of our programmes.

TEACHING EVANGELISM

My search has been for some simple way to enable people to share their faith — a way which fits the social realities of cities. Most fruitful evangelism comes through the primary networks of believers, so the key is to help people to identify them, and then teach them how to share their faith. People are not motivated by books on evangelism, or by your saying, 'Would you go to this conference? It will teach you how to become an evangelist.' Few lay people get excited by that. They need to be trained singly or in small groups, first, to give a simple testimony. This should have three parts:

My life before I met Jesus.
How I met Jesus.
The difference in my life since I met Jesus.

Then they need a few simple questions to start a conversation:

Are you interested in religion these days?
Can I take a couple of minutes and tell you what Jesus means to me?
Would you like to become a Christian?
Can I tell you how I became a Christian?

Most denominations have evangelism material in their churches, and some is superb. There is no room, however, for subterfuges, or 'foot-in-the-door' play for other agenda. Pastors need to develop the expectation that their church members will share the Gospel as a matter of course and in ways appropriate to their personalities, and to the time, place and audience. This is friendship evangelism — teaching lay people how to approach their friends and serve them in love.

Another training principle I recommend for pastors is never to do anything alone. It is more efficient to make a hospital visit alone, but I went alone only in an emergency. I would take Tom with me to visit Mrs Skulsky, and on the way I would say, 'By the way, Tom, Mrs Skulsky wasn't in church on

Sunday. Would you be able to tell her about the service?' Or, 'I think Mrs Skulsky would enjoy hearing your testimony; would you mind telling her how you became a believer?' In the hospital I would introduce Mrs Skulsky to Tom and ask her to introduce her friend in the next bed. The visit might include Tom's story of how he met Jesus, and prayer in which both our church member and her neighbouring patient are involved. Afterwards I would help Tom to recall and interpret the experience so that he could begin to make calls on his own. 'Tom, I think you are ready to make calls now yourself. And you know something? They expect me to make calls because they pay me, but when you come to the hospital they are really excited because they know you must care. Nobody expects lay people to come.'

In these ways your people will become evangelistic and they will draw upon their pastor for follow-on, or help with problems as they arise. Encourage your people to share testimonies — not 'bragimonies' — that illustrate who Jesus is and what he does. Conversion has been described as a radical act. Set people free from sin's awful bondage, and you may start an urban social revolution.

Signs for mission

John Vincent

Gordon Ashworth, minister in Bermondsey, has recently produced some significant figures for the London South-West Methodist District, showing how many people in the total population of an area correspond to one Methodist, one church, or one minister. Gordon worked it out for twelve London boroughs. I show it for only two.

	England as a whole	Sutton (suburbia)	Kensington (inner city)
One Methodist to every	94	148	362
One church to every	5,520	20,837	39,875
One minister to every	22,596	41,675	53,166

The moral is plain. Your chances of becoming a Methodist more than double if you move from inner city to suburbia, and are half as good again if you leave surburbia for the rest of England (small market towns, etc.). The sociologist David Martin states that the larger the town or city you live in, the less likely you are to go to church; and the further down the social class scale you are, the less likely you are to go to church.

Moreover, the churches subsidize mission to the salaried, professional, clerical and managerial classes by allowing a concentration of resources in suburban churches. Equally, the churches subsidize mission to the employed, and those favoured with skilled and well-paid jobs in factories, by supporting industrial mission. Clearly, we must stay in suburbia and in industry. We must mission to the middle class and to the working class. But the growing non-working class also needs us. We need a mission to people in their weakness as well as in their strength, a mission to the places we fail in as well as to those we succeed in, a mission to the unemployed as well as to the employed, a mission to the failures of our society as well as to its technocrats and managers, a mission to those called to be alternatives to the current socio-economic system as well as to those who become its masters and its slaves.

And there can be no doubt in anyone's mind where the priority of a Jesus-centred mission would be. It would be precisely with the weak, the unemployed, the failures, the alternative-seekers.

How, then, can we participate in Jesus's mission?

In 1978, I did a series of BBC 'People's Services'. Each of them featured various members of the Mission. Each of them, too, featured directions in mission strategy that we had discovered. We thought about them a lot, and made them the theme of our 1979 Annual Report. After a paragraph about 'wilderness' we listed our 'signs for mission' thus:

1. A JOURNEY BACKWARDS

Jesus began his ministry with a call for a Jubilee, a cancellation of debts and injustices by 'going back' to a state of freedom and authenticity. Churches today need to return to a simple, do-it-yourself, modest, grass-roots style. So we, in the Mission, began by saying to little surviving churches, 'There is no hope for you with the vast, irrelevant buildings of the immediate past. Rather, go back to the simpler, cheaper ways of those who met in houses and halls before they built your churches.' The journey backwards has led us to affirm churches which the denominations had been trying to close for nearly twenty years. Lopham Street returns to being a small church, part of a multi-activity centre, sharing premises with a Community Youth Workshop and two West Indian congregations. Wesley Hall sells its large building to the West Indian Testament Church of God (ravaged by National Front slogans in October), and buys a small shop around the corner to be a new style mission. Both are more modest, more people-centred, more like the earliest churches of Christendom, and the little improvised rooms of early Congregationalism and Methodism.

2. A JOURNEY SIDEWAYS

Jesus invited people to leave the Israel of his day and form an 'alternative community', represented first in the Twelve, and then in the earliest church. Churches today need to discover themselves, not as reflections of the world, but as prophetic communities alongside it. So, SICEM has become a kind of haven for people looking for alternatives. The Urban Theology Unit is a place where people step aside for twelve months to discover who they are, what they ought to be doing, and where they ought to be living. The Eucharist Congregation has become a place where people from inside and outside of denominational churches can discover what being an alternative congregation might mean. Pitsmoor Centre and Foundry Housing have given us the chance to experiment with a new style — of church and housing together — and to ask what new things are possible there which are impossible for the non-resident commuter church. The Mission itself has been for all of us a step aside from the usual expectations of churches, and a new search, apart from the old demands and ways of looking at things.

3. A JOURNEY DOWNWARDS

Jesus took their money and livelihoods away from the Twelve, and then proclaimed: 'Happy are you poor.' Churches today need to abandon their success images, their middle-class exclusivism, and discover life again at the bottom. So in the Mission we have little money, no investments, and discover what it means to have 'long-term commitment with short-term financing'. Every year, our finances are radically different. The support of our team ministry is possible by a juggling of monies from countless sources which would make any church treasurer quake. Our people accept modest standards, even poverty by comparison with their success-orientated relatives. St James and Shiregreen commit themselves to stay with the multicultural and housing estate communities they are part of. Ashram House has people who 'give up all' and 'possess things in common'. Eucharist Congregation helps run a Whole Foods Shop and adopts fasting disciplines. All are ways of setting ourselves beside Jesus, the man for others, and beside the world's majority of people, who are poor. The journeys backwards, sideways and downwards are neither easy nor straightforward. They are highly questionable, infinitely difficult, and often quite devious. They are only to be heard, we have found, by shutting off other voices, and listening to the voices around us: the voices of the poor, the voices of the dispossessed, the voices of the small surviving churches. In them we have heard the voice of Jesus.

So it has to begin in wilderness. As we also wrote in our 1979 Report:

Before Jesus began his ministry, he was driven out into the desert and spent forty days in isolation, self-doubt and testing. Today, his followers seeking new ways often have to go through periods of loneliness, confusion and alienation from others, when they find themselves in a strange, unwanted situation with unexpected, unwanted questions. It was so with us. We first had to reject all available solutions and go through a few years of darkness, when old friends deserted and survivors huddled together for warmth. Each part of our Mission has to face its own wilderness. For some it is past, for some it is present, for some it is yet to come. But new things only grow in wildernesses, we have found.

4. SIGNS FOR CHURCHES

The churches' answer to the situation of the inner cities and other urban areas has in the past not been a very useful one.

1. The church has been a *social escalator*. Get on it poor, you get off it rich.
    Get on it simple, you get off it qualified. Get on it working class, you get
    off it middle class. People from small inner city working-class churches
    on street corners have got on and got out. They took their churches with
    them, and Christianity is strong now in the south-east of Britain rather
    than the north, in suburbia rather than inner areas.
2. The Christian Church in Britain has become almost a *one-class* church.
    The poor are left out. The unacceptable, the odd, the immigrants, the
    one-parent family, the unemployed, are not often found in our chur-
    ches.
3. The church in Britain has become a *one-culture* church. Only middle-
    class, educated people feel really at home enough to decide things. Other
    cultures hardly exist among churchgoers.

Efforts are made to overcome these deficiencies. Whole denominations often
help city work. But this does not remove the divisions. At a recent Methodist
District Home Mission Division meeting, it was reported that an inner city
circuit accounted for £43 per head in a year, while a suburban circuit
accounted for only £22. And this is not to deny the help that some suburban
churches give to funds which support the inner city.

Our experience has been that while the churches have remained largely
one class and suburban-based, we have been able to rediscover the gospel 'at
the bottom'.

1. *The gospel acts as a social de-escalator*. Every year, we get people
    coming to live and work with us in the inner city. Often they come to
    study at the Urban Theology Unit. Often they change their lives. Often
    they change the place where they live. Rich, learned, middle class, they
    become poor, ignorant, non-working class. They discover themselves
    through a freely taken alternative journey, a journey downwards.
2. *The poor learn to share among themselves*. Within the Sheffield Inner
    City Ecumenical Mission, the ten little congregations and units meet
    together to sort out how they can survive. Each of them has a radically
    different style, and radically different financial support. But together
    they sort out their survival. And we have learnt: it's the poor that help the
    poor.
3. *The cosmopolitan kingdom comes into being*. A truly 'alternative
    church' has come to exist. It is alternative because instead of the able, the
    white, the qualified, and the decision-makers, we have the old, the black
    and the white, the unemployed, and the artisans. But it is also alternative
    because it bears witness to the radical pluralism ('many things going on')
    of the contemporary world, with the radical pluralism of the gospel ('all
    kinds of people getting their foot in the kingdom').

    Thus, we have ten completely different liturgies for Holy Communion
    in the Mission, we have ten different times and days of worship, we have
    eight different styles that people can fit into. The 'unity' we find is in
    recognition of a constantly growing 'diversity'.

So, we rediscover the gospel, and rediscover the Lord.

1. We reflect his *'journey downwards'*. As he constantly sought out new
    places and people where he had to be and become incarnate again, so we

in the inner city constantly seek new places where we must journey downwards to find places where incarnation is demanded.

2. We reflect his *'Blessed are the poor'*. This Jesus meant for his disciples. They are those who had become poor for the kingdom. Precisely this lifestyle of reversals is our experience and our joy.

3. We reflect his *'undistinguishing regard'*. Jesus welcomed all. But especially he welcomed bottom people, outsiders, foreigners, the unexpected. So we seek out those outside the conventional Christian folds, and encourage new forms of disciple groups or para-church arising around and for them.

Thus, is even a divided Britain challenged. But it cannot be challenged by churches which belong to only one side of the division — the top. We challenge it from the other side — the bottom. Through political groups, action groups, community organizations, mini-congregations, alternative lifestyles, through constant debate, through night fasts, through acted parables, through public statements, we seek to speak a contrary word in our monochrome political, social and economic world.

The message to the churches is that a recapitulation of some gospel marks becomes possible when the typical hopes and preoccupations of 'successful' churches are abandoned. The signs of the kingdom we have experienced can take place in any church. If it can happen here, it can happen anywhere! It is the good news for churches everywhere that we rediscover the man of Nazareth and the possibility in the unlikeliest places of people gathered around him as his community and his prophets.

5. SIGNS FOR DISCIPLES

It is hard enough to suggest contrary signs for citizens and cities. To suggest them for churches produces bitterness, anger, and defensiveness. But to produce them for Christians and their lifestyles, in my experience, produces near hysteria. I tried it in June 1979 with 300 lay people at the Methodist Missionary Laymen's Conference at Swanwick. I asked those present to indicate the jobs they did in relation to the Registrar General's six classifications of income groups. I then asked them to indicate which groups their parents belonged to. I asked them to indicate their present income, and the area and housing they lived in; then the same facts for their parents, when they were growing up.

Predictably, 95 per cent of them showed that their job classification, income and housing value had improved by two or three points over that of their parents. Even more significantly, the vast majority showed that they had grown up in cities or small-town working-class areas, but now lived in suburbs or small suburban towns. Many had moved from the north-west or the north-east to the west Midlands, the west or the south-east.

That is to say, Methodists tend to move from one side of the divided Britain to the other side in a single lifetime! Wherever the divide is placed — at jobs, at incomes, at housing, at areas, the position is the same. Moreover, on the line drawn between the Severn and the Wash, Methodists tend to start life north of it, and end life south of it! A recent survey shows only 7 per cent of those joining the Methodist Church are manual workers — though 68 per cent of the population. It is not my impression that the facts are different for any other denomination: I record merely the one I know best.

Can the inner city help?

Only, I think, by being a 'contrary sign' — perhaps even a thorn in the flesh. Because my experience is that many human, modest, small-scale, supportive things become necessary and thus possible in the inner city which are hardly necessary and thus not possible elsewhere.

But it will mean an about-turn for many Christians, and there is much evidence to suggest that most of us are not ready for it. I do not believe it is impossible, but it is a matter of turning back our history!

Nineteen centuries of triumphalist language and policy within the Christian churches mean that we are ill-equipped to lead the journey downwards. The Christian stories, images, paradigms have been so long employed in the service of extension, progress, development, aggrandizement and glorying in what is successful. It is a whole new ball-game to try to raise the question whether in fact some of our stories, images and paradigms ... are those of retraction, withdrawal, development, retreat and the glorying in what is failing.

The New Testament is a striking object lesson here. The people of the earliest Church were, in the main, people either from Galilee, a mixed, cosmopolitan but not notably upper-crust part of Palestine, or else from cultures on the edges of Jewish or pagan orthodoxy. What attracted them to the third estate of Christianity was that it represented a way by which, uniquely in its time, nobodies could become somebodies, and people near the bottom could become people who at least in the community of the church could become 'kings and priests, heirs and joint heirs'.

The call to conversion

Jim Wallis

From the outset, the life of the Christian community is dependent upon the coming of the Holy Spirit. Here again, the connection between the anointing and the carrying out of God's purposes is crucial. Just as the baptism of Jesus identified him as the one with whom God was pleased and whom God would use, so the baptism of the Spirit at Pentecost identifies the church as the community beloved of God and created by the Holy Spirit for the purposes of Christ in the world. Such a life means that believers are bound together as never before. They are brothers and sisters in the family of God and have become united in a deep love and a common task. The vocation of God's suffering servant had been embodied perfectly in one life, but now that same vocation can be seen, with the same authority, in the body of Christ as its members experience the gifts of God's Spirit.

The vocation and the very identity of the Christian community, therefore, are directly in line with Isaiah's description of the suffering servant. The same servant posture and style we saw in Isaiah and witnessed in Jesus characterizes the believing community. We are a people drawn into relationship to the Lord for the sake of God's purposes in history. The body of Christ has been anointed and empowered for God's mission to bring justice and reconciliation. The followers of Jesus, after his example, will lay down their lives for the kingdom; their life together will be laid down for the sake of the world. The coming of the Spirit at Pentecost resulted in a bold proclamation of the gospel, the repentance of thousands, and the establishment of a common life among the believers. But the anointing of the Spirit is not just for our own religious experience; it is for the intentions of God in the world. The Spirit is the sign and seal of the Church's vocation as a suffering servant. The question always before the anointed community is where and how to give its life in service of a broken world.

Community is the great assumption of the New Testament. From the calling of the disciples to the inauguration of the church at Pentecost, the gospel of the kingdom drives the believers to community. The new order becomes real in the context of a shared life. Throughout the book of Acts and in the epistles, the Church is presented as a community. The community life of the first Christians attracted many to their fellowship.

The preaching of the gospel is intended to create a new family in which those alienated from one another are now made brothers and sisters in Jesus Christ. 'There is neither Jew nor Greek, there is neither slave nor free, there is neither male nor female; for you are all one in Jesus Christ' (Galatians 3:28). The existence of the church itself, that inclusive community which knows no human boundaries, becomes a part of the good news.

When we understand that community is the form of the Church's life in the New Testament, the letters of Paul take on a clearer meaning than ever before. Reading them in the context of Christian community illuminates their message. That is not surprising when we realize their original purpose as pastoral letters to new communities. Paul was a theologian of community. His central ministry was the apostolic task of forming and nurturing new communities. Paul hoped his preaching would create new communities; he often stayed with these embryonic fellowships until they were on a solid basis; and he corresponded with them for years afterward, offering sound teaching and practical assistance in working out their life together. The love of Paul for these little growing fellowships is evident throughout his writing. The preaching of the gospel produced neither a new school of thought nor a new political party; the legacy of Jesus was a new people sharing a new life together. Different from an institution or an organization, the church would have the style and the feel of a family, an extended family created not by blood but by the Spirit.

Paul presents us with the cosmic sweep and meaning of community. In Ephesians he says 'the mystery of Christ ... hidden for ages' is now being revealed. The mystery is that Jews and Gentiles are to be united in one body in Jesus Christ. The dividing wall has been broken, the former hostility has come to an end, and a new humanity has been created in Christ Jesus. In Ephesians 2:13–22, Paul describes this new community in a way that reveals the power of God in Jesus Christ. But that is not all. Paul goes on to describe the community of believers in terms of God's plan for the world. The unity and reconciled fellowship of the new community is 'to make all men see what is the plan of the mystery hidden for ages in God who created all things — that through the church the manifold wisdom of God might be made known to the principalities and powers in the heavenly places' (Ephesians 3:9–10).

The testimony of such a community is living proof that the oppressive and divisive facts of the world system need no longer hold sway and determine the course of men and women. The whole of God's creation will someday be brought into community in Christ (Colossians 1:15–20). The community of the Church is the beginning of that great reconciliation, the sign and first fruit of God's cosmic purposes in Christ. The Church is an integral part of God's plan to reconcile all things. Through its ministry of reconciliation, the Christian community becomes both an instrument and a foretaste of God's purposes for the world. Paul describes the power of this reconciling force in his second letter to the Corinthians (5:16–20) . . . .

Therefore, those who would limit Jesus to the saving of souls and those who see him merely as introducing new ethical principles are both wrong. The purpose of God in Christ is neither simply to redeem individuals nor merely to teach the world some new thoughts. God's purpose in Christ is to establish a new community that points to the plan of God for the world. Forming community has been the social strategy of the Spirit since Pentecost.[1] Community is the basis of all Christian living. It is both the lifestyle and the vocation of the Church. The living witness of the Christian community is intended both to demonstrate and to anticipate the future of the world that has arrived in the person of Jesus Christ.

Conversion, then, has everything to do with community. A good test of any theology of conversion is the kind of community it creates. In the biblical descriptions, conversion is from one community to another, or from no community to community. Especially in an age of individualism and personal isolation, community becomes central to any idea of conversion. Evangelism can no longer mean simply taking people out of the world, running them through a process of conversion, and then placing them back in the same world and somehow expecting them to survive. If conversion is the translation of persons from one world to another, from one community to another, then conversion to Christ requires a new environment in which it is more possible to live a Christian life.

Nor is community simply a collection of the already converted. Community is the place where we lay ourselves open to genuine conversion. It is the corporate environment that preserves and nurtures the ongoing process of conversion. Once we have set our feet on a new road, community is what helps us along the way. In community we begin to unlearn the old patterns and to learn what the kingdom is all about. In relationship to one another, we understand more deeply the message of the gospel, and our relationships reinforce our ability to be faithful to it. The community of faith enables us to resist the pressures of our culture and to genuinely proclaim something new in its midst. Community is never withdrawn from the world, because its biblical purpose is to make Jesus Christ visible in the world.

Community is the arena in which the struggle for a faithful church will first take place. Community, therefore, does not exist for itself nor as an alternative church. Christian community is for the church. It is the battleground of the movement from captivity to renewal, from conformity to transformation. Community, then, is a living sacrament for the church. The historical issues confronting us will be first joined in communities of faith. Community can be the demonstration and the incarnation of a new word of renewal preached to the churches. As a result, community will be a place of struggle, conflict, pain, and anguish as we wage the battle with the false values around us and within us. It is where our personal and corporate sin is first revealed.

But community can also be a place of new freedom, of deep healing, of great love and joy as the power of conversion is experienced. Community helps us to grow, and it helps us to convert. We are enabled to turn from our cultural myths and illusions, and we are pointed toward the reality of the kingdom of God. Community is a place to grow in truth, wholeness, and holiness. The only way to propagate a message is to live it. That is why there can be no conversion without community. Community makes conversion historically visible.

The principal cause of the church's accommodation to the values and spirit of our age is the fragmentation of our common life. We are easy prey, because we are rootless and confused. In many places in the world today, the church suffers from brutal persecution. But in the United States our chief enemy is not persecution. It is seduction. We are a people seduced by a way of thinking, a way of living, that is irreconcilable with the lordship of Christ.

When I visit with Christians in local churches, I sometimes ask them, 'What is the most important social reality of your life? What place, what group of people do you feel most dependent upon for your survival?' Very seldom have people responded by pointing to their local church, their community of faith. Instead, their answer is their workplace or some other economic, educational, or political institution. People usually name something associated with economic livelihood, personal advancement, or social influence.

If in fact most Christians are more rooted in the principalities and powers of this world than they are in the local community of faith, it is no wonder that the church is in trouble. Clearly, the social reality in which we feel most rooted will be the one that will most determine our values, our priorities, and the way we live. It is not enough to talk of Christian fellowship while our security is based elsewhere. We will continue to conform to the values and institutions of our society as long as our security is grounded in them.

We need to know where our securities lie because they can and will be used against us, even as we begin to enter deeply into Christ's community. Our securities will be used to intimidate and control us, to rob us of our freedom in Christ. Just when we begin to respond to God's calling, we often move out into insecure places; this is when the powers of this world reach out, hook us, and reel us back into their circle of control. Where they hook us is at the point of our deepest insecurities. We are attacked in the places where we are most vulnerable and most easily controlled by the rewards, threats, and punishments of the system.

The only alternative is to create a faith community that generates a faith strong enough to enable us to survive as Christians. This strength is important at two points: in helping us to disengage from the securities of the old order and, at the same time, in empowering us to be actively engaged in the world as witnesses to the new order in Christ. Community is the place where the healing of our own lives becomes the foundation for the healing of the nations. The making of community is finally the only thing strong enough to resist the power of the system and to provide an adequate spiritual foundation for better and more human ways to live.

At a minimum, the Church should be known as the kind of community that makes it more possible, not less possible, to follow Jesus. But this is not always the case in today's churches. A New Testament scholar once told me, 'I have a hard time teaching my subject because, when I get to the idea of the community of faith, there is little I can point to today to show my students what it means. There's no problem, of course, describing what it meant back then. But I don't know how I can help them to understand when there are few examples I can point to now.' The statement is enough to make one more than sad; it should make one angry — angry at the control the system has over the church's life today. There is reason to be angry about a system that crushes poor people and defines whole populations as expendable in a nuclear exchange. And there is justification for anger at the ways the system has crippled and co-opted the faith of the churches. But the target of that anger is misdirected if it is aimed at the people who are trapped.

Jesus was full of anger when he entered the temple and thoroughly disrupted the business of the day. But he was more angry at what the people were doing than at the people themselves. He was angry at how the economic system was making a sacrilege of religion in the temple. Are we angry at the way the economic system has made a sacrilege of faith in the local church? The deeper our identification with the church, the angrier we ought to be. However, we must get beyond an adversary relationship with the people. The powers that be must take great pleasure in the way we constantly fight each other. We have to get beyond the spirit of accusation.

Those who have experience in pastoral counseling know what it means to be involved with persons who have lost all vision for their lives. The pastor's task is to hold before those people the vision of their wholeness and healing until they can grasp it and claim it as their own. So it is with the church. The church has lost any vision for its life together. Without that vision, the people are perishing. The vocation of those committed to rebuilding the church must therefore be to hold forth the vision of a renewed people, the vision of healing and wholeness. This is the role of conversion. Conversion begins by calling the church to repentance, by calling God's people back to a new understanding of who they are and to whom they belong as God's people. To hate the church for its failures is like a pastor hating the person who needs healing. Only those who have come to feel a genuine love for the church will be able to confront it with its own faithlessness and call it back to its true vocation.

I am often asked if I believe that real Christian community is possible in the established denominational churches. The question reminds me of what Mark Twain once said when asked if he believed in infant baptism. Twain replied, 'Believe in it? Hell, I've seen it!' That's my answer to the question about the established churches. I've seen Christian community take root and grow in these churches. Many people in the institutional churches admire these noble ventures into community but consider them irrelevant to their own or other local churches. The church has a tendency to put radical communities up on some inspirational pedestal, something to point at but not to imitate. Catholic Worker founder Dorothy Day once spoke to the danger of being admired into irrelevance. She said, 'Don't call me a saint. I don't want to be written off that easily.'

There was a time when I almost regarded alternative communities as the 'real church' and the institutional churches as the 'apostate church'. I don't do that any more, for a number of reasons. First, I have discovered that most of the problems that exist in the church also exist in my community and in my own life. Sojourners community is a microcosm of the problems that are faced in the larger church's life. We are full of this world, full of this culture, and we are in a slow process of being converted. Increasingly, we are able to identify not just with the strength of the church but also with its many weak and broken places.

Second, most of the churches today began their tradition by deciding to split off from the 'apostate' church and become the 'real' church. The cycle goes on and on, creating more versions of the apostate church. Personally, I am not of a mind to create new denominations and new divisions in the church's life. I am more anxious to speak of a new vision for the church, realizing that this new vision is in fact two thousand years old and, in most cases, is a vision that exists somewhere in the theological tradition of most churches. The task is to point these churches to the seeds of renewal in the Bible and in their own traditions. In most of the churches where renewal is taking place, there is a fresh emphasis on Bible study. The Bible is coming alive again as congregations reflect on their own experiences and relate the biblical word to their present historical situation. When the Bible is used simply to affirm and sanctify the present order of things, it is emptied of its power. But studying the Bible in a way that calls present realities into question will uncover its tremendous power to heal us and to change the world. The biblical word creates in us both the need for conversion and the hope of conversion.

Many of us tend to underestimate the hunger in the churches for something different, some new vision and focus and power. I often sense in the churches an underlying uneasiness about feeling so at home in this culture. There are people scattered throughout the churches who sense that their commitment to Jesus Christ ought to mean more than it does. There is a desire and a fragile hope for something new. In spite of all we have said about the American captivity of the churches, an integrity of faith remains in the church's life. In most churches I have visited, a small flame flickers that invites rekindling. As a result, I'm not ready to give up on the churches, and I'm certainly not willing to give up on the gospel.

Finding a new way of life for the churches, a new shape for our corporate existence, is finally a question of pastoral leadership. If the fullness of the gospel is to be preached and lived in the churches, the responsibility for this begins with our pastors. The pastoral vocation is to testify to what we know of the gospel. We cannot suppress the gospel in response to some mistaken notion of 'being sensitive' to the needs of our church members. When for any reason we fail to preach and to live the gospel in its wholeness, we fail not only our prophetic calling but our pastoral calling. To fail to lift up Jesus in the midst of our congregations and in the midst of our history is a failure of love — a failure to love one another and to love the church. Ultimately, of course, it is a failure to love God deeply and to trust God's deep love for us.

The prophets of the Bible spoke the hard word to a captive people. They were angry at the people's infidelity. They spoke the Word from the Lord, and often the people didn't want to hear it. But when the prophets spoke, they spoke with broken hearts, because they knew the people, loved them, identified with them, and held them as their own. Undergirding the prophetic rebukes was the vision for the faithful life of the people of God. The prophets didn't speak from arrogance, pride, bitterness, or despair. They spoke from love and hope for the people. Hope is ultimately rooted in love. So our hope for the church must be rooted in our love for the church. And love is the great enemy of fear. So our love for the church must overcome our fear of being the church, our hesitancy to preach God's word and to give visible demonstration of God's vision for the community of faith.

In Sojourners community, we are still learning what it means to love. God has taught us much, softening our hearts and expanding our capacity to love one another and the whole of God's creation. The process is always one of conversion. The 'turning to' part of conversion has enabled God's love to deepen among us in some exciting ways. But the 'turning from' part of conversion has never been easy. In the early days of our community, the conversion taking place among us was especially painful. We learned that all our models and schemes for community had to die before God's creative work among us could begin. Our plans and pride over what we could build with our own strength and resources had to be shattered before the Spirit had any room to work. And we had to learn that the necessary building materials of Christian community include two characteristics of love: forgiveness and a humble spirit. Being human, we could not avoid conflict and hurting one another. It took us a while to realize that we were utterly dependent on God's forgiveness in our corporate life. Learning to forgive one another, and to know our own need for forgiveness, were early lessons that tested the survival of the community. We also had to get over any notion of being perfect people building the perfect community, which could then take on all the big issues of the church and the world. The big issues overwhelmed us, because we forgot to tend to the simplest things, like learning to love and serve one another in our imperfection. The lesson here is a basic one: The church will never discover what it means to lay down its life for the world until its members begin to lay down their lives for one another. An authentic public witness requires an authentic community existence. The love, care, justice, and peace we desire in the world must also be practised among ourselves.

The first members of Sojourners community did not come to learn these things in a vacuum. The words of Scripture began to take on new meaning for us. Jesus said, 'A new commandment I give to you, that you love one another; even as I have loved you, that you also love one another. By this all will know that you are my disciples, if you have love for one another' (John 13:34–35). Jesus tells us to love each other, not simply *because* he loves us, but also *in the same way* that he loves us. We are to extend to one another the very same love that God has extended to us in Christ. We are told to love as we have been loved, to forgive as we have been forgiven, to share as we have been shared with, to sacrifice as we have been sacrificed for, to reconcile as we have been reconciled, and to make peace as peace has been made with us.

Conversion means a radical reorientation in terms of personal needs and ideas of personal fulfilment. When we enter community we bring with us an emptiness that seeks filling, but we also bring clear notions of what we think might fill that emptiness. We know our own needs best of all, and we are fairly sure about how they can be met. All of us, sooner or later, have to put aside the primacy of our own needs; we have to relinquish our narrow expectations of self-fulfilment and our agendas for self-assertion. Conversion is ultimately dying to self and becoming part of something that is larger than any of us. Community is the environment which can enable that conversion, and community is the fruit of that conversion. Our perspective changes from 'what can the community do for me?' to 'what can I do to best serve the community?'[2] The ramifications of this conversion are profound. The change affects us spiritually in terms of our identities, politically in terms of our loyalties, economically in terms of our securities, socially in terms of our commitments, and personally in terms of our vocations. Through it all, the most profound change is finally the most simple: discovering the meaning of love.

NOTES

1. A helpful discussion of community and its relationship to conversion, social change, and the overall plan of God for reconciliation can be found in *The Spirit and the World* (New York: Hawthorn Books, 1975) by James W. Jones, professor of religion at Rutgers College.
2. See Jean Vanier, *Community and Growth: Our Pilgrimage Together* (New York: Paulist Press, 1979), p. 5. 'A community is only a community when the majority of its members is making the transition from "the community for myself" to "myself for the community".'

Further reading

Geoffrey Ahern and Grace Davie, *Inner City God: The Nature of Belief in the Inner City* (London: Hodder and Stoughton, 1987). Drawing on empirical research into the variety of beliefs and implicit religions that are to be found in the inner city, the authors identify 'us' and 'them' attitudes towards the churches as the principal obstacle to churchgoing. They argue that secularization can be challenged in inner cities through effective use of the rites of passage, through better use of the mass media by the churches, and through the adoption of distinctive 'sectarian' styles of mission and discipleship.

Roland Allen, *Missionary Methods: Paul's or Ours?* (Grand Rapids, Michigan: Eerdmans, 1970). Allen's examination of the failures of modern missionary methods in the 1930s and his discovery of the missionary principles of self-reliance and inculturation which informed Paul's mission strategy was prophetic and ahead of its time. It is now recognized as a missiological classic of the greatest significance.

Trevor Beeson, *New Area Mission: The Parish in the New Housing Estate* (London: Mowbray, 1963). Well-written portrait of a new church in a new housing area whose clergy drew on the rich liturgical, theological and socio-logical resources of the liberal Catholic tradition in constructing a diverse and multi-faceted approach to the ministry and mission of the parish on a large public housing estate in the North East of England.

David Bosch, *Transforming Mission: Paradigm Shifts in the Theology of Mission* (Maryknoll, NY: Orbis Books, 1991). Ground-breaking and masterful survey of the theology of mission which presents a holistic missiological paradigm for a postmodern world.

David Cockerell, *Beginning Where We Are: A Theology of Parish Ministry* (London: SCM Press, 1989). Down-to-earth study of mission in the urban church which argues for radical contextualization of ministry and mission in relation to the needs and aspirations of local communities.

Jeffrey Cox, *The English Churches in a Secular Society: Lambeth 1870–1930* (Oxford: Oxford University Press, 1982). Fine socio-historical study of the ministry and mission of the churches during a crucial period of urbanization in South London which identifies the most successful churches as those with the greatest range of social activity, and with a strong sense of religious tradition, whether Catholic or Evangelical.

David Donnison, *Act Local: Social Justice from the Bottom Up* (London: Institute for Public Policy Research, 1994). The vision of socal justice and social renewal at street level which this paper presents is not only a model for community development and service delivery in urban regeneration but also a model for the church's ministry and mission in urban priority areas.

David F. Ford, 'Transformation', in Peter Sedgwick (ed.), *God in the City* (London: Mowbray, 1995). pp. 199–209. The dynamic of Christian mission in the inner city is the dynamic of Christian community wherein urban Christians affirm their shared dignity as the children of God, and encourage one another in the stresses and coping strategies of urban reality and in efforts to transform that reality into face-to-face community: 'there is a special promise from God attached to the creation of community around the weak, marginalized and those not valued by society'. 'It is not about exclusive boundaries but about getting the centre right: Jesus Christ crucified, and the good news for the poor, the broken-hearted and the oppressed. The open boundaries are created by the sorts of communication that this message generates.'

Robin Gill, *Beyond Decline: A Challenge to the Churches* (London: SCM Press, 1988). Explores the insights of the church growth movement and their relevance to structural reform, clergy deployment and evangelistic strategy in the Church of England.

Timothy Gorringe, *Alan Ecclestone: Priest as Revolutionary* (Sheffield: Cairns Publications, 1994). Engaging account of the life of one of Britain's foremost urban parish priests whose life and ministry were characterized by a passionate engagement with local politics and with the spiritual quest.

Michael Green, *Evangelism in the Early Church* (London: Hodder and Stoughton, 1970). A significant work of historical reconstruction from a well-known Anglican evangelist which succeeds in communicating the excitement of Paul's evangelistic project, and the principal reasons for his success.

Margaret Hebblethwaite, *Basic is Beautiful* (London: HarperCollins, 1994). A theological and empirical investigation of the meaning and significance of Basic Christian Communities as the distinctive mode of being church in the cities of the late twentieth century, including examples from Latin America, North America and Britain.

Trevor Lockwood, *The Church on the Housing Estate: Mission and Ministry on the Urban Estate* (London: Methodist Church Home Mission, 1993). A passionate account drawn from twenty years of experience of ministry on public housing estates which emphasizes the local, ecumenical and collaborative character of effective mission and ministry in these areas.

Mervyn Stockwood, *Chanctonbury Ring: An Autobiography* (London: Hodder and Stoughton, 1982). Wonderful description of his extensive and pioneering parish ministry in the East End of Bristol, and his later engagement as Bishop with the ferment of ideas and experiments in urban ministry in the Diocese of Southwark.

Benjamin Tonna, *A Gospel for the Cities: A Socio-Theology of Urban Ministry* (Maryknoll, NY: Orbis Books, 1985). Comprehensive study of the mission of the church in the city which is both sociologically rich and replete with examples of the mission of the churches in the cities of the non-Western world.

12

Faiths in the city

A second time the word of the Lord came to Jonah: 'Go to the great city of Nineveh; go and denounce it in the words I give you.' Jonah obeyed and went at once to Nineveh. It was a vast city, three days' journey across, and Jonah began by going a day's journey into it. Then he proclaimed: 'In forty days Nineveh will be overthrown!'

The people of Nineveh took to heart this warning from God; they declared a public fast, and high and low alike put on sackcloth. When the news reached the king of Nineveh he rose from his throne, laid aside his robes of state, covered himself with sackcloth, and sat in ashes.

When God saw what they did and how they gave up their wicked ways, he relented and did not inflict on them the punishment he had threatened.

This greatly displeased Jonah. 'It is just as I feared, Lord, when I was still in my own country, and it was to forestall this that I tried to escape to Tarshish. I knew that you are a gracious and compassionate God, long-suffering, ever constant, always ready to relent and not inflict punishment. Now take away my life, Lord: I should be better dead than alive.' 'Are you right to be angry?' said the Lord.

(Jonah 3:1–6, 10; 4:1–4)

Faith in the City

There are places where Christian service to the community may take the form of helping others to maintain their religious and cultural heritage in freedom and dignity. Many Christians have found that such service, though apparently incompatible with traditional styles of evangelism, in fact represents a faithful and sometimes compelling witness to Christ. For Christ came to serve amid the complex realities of his own time and is still glorified by the service of those who take seriously the religious quest and the religious inheritance of those around them. This task may require a generous approach to the use of church resources. ... We have been told that it is the withholding of these resources which has often been most resented and has robbed the Church of credibility in the eyes of members of other faiths. It is the offering of them which is often the most eloquent and valuable gift we can make. (3.28)

Introduction

When I moved to South Manchester in the summer of 1980 to be curate of a parish close to Moss Side I remember touring the area with the Rural Dean David Bonser and asking him if there had been any riots there. A few weeks later the most sustained and destructive riots Manchester had ever seen began. Since then riots have erupted periodically in every inner city area in Britain with significant ethnic minorities, from Brixton in 1981 to Tyneside in 1992. Curiously, *Faith in the City*, the report of a commission established partly in the wake of rioting across a swathe of inner-city Britain in 1981, devoted little space to a considera-tion of the ethnic issues (Pityana). And yet a map of the urban priority areas of Britain's cities, identified by the multiplicity of their social problems, also provides a reasonably accurate guide to those areas where the largest proportion of ethnic minorities in Britain currently reside.

British cities, like many cities across the world, are marred by ethnic conflict and racism. Verbal and physical abuse at school, violence on the street, harass-ment in the corner shop or through the letter-box, racist graffiti, name-calling and intimidation by neighbours, discrimination by landlords and employers, all are manifestations of a culture of racism which the social changes of the 1980s exacerbated. Discriminatory changes in immigration law — changes which were often accompanied by racist remarks by prominent politicians, such as Margaret Thatcher and Norman Tebbit, and which make it difficult for West Indian or Asian family members to join their parents or children here while white South African and Zimbabwean exiles have no difficulty emigrating to Britain — provide an official legitimation of racism on the streets (**Leech**). The demise of public investment in social housing, and the decline of manufacturing jobs in the 1980s, enhanced pre-existing ethnic tensions in inner city areas in relation to housing and jobs.

A significant minority of social commentators including politicians, journalists and some academics have argued consistently that the confluence of social and ethnic problems in Britain's inner cities is not the result of explicit malevolence by the white population of Britain but the simple consequence of allowing so many people from Britain's former Empire to settle in the 'mother' country. They contend that conflict between people of different ethnic origin is inevitable because people are fundamentally tribal, loyal to their own group, defensive of their own territory against aliens and migrants. Other commentators argue that there is no inevitability to ethnic conflict, that children only learn to discriminate between children of colour and white children from their parents, that British identity itself is a multi-ethnic identity incorporating a series of immigrant cultures including Celtic, Scandinavian, Norman, Jewish, and more recently Afro-Caribbean and Indian.

Theologians might agree that tribalism is a fundamental feature of the sinful human condition but they would also point to those significant parts of the Christian and Jewish scriptures which not only forbid maltreatment of foreign-ers, but contend that since God's people are themselves migrants in this world they should positively embrace the stranger as an exemplar of their own identity and calling (**Leech**). This theme is very strong in the New Testament from the story of the journey of the magi who come to worship the Christ child to the conversion of the Ethiopian and the dramatic abolition of ethnic barriers in the early Christian Church which though it began as a Jewish movement soon became more Gentile than Jewish. It is an even stronger theme in the Old Testament despite the incipient or explicit tribalism of many Old Testament stories and texts. The story of Ruth testifies to the openness of Israel to the peoples and faiths of other nations where these faiths did not conflict with their own moral codes. The books of Deuteronomy and Leviticus include many legal injunctions to care for the stranger and the sojourner, while in Genesis Abraham entertains angels unaware, exercising that natural hospitality to the traveller which is still expressed by many Arab and Persian communities today.

The story of Jonah is one of the most powerful exemplars of the increasing openness of the later Hebrew prophets to non-Jewish peoples and cultures, a feature no doubt of their own experience of exile and enforced migration. It is the story of a reluctant, even malevolent, and certainly racist, missionary who at every stage in the narrative shows less reverence and less faith in God than his non-Jewish neighbours, whether the pagan sailors or the people of Nineveh themselves. After preaching to the wicked city of Nineveh he sits outside the city hoping God will visit his wrath on its people whereas inside the city the people from the lowest to the highest respond to his preaching with outward and inward repentance. God responds not with judgement as Jonah hoped but with grace and salvation. The narrative structure of this short book gives powerful emphasis to the contrast between a judgemental prophet who can find no good in a pagan city and a gracious God whose will is to save all people who show signs of repentance and seek after goodness. The tribal God of the Fathers is in this story completely absent. Instead, we see a God of love who sees no boundaries to love where his own people and prophets would set up boundaries, whose will is not to judge but to save even the most pagan of cities (Cracknell and Lamb).

The story of Jonah finds an interesting echo in the remarkable story of the revival of religion amongst ethnic minorities in Britain's inner cities, a revival which has taken place even as the mainstream churches have struggled to sustain a remnant of viable inner city congregations and church buildings in many areas (Smith). Many Asians, and a small if growing number of mostly young Afro-Caribbeans, find hope and confidence in their identity through their embrace of the radical missionary style of Islam or Da'wah, which has grown in prayer houses and mosques in the inner cities throughout Britain, as in communities of Diaspora Muslims throughout the world in the last thirty years. Islam, with its communal and embodied style of worship and its strong tradition of education in the faith and language of the Quran, seems to provide a bulwark against the tides of secularism which have swept through the cities of Britain in the twentieth century.

Strong groups of active 'believing Asians' are to be found in every inner city area in Britain today. At the same time, many Asians, particularly from Hindu and Sikh backgrounds, have mobilized elements in their own culture and family structures in such a way as to enable social and economic advancement in spite of racial discrimination and the deprivation of inner city areas. 'Achieving Asians' embrace the value of education and of hard work and show the way out of the morass of downward social mobility which is affecting their white neighbours in the post-industrial and privatized cities of the late twentieth century (Modood). The achievement of Asian social advancement in the context of racial discrimination, though by no means universal, none the less indicates the complexity of the ethnic situation in contemporary Britain which simplistic accounts of racial dualism adopted by many anti-racists cannot explain (Modood). Similarly, the mobilization of religion and tradition by ethnic minorities in successfully resisting both secularism and racism indicate that white Christians and white atheists, especially in inner city areas, may have much to learn from their non-white neighbours about God and the ways of the world, just as Jonah learnt more about the nature of God from the people of Nineveh than he had from reading his own scriptures (**Pityana**).

White British Christians, like Jonah, are often unwilling to welcome their non-white neighbours into their churches, seeing them primarily as alien, and hence pagan, peoples, rather than, as many of them were, fellow Anglicans, Methodists and Presbyterians raised in the mission churches which had been planted by British missionaries in every corner of the Empire (**Pityana**). In consequence, many black and Asian Christians formed their own churches. The growing rather than the declining churches in many UPA areas are black-led or Asian churches, many of them having informal or formal links with African or Caribbean independent churches, with Pentecostal churches in Asia or the Caribbean, or with indigenous Asian churches such as the Mar Thoma church (Marchant).

These new religious communities are characterized by exuberant praise, by faithful committed worship, and by a profound affirmation of ethnic identity and solidarity. Their worship is characterized by informality and biblical preaching, they form close-knit communities of mutual support and care (Kerridge). They also manifest a significant pride in their cultural identity which many see as the way through and beyond ethnic conflict to a mutual confidence amongst all ethnic groups in their own ethnicity, a confidence from which bridges can then be built to welcome the difference of other cultures and traditions (**Pityana**).

The prevalence of racist beliefs and behaviour amongst communities suffering for generations from economic and cultural oppression, most notably in the East End of London, indicates that insecurity and lack of confidence amongst unemployed or poor working-class people are instrumental in the adoption of racist beliefs, though racist attitudes are also fairly prevalent amongst the 'comfortable' (**Leech; Carnelly**). The racist statements or speeches of politicians from Oswald Moseley in the 1930s to Norman Tebbit in the 1980s will often seek to mobilize such insecurities in efforts to stir up racism for political ends. In the light of these insecurities, the melting-pot approach of cultural assimilation is a positively unhelpful strategy for countering racism. Instead, each ethnic or people group — black, Asian, white, working class or unemployed — needs to recover a sense of its own particular identity and giftedness in order that members of the different people groups can, from a new sense of confidence, embrace the difference of other cultures and people groups (Modood). New ethnic religious groups may thus have a vital part to play in countering racism, and fostering a new collective confidence and communal self-respect despite the deprivation which in many ways they share with their white neighbours.

Ethnic religious practice in inner city areas is a significant source of concerted action in the civil and social realms as people inspired by their respective faith traditions co-operate in a common struggle against discrimination, violence, criminality, and against the systemic roots of social and economic deprivation (Haslam). Different religious traditions agree on many of the fundamental moral values including respect for persons, and especially the vulnerable, the preserving of family life, the acceptance of responsibility for one's actions: not least in fathering children, compassion for the poor and love for children, obedience to legal authority, the avoidance of violence, and care for the environment. Ethnic minorities perhaps more than mainstream white Christians are aware of the determinative links between religion, moral values and social cohesion. It is notable, for example, that Asian intellectuals are now some of the strongest supporters of the establishment of the Church of England as a symbolic bulwark against secularism and atheist religious intolerance which is often also a veiled form of racial discrimination (Modood), even though Leech and others argue that the links of the Church of England with the British state involve it also in reinforcing cultural nationalism and racism (**Leech**). It is also notable that the recent growth of broad-based community organizing in inner-city Britain has taken place on multi-faith lines, drawing the different faith communities together in a common struggle to rebuild the weakened sinews of civil society and to resist the twin tides of criminality and official neglect which blight so many inner-city communities.

The strength of ethnic minority religions — black or Asian Christian, Muslim, Hindu, Sikh — in inner-city areas is a reminder to the churches in Britain's cities that religion may thrive in Urban Priority Areas, and can make a real difference to the culture of these areas by providing hope and confidence where the wider society has denied both (**Smith**). Again, as in the story of Nineveh, Christians in comfortable Britain may need to look to the vibrant ethnic religious communities of the inner city for exemplars of faithfulness in the face of triumphant secularism, and of spiritualities which still find ultimate meaning in divine worship and praise rather than in the rampant consumerism which dominates mainstream popular culture, and whose shadowside is the growth of real poverty, crime, violence and homelessness in Britain's inner cities (**Smith**).

Prophecy, race and Eastenders: ministry on the Isle of Dogs and celebrating the difference

Elizabeth Carnelley

What does it mean to stand in the prophetic tradition today? The experience of the churches on the Isle of Dogs over the past 12 months, since the by-election of a British National Party candidate in September 1993, has been that it can mean being rejected and vilified by some people while standing in solidarity with others.

Rosemary Radford Ruether has written that the liberation theologian and the prophet 'speak a judgmental word of God against the sins of the community in order to call it back to ... the faith of the covenant'.[1] This brings the prophet into conflict with those who represent the establishment: 'Established religion sees religious faith as the sacred ideology of the dominant social order ... [but prophetic faith] sets God in tension ... as advocate of the poor and oppressed.'[2] Those among the white community sympathetic to the BNP protested to the church leaders at a large meeting 'you should be representing us ... not Asians'. A BNP leaflet reporting this meeting quoted Nick Holtam, Vicar of Christchurch on the Isle of Dogs, as saying that he was 'working for God, not the community'.[3] Members of the white community were shocked and angry that the churches on the Island[4] did not legitimate their views that Bangladeshi people had 'invaded the Island', 'taken the best housing' and 'should be repatriated',[5] but that the church was presenting the gospel. 'Don't quote the Bible at us', they argued at the meeting. For them the church should represent the established social order and the secure place of Islanders — the indigenous white community — and not the Bangladeshi minority. It is true that many of the whites on the Isle of Dogs are themselves the victims of poverty and, as far as Britain as a whole is [concerned], are certainly deprived, in terms of health, housing, and employment, for example. None the less in the context of this community they are better off than the ethnic minorities who live on the Island.[6] Further, many of the key BNP supporters here are householders who have done fairly well for themselves and want to keep a secure grip on the achievements they have made. Therefore in this context they represent to an extent the establishment, even though they were themselves fighting 'the establishment' — the three-tier system of government: the Conservative Government, the Liberal Council (the Borough of Tower Hamlets), and the local Neighbourhood (the Liberals divided Tower Hamlets into seven Neighbourhoods) which is Labour-controlled.

The churches were in a difficult position. They wanted to convey a clear message to the local community that the politics of racism and violence that the BNP represented were no answer to the needs of our community, and that the policies of the BNP (such as repatriation of all non-whites, and a promise if elected to give no funding to any non-British [non-white] groups) were contrary to the gospel. At the same time they wanted to represent the real concerns and needs of the community: the lack of decent and affordable housing; the shortage of school places; the poor health provisions, and so on, which had made this such a fertile ground for racist groups to sow seeds of discontent and racial division. Feeling powerless, in competition for scarce resources, frustrated and angry, many people made a protest vote for the BNP in September 1993. Moreover, there were others happy to scapegoat the Bangladeshi community, whites who viewed those of colour around them with fear, mistrust and bigotry. Although most of the activists who swarmed on to the Island on Saturdays to leaflet and canvass were not local, there were key members of the local community who were happy to ally themselves with the BNP. Thus in the September election the BNP won, by the narrowest of margins — seven votes.

A group of people drawn from the churches on the Island (RC, URC, Baptist and Anglican) met together monthly to respond to the election result and to try and see a way forward. There was a feeling of fear and uncertainty; racial attacks were increasing and there were a couple of horrific assaults on Asian boys in the locality. The election of all three seats on the Island was due in eight months and if the BNP achieved a similar vote then, they would win control of the Isle of Dogs Neighbourhood and a £23 million budget.

A support worker was employed for three days a week to work on behalf of the churches, supporting and enabling their work. She began before we had secured funding and we set out in faith! The work was at many different levels, and Sue Mayo's skills were used in very different ways: they ranged from arranging story-writing sessions in local schools; having lunch and making links with the Island Women's Group; dealing with Radio 4, the BBC, Sky News and the multifarious media circus which invaded for six months; and arranging for literature on how to vote to be translated into several languages; to answering the phone in the parish office.

First it was vital to try to build bridges in the community. This was begun in small but significant ways: meeting and making links with some local Bangladeshi groups (there is a diversity of groups and organizations — they are not a unity), and organizing two multicultural events — a New Year party, and a party with a story-teller to launch a collection of writing by adults and children about life on the Island. The links were informal as well as formal and meant that friendship and trust could grow and we could co-operate as time went on in specific ways around the election in May.

Second, we tried to alter the atmosphere of hatred and mistrust. The BNP had leafleted the area with misleading 'facts' about the area — saying for example that the number of Asians on the Island is now 40 per cent (in fact 20.9 per cent are non-white; of 18,551 people on the Isle of Dogs 1,957 are Bangladeshi: 10.5 per cent).[7] We liaised with other groups trying to disseminate accurate information like the Docklands Forum and the Institute of Community Studies, and we did a lot of work negotiating with the media and using local and national newspapers and TV to get our message across. Perhaps the most effective single thing was the Rainbow Ribbon Campaign. The Churches' Peace Group came up with the idea of distributing ribbons in rainbow colours for people to wear, and rainbow maps of the Island with the slogan 'celebrate the difference', as a symbol of celebration of the multicultural community, peace, and God's covenant with all people on the earth. This was in stark contrast to the BNP's view that this is a 'multi-racial hell' and that 'if we don't have this multi-racial society anywhere, there wouldn't be any problems' (sic).[8] 10,000 ribbons were distributed, and many of these were worn around the Island, given out to friends, and picked up in schools, in churches, community groups and doctors' surgeries. This was very effective in changing the feel of the Island to one of positive celebration and support for everyone in the community. The Rainbow Ribbon Campaign featured in BBC TV and ITV local news in London, local newspapers and local radio, as well as in the *Independent* and the *Sunday Times*.

Third, there were attempts to move things forward on the problematic question of a lack of affordable housing for rent. This meant careful study of Housing Law and negotiations with the London Docklands Development Corporation and the Neighbourhood as well as housing associations. This is a long slow process but at the time of writing (August 1994) it does seem as if there will be some new housing aimed particularly at the hidden homeless on the Isle of Dogs — families in overcrowded, damp or unsuitable accommodation. This of course would be a drop in the ocean and we feel as frustrated as those who voted BNP that it is government policies which have caused local people to feel that their fears and needs, which led some of them to seek answers in extremist policies, are not being heard, and there seems little sign of any change.

Fourth, we tried to deal specifically with issues around the election in May. We joined with other community groups to encourage voter registration, and to provide transport for polling day (intimidation at the September election prevented many people from leaving their homes to vote). We met with the police and arranged a meeting between Bangladeshi leaders and representatives of the mainstream parties who were standing to ensure a safe and fair election. Liberty and the Society of Black Lawyers provided a team of Observers at the election — the first time this has happened in the UK. A 67 per cent turnout was the result of a great deal of hard work on the part of the churches as well as the high media profile the Island received.

The result of the election brought a huge sense of relief and celebration: Labour won all three seats. However, we knew that we could not be complacent. The anger of those whose vote had won them nothing was expressed in verbal abuse of the church, graffiti all over the Island: 'Election Fix', 'Traitor Scum' (on the church door) and an assault on someone wearing a rainbow ribbon outside a pub. The number who voted BNP had actually increased — from 1,400 to 2,000. Labour's candidates received between 3,400 and 3,600 votes.[9]

Whilst the situation is still tense, with feelings bubbling under the surface, and BNP graffiti continuing to appear, the church has managed to maintain an ongoing relationship of conversations with both the BNP and the key members of the community who allied themselves with them, as well as members of the white community who, although they did not support the BNP, felt that they had a point and that the churches should not be 'involved with politics'. All of these three groups were represented in the church congregations on the Island. Interestingly some other local clergy also were critical of the firm stance the churches on the Island took. 'You'll alienate the whites', 'you'll get your fingers burned'. It was sometimes very frightening and we sometimes felt very isolated; faced with extreme verbal abuse, threatening phone messages on the parish office phone (which we took very seriously) and some difficult relationships with those members of the churches who felt very unsure or were even hostile about the stance the Churches' Group were taking. On both of the election days in May and September there was a prayer vigil at lunchtime for local people, and after the first a car full of BNP activists drove past shouting as people left the church. However, we did feel supported by the wider church; people wrote to say we were in their prayers, and we received support from our Bishops, from many Christian organizations, and from people of goodwill — emotional, practical and financial.

The climate has changed somewhat on the Island but the work remains the same. There are still needs which need to be addressed, and to rebuild the community which became so divided is a long slow struggle. The BNP are withdrawing only to regroup, and to find new targets, and must not be underestimated. It is imperative that the churches who worked together so closely do not lose their focus as the real work begins, and that they remain firm in the fight against those who seek to destabilize and undermine the community here.

The history of the Jewish people is full of those who were not afraid to criticize the dominant social order and to represent God as advocate of the poor and oppressed. One such was Amos who criticized those who 'trample the head of the poor into the dust of the earth, and turn aside the way of the afflicted' (Amos 2:7). The social problems on the Island are suffered most by the Bangladeshi minority who have higher unemployment, worse housing and so on than the white population on the Island, and are also the victims of racial attacks. The Limehouse Police Station report that racial attacks, two-thirds of which are whites on Asians, increased threefold between January 1993 and January 1994.[10] It is vital that the churches continue to support the ethnic minority groups here and do not allow groups like the BNP to gain a voice in local politics where they could further divide our community. The voices of prophets are still vitally needed as the poor continue to be trampled upon. Urban theology is a contextual theology and like liberation theologians, those trying to do theology in the city must be aware of the local context. As others have said, urban theology is not so much about focusing on specific issues but 'is a way of doing things in relation to our context'.[11] One strand of this is to stand alongside those who are victimized, the poor and the powerless. However, this is not necessarily straightforward in a particular context.

It is true that many white people who live on the Isle of Dogs are at the bottom of the pile themselves. This is not the clear-cut situation portrayed by some of the media. Unemployment is 26 per cent in the Isle of Dogs[12] and in Tower Hamlets the number of people in overcrowded housing is one in ten — twice the average for Inner London.[13] There are many complex factors involved. It is not simply bigotry about race which causes racism, but there are deep-rooted fears of difference which are to do with power and insecurity, dominance and tribalism, and the struggle to reach the top of the pile, which cause resentment of the Bangladeshi community, not only from some whites but also some members of the Afro-Caribbean community. There are real needs on the Island which must be addressed if things are going to change.

The command to love our neighbour has been the key for the Island churches in the fight against the far Right, and it is necessary both to condemn racist politics and to try to unite the community and also to work for the needs of all the people living on the Isle of Dogs. To stand in the prophetic tradition has meant for us, as Ruether said, speaking out against the sins of the community and standing with the poor; 'celebrating the difference' also means assessing complex situations and trying to make positive responses to the needs of the community in living out the Gospel.

NOTES

1. Rosemary Radford Ruether, 'Prophetic tradition and the liberation of women', *Feminist Theology* 5 (January 1994) (Sheffield Academic Press), 58.
2. Ruether, 'Prophetic tradition', p. 58.
3. *Island Patriot*, June 1994 (BNP, PO Box 300, Emma Street, Hackney, London E2).
4. It is almost literally an Island, surrounded by the river on three sides and docks across the top, and this focuses the feeling of being in a tight-knit community, and conversely of being very inward-looking.
5. The BNP's slogan was 'Rights for Whites' and clearly stated their views and still found much support.
6. *Once Upon a Time In Docklands: Facts and Figures in the 1990s* (London: Docklands Forum, 1994), p. 14.
7. In the 1991 census; quoted in *Once Upon a Time*, p. 7.
8. Derek Beackon, BNP councillor for Millwall, September 1993–May 1994, quoted in *Once Upon a Time*, p. 6.
9. These figures are rounded to the nearest 100.
10. *Once Upon a Time*, p. 21.
11. Paul Hackwood and Phil Shiner, 'New role for the Church in urban policy?', *Crucible* (July–Sept. 1994), 148.
12. *Once Upon a Time*, p. 14.
13. *Once Upon a Time*, p. 20.

Racism and the proclamation of the gospel

Kenneth Leech

In confronting racism with the prophetic word, we need to realize its own intrinsic power as an alternative world view and an alternative hope. At heart the racist mythology offers a different view of what it is to be human. Historically this mythology has been linked with alleged truths of natural science, in particular the 'truth' of superior and inferior racial types. Today, we have what has been called a 'new racism',[1] which does not use the concepts of superior and inferior but rather those of differences, of the nation as a racial unit, and of an unchanging 'human nature'.

In this way of thinking there are a number of recurring themes. The nation takes precedence over the human race: loyalty, devotion and responsibility can only be to the nation, not to humanity as a whole. The state of nationhood becomes the truly human state. But the sense of unity as a nation is only possible among people of a common racial stock. Thus the Northern Irish and the Falkland Islanders are part of the British nation in the sense that black people born here can never be. And throughout, there is a constant appeal to 'human nature'.

Thus Enoch Powell, speaking at Eastbourne in 1968, described the English as being 'dislodged' from their homeland, a process which he argued could not continue without resistance.

> My judgement then is this: the people of England will not endure it. If so, it is idle to argue whether they ought or ought not to. I do not believe it is in human nature that a country, and a country such as ours, should passively watch the transformation of whole areas which lie at the heart of it into alien territory.[2]

In later speeches, Powell spoke of 'operating with human nature as it is', rather than seeking to alter it.[3]

The theme of 'working with human nature as it is' is a common one among those who seek to defend racial nationalism. Thus Ivor Stanbrook said in a Commons debate: 'I believe that a preference for one's own race is as natural as a preference for one's own family. Therefore it is not racialism if by that one means, as I do, an active hostility to another race. It is simply human nature.'[4] Other writers have not been so concerned to avoid the word 'racialism'. Thus Andrew Alexander, writing in the *Daily Mail* in 1981: 'The time has come to make a stand in favour of racialism ... racism, racialism, racial discrimination — call it what you will ... means discerning real and substantial differences between the human races, and maybe their subdivisions too, and to act on the basis of that discernment.'[5]

This kind of language, and the view of 'human nature' which underlies it, are in fundamental conflict with traditional Christian theology. Biblical language contains no word for race in the modern sense: *ho genos ton anthropon* refers to the human race, as distinct from animals and plants. There is a solidarity and kinship among human beings by virtue of their humanity. Human beings are the offspring of God: *tou gar kai genos esmen* (Acts 17:28). This solidarity of all humankind in God is emphasized particularly within the Eastern Orthodox tradition as being a solidarity which is rooted in human nature as created. The contemporary Orthodox theologian John Meyendorff expresses the doctrine in this way: 'Man is truly man when he participates in God's life. This participation therefore is not a supernatural gift but the very core of man's nature.'[6] Human nature is thus fundamentally open to God and to the activity of grace. Orthodox theologians sometimes express this doctrine by saying that humanity as created is deiform, made in the image and likeness of God. In the West the fourteenth-century mystic Julian of Norwich expressed the same idea: 'our nature is wholly in God ... for our nature ... is joined to God in its creation'.[7] This openness to God is not something added to humanity at a later stage: it expresses what human beings are in their essential nature.

There is thus, according to Christian theology, a radical openness to God and to our sisters and brothers who share God's image. Human nature is not fixed and static, irredeemably narrow and tribal. It is open to change and transformation. 'You can't change human nature' is so profoundly anti-Christian that, if taken seriously, it would undermine the whole of Christian faith which is based on the assumption that human nature can be, and has been, changed. In racist doctrine, what matters most about human beings is their birth and ethnic origin: in Christian doctrine, what matters is that they are made in the divine image and shine with the divine light.

It is this image and glory which Christ in the incarnation both shared and further transformed, introducing a new phase in the divine–human relationship. Christian faith is rooted and grounded in the doctrine of the incarnation, the belief that in Christ God took human nature to himself, raising it up to share the divine nature. In Mascall's words:

> Human existence and human history can never be the same again since the moment when God the Son united human nature to himself in a union which will never be dissolved. It will be one of the tasks of the theology of the future to work out the implications of this amazing truth, for, apart from occasional adumbrations in such fathers as St Irenaeus, the theology of the past, especially in the west, has paid little attention to it.[8]

If we are to preach effectively against racism, we need to grasp the two basic truths of creation and incarnation, and their consequences for our view of human nature. It was orthodox Christology which formed the heart of the anti-Nazi movement in the churches. Bonhoeffer was writing his book on Christology at the very point at which Hitler came to power, and it was out of this book that the Confessing Church was to draw much of its material in the resistance to Nazism.

As racism offers an alternative view of human nature, so it offers an alternative view of human love, care and relationship. In Powell's view, a successful multiracial society is impossible. Such ideas of intrinsically limited human love and care are not new. They occur, for example, in Hume's *Treatise of Human Nature*. Altruism, Hume argues, is natural to humankind, but only within limits.[9] In recent New Right thinking we find the same idea. What we call racism is no more than a 'feeling of loyalty to people of one's own kind'.[10] As one journalist wrote: 'It's in our genes. It is part of every person's nature, black or white.'[11] The war in the Falkland Islands reinforced such notions of 'kith and kin'. The war was defended on the grounds that the inhabitants were 'our own people', genuinely British.

Those who hold such ideas of the impossibility of loving people beyond limited kinship boundaries have in recent years looked for scientific support in the new discipline of sociobiology. This is not to say that sociobiology is in itself racist, but that those who seek a scientific basis for their racist ideas have, rightly or wrongly, found sociobiology a convenient source. They have been impressed by claims from within this discipline which appear to support their views. Thus the popular writer Desmond Morris has described the idea of 'a worldwide brotherhood of man' as 'a naive utopian dream. Man is a tribal animal and the great supertribes will always be in competition with one another.'[12] According to Edward Wilson, 'nationalism and racism . . . are the culturally nurtured outgrowths of simple tribalism'.[13] Such simple tribalism is in fact kin altruism in action, the extension of love of family. Richard Lynn sees a line of succession from Darwin through the psychologist William MacDougall to contemporary sociobiology.

> The first stage was initiated by Charles Darwin and reached its apogee in the second decade of this century in the work of William MacDougall who listed a dozen or so instincts which motivated most of human behaviour. ... The third phase can be dated from around the mid-1960s and has resurrected the older doctrine of instincts. This swing back to the Darwin–MacDougall position is represented, among others, by Konrad Lorenz, Lionel Tiger, Robin Fox and Edward O. Wilson.[14]

According to MacDougall, racism is no more than preference for one's own kind, and he sees it as a necessary part of 'conservatism'.

> The essential expressions of conservatism are respect for the ancestors, pride in their achievements, and reverence for the traditions which they have handed down: all of which means what is now fashionable to call 'race prejudice' and 'national prejudice', but may more justly be described as preference for, and belief in the merits of, a man's own tribe, race or nation, with its peculiar customs and institutions — its ethos in short.[15]

MacDougall saw black people as 'a race which never yet has shown itself capable of raising or maintaining itself unaided above a barbaric level of culture'.[16]

Again, such ideas of essentially limited love and concern are in conflict with Christian faith, which stands or falls on the belief that love is possible among people of differing races and nations, that love is more fundamental to the nature of the human person than is selfishness, and that such love is rooted in our own openness to the love of God. That self-giving love represents that which is most true to human nature as created, that it is in fact most natural, is basic to the Christian understanding of God as love and of humanity as made to reflect that love. If human beings are incapable of transcending the limits of tribal and national boundaries, then we must revert to the 'culture religions' of paganism. And indeed it is significant that many racist and fascist movements show a strong preference for the pagan gods, the gods of race and nation.

Fundamentally, what is at issue here is the potential and scope of the grace of God in the work of redemption. By focusing on a fixed and unchangeable 'human nature', the racist doctrine ignores or rejects the Christian view that human nature has been transformed, that a new humanity has been created, and that therefore humanity is greater than its most limited and most base and corrupt aspects. By appealing always to these base and corrupt aspects as the rationale for policy, racism reinforces the notion of irredeemable human degeneracy. In theological terms, fallenness comes to dominate and to obscure the gift and power of grace. If grace is seen to operate, it is only within a restricted field.

And here we encounter a more pervasive problem which affects many Christians: the fact that the transforming power of the grace of God is widely seen as only operative within a closed realm, identified as the sacred, the sacramental world, the realm of the personal, or whatever. Transformation is not seen as affecting the way in which life in the real world goes on. So lip service is paid to themes such as liberation, sanctification, transformation, but they are all seen as making no effective difference to reality. The spiritual world is carefully insulated from the world of concrete social and political action.

This dualistic theology is not new. Martin Luther responded to the peasants who demanded an end to serfdom in the name of the redemption wrought by Christ with precisely this kind of theology: 'It is a malicious and evil idea that serfdom should be abolished because Christ has made us free. This refers only to the spiritual freedom given to us by Christ in order to enable us to withstand the devil.'[17] Two hundred years later an eighteenth-century Bishop of London made the same point:

> The freedom which Christianity gives is a freedom from the bondage of sin and Satan and from the dominion of men's lusts and passions and inordinate desires: but as to their *outward* condition, whatever that was before, whether bond or free, their being baptized and becoming Christian makes no matter of change in it.[18]

Against such false spiritualizing, Christian preaching needs to assert that redemption is not limited to the realm of the inward or contained within a protected area, but affects all social, economic and political relationships. Unless redemption is total, it does not occur at all.

Since racism offers an alternative understanding of the gospel, its view of the nature and function of the Church is different. The Church comes to be seen as a religious arm of the nation, a unifying force for national pride and identity, a community of common stock and of the like-minded. So the Union Jack (or its equivalent elsewhere) is flown over the church. Its role is to reinforce the national character and aspirations. But Christian theology sees the Church as the social aspect of Christ's humanity, incomplete until all humanity is redeemed. It is therefore potentially as inclusive as creation itself. The Church is, by its very nature, international, non-racial, cosmic in its range and scope. In the New Testament, the terms race (*genos*) and nation (*ethnos*) are used of the Church itself, that is, not of an ethnic community but of a spiritual community into which entrance is by repentance and baptism (1 Peter 2:9). So the doctrine of the Church becomes a subversive doctrine in relation to ideologies of race and nation. John Davies has written, with the South African Church struggle in mind:

> The most powerful weapon in Catholicism's armoury of imagery in the struggle against injustice is the doctrine of the Body of Christ ... There has been nothing radical or intellectually daring about this: the South African situation has required Catholicism to be thoroughly conservative and oppose the moral nonsense of upstart racism with a traditional orthodoxy which insists that there must be a visible fellowship of believers and that Christian love must be acted out in visible terms.[19]

The apartheid theology, Davies claims, involves a version of the old Eutych-ian heresy, which denies that the love and fellowship of the gospel needs to be structurally embodied.

Thus on the four central questions of the nature of humanity, the potential for human love, the nature and scope of grace and the character of the

Church itself, racism offers a different and incompatible gospel and world view. The conflict between the Christian gospel and racism is therefore not a mere side-show, an incidental aspect of Christian action, but is deeply theological, a conflict which touches the very heart of the gospel message.

In the twentieth century the most dramatic point at which these two theologies came into collision was the Nazi period, and Christians today need to learn from the witness, and the failure to witness, of the Church in Nazi Germany. Most of the features which we have considered in this chapter as distortions of, or alternatives to, the gospel were present there: the neglect of the Old Testament and the Jewish prophetic tradition; the false dualism of social and spiritual; the neglect of Christology and its ethical dimensions, and of discipleship; and the close link between Christianity and national identity. Richard Gutteridge, who studied anti-Semitism in the evangelical churches from 1870 to 1950, found virtually no evidence of theologically based critique of the treatment of the Jews or of the anti-Semitic ideology which was so pervasive within the Church. What he did find was a prevailing tendency to identify the Church with race and nation. 'The Protestant tendency to anti-Semitism was part and parcel of the well-established tradition of close identification between Christianity and a mystical interpretation of nationality in manifestly untranslatable terms such as *Deutschtum* and *Volkstum*.'[20] And this identification had disastrous consequences for the understanding of the nature of the Christian community, as Bonhoeffer saw in 1935: 'Under the onslaught of new nationalism, the fact that the Church of Christ does not stop at national and racial boundaries, so powerfully attested in the New Testament and in the confessional writings, has been far too easily forgotten.'[21]

Yet Bonhoeffer's voice was a lonely one. More typical was that of the distinguished theologian Gerhard Kittel, an enthusiastic Nazi, who contrasted the internationalism of Jewish faith with the racial nationalism of Hitler — making his own preference very clear.

> At the cradle of modern Judaism stands the idea of humanity as superior to the concept of the race ... To him [the Jew] racial culture is but a preparation for a culture embracing all humanity.

However, Kittel assured his readers:

> A new movement full of life has broken out in our midst, to which not world citizenship and universal culture is the ideal, but a culture bound up with the people. ... What it can contribute in spiritual values, it can give best by developing its own inherent culture which springs from blood and soil, and by killing as poison all that opposes it.[22]

We know only too well the terrible consequences of this view. It was a reduced and watered-down gospel which helped it to flourish, while its effects on the preaching of the gospel were that many sermons were preached from which all Christian references had been removed.

Reinhold Niebuhr and others have argued that Germany's plight was in part the result of the theology of the Lutheran Reformation, with its dualism of 'two kingdoms' and its lack of interest in issues of justice.[23] Certainly one major factor in the capitulation of the churches to Hitler was the fact that the proclamation of the gospel had gone seriously astray. It is equally clear that out of the terrible experience of Nazism came a thorough and continuing critique and reappraisal of Christian theology itself.

Today, the experience of racism can act as a force for the renewal of the wholeness of Christian proclamation. We shall need to hear the voices from the Third World, the theologies of liberation, which are seeking to end the identification of the Church with oppressive power structures and false spiritualities. We shall need to recover neglected emphases — on the creation, on incarnation, on the social and political dimensions of redemption, on the meaning of the Kingdom of God. The experience of racism, much of it based upon, or feeding upon, defects and distortions of Christian faith, should lead us to renew our theology and our preaching. It should, more than anything else, lead us to see that the gospel is not merely about certain truths: it is about the truth which makes us free, truth in action, truth in concrete struggle with the forces of evil. As J.H. Oldham wrote in 1924:

> Christianity is not primarily a philosophy but a crusade. As Christ was sent by the Father, so he sends his disciples to set up in the world the Kingdom of God ... He was manifested to destroy the works of the devil. Hence when Christians find in the world a state of things which is not in accord with the truths which they have learned from Christ, their concern is not that it should be explained, but that it should be ended.[24]

NOTES

1. See Martin Barker, *The New Racism: Conservatives and the Ideology of the Tribe* (London: Junction Books, 1981); Paul Gordon and Francesca Klug, *New Right, New Racism* (London: Searchlight Publications, 1986).
2. *The Times*, 18 November 1968; Bill Smithies and Peter Fiddick, *Enoch Powell on Immigration* (London: Sphere, 1969), pp. 73–4.
3. *The Daily Telegraph*, 22 January 1977.
4. House of Commons, *Hansard*, 914.137 (5 July 1976), p. 1409.
5. *Daily Mail*, 9 November 1981.
6. John Meyendorff, *Christ in Eastern Christian Thought* (New York: St Vladimir's Seminary Press, 1975), p. 11.
7. E. Colledge and J. Walsh (trs and eds), *Julian of Norwich: Showings* (London: SPCK, Paulist, 1978), ch. 57, p. 291.
8. E.L. Mascall, *Theology and the Future* (London: Darton, Longman and Todd, 1968), p. 133.
9. David Hume, *A Treatise of Human Nature*, ed. by P. Ardal (London: Collins, 1972), pp. 73, 219.
10. John Casey, 'One nation: the politics of race', *Salisbury Review*, 1 (Autumn 1982), pp. 14ff.
11. Robert McNeill, *Daily Star*, 18 April 1984.
12. Desmond Morris, *The Human Zoo* (London: Corgi, 1971), p. 126.
13. E.O. Wilson, *On Human Nature* (Cambridge, MA: Harvard University Press, 1978), p. 92.
14. Richard Lynn, 'The sociobiology of nationalism', *New Society*, 1 July 1976, cited by Barker, *The New Racism*, p. 108.
15. William MacDougall, *Ethics and Some Modern World Problems* (London: Methuen, 1924).
16. MacDougall, *Ethics*, p. 15.

17. Cited in Reinhold Niebuhr, *The Nature and Destiny of Man* (New York: Scribners, 1964), vol. 2, p. 194.
18. Cited in Charles Jones. *The Religious Instruction of Negroes in the United States* (Savannah: T. Purse Co., 1842), p. 20.
19. John Davies in Kenneth Leech and Rowan Williams (eds), *Essays Catholic and Radical* (London: Bowerdean Press, 1983), pp. 188ff.
20. Richard Gutteridge, *Open Thy Mouth for the Dumb: The German Evangelical Church and the Jews 1879–1950* (Oxford: Blackwell, 1976), p. 2.
21. Dietrich Bonhoeffer, *No Rusty Swords* (London: Collins, 1965), p. 326.
22. Gerhard Kittel, *Die Judenfrage* (1933), cited in Olga Levertoff, *The Jews in a Christian Social Order* (London: Sheldon Press, 1942), pp. 13, 14.
23. Reinhold Niebuhr, 'Christianity and Political Justice', in *Christian Newsletter*, supplement no. 11 (10 January 1940). See also Niebuhr's comments on the period in his various works.
24. J.H. Oldham, *Christianity and the Race Problem* (London: SCM Press, 1925), p. 26.

The unsecular city: the revival of religion in East London

Greg Smith

In the nineteenth century the urbanization which accompanied the Industrial Revolution sent waves of panic through the religious establishment (especially as they looked across the Channel and saw the results of Enlightenment philosophy in the secular revolution of 1789). Despite the successful evangelism of the Methodists among some sections of the working classes, the 1851 religious census showed how unchurched the urban masses remained.[1] The second half of the century saw ambitious programmes of church-building and urban mission.[2] *The Daily News* census of 1903 showed the same picture.[3] Inner urban areas of London (especially the East End) still reported much lower church attendance than the emerging suburbs or the West End. As the twentieth century proceeded churches saw numerical decline both nationally and locally. From 1945 churches were closed and demolished at an ever increasing rate. When I came to live in East London in 1975 and began employment as a community worker with a Christian organization, I was told that if current trends continued and Christians continued to migrate towards the coast (like lemmings!) there would be no churches left in Newham by the year 2000.[4] As late as 1985 the *Faith in the City* report was bemoaning the continuing decline of urban congregations; in urban priority areas Anglican attendance averaged 0.85 per cent or half the national average.[5]

In none of these statistics was there any attempt to control for population decline, the age profile of urban areas, or to analyse in any depth the effect of social class or ethnic composition of communities and congregations. It was taken as gospel that 'urban' was bad news for the church, and when Colin

Marchant and I began to suggest that a new wave of urban church-planting was beginning to transform the Christian scene in Newham, and other parts of London, our observations were hard for many people to accept.[6] Evidence in our favour is now building up as this paper will attempt to show.

The borough of Newham according to the 1991 Census is the second most ethnically diverse in the whole of Britain, with only 58 per cent of its people describing themselves as white.[7] Religious pluralism is unparalleled and recognized by the local authority in the provision of school holidays at festivals such as Eid-ul-Fitr (Islam), Diwali (Hindu), Guru Nanak's Birthday (Sikh), as well as the traditional Christian ones of Christmas and Easter. Local politics increasingly reflects religious interests; recent arguments in Newham Council and Labour Party have focused on the following issues:

- the sale of land to provide car parking for a mosque as opposed to a building site for housing;
- the inappropriateness of scheduling a race equality sub-committee on the eve of Eid;
- whether Muslim representation on the Standing Advisory Committee for Religious Education should be increased;
- selection contests in the Labour Party for council candidates involving Muslim, Hindu and Sikh candidates, sometimes with accusations of dubious membership recruitment practices within religious communities;
- the nomination of two Christian Independent candidates for the May 1994 Council elections;
- conflicts over the funding of community centres; the Council substantially funds what in practice is a Hindu centre, but is uneasy about the prospect of backing a Muslim women's centre (rather than an Asian women's centre), while at least one Christian centre has ceased to be funded by the Council following a debate over religious/moral values around equal opportunities for gay and lesbian people and equal access to Muslim groups;[8]
- churches taking a lead in campaigns against the neo-Nazi BNP in Docklands, and in support of asylum seekers and refugees fighting deportation, to the extent of offering sanctuary in their buildings.

The history of religious institutions in the borough of Newham is a rapidly changing one and is well documented, especially in the writing of Colin Marchant[9] and in historical studies such as the volume edited by F. Sainsbury.[10] Before 1850 there were the three ancient parish churches of Little Ilford, West Ham and East Ham, a congregational chapel and not much else. The second half of the nineteenth century saw the establishment of over forty Church of England parishes, five large Roman Catholic parishes, and a very strong Free Church presence with ninety-seven Methodist, Baptist and Independent churches . . . as well as numerous settlements and mission halls. There was also a significant Jewish presence with several synagogues and cemeteries. The post-1945 exodus and decline in local population on top of a general decline in church-going habits, and the loss of a number of church buildings in the blitz, led to rationalization and closures on the part of the denominations, the Church of England merging parishes and the Free

Churches selling off buildings. There were by the mid-1970s only eighteen Anglican buildings and twenty Free Churches. However, by the mid-1980s Colin Marchant, a local Baptist minister whose doctoral research produced the groundbreaking study of the religious history of Newham, was becoming less pessimistic as he had noticed a wave of church-planting.[11] David Driscoll (a local Anglican vicar) and I, in a report submitted to the Archbishop's Commission on UPAs, documented some of the new church-planting and the renewal of congregational life in some parts of the mainline churches.[12]

Several factors have contributed to the stemming of the tide of secularization in Newham. The first of the 'black Pentecostal' churches were founded in the area before 1970 by immigrants from the Caribbean. By about 1975 a new awareness of East London as a mission field was emerging in the mainline churches spurred on by David Sheppard's book *Built as a City*[13] and the creation of groups such as the Newham Community Renewal Programme and In Contact. A wave of educated Christian incomers (including the present author) moved into the area, full of zeal to do evangelism and/or community work, and many of them have now stayed nearly 20 years. They have been joined more recently by several groups of 'religious' from the Roman Catholic orders. From 1975 to the present several new independent congregations have emerged in the 'white-led' evangelical charismatic sector of the church. Many mainline denominational churches which were on the verge of closure in the mid-1970s have found new congregational life. These include both charismatic/evangelical congregations and (more recently) broad and Anglo-Catholic congregations. Caribbean-led majority black Pentecostal churches continue to be formed, although there is some evidence that their growth had peaked by the mid-1980s. In the last ten years the most significant growth point has been among African Christians.[14] Many mainline denominational churches have doubled in numbers because of the involvement of African Anglicans, Methodists, Baptists and Pentecostals, while a thriving independent African-led sector has mushroomed. These newer churches are mainly from Pentecostal/Holiness or the Aladura/African indigenous traditions and serve Ghanaians, Nigerians, Ugandans, Zaireans and Zimbabweans usually in their national or ethnic grouping.[15]

Alongside this Christian growth has been the development of Hindu, Sikh, Muslim and other faith communities. There are now more than a dozen mosques, at least three Sikh and four Hindu temples in Newham. There are also two Buddhist centres and Bahai, Pagan, Rastafarian and other groups. In the white community there is a traditional Spiritualist presence, which is arguably a product of Cockney folk religion with its excessive reverence for departed relatives.[16] Similar informal, folk or implicit religions are to be found in the various ethnic minority communities, although there is little research in this hidden and sensitive area. There are, in addition, some proponents of New Age spirituality, although because of its privatized and consumerist nature and local focus in more 'trendy' places such as Glastonbury and Brighton, little organized activity is to be observed in Newham.

The Newham Directory of Religious Groups (second edition) published in 1994 lists 275 groups. Statistics for all faith communities (based on a survey with a response rate of 78 per cent of all congregations, and 96.5 per cent for the mainline Christian churches) show that in Newham in 1994 there were:

- 198 'congregations', 117 of whom owned their own meeting place;
- 163 of these congregations were in the broadest sense of the term 'Christian';
- 77 religious organizations, centres, agencies, orders, networks, etc.

A breakdown by denomination shows that Pentecostal congregations are by far the most numerous category, followed by Anglicans (Church of England), independent evangelicals and Muslims. But when it comes to owning their own buildings the Anglicans are in a league of their own, although almost all Muslim, Baptist, Methodist, Salvation Army and United Reform Church (URC) groups do own their buildings. Many of the newer Pentecostals and Independent Evangelicals and some of the Roman Catholic groups meet in rented church halls and community centres. There are also a handful of examples where two or more congregations of different denominations have a formal agreement to share a church building such as the ecumenical St Mark's Centre in Beckton.

* * *

Church attendance figures are one of the most frequently used measures of trends in secularization, perhaps because the measurement is relatively easy to put into operation (usually by counting all attenders on a given Sunday) and is therefore thought to be reliable and replicable at different times. The only national religious census for England in 1851 showed that in West Ham, there was a 40 per cent church attendance rate (65 per cent of it Anglican). Since urbanization had hardly begun in the area in 1851 this can hardly be used as a baseline for later comparisons.

In London in 1903 *The Daily News* survey of religious life indicated that the attendance rates in inner, and especially East, London were low.[17] In West Ham church attendance was put at 20 per cent (55,649 people in 137 churches and chapels). Nonconformists accounted for 65 per cent of the church-goers, 32 per cent were Church of England and the Roman Catholic congregation had grown to 12 per cent. There was also one synagogue with 68 worshippers. The church authorities were most concerned over even lower attendances in the southern working-class neighbourhoods of the borough. Marchant's doctoral work suggested the pattern continued in the 1970s and he summarized the historical situation by saying that in East London the decline in national church attendance was reflected locally, but rates were consistently half to a third of the national average.[18] Yet by 1988 my own research was suggesting that in Forest Gate church attendance rates were not far behind the national average, and really quite high in a community where around half the population was from Muslim, Hindu and Sikh communities.[19] My estimates of numbers for the mid-1980s, based on extensive visiting and participant observation, were that about 2 per cent of the predominantly white working-class population of Plaistow and Canning Town might be regular attenders at Christian churches, while at least 7 per cent of the multiracial, more socially mixed population of Forest Gate might attend.

The most recent church censuses with any claim to comprehensive national coverage were those of 1985 and 1989 conducted by MARC

Europe based on a head count on a specified Sunday in each year.[20] They showed a 10 per cent increase over four years in adult attenders in Newham from 6,800 to 7,500 and a growth in membership of 16 per cent from 13,300 to 15,400. But this attendance level still only represented some 5 per cent of the adult population. There are many problems about the reliability and coverage of this data, but it does not seem implausible to those with local knowledge of the churches, and it is matched by similar trends in other parts of inner London especially the inner south-east and inner north-east sectors.[21] The 1989 MARC census put church attendance rates for England as a whole at 9 per cent and follow-up work suggests they are still declining.[22]

The 1994 *Newham Directory of Religious Groups* gives estimates of attenders at congregations in the Christian tradition which are at least one and a half times as high as the 1989 Census figures. Between 15,000 and 18,000 people are likely to attend services in the borough. This is around 8 per cent of the whole population and 10 per cent of the non-Asian population.

It is important to ask why even our lower estimate for church attendance in Newham is so much higher than the MARC Europe 1989 figures. The research discovered many churches which were not included in the MARC census and elicited a much higher response rate. MARC researchers worked from a list of only 65 churches and achieved only a 65 per cent response rate. The directory's key question invited church leaders to estimate the number who usually attended the largest worship event regularly held, rather than insisting on an actual count on a given Sunday. The temptation to round up numbers and to count every person who might attend would have been irresistible for many. Despite this caveat it is impossible to discount the possibility that there has been a substantial growth in religious observance among Christian groups in Newham in recent years.

The major growth area has been among Pentecostal and African Independent congregations. Almost all of these churches are black-led, and have predominantly black congregations. In the last decade the African element has predominated, and in addition many mainline white-led congregations have benefited from an influx of African Christians, and the lively faith and style of worship they bring with them.

But even the predominantly white communities of Docklands are affected. A recent local study by Oliver[23] has looked at adult Christian learning and church attendance in Canning Town and Custom House, an area of council estates, which is well researched and documented in earlier urban mission literature.[24] Oliver estimated 2.86 per cent of the local population were church-goers (230 of them attending 7 local churches). Nearly three-quarters of them were female and just under a quarter were black. Oliver characterizes church-going as 'deviant' behaviour in the local (white) working-class Cockney culture, especially for men. Yet significantly he reports growth in attendance; a doubling of estimated numbers from 150 (in 8 buildings) in the early 1980s to 300 (in 7 buildings) in 1991/2. Only a small part of the growth can be put down to active Christian incomers including black people. There has been some significant 'conversion' growth, of which Oliver documents a number of individual cases.[25]

* * *

What then can we say about religion in Newham, and more widely about religion in the inner city?

In the first place, whatever Newham is in the 1990s it is not a godless or unchurched community. Although religion is by no means a majority interest and attendance at worship is far below Irish or American levels, faith persists and if anything is growing in numbers, influence and significance. New churches, mosques, temples and organizations are being formed to cater for unmet religious and community need. Some important questions are raised which I will address in the remainder of this section:

Is the revival of religion purely a result of ethnic diversity? This is a compelling suggestion in as far as the tendency for religious organizations is to be ethnically homogeneous. Indeed, there is a case that in many plural urban settings around the world the prime focus for belonging, identity, community, *gemeinschaft* is located in some notion of ethno-religious-linguistic identity. However, there may be some counterevidence especially if the growth of churches, mosques and other religious communities which cut across some of the ethnic, national and tribal identities can be sustained. Yet even in Christian congregations which have attracted roughly equal numbers of black and white worshippers, there are often observable social divides, cliques with ethnic boundaries, and an imbalance in patterns of participation and power that can be seen as racist exclusion. The same may be true in some of the other faith communities that cross ethnic lines.

The answer to the ethnic question and the future of Christianity in Newham will depend on whether a long-term measurable revival in religious activity among the deprived white communities in Newham can be sustained. At this moment there are only hopes and hints to counter long-established trends. Will church attendance, or 'getting religion', continue to be deviant behaviour in the Cockney culture? Will young white people start to attend church, or will older congregations simply die out? If numerical growth is established among both white and black communities, and the church can overcome its own racism, then religious community identity might become a significant factor in its own right. Specifically it could emerge as the polar opposition to the sense of Islamic identity found among some young local Muslims. For Christians at least the dream of evangelical unity which rests on the vision of 'people of every language, tribe and nation worshipping before the throne of the Lamb' (Revelation 7) could just be realized in Newham as it is in heaven.

More generally will religion diminish in significance as immigrant communities mature and become established in Britain? There are inevitably many pressures towards secularization including economic forces, the professed value neutrality of the state and its education system (which is now being questioned), the mass media and the McDonaldization of global culture. But all of these forces encounter some resistance at the level of human communities, and a feature of postmodern culture is that there is some recognition and space in which subcultural forms can flourish. In North America it is significant that ethnicity has undergone a strong revival in recent decades, and that for many ethnic groups it is their churches which maintain ancestral traditions, values, cultural forms and 'roots' long after other markers of ethnic community identity have gone. The same forces could be at work in Britain. In addition, there is the dimension of racism. As minority groups, most of them 'Black' in the political sense of the word, continue to meet hostility, discrimination and social exclusion, their religious identities and organizations will prove to be a powerful resource in their struggles. Already we are seeing a mobilization of Islamic (rather than Asian or Pakistani) identity around such issues as the publication of *The Satanic Verses*, and the Muslim Parliament. In this setting it is hard to believe that an irresistible force of secularization will sweep away the religious aspects of minority cultures.

The ethnic dimensions of religion clearly portray faith as a social phenomenon, involving belonging as much as believing. An alternative approach to religion, quite widely held in mainstream white British culture in the twentieth century is that faith is a purely personal matter between the individual and God. In this view, derived in large part from the Protestant view of individual conscience, the role of the church is merely to be available as a solace in time of need. One can certainly be a good Christian without attending church, and the congregation as community, or the church as a political force is not on the agenda. Undoubtedly there are many people in Newham, particularly among older white nominal Christians who subscribe to this view of believing in an ordinary God, as opposed to a supernatural interventionist one, without belonging to any church. However, most churches in Newham, of all denominations, are increasingly operating on the model of the congregation as the gathered community of God's people, distinct from the non-Christian world, but committed to being involved in that wider world according to the biblical metaphors of salt and light, in service and evangelism. This trend has theological roots, but also resonates with an important social need. As neighbourhood community and kinship networks have fragmented, perhaps more rapidly in East London than elsewhere, many people recognize a deep personal need for belonging, for solidarity, for social support, for communion. At the local level it is churches and other religious groups that are best placed to meet such needs.

In a deprived urban area such as Newham a crucial question must be the relationship of poverty and religion. Religion was criticized by Marx as 'the opium of the people' and with some justification as an ideological tool of the ruling classes. But in the light of the collapse of Soviet-style communism and the resurgence of religion in Eastern Europe and in the Islamic world it is time to re-evaluate. There is a long Christian tradition of concern for and involvement alongside the poor, of voluntary poverty for the sake of the Gospel, and of struggling to see the Kingdom of God established as social and economic reality on earth. That tradition continues in Newham as church and other groups play a major, and growing role in community development work, anti-poverty programmes and the provision of social services. It would appear that such social involvement is widely spread across the denominations in Newham. Pentecostals, Adventists, Catholics, Methodists and Anglicans all play a part. The media stereotypes of a church divided between the evangelical fundamentalists who reject social involvement and the liberals who have lost all confidence in God and the Gospel do not in my experience seem to fit. There are differences in emphasis, more among clergy than lay people, and some Christians see their social mission as little more than 'bait' with which to entice converts. For them church growth and numerical success is a priority. On the other hand, there are those who put political action as a high priority and who are very cautious about evangelism, especially in its American mass meeting form, or when it targets people from other faith communities. Such Christians stress faithfulness to the Gospel and quality of discipleship over numerical growth. But there are many individuals and congregations that seek to bridge these divides and there are a range of projects, organizations and networks that enable Christians of diverse viewpoints to co-exist and even collaborate.

It would appear that the social context in which the Church operates is having an increasingly strong influence on its theology. Internationally there is a vigorous theological debate both in Catholic and evangelical circles about social justice and the Gospel, in which Christians in the 'Two Thirds World' and in British inner cities often make common cause on 'the option for the poor' and the need to root the gospel in local realities. Some Muslims too are exploring their traditions in the light of longings for equality and liberation. As the social and economic statistics about Newham show that it is consistently the African, Pakistani and Bangladeshi groups that are bottom of all the deprivation leagues, and it is these very groups that are most religiously active, then we can expect struggles for racial and social justice to take on a religious form. There may still be some vestiges of the 'pie in the sky when you die' syndrome, a reluctance among heavenly-minded people to engage with the everyday world, and a global culture which seeks to privatize spirituality, but it seems to me unlikely that this will be the dominant feature of religion in East London in years to come.

A final question is whether religious and ethnic divisions will sharpen and lead to conflict, segregation, and the brutality of competing fundamentalisms. In short will Newham become like Belfast or Beirut? Clearly there are such dangers, especially if the discourse of nationalism, racism and tribal loyalties are superimposed on deeply held religious, social and 'moral' values in a context of conflict over diminishing economic and social resources. At the time of writing, a recent murder in Newham has been reported as having some such dimensions of religious conflict. However, such fragmentation might be mitigated by the inability to avoid contact with a common mass culture, the complexity of ethnic interaction in Newham (compared with say the bipolar conflict in Belfast) and by deliberate policies in education, housing and community relations work.

Will the majority of Muslims in Newham follow a line that can be described as 'fundamentalist'? Will Hindus and Sikhs develop radical versions of their own religions? Will Christians be pushed towards a fundamentalism of their own, or will the liberal tolerance of broad church Anglicanism and the Free Churches survive and grow? Interestingly enough the material from the Newham Association of Faiths survey does not suggest that the majority of people are willing to go to war over religion, but rather see religion potentially as a force for harmony. Although 75 per cent of respondents agreed that 'there are always going to be conflicts between religions' only 10 per cent agreed with the statement 'I think of other faiths as the enemy of my own'. By contrast 69 per cent agreed that 'all religions have a lot in common' and an overwhelming majority of 92 per cent agreed that 'different religions should work together to help people in need'. There is in these findings a potentially more hopeful scenario in which religion, in all its diversity, becomes the building blocks out of which a new wider sense of community can be constructed.

NOTES

1. R. Currie, A. Gilbert and L. Horsley, *Churches and Church-goers: Patterns of Church Growth in the British Isles Since 1700* (Oxford: Clarendon Press, 1977); E. Wickham, *Church and People in an Industrial City* (London: Lutterworth, 1957).
2. H. McCleod, *Class and Religion in the Late Victorian City* (London: Croom Helm, 1974). H. Walker, *East London: Sketches of Christian Work and Workers* (1896) republished in 1987 by Peter Marcan Books, High Wycombe.
3. J. Hart, *The Religious Life of London 1903* (EUTP, PO Box 83, Liverpool L69 8AN); C. Marchant, 'Religion', in *A Marsh and a Gas Works: One Hundred Years of Life in West Ham* (WEA/Newham Parents Centre Publications, 745 Barking Road, London E13 9ER, 1986).
4. C. Hill, *Renewal in the Inner City* (London: Methodist Home Mission Dept., 1976).
5. ACUPA — Archbishop's Commission on Urban Priority Areas, *Faith in the City*, (London: Church Information Office, 1988).
6. Marchant 'Religion'; Greg Smith, *God's in E7* (London: Evangelical Coalition for Urban Mission/British Growth Association, 1986); G. Smith, *Inner City Christianity: Some Sociological Issues* (London: MARC monograph series, Number 17, 1988).
7. G. Smith, '(Almost) All you could ever want to know: Newham in the 1991 Census, implications for community work', in *Newham Needs and Responses; CIU Annual for 1994* (London: Aston Community Involvement Unit, 1994).
8. P. Watherston, *A Different Kind of Church: the Mayflower Family Centre Story* (London: Marshall Pickering, 1994).
9. Marchant, 'Religion'; C. Marchant, *The Inter-relationship of Church and Society in a London Borough*, unpublished PhD (London: Thesis, London School of Economics, 1974).
10. F. Sainsbury (ed.), *West Ham 1886–1986* (London: London Borough of Newham, 1986).
11. Marchant, 'Religion'.
12. G. Smith and D. Driscoll, *West Ham Christians: 1984* (London: Evangelical Coalition for Urban Mission, 1985).
13. David Sheppard, *Built as a City* (2nd edition) (London: Hodder, 1975).
14. J. Ashdown, *Guide to Ethnic Christianity in London* (London: Zebra Project, 1993).
15. Booth, *We True Christians*, unpublished PhD thesis, (Birmingham: Birmingham University, 1985).
16. G. Ahern, 'Cockneys and clergy speak', in G. Ahern and G. Davie, *Inner City God* (London: Hodder & Stoughton, 1987).
17. Marchant, 'Religion'.
18. Marchant, *Inter-relationship*.
19. Smith, *Inner City Christianity*.
20. P. Brierley, *Prospects for the Nineties: Trends and Tables from 1989 Census of Churches in England* (especially volume on Greater London, including commentary by G. Smith) (London: MARC Europe, 1991); P. Brierley (personal communication) Data for LB Newham in 1989 Churches Census.
21. Brierley, *Prospects*.
22. P. Brierley and V. Hiscock, *UK Christian Handbook*, 1994/95 edition (London: Christian Research Association/Evangelical Alliance, 1993).
23. J.K. Oliver, *Christian Lay Learning in an East London Community*, unpublished MA

dissertation, Youth and Community Work, Faculty of Education & Design, Brunel University, 1992.

24. Marchant, *Inter-relationship*; Sheppard, *Built as a City*; Smith and Driscoll, *West Ham Christians*.

25. There is a (spurious?) correlation between the take-off of this growth and the fact that the present author ceased to be a pastor in the area in 1984!

Towards a black theology for Britain

Barney Pityana

The sum total of racial disadvantage caused by prejudice and fortified by the ability to exploit and exclude black people from resources and from effective decision-making because of the colour of their skin, equals racism. But it must be remembered that in Britain racism is a sub-class within the overall structural inequality caused by class stratification. Class differentiation, together with its attendant privileges and social esteem for those at the top, is at the heart of British social organization. It is therefore not surprising that racism is so endemic in Britain.

Racism entails, at one level, a confusion about nationality and, at another, various confused perceptions about the nature of nationalism which in Britain serve to fuel racial intolerance. There is a prevailing tendency to speak about black people wholly as if they were immigrants or aliens. To wear a black skin confirms that one does not belong. The truth is, of course, that more and more black people are British by birth, loyalty and commitment. What distinguishes them from white British people, besides the colour of their skin, is that their ideas and culture convey a language and way of life rooted in Africa or the West Indies. Yet there is in British society a strong reluctance to accept the cultural diversity that this entails — an emerging British culture that is affected by the customs of the wider Commonwealth peoples. In the frontline of the urban uprisings of recent years are black British youth who will not trade off their Britishness and yet will not be assimilated into a stagnant British culture. However, hostility and rejection are part of their daily experience in their dealings especially with the police; and they meet with mistrust on the dole queue and suspicions from their white neighbours. Yet many black people have been making a contribution to the sporting, musical, political, religious, intellectual and business traditions of this country for a very long time. They pay taxes, they go to war; as Peter Fryer notes, 'Black people born in Britain are a permanent part of British society.'[1]

However, black people in Britain do not simply have to cope with the burden of having to prove their belonging by assimilating British values; voices have been raised which suggest that it is logically impossible for black people to acquire British nationality. Enoch Powell argues that black people are 'unassimilable and unassimilated populations ... alien weeds in the heartland of the state'.[2] He has the support of Sir Alfred Sherman, a former adviser to the British Prime Minister, who invited the French racist politician Jean Marie Le Pen to the Conservative Party Conference in 1987. Sherman asserts that it is impossible to acquire British nationality by mere legislative fiat; 'a passport or residence does not implant national values or patriotism', he argues.

Of course, the fundamental flaw in these arguments is the assumption that a precondition of being a national of another country is to become totally assimilated into its values and lifestyles and culture. Furthermore, implicit in these views is the notion that a white skin conveys a kind of assimilability that makes it possible for white aliens to become British citizens. Enoch Powell and those of his ilk need to be reminded that nationhood is a dynamic process and is not solely dependent upon one's ability to trace one's roots to an ancestry long past. If that is the case, then there can be *no* purely 'British' citizens, since there is a diversity among the constituents of British society: English, Scot, Irish, Welsh, Cornish, etc. Besides, a large number of leading British personalities came into Britain as refugees or immigrants, many as recently as the end of the Second World War.

Of course, the truth is that British nationality is less culture-determined than it is constituted by a common bond of loyalty to the Crown. That was what a British passport meant and, traditionally, it was not even geo-graphically circumscribed. Besides, cultural diversity is not inimical to the concept of nationhood. The United States of America has grown out of an acceptance of diversity and is enriched thereby.

The Commonwealth is an expression of such a diversity on a grand scale. It therefore must not be surprising that great diversity is represented in British national life. A tangible example of that diversity is the presence of Japanese Buddhist Peace Pagodas in London and elsewhere. These are a measure of the Japanese cultural incursion that has come with the advent of the Nissan factory and the earlier influx of electronic goods and compo-nents.

All nations require injections of cultural dynamism from other lands, and these can be creative and enriching experiences. Society — and *a fortiori* a nation — is a self-creating entity: it can never be fossilized. Rejecting calls for the repatriation of black people (which calls have since died down), the Archbishop of Canterbury, Dr Robert Runcie, said in a lecture to the Birmingham Council for Community Relations in 1982:

> Any talk of repatriating people who have sometimes lived here for more than two generations or who are no longer welcome in their own countries of origin is a dangerous fantasy. We are in fact a multiracial society, and the choice we have is between working to make this fact a matter of pride and celebration, or drifting into a situation where this fact is a matter of lament and despair.[3]

In the light of the above social analysis, we can turn to *Faith in the City*, the 1985 report of the Archbishop's Commission on Urban Priority Areas. Here the concerns of the black community receive understanding and the prob-lems of poverty are firmly addressed. As the commissioners went among inner-city communities they bemoaned the evidence of a divided Britain. It is the poor and deprived who speak through the pages of the Report. The commissioners listened and saw for themselves. The Report restates the fundamental Christian values of social responsibility. It proposes a sharing and a wider distribution of resources and a redressing of the balance of power and opportunity to give the poor and the deprived an even chance.

Significantly, however, the Report fails to address the question of nationality, nor does it face up to the essential or structural inequality in British society. A question that needed to be asked is: How can the structures of Church and society so change as to be more fully representative of contemporary British life? The report is Eurocentric in its mould. No effort is made to examine the history and culture of the black communities. The tone is one of benevolence towards the deprived. It appeals to the conscience of the wealthy and powerful to give due regard to the needs of the poor, the implication being that *they* hold the key to change towards a more just and caring society.

It is not surprising, therefore, that the Report's theological stance articulates what may be termed 'Christendom values': an assertion of Christian values and triumphalism. But there must be a revision of the theological outlook that has for so long undergirded British church and social life. The Church's theological frames of reference, language and world-views, styles of leadership and organization need to be tempered if it is to identify fully with and help black people develop a sense of belonging to it. Belonging presupposes a freedom to make one's contribution to the life of the Church in such a way that change may be discernible. Black people need to own the Church and exercise their freedom within it.

A major defect of the Report is its inadequate and potentially misleading exposition of the nature and task of the Church. One can so easily take away from it the impression that the Church in the inner city is a social welfare or employment agency. Granted, the Church can become the focus of community life and endeavour, but it can hardly possess resources sufficient to accomplish the necessary inner city regeneration. That is and must be the task of government. There is a further danger, that the Church might be associated too closely with the various government agencies and initiatives such as the Social Services departments and the Manpower Services Commission employment schemes to the extent that the faults within the system could become attributable to the Church.

The Church can hardly be accountable for resources which it does not ultimately control. However, even if the Churches were to set up their own schemes, the energy required to find adequate resources and manage them would be disproportionate to the time and energy needed to tackle deprivation. Allegedly poor people will need to find large sums of money, negotiate with government agencies or industry or local authorities and be adept at operating through a maze of bureaucracies. And yet such initiatives, especially if they lead to enterprise and accomplishment, could boost community life remarkably.

The concept so beloved of the Victorian Catholic Renewal movement, that the Church of God stands at the centre of human deprivation to proclaim the glory of God, urgently needs revision. We need to draw attention to the Church built not of walls but of people; we need to identify with the people whom we serve and so empower them that they may more fully take control of their lives. I am referring to the biblical idea of 'the ark of God' which dwelt among God's people and with whom God tasted both victory and defeat. The Church is accordingly a sign of the immanence of God. Communities dwelt in by God are spiritually privileged. At the heart of the community, God shares in the struggles and the hopes of his people.

This model of the Church raises theological possibilities for pastoral care — possibilities which I have always believed are the privilege of the Church of England. A significant one is that of an interaction between the Church (as the gathered ecclesial and eucharistic or charismatic community) and the wider community which it seeks to serve, such that the people of faith are indistinguishable from their community save in the deeper spiritual understanding of witness and service which undergirds their participation in community. Prayer, worship and action would then become part of the activity of the community. This ties in with Philip Berryman's judgement — in the context of a discussion of the development of basic ecclesial communities — that a community emerges only when people 'understand their life in the light of God's Word, and form among themselves bonds of support and experience [the] unity that is the germ of a future united community'.[4]

The call to community is a call to neighbourliness. Community is emphatically not merely the aggregate of individuals who make up the whole, despite Margaret Thatcher's philosophy that 'there are no communities, only individuals'. In fact this ideology of individualism serves only to undermine *koinonia* and interdependence.

Finally, I want to make a passing reference to renewal: a need for change. As the Church, we should resist the temptation to model ourselves along the lines of the prevailing social norms and traditions. A living Church is one which is conscious of its need to be renewed; a society in search of truth and justice must be prepared to change. The Creator God accomplishes his purposes because he has been ready to change so that creation can be made perfect. One understands only too well that there is a certain amount of cosiness, charm and security under the cover of tradition and unchanging norms and values. But that is a denial of the incarnation: 'The Word became flesh and dwelt among us' (John 1:14). Out of the activity of God's people we see a vision of the struggles which will bring blessings. Kenneth Leech, in a Jubilee Lecture, 'The Resurrection of the Christian Social Voice' (1976), has this to say: 'We have lost the hope of renewal, of a new order, the Kingdom of justice, love and peace.' He goes on to make reference to what could be described as the spiritual liberative programme of local parishes so that they become (i) centres for deepening the inner life; (ii) centres for local community action and caring and (iii) campaigning centres for righteousness and peace, so that all individual caring is set firmly in the context of the Kingdom of God and his righteousness.[5]

Rudolf J. Siebert aptly summarizes our concerns in this section: 'Only the reconciled society is a free society and only a free society is reconciled.'[6]

How does all this impinge on the theological practices of black people in Britain? How does the black experience inform theological understanding and theology affect the black people's action for justice? And what is so distinctive, in any case, about the theology done from a black perspective?

In this section I want to look at five areas which involve an appreciation of

the contribution of black Christians to the theological task. But I would like
to preface my remarks with the following three observations:

1. Black religious practice in Britain has a common thread that runs
    through all denominations.
2. Racial discrimination in Britain has imposed a common objective on
    black people as a group to work together for racial justice, and indeed
    this is the only basis on which they will overcome.
3. The black theology of liberation expresses the deepest yearnings of the
    black people of faith in Britain, affirms black personality and nourishes
    their hopes.

Any understanding of the spirituality of black people has got to begin with
community.

Community is the substance of life and belonging. The people of God are
an expression of God's community with his people. As among the ancient
Israelites, community breaks down through sin and selfishness, and when it
breaks down God deserts his people and they become prey to the ravenous
wolves.

But community is also a means of self-realization when, in the African
idiom, we are who we are because of others. A community expresses the
common will, realizes and dispenses the common wealth. Out of it life's
values are sustained and through it common tasks are accomplished.

A community is an organizational unit that devises common strategies,
promotes dialogue within and, externally, with institutional forces and
engages in action for change and mutual fulfilment. Paul Gilroy quotes with
approval one Mellucci, who identifies the spiritual component as one which
connects the diverse social and political movements. 'Spirituality', he writes,
'has acquired powerful radical dimensions not only because religious language can express the intensity of aspirations for which no secular alternative
is available but because the political order which these movements criticise
and oppose is itself increasingly secular in its rationalisations.'[7] Such a view
of community is considered part of the natural order in the black world and
needs no justification, whereas the Western philosophical mindset perceives
a dichotomy between the sacred and the secular. The coherence and homoge-
neity of all creation with all humanity explains why community is considered
holy and nature sacred in many traditional religions.

British blacks share together the *pilgrim* experience. It must have taken the
faith of Abraham for many to travel to unknown lands. They all come from
places far away to claim a sense of belonging in this land where God will help
them to take root (Genesis 12:1–3), and they bring blessings to their adopted
country.

Black people have a right to claim Abraham the wandering Aramaean as
their ancestor. If they do so, then they are assured of the privilege of seeing
the day of the coming of Christ and rejoicing (see John 8:56). But, for a
Christian, there is also the consciousness that this is no final resting place,
and so the pilgrim fathers dwell in tents or tabernacle, getting themselves
ready for the call of God. Meanwhile there are blessings to be bestowed, the
household of faith to be built and the world to be made more perfect.

The fate of the cities which reject God's messengers is stated in Luke
10:10–12. And so we are called to proclaim judgement–'nevertheless know

this, that the kingdom of God has come near' (v. 11). Black people live through the crisis of faith, in the tension of seeking fulfilment even within the society that they believe is under judgement. They are on the frontiers, straddling the divide between those who make a positive affirmation of faith and others who, while unable to make a faith testimony, yet share identifiable concerns about justice.

Blacks can lead the way towards radical ways of collaborative activity. They can identify with an impotent and weeping God of the ghetto, one who suffers crucifixion each time black humanity is insulted. He shares their powerlessness in the face of human complicity in evil. And yet out of their belief in that God, they can rejoice that they are 'no longer aliens in a foreign land, but fellow-citizens with God's people, members of God's household' (Ephesians 2:19).

Next I turn to that cluster of issues relating to *justice, liberation* and *peace.* Indeed, a great deal of black theology and liberation theology has concentrated so much on these matters that I must simply draw out pointers. Yet, in the British context and arising from my South African experience, I do not want to trivialize the significance of liberation.

I do not want to suggest that the British democratic institutions are without integrity or that they absolutely block access for blacks and that it is necessary to seek to break them up. It is only in those matters relating to the denial of nationality or citizenship that I would hazard to make reference to liberation. And yet it can be argued both that the incidence of police brutality has reached such proportions that black people can no longer identify with the State which they represent and that immigration policies are such that they can be considered repressive. And so we have recourse to the Jubilee proclamation in Isaiah 61 and Luke 4, and the liberation theme in Exodus: 'I have seen the affliction of my people who are in Egypt, and have heard their cry ... I know their sufferings, and I have come down to deliver them' (Exodus 3:7–8).

The link between Exodus and Jubilee is precisely in the fact that the God who frees his people from external domination will not countenance the assumption of practices within the liberated Israelite community that are contrary to the principles of justice and cause God to act to liberate them. But, more importantly, liberation–justice is about the restoration of community; about 'shalom'; about just and peaceable relations; about harmony. Justice is an obligation of all societies, because to practise injustice is to deny one's own freedom.

Following the disturbances in Handsworth in September 1985, the Handsworth Forum, an association of clergy based in Handsworth, issued this statement: 'God has given us a vision and a task. The vision is of a society where, under God, everyone has equal value, and where justice and peace are seen to prevail over the forces of oppression and destruction. The task is to work together with God towards that end by all just means.'[8] We have the capacity to work towards that vision because we can see that it is an achievable goal. That is hope. As we progress the struggle for liberation and justice, we celebrate now all manner of victories: the victory of Christian conviction, the victory of hope, the victory of love and the will to persevere. And so, in the words of the South African theologian Dr John de Gruchy, we are urged to rejoice in the Lord always: 'So our little or large penultimate, proximate victories, those moments when justice is done and reconciliation becomes a reality, become pointers to the ultimate judgment and redemption of God.'[9]

We need to adopt a healthy scepticism about the claims of ownership of theology. We need to develop a theological model that has intellectual rigour and yet is earthed in the reality of black life and experience. That can best be done by taking the disciplines of the humanities seriously and by drawing from the consensus of faith and wisdom embedded in black culture.

The history of black peoples, their culture and philosophy of life, do not all deserve to be thrown overboard but need to be nurtured and reinterpreted with conceptual tools that affirm the black experience. Therefore we should affirm the narrative model of biblical interpretation, which is a return to the primacy of the oral tradition that is in danger of being lost. Likewise, spontaneity in song and dance, as well as the absence of inhibitions, needs to be revived again. Note how David 'danced before the Lord with all his might', brushing aside the embarrassment of his wife Michal (2 Samuel 6:14, 21–2).

Black Christianity in Britain has grown into an understanding of its true self, especially in culture and worship. Gilroy explains the effect of this phenomenon in these terms: 'Affection and intimacy are created in collective rituals, and a view of society which stresses its "ontological depth", demanding specific standards of truth from the forms of knowledge which will guide the community towards authentic freedom in the future'.[10] We have begun to see representatives of black worship in the media — for example, gospel music has become very popular — and the annual West Indian carnivals in Notting Hill and Handsworth express black personality. But deep down these manifestations of black culture are also a politico-religious testament to the pain and aspirations of black people. Precisely because of that, black music, dance, poetry and other forms of creative cultural expression are legitimate vehicles of black theology.

Finally, all this has some implications for those who practise their religion within such an ethos of alienation. Black theology essentially relates to black people. It is the black person's tool for affirmation of personhood and understanding of God's activity. It can function with credibility in the hands of blacks, but white people too will need tools of interpretation to unravel its meaning and significance. I therefore take the view that black people must themselves take charge of the business of religious affirmation from their context.

However, black people live with the reality of the dominance of white society. For many black people black theology will be exercised within the white-led Churches. In that case it can become a means of mutual mis-understanding. White people need to understand the religious dimension of black life in its authentic and primal sense. In that sense it can mark a contribution to race relations. But much more than that, this understanding should lead to the formation of alliances for justice across the colour spectrum — what in the United States has come to be known as the 'Rainbow Coalition' associated with the presidential candidacy of the Revd Jesse Jackson.

One can therefore envisage a revised system of training for ministry. Black people will lay the foundations for their participation in the Church by undertaking a programme of learning that explores their deeper being in order to offer the experience of faith of the black Christians to the wider Church. Only fully liberated people can freely participate and contribute to Church and society.

In order to open up black culture and share its riches with the community Gayraud Wilmore suggests that we have to call for the tools of interpretation vested in the black experience, culture and systems of knowledge, which reveal that the God of history has been at work in black communities for many hundreds of years.[11] The paradigmatic shift required here will give a more authentic statement of black understandings of God and how the vision of a just and reconciled society flows from such a vision.

NOTES

1. P. Fryer, 'The history of English racism, Part 2', *Ethical Record*, 93 (4) (April 1988), 22.
2. P. Gilroy, *There Ain't No Black in the Union Jack* (London: Hutchinson, 1987), p. 59.
3. 'Racial attitudes in Britain – the way forward', published by the Church Information Office, London, 2 July 1982.
4. P. Berryman, *The Religious Roots of Rebellion* (London: SCM Press, 1984), p. 334.
5. K. Leech, 'The resurrection of the Catholic social voice', *Theology*, 77 (1974), 654.
6. R.J. Siebert, 'Jacob and Jesus: recent Marxist readings of the Bible', in N.K. Gottwald (ed.), *The Bible and Liberation* (New York: Orbis Books, 1984), p. 501.
7. Gilroy, *There Ain't No Black*, p. 227.
8. Unpublished statement issued by the Handsworth Forum, September 1985.
9. J. de Gruchy, 'The struggle for justice and ministry of reconciliation', *South African Journal of Theology*, 62 (1988), 52.
10. Gilroy, *There Ain't No Black*, p. 218.
11. G. Wilmore, *Black Religion and Black Radicalism* (New York: Seabury Press, 1980).

Further reading

Wesley Ariarajah, *The Bible and People of Other Faiths* (Geneva: World Council of Churches, 1985). Superb exposition of the openness to cultural exchange and dialogue which is to be found in the Old and New Testaments, and which deeply marks the expansion of Christianity from Jewish sect to Gentile religion in the first and second centuries.

Kenneth Cracknell and Christopher Lamb, *Theology on Full Alert* (London: British Council of Churches, 1986). Proposes a radical reorientation of theological education and ministerial training for clergy and laity towards a multi-faith awareness which will include serious study of the scriptures and traditions of other religions and of the implications for religious pluralism for mission in Britain's cities.

Peter Fryer, *Staying Power: The History of Black People in Britain* (London: Pluto, 1984). Definitive account of the black presence from the Roman occupation to the present day. Addresses the historical roots of racism while retelling stories of the major contributions of black people to national life over the centuries.

Roswith I.H. Gerloff, *A Plea for Black British Theologies: The Black Church Movement in Britain in its Transatlantic Cultural and Theological Interaction* (Frankfurt: Peter Lang, 1992). The director of the Centre for Black and White Christian Partnership explores the impact and dynamics of black-led churches and groups, and calls for engagement with a developing black British theological process.

Paul Grant and Raj Patel, *A Time to Speak: Perspectives of Black Christians in Britain* (London: CCBI & Evangelical Christians for Racial Justice, 1990). Painful stories and hard-hitting analysis of the failure of the British churches to understand the exclusion of black Christians. There can be no reconciliation without repentance and justice.

David Haslam, *Race for the Millennium: A Challenge to Church and Society* (London: Church House Publishing, 1996). Analysis of structural, pastoral and theological responses to racism. Draws on the black experience in USA and puts Britain firmly in the European context.

Roger Hooker and Christopher Lamb, *Love the Stranger: Christian Ministry in Multi-Faith Areas* (London: SPCK, 1986). In a rich account of ministry in multi-faith areas, the authors argue that building friendships between Asians and Christians is a central task of ministry to other religions where the aim is not evangelism (though this may be involved), but community building and the generation of Christ-like love between neighbours.

Roy Kerridge, *The Storm is Passing Over: A Look at Black Churches in Britain* (London: Thames & Hudson, 1995). Fascinating photographic and journalistic record of an encounter with four black-led churches.

Colin Marchant, *Signs in the City* (London: Hodder and Stoughton, 1985). Includes a number of references to the growth of African-Caribbean churches and church styles in London.

Tariq Modood, *Not Easy Being British: Colour, Culture and Citizenship* (Stoke-on-Trent: Trentham Books, 1992). A finely nuanced study which examines the complex social and cultural interactions between white and non-white communities in contemporary Britain.

Robert Solomos, *Race and Racism in Contemporary Britain* (London: Macmillan, 1989). Valuable introduction to the sociology and politics of race and racism in post-war Britain and in particular the racialization of Englishness in the 1970s and 1980s, its use for political ends and in the framing of new immigration law.

Novetter Thompson, 'Labouring for a new birth: the black experience', in Peter Sedgwick (ed.), *God in the City* (London: Mowbray, 1995), pp. 153–62. Racism and disadvantage have generated a struggle amongst British black people for recognition in the mainstream culture and for recovery of their own distinctive cultural identity. This dual movement is reflected in efforts towards spiritual regeneration which are exemplified in the movement 'Claiming the Inheritance': 'Being born again for black people in Britain will not mean being accepted by others, but will mean being accepted by ourselves. As long as we try to remake ourselves in the image of other people, we shall never be at peace. Being born again must mean celebrating and reclaiming our own cultural and spiritual inheritance.'

John Wilkinson, *Church in Black and White: The Black Christian Tradition in Mainstream Churches in England. A White Response and Testimony* (Edinburgh: St Andrew Press, 1994). Written by a parish priest with extensive experience of working in mixed-race churches in Birmingham, Wilkinson argues that the mainstream churches have done too little to overcome racism within their own structures and organization and to understand, let alone welcome, the distinctive voice and experience of black Christians.

Andrew Wingate, *Encounter in the Spirit: Muslim–Christian Meetings in Birmingham* (Geneva: World Council of Churches, 1988). A wonderful account of Christians and Muslims both sharing their faith together, and praying together in prayer houses and churches in Birmingham.